Macroeconomic Policies for Sustainable Growth

Munasinghe Institute for Development
'making development more sustainable-MDMS'

Munasinghe Institute for Development (MIND) Series on Growth and Sustainable Development

***Series Editor*:**

Mohan Munasinghe
Chairman, Munasinghe Institute for Development, Sri Lanka
Honorary Energy Advisor to the Government, Sri Lanka
Visiting Professor, Yale University, USA
Vice Chair, Intergovernmental Panel on Climate Change, Switzerland

This series of three volumes deals with the interaction between conventional economic growth and the more recent paradigm of sustainable development. A distinguished group of international experts drawn from a broad range of disciplines examine this nexus, and suggest ways for making development more sustainable in the future. The volumes cover both theory and practical applications at the global, national and local levels:

1. The Sustainability of Long-term Growth: Socioeconomic and Ecological Perspectives – Mohan Munasinghe, Osvaldo Sunkel and Carlos de Miguel
   (Edward Elgar, 2001)

2. Sustainable Energy in Developing Countries: Policy Analysis and Case Studies – Peter Meier and Mohan Munasinghe
   (Edward Elgar, 2005)

3. Macroeconomic Policies for Sustainable Growth: Analytical Framework and Policy Studies of Brazil and Chile – Mohan Munasinghe, Raul O'Ryan, Ronaldo Seroa da Motta, Carlos de Miguel, Carlos Young, Sebastian Miller and Claudio Ferraz
   (Edward Elgar, 2006)

Macroeconomic Policies for Sustainable Growth

Analytical Framework and Policy Studies of Brazil and Chile

Mohan Munasinghe
Munasinghe Institute for Development (MIND), Sri Lanka and Yale University, USA

Raul O'Ryan
University of Chile (UC), Chile

Ronaldo Seroa da Motta
Research Institute for Applied Economics (IPEA), Brazil

Carlos de Miguel
UN Economic Commission for Latin America and the Caribbean (ECLAC), Chile

Carlos Young
Federal University of Rio de Janeiro (UFRJ), Brazil

Sebastian Miller
University of Chile (UC), Chile

Claudio Ferraz
University of California, USA

Edward Elgar
Cheltenham, UK • Northampton, MA, USA

Research supported by the World Bank, Washington DC, and the Munasinghe Institute for Development (MIND), Colombo.

Published by
Edward Elgar Publishing Limited
Glensanda House
Montpellier Parade
Cheltenham
Glos GL50 1UA
UK

Edward Elgar Publishing, Inc.
136 West Street
Suite 202
Northampton
Massachusetts 01060
USA

A catalogue record for this book
is available from the British Library

Library of Congress Cataloguing in Publication Data

Macroeconomic policies for sustainable growth : analytical framework and policy studies of Brazil and Chile / Mohan Munasinghe ... [et al.].
p. cm.
Includes bibliographical references and index.
1. Sustainable development–Case studies. 2. Sustainable development–Brazil. 3. Sustainable development–Chile. 4. Brazil–Economic policy. 5. Chile–Economic policy. I. Munasinghe, Mohan, 1945–

HC79.E5M313 2006
338.981'07–dc22

2005050155

ISBN-13: 978 1 84542 494 7
ISBN-10: 1 84542 494 8

Printed and bound in Great Britain by MPG Books Ltd, Bodmin, Cornwall

Contents

Acknowledgements

This volume is based on applied research studies funded principally by the World Bank and the Munasinghe Institute for Development (MIND). The work was carried out in association with the International Society for Ecological Economics (ISEE), USA, the Research Institute for Applied Economics (IPEA), Brazil, the Federal University of Rio de Janeiro (UFRJ), Brazil and the University of Chile (UC).

The overall study was led by Mohan Munasinghe. The Brazil country team consisted of Ronaldo Seroa da Motta, Carlos Young and Claudio Ferraz, while the Chile country team included Raul O'Ryan, Carlos de Miguel and Sebastian Miller.

We thank Jorge Araujo for suggestions and support. Additionally Eustáquio J. Reis provided part of the data used in this volume and gave insightful comments and suggestions. Edward Barbier, Sergio Margulis, Robin White, Octávio Tourinho and Sven Wunder also provided comments on a previous version and Rosane Campos contributed with research assistance.

We are grateful for the contributions of researchers and assistants from the Research Group on Environmental Economics and Sustainable Development, the Federal University of Rio de Janeiro (UFRJ), Brazil (GEMA/IE-UFRJ), namely Maria Cecília Lustosa, André Santos Pereira, Edgar Assis, Luisa Schwartzman, Bárbara Hartje, André Andrade Pereira, Josiane Carvalho and Marcos Thanus.

Finally, we are deeply indebted to Nishanthi De Silva and Yvani Deraniyagala of MIND for helping to prepare the manuscript.

All the views expressed in the book, as well as any remaining errors, are the authors' responsibility, and should not be ascribed to any organization.

Abbreviations and acronyms

AIM	action impact matrix
BEN	national energy balance
BOD	biochemical oxygen demand
CGE	computable general equilibrium
EE	externality cost
EKC	environmental Kuznets curve
ELES	extended linear expenditure system
EMD	environmental marginal damage
EPPA	emissions and public policy analysis
ES	economic subsidy
EX	external balance
GDP	gross domestic product
GTAP	global trade analysis program
IBGE	Brazilian Institute of Geography and Statistics
IMF	International Monetary Fund
I–O	input–output
IPPS	industrial pollution projection system
ISEE	International Society for Ecological Economics
ISEW	index of sustainable economic welfare
MCA	multi-criteria analysis
MCPF	marginal cost of public funds
NIC	newly industrializing countries
NNP	net national product
OECD	Organisation for Economic Cooperation and Development
PAM	Pesquisa Agrícola Municipal
PPM	Pesquisa Pecuária Municipal
SAM	social accounting matrix
SAP	structural adjustment program
SEEA	integrated system of environmental and economic accounting (United Nations)
SNA	system of national accounts
WB	World Bank
WTO	World Trade Organization

Preface

This volume is the third major publication emerging from a multi-year research project on the sustainability of long-term growth, funded principally by the World Bank, Washington DC, and the Munasinghe Institute for Development (MIND), Colombo. The work was carried out in association with the International Society for Ecological Economics (ISEE), USA, the Research Institute for Applied Economics (IPEA), Brazil, the Federal University of Rio de Janeiro (UFRJ), Brazil and the University of Chile (UC).

The origins of this research effort date back to 1990, when I was requested to lead two major research programmes at the World Bank. These initiatives, carried out in collaboration with senior colleagues, have helped to shape a range of subsequent Bank policies. The first research project explored a more balanced and practical approach to sustainable development based on its economic, environmental and social dimensions. The results fed into the 1992 Earth Summit in Rio de Janeiro. Subsequently, the creation of the Vice Presidency for Environmentally and Socially Sustainable Development institutionalized this approach in the Bank. The second research initiative was a comprehensive study that traced the linkages between economywide policies and the environment, and suggested practical policy remedies in response to mounting criticisms of the adverse environmental impacts of structural adjustment programmes. The findings were approved by the Bank's Board of Executive Directors in 1994, and then presented to the world's finance ministers at a special seminar at the World Bank–International Monetary Fund fiftieth anniversary celebrations in Madrid.

Building on the earlier research, the volumes in this series amply illustrate practical applications of the sustainomics methodology – a comprehensive, trans-disciplinary framework for making development more sustainable. The results have been fed into the 2002 World Summit on Sustainable Development (WSSD) in Johannesberg, and ongoing work on the United Nations Millennium Development Goals (MDG),

The first volume was published in 2001 (Mohan Munasinghe, Osvaldo Sunkel and Carlos de Miguel (eds), *The Sustainability of Long-term Growth: Socioeconomic and Ecological Perspectives*, Edward Elgar). It contains state-of-the-art papers presented by internationally renowned researchers at the fifth ISEE biennial international conference held in Santiago, November 1998. This book helps to improve our understanding of the complex issues arising from the interactions among key policy objectives that will shape sustainable development strategies in this century – including economic growth, poverty eradication, environmental protection, social inclusion and good governance.

The second book, published in 2005, takes a comprehensive look at the energy dimensions of the growth-sustainability nexus (Peter Meier and Mohan Munasinghe, *Sustainable Energy in Developing Countries: Policy Analysis and Case Studies*, Edward Elgar). It describes an in-depth country case study of Sri Lanka, covering four major dimensions of energy – conventional power and energy, renewable energy, transport and greenhouse gas emissions. The authors present an innovative analytical framework. They apply it to resolve key issues and identify robust policy options, in the presence of risk and uncertainty.

The material presented in this third book in the series continues the same broad theme, by examining how macroeconomic strategies influence the sustainability of growth. The theoretical framework seeks to explain the manner in which haphazard growth might exacerbate existing economic imperfections, and give rise to serious economic, environmental and social unsustainability. Country case studies of Brazil and Chile illustrate the theory – covering a broad spectrum in terms of macroeconomic policies and analytical models tested, physical scale and demographics, and resource endowments. Various policy options are discussed, to restructure the pattern of growth and make development more sustainable.

Mohan Munasinghe
Series Editor

PART I

Overview

1. Historical evolution of ideas

1.1 INTRODUCTION

This book focuses on the sustainability of growth-oriented macroeconomic strategies. The analytical framework highlights how growth might combine with economic imperfection to produce unsustainable outcomes characterised not only by serious economic, but also environmental and social problems. Various remedial policy options are discussed, to make development more sustainable by reshaping the structure of growth.

The two detailed practical case studies of Brazil and Chile span a wide range, in terms of geographic size and demographics, resource endowments, macroeconomic policies and analytical models used. They were carried out by a team consisting of Mohan Munasinghe (Project Leader), Ronaldo Seroa da Motta, Carlos Young and Claudio Ferraz (Brazilian study), and Raul O'Ryan, Carlos de Miguel and Sebastian Miller (Chilean study). Valuable advice was provided by Jorge Araujo (World Bank).

The chapters in the volume are organized as follows. The remainder of Chapter 1 contains a brief review of the historical evolution of ideas linking macroeconomic policies, growth and sustainability. Next, more recent empirical evidence is presented, including a discussion of the environmental and social impacts of structural adjustment programs since the 1980s. One important conclusion is that it is the combination of growth and economic imperfections that lead to unsustainable outcomes, characterized by environmental and social harm. Chapter 2 develops a framework for analysis, including both macroeconomic and microeconomic analyses of the linkages between the economy and the environment. The chapter concludes with a summary and directions for future work.

The Brazil case study begins in Chapter 3, with a background description of the indicators of production and consumption patterns of industrial output, personal consumption and agricultural expansion in Brazil in the last decade and the environmental pressure associated with urban and forest issues. Chapter 4 examines the impact of trade liberalization policies on the level of urban pollution in Brazil, due to rising industrial exports. It uses input–output modeling techniques, whereby pollution coefficients are linked with industrial activities, to estimate the total emissions required to produce a specified volume of industrial exports. In Chapter 5, the authors analyze how the environment is stressed by consumption patterns of different income classes in Brazil. Environmental pressures include polluting discharges and natural resource uses related to production and direct consumption of goods. Again, input–output modeling links environmental degradation to both production and consumption. Chapter 6 analyzes deforestation taking place due to agricultural and cattle ranching expansion in eight states of the Brazilian Amazon from 1980 to 1995. The model separates direct government interventions (such as government credit and road building), from market incentives that work through prices. The Brazil case study is concluded in Chapter 7, with a summary of the main findings and policy recommendations.

Chapter 8 launches the Chile case study, with a description of computable general equilibrium (CGE) models as an integrated tool to evaluate environmental, social and economic impacts of different policies. It discusses various models developed to analyze environmental policies, including specific models developed for Chile. In Chapter 9, the main features and underlying equations of the detailed CGE model used in the present study are set out, especially how environmental aspects have been included. Chapter 10 summarizes background information on Chile during the past decade, including the macroeconomic performance, social and environmental situation, policies adopted and objectives behind them, and key social and environmental impacts. In Chapter 11, four practical examples are presented that use the CGE model to analyze both the impacts of, and mutual interactions among, sets of specific environmental and social policies. Finally, Chapter 12 summarizes the main conclusions of the Chile case study and suggests areas for further research.

1.2 REVIEW OF PAST EXPERIENCE

Sustainable development or 'development which lasts', is a concept that is receiving increasing attention from world decision makers, in their search for new solutions to many critical problems including traditional development issues (such as economic stagnation, persistent poverty, hunger, malnutrition and illness), as well as newer challenges (like worsening environmental degradation and accelerating globalization).

Following the 1992 Earth Summit in Rio de Janeiro and the adoption of the United Nations' Agenda 21, sustainable development has become well accepted worldwide (WCED 1987; UN 1993).

In this context, the role of macroeconomic policies has come under increasing scrutiny, because of their powerful and pervasive impacts throughout the economy. In particular, the linkages between such policies and the environment have been studied by several researchers in recent years (see for example, Munasinghe and Cruz, 1994; Reed, 1996; Munasinghe, 1996). Key questions raised include the extent to which growth-inducing economic policies are linked to environmental and social harm, the nature of the mechanisms underlying such interactions and the appropriate policy conclusions to be drawn.

For our purposes, sustainable development may be defined as a process for improving the range of opportunities that will enable individual human beings and communities to meet their needs, as well as to achieve their aspirations and full potential, over a sustained period of time, while maintaining the resilience of economic, social and environmental systems (Munasinghe, 1992, 2002a).

The analytical approach used in this book is based on the sustainomics framework (see Box 1.1 for details). First, we seek policies and measures that *make development more sustainable* and lead to continuous improvements in the present quality of life at a lower intensity of resource use, thereby leaving behind for future generations an undiminished stock of productive assets (i.e., manufactured, natural and social capital) that will enhance opportunities for improving their quality of life (Munasinghe 1992, 2001).

Second, the sustainomics approach uses the sustainable development triangle (Figure 1.1), to analyse economywide policies in terms of their economic, social and environmental implications. This wider perspective on human well-being is important, since most traditional economic policies have focused on maximizing economic output, sometimes at significant environmental and social cost.

Third, the analysis explicitly seeks to transcend conventional boundaries imposed by discipline, space, time, stakeholder viewpoints, and operationality. Fourth, sustainomics mobilizes a variety of practical analytical tools to facilitate governance over the full cycle from initial data gathering to ultimate policy implementation (e.g., Action Impact Matrix – AIM, and policy-tunneling methodologies described in Chapter 2).

Box 1.1 Sustainomics framework - summary of basic principles and methods

The core sustainomics framework summarized below was developed from 1990 onwards and first presented at the 1992 United Nations Earth Summit (UNCED) in Rio de Janeiro. It is based on the following principles and methods (Munasinghe 1992, 2002a, 2006).

(a) Making development more sustainable (MDMS)

The step-by-step approach of 'making development more sustainable' (MDMS) becomes the prime objective, while sustainable development is defined as a process (rather than an end point). Since the precise definition of sustainable development remains an elusive and perhaps unreachable goal, a less ambitious strategy that merely seeks to make development more sustainable does offer greater promise. Such a gradient-based method is more practical and permits us to address urgent priorities without delay, because many unsustainable activities are easier to recognize and eliminate. Although MDMS is incremental, it does not imply any limitation in scope (e.g., restricted time horizon or geographic area – see item (c) below). While pursuing the MDMS approach, we also follow a parallel track by continuing our efforts to better define the ultimate goal of sustainable development. Finally, MDMS encourages us to keep future options open and seek robust strategies which meet multiple contingencies and increase resilience.

(b) Sustainable development triangle and balanced viewpoint

Sustainable development requires balanced and integrated analysis from three main perspectives: social, economic and environmental (see Figure 1.1). Each viewpoint corresponds to a domain (and system) that has its own distinct driving forces and objectives. The economy is geared mainly towards improving human welfare, primarily through increases in the consumption of goods and services. The environmental domain focuses on protection of the integrity and resilience of ecological systems. The social domain emphasizes the enrichment of human relationships and achievement of individual and group aspirations. The sides of the triangle representing interactions among the vertices are also important for the analysis. Finally, key issues like poverty and economywide policies may be analysed within the triangle, to underline that they have economic, social and environmental dimensions.

(c) Transcending conventional boundaries for better integration
The analysis transcends conventional boundaries imposed by discipline, space, time, stakeholder viewpoints, and operationality. The scope is broadened and extended in all domains, to ensure a comprehensive view. Trans-disciplinary analysis requires coverage of economics, social science and ecology, as well as many other disciplines. Spatial analysis must range from the global to the very local, while the time horizon may extend to decades or beyond. Diverse stakeholders from the government, private sector and civil society should participate equally, and the analysis needs to encompass the full operational cycle from data gathering to practical policy implementation and monitoring of outcomes.

(d) Full cycle application of practical analytical tools
A variety of practical analytical tools facilitate governance over the full cycle from initial data gathering to ultimate policy implementation.

The Action Impact Matrix (AIM) process is the key link from initial data gathering to practical policy application and feedback. Critical sustainable development concerns are incorporated into conventional national development strategy and goals in two main ways: an upward link where sustainable development issues are embedded in the macro-strategy of a country via the medium- to long-term development path; and a downward link where sustainable development issues are integrated into the national development strategy in the short- to medium-term, by carrying out sustainable development assessments (SDA) of micro-level projects and policies.

Two complementary approaches based on 'optimality' and 'durability' may be used to integrate and synthesize across economic, social and environmental domains, within an integrated assessment modeling framework. An issues-implementation transformation map (IITM) helps to translate issues in the environmental and social domains, into the conventional national economic planning and implementing mechanisms within line ministries and departments.

Restructuring the pattern of development to make economic growth more sustainable is explained through a 'policy tunneling' model, especially useful in developing countries, where poverty alleviation will require continued increases in income and consumption. Other practical tools include integrated national economic–environmental accounting (SEEA), sustainable development assessment (SDA), environmental valuation, extended cost–benefit analysis (CBA), multi-criteria analysis (MCA), integrated assessment models (IAMs), and so on. A range of sustainable development indicators help to measure progress and make choices at various levels of aggregation.

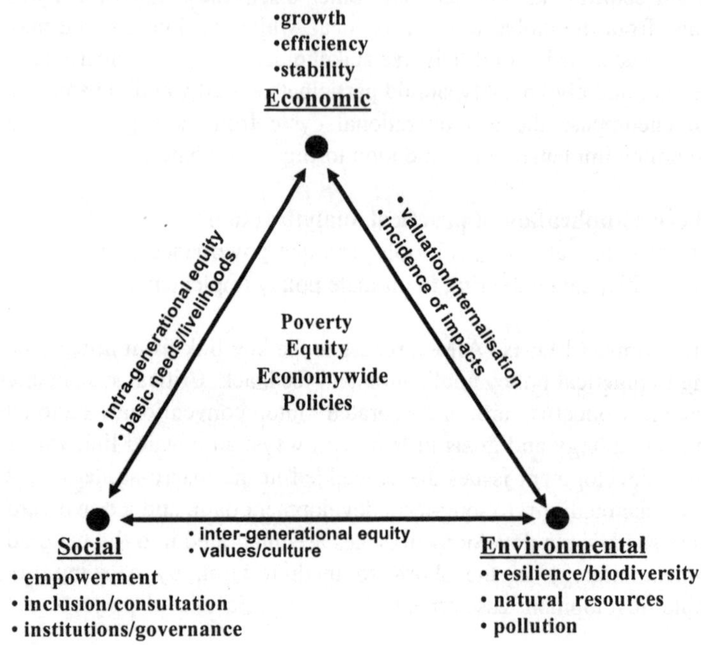

Source: Munasinghe (1992).

Figure 1.1 Key elements of sustainable development and interconnections

Macroeconomic policies and strategies have widespread effects – typically, they range from exchange rate, interest rate and wage policies, to trade liberalization, privatization and similar programs. They are invariably coupled with sectoral measures that involve a variety of economic instruments, including pricing in key sectors (for example, energy or agriculture) and broad sectorwide taxation or subsidy programs (for example, agricultural production subsidies and industrial investment incentives). Such economywide policies (both macroeconomic and sectoral), are often packaged within programs of structural adjustment, stabilization and sectoral reform, aimed at promoting economic stability, efficiency and growth, and ultimately improving human welfare. Although the emphasis is on economic policies, other non-economic measures (such as social, institutional and legal actions) are also relevant.

Many key ideas on macroeconomics and the environment have been developed within the last two decades, although some historical roots are discernible in several classical papers. We focus below on selected papers describing macro socioeconomic–environment interactions.

Tracing Macro Socioeconomic–Environment Linkages

There are three relevant, interwoven lines of enquiry in early articles. First, both production and consumption give rise to polluting emissions on the output side. This approach draws on the classic work of Leontief on input–output (I–O) analysis, developed during the 1930s.

Second, economic activities result in the use of resource inputs. The crucial role played by natural resource scarcities in limiting growth were recognized as far back as Malthus (1798), in his analysis of impoverishment due to agricultural land constraints and exponential population growth. Subsequently, Ricardo (1817) explained how diminishing returns to land would impose checks on wealth and population. This avenue also has roots in the theory of exhaustible resources, as developed in the classic article by Hotelling (1931). More recently, attention has been focused on the distinction between optimal growth and the sustainability of long-term growth (Munasinghe et al., 2001).

Third, attempts have been made to incorporate environmental considerations into more conventional macroeconomic models used in policymaking. Proposed frameworks range from extensions of the Keynesian IS–LM type used in analyses of comparative statics, to sophisticated computable general equilibrium (CGE) models that include environmental variables – as both inputs to, and outputs of, economic activities.

The core of Leontief's approach is the I–O table, which describes both the inter-industry relations and industry–consumer relations in a given time period (for example, a base year), in terms of the volume and mix of inputs required to produce or consume one unit each of a range of outputs. In the late 1960s, Leontief extended this system to examine pollution issues. Leontief (1970) sets out a seminal framework to analyze polluting outputs from productive sectors, and the impact of policies to reduce such emissions in pollution abatement sectors. It seeks to incorporate issues raised by undesirable environmental externalities into the conventional I–O analysis of modern economies. Many subsequent studies have elaborated on the basic I–O approach, by linking it with vintage models specifying labour demand and capital stock, as well as by endogenized consumer demand based on linear expenditure systems. More sophisticated models made the technical I–O coefficients (which were constant in Leontief's original analysis) endogenous and dependent on prices. Present state-of-the-art computable general equilibrium models used for macroeconomic–environmental analysis, as well as the integrated frameworks for environmental–economic accounting, draw on the I–O approach, as described later.

Koopmans (1973) paper focuses on natural resource use, and starts from the so-called 'cake-eating' problem, first analyzed by Hotelling (1931). The objective here is to find the optimal consumption rate over time of a finite stock of raw material, which is the sole source of well-being. A key macroeconomic parameter, the rate of interest, plays a significant role in the analysis. Koopmans seeks to combine the exhaustible natural capital in the simple cake-eating problem with accumulating manufactured capital, within a Ramsey-type growth model. Subsequent work (Withagen, 1990) have explored many ramifications of this approach, leading to recent work by Hartwick and others (see below).

Stiglitz (1974) continues in the same vein, by examining the conditions underlying feasible sustainable per capita consumption paths, the characteristics of steady state paths in economies based on natural resources, and features of optimal growth paths. His model includes an aggregate production function with capital, labor and natural resources as substitutes in production. An important result is that declining stocks of natural resources could be offset by increasing technological progress in substitution. Higher levels of consumption may be sustained by imposing more stringent requirements on the rate of technological advance, thereby implying that exhaustion of (substitutable) natural resources need not be a constraint on long-term sustainability of growth.

Solow's (1993) paper also examines links between natural capital and growth, from the viewpoint of sustainability. It is an important departure from his earlier work, which paid little attention to sustainability concerns. This article argues that the net national product (NNP) of an economy should be adjusted to reflect both the depletion of natural resource stocks and changes in the quality of environmental amenities. He goes on to define NNP as a measure of the maximum level of consumption that can be sustained forever (assuming undistorted prices). Therefore, sustainability depends on the maintenance of adequate stocks of productive resources in the future. These arguments link conventional neoclassical economic theory with earlier work in environmental economics and environmental accounting

Daly (1991) sets out some important criticisms of conventional macroeconomic theory, from the environmental viewpoint. Macroeconomic textbooks emphasize the circular flow of income, and how it is accompanied by the use of natural resources and emission of pollutants. However, they pay little attention to the fact that as the scale of economic activities grow, both the resource depletion and pollution impose an increasingly unsustainable burden on the natural resource base. Daly points out that getting the prices right may ensure optimal resource allocation, but does not address the issue of scale, and goes on to draw appropriate policy conclusions.

England's (2000) paper reviews the state of the debate between growth theorists seeking the conditions under which long-term steady state growth paths become feasible, and ecological economists who emphasize the biophysical limitations on unrestricted exponential growth of aggregate output. He draws attention to three conditions that would curtail growth and lead to a steady state economy – the scarcity of natural capital essential for growth; the complementarity (non-substitutability) between manufactured and natural capital in production; and constraints on technological progress that raises the productivity of natural capital use.

Environmental considerations are increasingly examined in macroeconomic models, focusing on short-run Keynesian issues such capacity utilization, unemployment and cyclical movements in the economy. Longer-run environmental–macroeconomic models for both closed and open economies are built around supply-side issues like capital accumulation, natural resource depletion, long-run labour supply, discount rate and rate of technological progress.

Girma (1992) is a good example that starts from a conventional macreconomic modeling framework, to which an environmental sector is added. The simple model examines macropolicies (including those affecting aggregate demand, key economic sectors and income distribution) and their impacts on the environment.

Maler and Munasinghe's (1996) paper uses an explicit mathematical model to explore the circumstances in which macroeconomic policies might be modified to address environmental issues. They argue that we live in a second-best world, and it is this fact that gives rise to adverse environmental impacts of first-best macroeconomic policies. If the environmental side effects will be substantial, either the root causes (market failures or property rights problems) should be addressed, or if that is not feasible, the macroeconomic policy itself should be appropriately modified in order to reduce losses. The impacts on the environment from changes in macroeconomic policies are channeled most often through rather complex and less direct mechanisms in the economy that may be captured by computable general equilibrium models. Therefore, the authors conclude that amalgamating macroeconomic objectives with environmental objectives in the context of such models could yield useful insights, in spite of the rather severe data problems.

Empirical Surveys of Macro Socioeconomic–Environment Linkages

This section contains general surveys of the relationship between economic growth and environmental degradation, and empirical reviews of the environmental and social impacts of structural adjustment and other macroeconomic interventions that have been applied during the past two decades, especially in the developing countries.

Grossman and Krueger (1995) is a good example of the voluminous recent literature examining the links between economic growth and the environment. It studies the empirical relationship between per capita income and several indicators of air and water pollution. A central question, as yet unresolved, is whether the evidence proves the existence of an inverted ‘environmental Kuznets curve’ (EKC). There is agreement that environmental quality declines with increases in per capita income in the early stages of growth, but it is unclear whether continued growth reverses this trend, since the shape of the curve appears to vary widely across different countries and forms of environmental degradation (*Ecological Economics*, 1998; *Environment and Development Economics,* 1997 and de Bruyn and Heintz, 1999).

Opschoor and Jongma’s (1996) paper is a comprehensive review of the impacts of World Bank and International Monetary Fund structural adjustment and stabilization programmes on the environment and sustainable development in developing countries. They draw a number of important policy conclusions. In particular, they argue for complementary environmental policies to counteract any adverse impacts of growth oriented macroeconomic policies as a short-run remedy, but urge a more integrated approach in the long run.

Panayotou and Hupe (1998) point out that structural adjustment programs must pay as much attention to market and institutional failures as they pay to policy failures. Using environmental and social policies as supplementary and compensatory or parallel policies to cushion the environmental and social impacts of structural adjustment is second best, compared with the full integration of these policies with the economic reforms in the context of a sustainable development strategy. Structural adjustment programs can best ensure sustainability by providing for reinvestment of rents from the depletion of natural resources in natural, environmental, man-made and human capital, to maintain and expand the productive capacity of the economy and the quality of life. Partial reforms or incomplete implementation of reforms may do more harm than good if they are selectively applied without due regard to their social and environmental impacts.

Kessler and Van Dorp's (1998) paper describes methodologies for studying the impacts of structural adjustment programs. It also draws attention to the unpredictable of such impacts, focusing on key indicators relating to soils, water resources and forests. The importance of ex ante assessment of the environmental impacts of adjustment policy packages to assist in remediation efforts, is emphasized.

Mathematical Models

This section reviews selected papers with mathematical models seeking to incorporate environmental variables into macroeconomic frameworks, as well as practical country case studies that investigate the linkages between a variety of macroeconomic policies and different environmental issues, in both industrial and developing countries.

Jorgensen and Wilcoxen (1990) present an important case study from both the theoretical and empirical points of view. It analyzes the economic impact of environmental regulations on the US economy using a computable general equilibrium (CGE) approach. The paper was one of the first that applied inter-temporal analysis to a complex disaggregate model of long-term growth impacts. It focuses on critical energy–economy–environment linkages. The share of abatement costs in total costs is estimated for each industry, as are the share of investment in pollution control equipment and the cost of pollution control devices in motor vehicles.

Bergman's (1990) paper also uses a CGE model designed to simulate the effects of environmental regulation and energy policy on the Swedish economy. In this case, the environmental market failure is corrected by the creation of a market for emission permits. The cost of emission permits for carbon dioxide, sulphur, and nitrogen is incorporated in the cost functions.

Persson and Munasinghe (1995) describe a CGE model to examine deforestation in Costa Rica. The results support the conclusions of more conventional partial equilibrium approaches, that: (a) establishing property rights tends to decrease deforestation because such rights allow forest users to better capture the future benefits of reduced logging damage today; and (b) higher interest rates promote deforestation and vice versa. Further, the CGE approach shows indirect effects arising from intersectoral linkages, which are not captured by partial equilibrium analysis. The latter predicts that stumpage price increases will act directly to reduce logging, but the CGE model shows that while deforestation from logging will indeed decline, total deforestation nevertheless increases. This and other examples underline the importance of pursuing sectoral reforms in parallel with growth-inducing policies.

Glomsrod et al.'s (1998) paper uses a CGE model to study the impacts of structural adjustment policies on deforestation in Nicaragua. The model incorporates an informal food producing sector that encroaches on forest land, to help analyze how policy elements like tax reform, public expenditure and external balance, might affect the dynamic balance between subsistence farming and forested areas. Improving the fiscal balance by reducing public expenditure or through sales tax reform, both improve economic growth and conserve forests. Flexible urban wages would lead to more rapid deforestation than a fixed urban real wage regime. Some polices increase deforestation in the near term, but ease pressure on forests in the longer term, and this trade-off should be studied carefully during policy formulation.

Holden et al. (1998) develop a general model of a village economy, and apply it to study the effects of structural adjustment policies in Zambia. Six types of village economies are characterized by the degree of isolation from the outside world, and the internal differences in access to resources. Simulations show that adjustment policies have significant adverse impacts on the environment. The removal of policy distortions does not necessarily lead to well functioning markets, because of high transactions costs and imperfect information in remote areas. The model results are consistent with empirical findings.

Islam, Munasinghe and Clarke (2003) examine the sustainability of optimal growth. Their model analyzes economic–ecological interactions, including resource depletion, pollution, irreversibility and uncertainty. Key socioeconomic issues include savings, investment, technical progress, substitutability of productive factors, intergenerational efficiency and equity. Many policy options emerge to make growth more sustainable.

Trade and Environment

This section focuses on an important aspect of macroeconomic policy within an open economy – the linkages between international trade and the environment.

Steininger's (1999) paper provides a comprehensive review of general models used to analyze trade–environment issues, including three complementary categories of models – Heckscher–Ohlin (with added environmental variables), statistical–econometric and applied general equilibrium models. They are able to address a variety of issues such as, leakage, distribution, policy feedback effects, interlinkages between production sectors and markets, and specialization patterns. The author also points out that further work is required on spatial effects, technological innovation and developing country issues.

Batabyal (1994) presents a theoretical country case study that seeks to trace the impacts of domestic environmental policies on international trade. It shows that there are plausible circumstances in which a large developing country might be worse off by pursuing environmental policies unilaterally. The results depend on a variety of empirical factors. The government could use its market power to set a (second best) optimal pollution tax to correct for domestic economic distortions, and thereby capture trade gains.

Goldin and Roland-Host's (1997) paper examines the converse question – how growth in international trade might affect the local environment in Morocco. In the past, subsidized water charges artificially promoted production of water intensive crops. In the CGE simulation, liberalization of trade alone leads to economywide gains. However, elimination of duties leads to budgetary deficits, and economic expansion increases water use, causing water shortages. If the growth stimulating trade liberalization is coupled with water price increases, agricultural water use is substantially reduced. Thus, trade liberalization alone results in more efficient allocation of resources and expansion of exports, but also leads to environmental stress through increased water use. When complementary water price increases are simultaneously undertaken with trade liberalization, the beneficial expansionary economic effects of the latter are largely retained, but now with reduced water stress as well.

Mani and Wheeler (1998) review the empirical evidence to determine whether pollution- intensive industries seek havens in countries with lax environmental standards. They analyze data for the period 1960–95 for a variety of industrial sectors, in a wide range of countries. The initial results appear consistent with the 'pollution havens' hypothesis.

The share of pollution-intensive output in total manufacturing has fallen steadily in the OECD and risen correspondingly in the developing countries, especially in periods when the cost of pollution abatement rose sharply in OECD economies. However, the paper concludes that trade is not to blame for increases in the production of pollution-intensive goods, since production appears to have taken place primarily for domestic markets, rather than for export.

Green National Income Accounting

The greening of the system of national accounts (SNA) is an important prerequisite for environmental–macroeconomic policymaking.

Hartwick's (1990) paper captures key elements of his contributions to environmental accounting since the late 1970s. He develops a theoretical expression for net national product (NNP) of an economy as the current value Hamiltonian for an optimal aggregate growth problem (see Part I). This formulation includes not only the more conventional inputs like capital and labor, but also a variety of natural resources (that is, depletable, renewable and environmental resource stocks). Drawing down such natural resource stocks is the equivalent of economic depreciation, and therefore natural resource use should be netted out of gross national product (GNP), to derive NNP.

Repetto et al. (1989) is an empirical case study of Indonesia – a large, natural resource-rich, developing country. They argue that a nation's conventionally measured economic output could keep rising, while its natural resource base is being degraded, unless the use of natural resource stocks is recognized in the same way as the economic depreciation of manufactured capital.

Bartelmus et al.'s (1991) paper formalizes the environmental accounting approach through a basic framework called SEEA, for integrating environmental and resource accounting into the standard system of national accounts (SNA). Their methodology creates additional satellite accounts that facilitate the definition and compilation of modified indicators of income and expenditure, production, capital and value added, which reflect the depletion of natural resource stocks, degradation of environmental quality and human responses to these impacts. The practical application of the SEEA framework is provided through a typical country case study.

Hultkrantz (1992) applies resource accounting to a typical industrialized country. Focusing on forest resources in Sweden, the paper provides monetary estimates of changes in timber stocks, production of non-marketed and non-timber products and depletion of key environmental assets such as soil nutrients, biodiversity and carbon sinks.

Atkinson et al. (1997) describe various methods of adjusting the conventional system of national accounts to account for environmental effects, including a discussion of social accounting matrices. The concept of green national product or GNP (that is, conventional GNP revised to include changes in environmental services and resources) is extended, to develop the idea of 'genuine savings' (that is, national savings that include environmental effects). Genuine savings is a more useful measure than green GNP, since the latter could be higher or lower than conventional GNP without any particular implications for sustainability, whereas persistent negative genuine savings provide a potential danger signal.

Aronsson and Lofgren's (1998) paper reviews recent developments on the subject. Their theoretical framework summarizes the consensus concerning the current state of knowledge, and sets out some areas of uncertainty and key questions for further research.

1.3 STYLIZED RESULTS OF ENVIRONMENTAL EFFECTS OF STRUCTURAL ADJUSTMENT POLICIES

During recent decades, structural adjustment programs (SAPs) have emerged as a powerful form of macroeconomic intervention in the developing world. For many developing countries, the 1980s represented a period of economic hardship. Internal mismanagement of economies combined with external economic factors that were beyond their control, caused a situation now commonly referred to as the 'debt crisis'. The major oil price increases of 1974 and 1979 were a significant shock to most of these countries, which depended heavily on imported oil. Furthermore, restrictive monetary policies were adopted by Western countries during the late 1970s and early 1980s to curtail their own inflation rates. This caused real interest rates to rise and made it very difficult for developing countries to service their debts. As a result, developing countries experienced balance-of-payment difficulties, which forced them to rely even more heavily on foreign donors. Economic growth rates declined and unemployment worsened.

The International Monetary Fund (IMF) and the World Bank (WB) agreed to provide financial assistance with the primary objective of enabling countries to service their debts. Assistance, however, was conditional on the adoption of a broad reform framework currently referred to as structural adjustment programs (SAPs), including short-term 'stabilization' and more medium-term 'adjustment' measures. These stringent economic and fiscal reform policies, which were designed to reorient faltering economies back towards growth and development, also proved to have adverse environmental and social impacts, as they continued to be applied through the 1990s.

A major emphasis of stabilization policies was to reduce the pressure on foreign reserves by reducing domestic demand. Balance-of-payment problems were addressed through a monetary approach, designed to control inflation and reduce imports by both maintaining tight fiscal contractionary policies and restraining the supply of money. Simultaneously, currency devaluation policies were adopted to improve the terms of trade and make exports more competitive in international markets. Adjustment policies were applied to accelerate the economic recovery and growth of the export sector. These policies focused on the supply side and addressed inefficiencies of the internal economic structure. They also focused on reforming the public sector, through medium- and long-term measures. Together with reform programs at the macroeconomic level, sectoral policies were adopted to improve the efficiency of resource allocation and competitiveness of markets at the sectoral level. Unfortunately, these reforms often had recessionary effects, resulting in significant loss of jobs and livelihoods – before the promised export-led growth could materialize. Furthermore, budget cutting pressures often forced governments to abandon social 'safety-net' programs, thereby causing further hardship to low income groups.

Such reforms programs have not always achieved their economic goals, for a variety of reasons. Of greater relevance is the fact that even where macroeconomic gains have been realized through structural adjustment, both environmental and social problems have persisted or been exacerbated in several countries. The growing sustainable development literature is seeking to identify and remedy development strategies that lead to the unsustainable use of natural resources and the environment. One key question is whether the very economic policies being prescribed to alleviate economic problems are perhaps undermining the environmental resources and social fabric on which the long-term development of nations will ultimately depend (Munasinghe, 2001).

It is difficult to generalize about the environmental and social impacts of economywide policies, because the linkages tend to be extremely complex and country specific. For example, even the purely economic impacts of structural adjustment programs are difficult to trace comprehensively (Tarp, 1993). Nevertheless, in this section we attempt to summarize the main lessons learned from recent studies.

Economywide policy reforms are designed primarily to achieve broad economic objectives (for example, improving macroeconomic stability, enhancing efficiency and growth and alleviating poverty), and therefore, it is not surprising that their environmental and social consequences could be either positive or negative. Accordingly, it is convenient to consider three broad categories of countrywide policy impacts on various indicators of sustainability – beneficial, harmful and unknown. In the first group are the so-called 'win–win' policies, where it is possible to achieve simultaneous gains in all three areas of sustainable development (that is, economic, social and environmental) when economywide reforms are implemented. The second category recognizes important exceptions where such potential gains cannot be realized unless the macro-reforms are complemented by additional environmental and social measures that protect both the environment and the poor. The third and final category consists of impacts that are less predictable, mainly because of the complexity of the linkages involved, and the long-run time perspective.

Case studies of the environmental and social impacts of countrywide policies (including structural adjustment programs) have been presented in a number of recent articles and volumes (see for example, Reed, 1992; Munasinghe and Cruz, 1994; Abaza, 1995; Young and Bishop, 1995; Munasinghe, 1996; Reed, 1996; Opschoor and Jongma, 1996; Cruz et al., 1997; and Warford et al., 1997). We review some key results below, from these and other studies.

Beneficial Impacts

Several studies indicate that liberalizing reforms that seek to make desirable alterations in the structure of the economy could contribute to both economic and sustainability gains. Such changes include the removal of price distortions, promotion of market incentives and relaxation of trade and other constraints (which are among the main features of adjustment-related reforms). For example, reforms that improve the efficiency of industrial or energy-related activities could reduce economic waste, increase the efficiency of natural resource use and limit environmental pollution. Similarly, improving land tenure rights and access to financial and social services not only yields economic gains but also promotes better environmental stewardship and helps the poor.

In the same vein, there is evidence to show that shorter-run policy measures aimed at restoring macroeconomic stability will generally yield economic, social and environmental benefits, since instability undermines sustainable resource use and especially penalizes the poor. For example, price, wage and employment stability encourage a longer-term view on the part of firms and households alike. Lower inflation rates not only lead to clearer pricing signals and better investment decisions by economic agents, but also protect fixed income earners. These are essential prerequisites for encouraging environmentally sustainable activities.

Examples involving macroeconomic reforms

Two studies highlighted in Munasinghe and Cruz (1994) illustrate win–win situations. At the level of 'macroeconomic' pricing policies, a case study of Zimbabwe illustrates how foreign exchange reforms associated with adjustment efforts strengthen the economy and support tourism based on wildlife management – a key environmental sector. More indirect or systemic effects of economic policies on the environment have been analyzed using a computable general equilibrium (CGE) model for Morocco, which projected that a combination of trade liberalizing and water pricing reforms would not only increase economic growth rates, but also conserve water and help limit emerging water deficits – thereby providing significant environmental gains. An earlier CGE model of Thailand showed that combined economic and environmental gains would be possible with adjustment policies coupled with complementary measures, including the clear delineation of property rights in rural areas, and use of regulatory or economic instruments to limit urban pollution (Panayotou and Susangkarn, 1991). Although the quantitative results of CGE models should be interpreted with care, the qualitative results provide valuable insights and highlight the kinds of information needed to be able to anticipate with greater accuracy the environmental consequences of policy reform (Devarajan, 1990; Robinson, 1990; Persson and Munasinghe, 1995).

Other illustrative examples of the role of macroeconomic policies include the investigation of links between adjustment policy and environment in the agriculture sector in Sub-Saharan Africa (Stryker et al., 1989). Important contributions have also been made by environmental organizations through studies on the environmental impact of the adjustment process in Thailand, the Ivory Coast, Mexico and the Philippines (Reed, 1992; Cruz and Repetto, 1992). Another study suggests that trade policies that encourage greater openness in Latin

America have tended to be associated with a better environment, primarily due to environmentally benign characteristics of modern technologies (Birdsall and Wheeler, 1992).

Examples involving sectoral reforms

Energy and industry More specific or restricted policies affecting major sectors, such as industry and agriculture, or key resources, like energy, are also addressed in programs of economywide policy reforms. For example, Meier et al. (1995) demonstrate that raising subsidized energy prices closer to the long-run marginal cost of electricity supply will not only improve the efficiency of power use and accelerate GNP growth, but also reduce both in-country air pollution and CO_2 emissions that contribute to global greenhouse warming (for details, see Munasinghe, 1996). In Mexico, the potential for 'win–win' industrial policy reforms rests on removing subsidies and distortionary incentives to energy-intensive industries would result in large economic savings and reductions in industrial pollution. (for details, see Munasinghe and Cruz, 1994).

Water Experience in the water and sanitation sector shows that both targeting and reducing subsidies would have beneficial economic, social and environmental impacts. It would help to reduce wasteful use of water, improve cost recovery in a resource-scarce sector, eliminate the large subsidies that are captured mainly by the wealthy, expand facilities to low income areas and reduce water pollution (for examples involving Brazil, China and India, see World Bank, 1992b; World Bank, 1992c; and World Bank, 1993a).

Land use In Tunisia, the removal of livestock subsidies would produce significant economic gains and also improve the sustainable use of rangelands (Munasinghe and Cruz, 1994). Studies done for the Zambia Marketing and Processing Infrastructure Project (World Bank, 1992d) show that restructuring public expenditures for agriculture by eliminating maize, fertilizer and transport subsidies would improve the efficiency of food production, increase farm output, and encourage more sustainable farming practices. In the Amazon region, Mahar (1988) and Binswanger (1989) have analyzed the role of subsidies to agricultural and livestock expansion as the key factor leading to deforestation. Schneider (1993) focuses on institutional barriers at the economic frontier that prevent the emergence of land tenure services, such as titling and property rights enforcement, and thus undermine the potential for sustainable land use. Other studies have addressed similar adverse impacts of agricultural policies on the environment in Indonesia (on soil erosion), Sudan (on deforestation) and Botswana (on pastureland degradation) (Barbier, 1988; Larson and Bromley, 1991; Perrings, 1993).

Examples involving stabilization of inflation

The critical link between inflation and sustainability is illustrated in a case study of Costa Rica, using a CGE model, which demonstrates that lower real interest rates associated with a stable economy allow the logging sector to correctly anticipate the benefits from future returns to forestry – thereby leading to more sustainable logging practices (Persson and Munasinghe, 1995). Other studies have indicated that low and stable discount rates favor the choice of sustainable farming rather than unsustainable short-term cultivation practices (Southgate and Pearce, 1988). A study of Brazil also found that if interest rates are very high, farmers would tend to used less sustainable methods (Schneider, 1994).

Avoiding Harmful Impacts

A typical economywide reform program is implemented in stages, with the initial adjustment package aimed at the most important macroeconomic issues. Often, some distortions (policy, market or institutional imperfections) that policymakers intend to address later, or other constraints that have passed unnoticed in the initial screening, could combine with an adjustment program to cause environmental or social harm (Munasinghe et al., 1993). The remedy does not generally require reversal of the original reforms, but rather the implementation of additional complementary measures (both economic and non-economic) that remove such policy, market and institutional difficulties. These complementary measures are not only socially and environmentally beneficial in their own right, but also help to broaden the effectiveness of economywide reforms.

The results of a recent UNEP/World Bank workshop (Abaza, 1995) concluded that two major outcomes of structural adjustment programs often have adverse consequences. First, strong substitution effects in favor of exports could lead to environmental harm – for example, due to the increased profitability of export crops that may be more soil erosive in the long run, or through the deforestation of open access areas caused by export-oriented logging. Second, changes in both public expenditures and relative prices have often hurt the poor, and in turn led to further environmental degradation – especially when the landless poor have had no other alternative but to overexploit fragile lands.

Typical examples of potential environmental damage caused by unaddressed imperfections include:

Policy distortions Export promotion measures that increase the profitability of natural resource exports, will encourage excessive extraction or harvesting of this resource if it were underpriced or subsidized (for example, low stumpage fees for timber). Similarly, trade liberalization could lead to the expansion of wasteful energy-intensive activities, in a country where subsidized energy prices persisted.

Market failures Economic expansion induced by successful adjustment may be associated with excessive environmental damage – for example, if external environmental effects of economic activities (such as air or water pollution), are not adequately reflected in market prices that influence such activities. In the case of Indonesia, liberalization policies and industrial promotion accelerated growth in the modern sector, and reduced pollution. However, the scale of expansion has increased pollution externalities, which need to be addressed through complementary pollution taxes and environmental regulations (Munasinghe and Cruz, 1994).

Institutional constraints Often, the benefits of countrywide reforms are negated by unaddressed institutional problems, such as the poor accountability of state-owned enterprises (which would allow them to ignore efficient price signals), weak financial intermediation, or inadequately defined property rights. Such issues tend to undermine incentives for sustainable resource management and worsen equity.

Basically, the reform of regulations and institutions should not be allowed to lag too far behind economic restructuring, as shown in the case of energy pricing reforms and accountability of energy industries in Poland (Bates et al., 1995). In Peru, economywide reforms could have potentially increased harvesting pressures on Peru's over-exploited fisheries, unless complementary new fishing regulations to protect various fishing grounds were incorporated directly into the adjustment program (World Bank, 1993b).

Stabilization The shorter term stabilization process often has unforeseen adverse environmental and social impacts. For example, unless reductions in government spending to bring inflation under control are carefully targeted, they may disproportionately penalize expenditures on environmental protection or poverty safety nets (ECLAC, 1989; Miranda and Muzondo, 1991; Cornia et al., 1992). Other examples include increases in air pollution in Thailand and Mexico due to reductions in infrastructure expenditures (Reed, 1992), severe adverse impacts on low income groups in Africa (especially women and children), due to reduced government spending in areas like health (Nzomo, 1992), and underfunding of forest protection activities (World Bank, 1994b). Thus, both critical environmental and social expenditures need be protected by making government budget cuts judiciously.

Another important linkage is the short-term recessionary impact of adjustment on poverty and unemployment, whereby the poor are forced to increase their pressures on fragile lands and 'open access' natural resources – due to the lack of economic opportunities elsewhere. In this case, appropriate measures designed to address the possible adverse consequences of adjustment will be justified – on both social and environmental grounds.

Longer-term and Less Predictable Effects

Finally, economywide policies will have additional longer-term effects on sustainability, whose net impacts are less predictable. Some of these effects need to be traced through a general equilibrium framework that captures both direct and indirect links. In a study of Costa Rica, a CGE model that highlights the economic activities and factors affecting deforestation, shows that the economic and environmental implications of wage restraints in structural adjustment are different from the results obtained from partial equilibrium analyses (Persson and Munasinghe, 1995).

Several studies confirm that adjustment-induced changes often succeed in generating new economic opportunities and sources of livelihood, thereby alleviating poverty and helping to break the vicious cycle of environmental degradation and poverty (see for example, World Bank, 1992a). Higher incomes tend to increase the willingness-to-pay for better environmental quality which will lead to better protection of the environment. However, while such growth is an essential element of sustainable development, it will necessarily increase the overall pressures on environmental resources. At the same time, properly valuing resources, increasing efficiency and reducing waste, will help to reshape the structure of economic growth and limit undesirable environmental impacts. Both the economic and environmental consequences of adjustment programs will depend crucially on the mobility of capital and labor in the longer run. Finally, environmental policies themselves could have impacts on income distribution and employment.

Another set of studies has looked at the environmental implications of rural poverty and unemployment within the broader context of the social and demographic problems (Feder et al., 1988; Cruz and Gibbs, 1990; Lele and Stone, 1989). For example, inequitable access to land and rapid population growth exacerbate unemployment and income inequality, thereby forcing the poor to depend increasingly on marginal resources for their livelihood. The result is more pressure on fragile environments.

With regard to sustainable agriculture, one study found that shifting cultivation and grazing could worsen land degradation, in the context of limited capital and technical change, coupled with rapid population growth concerns (Cleaver and Schreiber, 1991). The importance of long-term links among adjustment programs, trade and agriculture, and the difficulties of analysing them, have also been emphasized by Goldin and Winters (1992). A Philippines case study (Munasinghe and Cruz, 1994) evaluates the policy determinants of long-term changes in rural poverty and unemployment that have motivated increasing lowland to upland migration, and led to the conversion of forest lands to unsustainable agriculture.

The foregoing evidence suggests that countrywide policy reforms may have counter-intuitive environmental and social impacts, through longer-term and indirect mechanisms. Considerable new work will be required to trace these complex linkages and improve the long-run sustainability of economic policies.

2. Framework for analysis

2.1 MICROECONOMIC VIEW OF ENVIRONMENTAL HARM – MAGNITUDE AND STRUCTURE OF GROWTH

Some linkages between economywide policies and the environment, which illustrate the interplay of both price and income effects, are summarized briefly below (see Munasinghe, 1995, for details). Consider a relatively stagnant economy, which has open access forest areas, as depicted in Figure 2.1. Initially, the demand for timber is given by the usual downward sloping curve D_0 in the figure, where the demand is assumed to be a function of both price P and income Y (that is, $D = D(P,Y)$). At the effective (subsidized) price P_S, which represents the marginal cost of logging, the initial rate of deforestation is Q_0. Suppose Q_L is the safe limiting rate of deforestation beyond which serious ecological damage occurs. As long as $Q_0 < Q_L$, the situation may continue undetected and uncorrected.

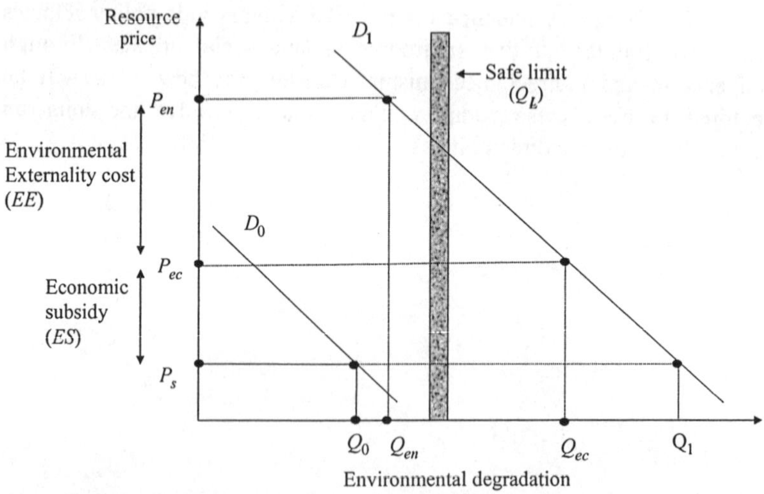

Source: Munasinghe (1995).

Figure 2.1 Restructuring growth to reduce environmental degradation

Next, suppose an economic reform package stimulates growth and shifts the timber demand curve outward to D_1. This 'income effect' could be the result of increased domestic demand (for example, timber required by a construction boom), and/or higher timber exports (for example, due to trade liberalization and devaluation that make such exports more profitable). Now, the deforestation rate could quickly shift to Q_1, greatly exceeding the safe limit Q_L and causing serious environmental harm.

Clearly, the remedy is not to stop growth (especially in a poor country), but rather to introduce complementary measures that establish a proper market price for timber. As a first step, property rights may need to be re-established in open access areas and an 'efficient' stumpage fee imposed – to eliminate the economic subsidy (*ES*) and correctly reflect the opportunity cost of the timber. The resulting efficient price (P_{ec}) would reduce the logging rate to Q_{ec}, which still exceeds Q_L. The next step might be to impose an additional environmental externality cost (*EE*) that reflects the loss of biodiversity or damage to watersheds, and thereby establish the full environmentally adjusted price (P_{en}). The deforestation rate would now fall to $Q_{en} < Q_L$.

Exactly analogous reasoning would apply if we considered fuel prices and polluting emissions from urban transport or industry. In this case, P_S might be a subsidized diesel price, P_{ec} the equivalent import (or export) opportunity cost, P_{en} the full price including a tax to cover the externality cost of air pollution, and Q_L the health-determined safety standard.

This rather simple example based on comparative statics helps to clarify how the expansionary effects of economic reform policies could combine with hitherto neglected economic distortions, to cause environmental harm. It also indicates that environmental damage need not be inextricably linked to economic growth (see the discussion on the environmental Kuznets curve, below), but might be moderated by sound policy measures. Thus, the parallel introduction of complementary measures that address the specific distortions would allow the broader reforms to go forward without adverse environmental (or social) impacts. These additional measures would need to be built (ex ante) into the macroeconomic reform package, rather than introduced as an afterthought.

The structure of economic growth is another important determinant of environmental degradation. Numerous studies during the past three or four decades have established that low income economies depend primarily on agriculture and primary products. As development accelerates, manufacturing becomes a more important contributor to the gross national product (GNP), starting with light industries (such as garments) and moving to heavy industries including steel and cement. In this stage corresponding to middle income or newly industrializing countries (NICs), intensity of natural resource use increases to support the urban-industrial centers, and pollution levels rise rapidly – especially where growth rates of GNP exceeding 5 percent per annum are commonplace. Finally, as countries move into the more mature, post-industrial phase of development like most of the Western market economies, the share of information technology and services in GNP rises, while industrial activity flattens out. Reductions in the intensity of raw material use and polluting emissions per unit of economic activity, help to diminish the environmental burden. Some theoretical aspects of this structural evolution are examined below in the section on the environmental Kuznets curve.

2.2 MACROECONOMIC VIEW OF ENVIRONMENTAL HARM

Up to now we have not seriously considered altering economywide policies merely to achieve sustainability objectives, but instead have chosen to rely on specific complementary measures to mitigate environmental and social harm. In this section, we examine whether circumstances exist, under which even macroeconomic policies might be tailored to satisfy environmental considerations.

Role of Second Best Policies

In a recent paper, Maler and Munasinghe (1996) developed a theoretical model in which they showed that pursuing first-best macroeconomic policies that seek to achieve a Pareto optimum will not maximize welfare, if an environmental externality exists. In such a situation, it is possible to contemplate whether second-best macroeconomic policies ought to be pursued – basically to trade off between broad macroeconomic goals and environmental damage.

More specifically, their mathematical analysis confirms the empirical observations made earlier in this chapter that it is the combination of growth-inducing economywide policies and residual imperfections such as policy distortions, market failures and institutional constraints that lead to environmental damage. The model also underlines the microeconomic analysis in the previous section, that such imperfections and resultant economic harm may well go unnoticed in a relatively stagnant economy, only to emerge quite visibly when growth rates begin to rise. Maler and Munasinghe explain further that the first-best solution would be to correct the imperfections using complementary policies while pursuing the original macroeconomic reforms. However, if political or other constraints prevent or delay the correction of the policy, market or institutional imperfections, then second-best macroeconomic policies may be justified – especially in cases where the environmental harm could be significant.

It is also relevant to examine the dynamics of the policy reform process. For example, such reforms might be intensified over a period of time (instead of being suddenly imposed), thereby allowing further time for residual imperfections that degrade the environment to be gradually phased out. In this context, the timing and sequencing of macroeconomic reforms may be critical, as explored below.

Timing and Sequencing of Policy Reforms

For illustrative purposes, suppose that the environmental damage due to an economic reform program is likely to be rather large. In such a case, is it possible to adjust the timing and sequencing of macroeconomic and sectoral policy tools, to avoid the worst environmental consequences?

In this same vein, there is a growing body of literature that seeks to examine the pros and cons of timing and sequencing stabilization and adjustment measures – to achieve economic goals (for a recent review, see Edwards, 1992), but not environmental ones. One may adapt some of this past work to obtain basic insights that help to deal with environmental issues.

Consider Figure 2.2, in which the X axis indicates aggregate expenditure in a national economy (for example, government expenditure) and the Y axis reflects the effects of domestic currency appreciation (for example, the ratio of domestic goods prices to foreign goods prices weighted by the exchange rate). Suppose that the initial state of the economy is at point A – below the line of internal balance IN (along which the economy is producing at the full employment income Y_F), and above the line of external balance EX (along which the current account CA is zero). In this situation, economywide policy reforms would seek to move the economy towards the equilibrium point B by reducing both the current account deficit (since $CA < 0$), and the excess demand (since $Y > Y_F$).

A movement in the (downward) direction AD could be achieved by a currency devaluation and removal of trade barriers, while a shift in the (leftward) direction AL would occur if government subsidies were eliminated (for example, by raising subsidized energy prices). Suppose that the reforms affecting AD could be achieved first and AL somewhat later. In this case, the opening up of the economy represented by AD alone might lead to greater foreign investment and expansion of energy-intensive industries that were attracted by the low energy prices. However, this apparent gain would also result in wasteful use of (the still subsidized) energy and more environmental pollution later, due to powerful vested interest (for example, transport or industrial lobbies).

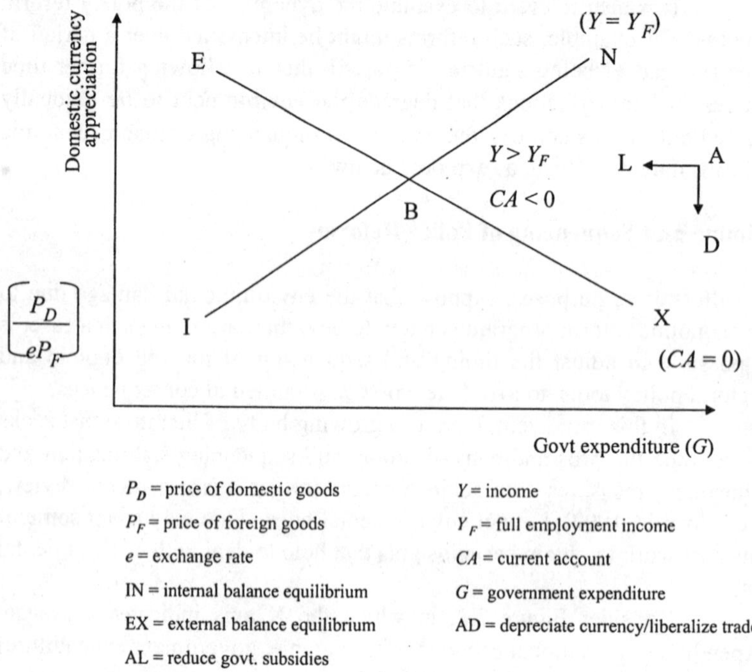

Figure 2.2 Timing and sequencing economic policies to make development more sustainable

Clearly, the foregoing analysis is limited by its simple, static and short-term nature. Nonetheless, some environmentally-related arguments such as the above could be used to fruitfully re-examine (and perhaps modify) the timing and sequencing of policy reforms. In extreme cases where significant environmental and social damage might occur, certain macroeconomic policies may have to be avoided altogether. Since hardly any work has been carried out in this area, and country circumstances vary widely, it would be difficult to generalize at this time. At the same time, restraint and good judgment is required to avoid the temptation of making major changes in economywide policies merely to achieve minor environmental and social gains. Once again, policy options that achieved 'win–win' gains would be the most desirable.

Extending the Conventional IS–LM Macroeconomic Analysis

Because the conventional IS–LM framework used in comparative static analysis of macroeconomic policies is so well known, it is useful to examine environmental concerns from this viewpoint (see for example, Heyes, 2000). In Figure 2.3, the familiar IS–LM curves are plotted in the (r,y) space, where r is the interest (discount) rate and y is aggregate demand.

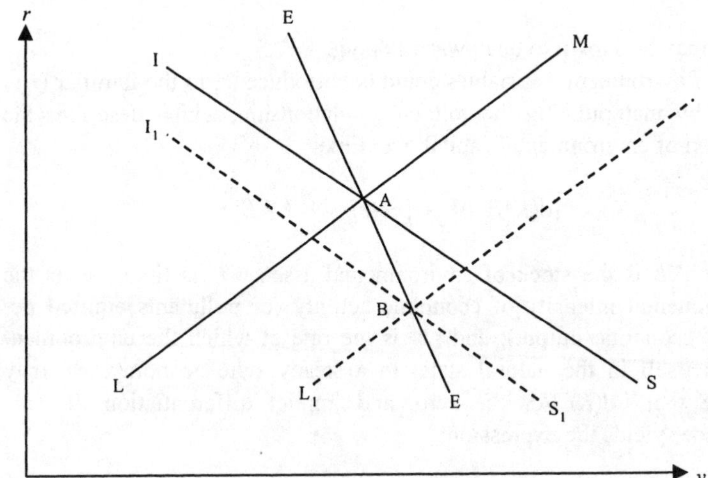

Figure 2.3 Extending conventional IS–LM analysis to include the environment

The IS curve is most simply derived from the identity indicating the equality of aggregate demand and supply, or equilibrium in the goods market:

$$y = [c(y) + i(r) + g] = [c(y) + s(y) + t.y]\text{ ; or equivalently}$$
$$[i + g] = [s + t];$$

where, c is consumption, i is investment, g is government spending, s is saving, and t is the tax rate. Simple calculus yields the equation for the basic IS curve:

$$[dr/dy]_{IS} = [t + ds/dy] / [di/dy];$$

which may be shown to be downward sloping.

The LM curve is derived from the corresponding money market equilibrium:

$$M/p = L(r,y)\ ;$$

where, M is the (fixed) money supply, p is the price level, L is the demand for money. Simple differentiation again yields the equation for the basic LM curve:

$$[dr/dy]_{LM} = -[dL/dy] / [dL/dr]\ ;$$

which may be shown to be upward sloping.

Environmental variables could be introduced into the familiar (r,y) space, by manipulating the following relationship, which describes the variation of environmental capital over time:

$$[d(KE)/dt] = [-e(r).y + k.KE]\ ;$$

where, KE is the stock of environmental assets, t is time, e is the environmental intensity of economic activity (or pollutants emitted per unit of economic output), and k is the rate at which the environment renews itself in the natural state. In a steady state economy, we may assume that $d(KE)/dt$ is zero, and implict differentiation of the remainder yields the expression:

$$[dr/dy]_{EE} = -[e] / [y.(de/dr)]$$

It is reasonable to assume that the environmental intensity would increase as the cost of capital rises, so that $(de/dr) > 0$. Therefore, $[dr/dy]_{EE}$ would be downward sloping. In Figure 2.3, the EE curve is shown to be steeper than the IS curve, assuming that e is relatively insensitive to r. One could postulate that e is also a function of some regulatory framework parameter Z, which determines how effectively the polluter is obliged to pay for environmental externalities. We might expect that $(de/dZ) < 0$; implying that the entire EE curve would shift leftward as regulatory enforcement improves.

A simple example of comparative statics analysis demonstrates the pedagogic value of the above approach. Initially, the economy shown in the figure is at equilibrium with the IS, LM and EE curves intersecting at the point A. An expansionary monetary policy would cause a shift from LM to L_1M_1. Restoring the tripartite equilibrium at point B, would now require a contractionary fiscal policy that yields the countervailing shift IS to I_1S_1 (assuming that the EE curve does not shift). Many similar policy exercises may be conducted, involving changes in various parameters and the shifting of all three curves.

2.3 ACTION IMPACT MATRIX (AIM): TOOL FOR POLICY ANALYSIS, FORMULATION AND COORDINATION

In the context of the foregoing discussion, economic–environmental–social interactions may be identified and analysed, and effective sustainable development policies formulated, by linking and articulating these activities explicitly. One tool that would facilitate the implementation of such an approach is the action impact matrix (AIM) – a simple example is shown in Table 2.1, although an actual AIM would be very much larger and more detailed (Munasinghe, 1993). Such a matrix helps to promote an integrated view, meshing development decisions with priority economic, environmental and social impacts. The far left column of the table lists examples of the main development interventions (both policies and projects), while the top row indicates some of the main sustainable development issues. Thus the elements or cells in the matrix help to: (a) identify explicitly the key linkages; (b) focus attention on valuation and other methods of analysing the most important impacts; and (c) suggest action priorities. At the same time, the organization of the overall matrix facilitates the tracing of impacts, as well as the coherent articulation of the links between a range of development actions – that is, policies and projects.

Table 2.1 A simplified preliminary action impact matrix (AIM)[a]

Activity/Policy	Main Objective	Impacts on Key Sustainable Development Issues		
		Land degradation	Air pollution	Resettlement
Macroeconomic & sectoral policies	Macroeconomic and sectoral improvements	Positive impacts due to removal of distortions Negative impacts mainly due to remaining constraints		
• Exchange rate	• Improve trade balance and economic growth	(−H) (deforest open-access areas)		
• Energy pricing	• Improve economic and energy use efficiency		(+M) (energy efficiency)	

Activity/Policy	Main Objective	Impacts on Key Sustainable Development Issues		
		Land degradation	Air pollution	Resettlement
• Others				
Complementary measures[b]	Specific/local social and environmental gains	Enhance positive impacts and mitigate negative impacts (above) of broader macroeconomic and sectoral policies		
• Market based	• Reverse negative impacts of market failures, policy distortions and institutional constraints		(+M) (pollution tax)	
• Non-market based		(+H) (property rights)	(+M) (public sector accountability)	
Investment projects	Improve efficiency of investments	Investment decisions made more consistent with broader policy and institutional framework		
• Project 1 (hydro dam)	• Use of project evaluation (cost–benefit analysis, environmental assessment, multi-criteria analysis, etc.)	(−H) (inundate forests)	(+M) (displace fossil fuel use)	(−M) (displace people)
• Project 2 (Re-afforest and relocate)		(+H) (replant forests)		(+M) (relocate people)

Notes:

[a] A few examples of typical policies and projects as well as key environmental and social issues are shown. Some illustrative but qualitative impact assessments are also indicated: thus + and - signify beneficial and harmful impacts, while H and M indicate high and moderate intensity. The AIM process helps to focus on the highest priority environmental issues and related social concerns.

[b] Commonly used market-based measures include effluent charges, tradable emission permits, emission taxes or subsidies, bubbles and offsets (emission banking), stumpage fees, royalties, user fees, deposit-refund schemes, performance bonds and taxes on products (such as fuel taxes). Non-market based measures comprise regulations and laws specifying environmental standards (such as ambient standards, emission standards and technology standards), which permit or limit certain actions ('dos' and 'don'ts').

Source: Munasinghe and Cruz (1994).

A stepwise procedure, starting with readily available data, has been used effectively to develop the AIM in several countries (for instance, Brazil, Chile, Ghana, Nepal, Philippines and Sri Lanka). This process has helped to harmonize views among those involved (economists, environmental specialists, sociologists and others), thereby improving the prospects for successful implementation (Munasinghe and Cruz, 1994, and MIND, 2005).

Screening and Problem Identification

One of the early objectives of the AIM-based process is to help in *screening and problem identification* – by preparing a preliminary matrix that identifies broad relationships, and provides a qualitative idea of the magnitudes of the impacts. Thus, the preliminary AIM would be used to prioritize the most important links between policies and their sustainability impacts. For example, in the second from top row of the table, a currency devaluation aimed at improving the trade balance, may make timber exports more profitable and lead to deforestation of open access forests. The appropriate remedy might involve complementary measures to strengthen property rights and restrict access to the forest areas.

A second example might involve increasing energy prices closer to marginal costs – to improve energy efficiency and decrease pollution (third row of table). A complementary measure involving the addition of pollution taxes to marginal energy costs will further reduce pollution. Increasing public sector accountability will reinforce favorable responses to these price incentives, by reducing the ability of inefficient firms to pass on cost increases to consumers or to transfer their losses to the government. In the same vein, a major hydroelectric project is shown lower down in the table as having two adverse impacts – inundation of forested areas and villages – as well as one positive impact – the replacement of thermal power generation (thereby reducing air pollution). A re-afforestation project coupled with adequate resettlement efforts may help address the negative impacts.

This matrix-based approach therefore encourages the systematic articulation and coordination of policies and projects to achieve sustainable development goals. Based on readily available data, it would be possible to develop such an initial matrix for many countries. Furthermore, a range of social impacts could be incorporated into the AIM, using the same approach.

Analysis and Remediation

This process may be developed further to assist in *analysis* and *remediation*. For example, more detailed analyses and modeling may be carried out for each matrix element in the preliminary AIM, which represented a high priority linkage between economywide policies and environmental impacts that had been already identified in the cells of the preliminary matrix. This, in turn, would lead to a more refined and updated AIM, which would help to quantify impacts and formulate additional policy measures to enhance positive linkages and mitigate negative ones.

The types of more detailed analyses that could help to determine the final matrix would depend on planning goals and available data and resources. They may range from the application of conventional sectoral economic analysis methods (appropriately modified in scope to incorporate environmental impacts), to fairly comprehensive system or multi-sector modeling efforts – including CGE models that include both conventional economic, as well as environmental or resource variables. Economic valuation of environmental and social impacts is a key (and often difficult) step, in integrating these concerns into conventional economic cost–benefit analysis (Munasinghe, 1992; Freeman, 1993). When such valuation is problematic, other techniques like multi-criteria analysis may need to be used. Sectoral and partial equilibrium analyses are more useful to trace details of direct impacts, whereas CGE modeling provides a more comprehensive but aggregate view, and insights into indirect linkages.

2.4 LINK WITH THE ENVIRONMENTAL KUZNETS CURVE (EKC) LITERATURE

The earlier sections help to bring several threads of thought together. First, one principal result of the empirical work summarized earlier was that imperfections in the economy could combine with growth-inducing economywide policies to cause environmental harm and, therefore, complementary policies that removed such imperfections would protect the environment. Second, this fundamental insight was confirmed by both the microeconomic and macroeconomic theoretical investigations carried out above.

The foregoing has relevance for growth-oriented policymaking in developing countries. Figure 2.4 is a stylized curve showing the relationship between economic progress (for example, GNP per capita) and environmental risk (for example, CO_2 emissions per capita). This type of curve has been dubbed the 'environmental Kuznets curve' or EKC. A typical industrial country might be at the point C, while a representative developing country would be at the lower point B. Ideally, industrial countries (which have exceeded safe limits), should seek to increase their environmental protection efforts and follow a future growth path such as CE. The developing countries could learn from the past experiences of the industrialized world, by adopting measures that would permit them to 'tunnel' through the path (as shown in Figure 2.4) – preferably below the safe limit beyond which at least some types of environmental damage (like climate change or biodiversity loss) could become irreversible. Munasinghe (1995) advances the argument that such a tunnel also corresponds to a more economically optimal path. He points out the resemblance here to the literature on 'turnpike' growth paths, which appeared in the 1960s and 1970s (Burmeister and Dobell, 1971).

The high peak in the path ABCE could be interpreted as the result of economic imperfections that make private decisions deviate from socially optimal ones. The adoption of corrective policies by the developing countries would help to reduce such divergences and permit movement through the tunnel BDE. They could thereby avoid the peak of environmental degradation associated with a conventional development path (like ABCE), which merely mimicked the evolution of the industrial economies. The viewpoint presented above is not concerned with issues such as the exact shape of the EKC, or whether the empirically estimated EKCs can adequately capture the growth characteristics of any single country. Instead, the emphasis would be on identifying policies that will help delink environmental degradation and growth, so that environmental harm will be reduced along the development path.

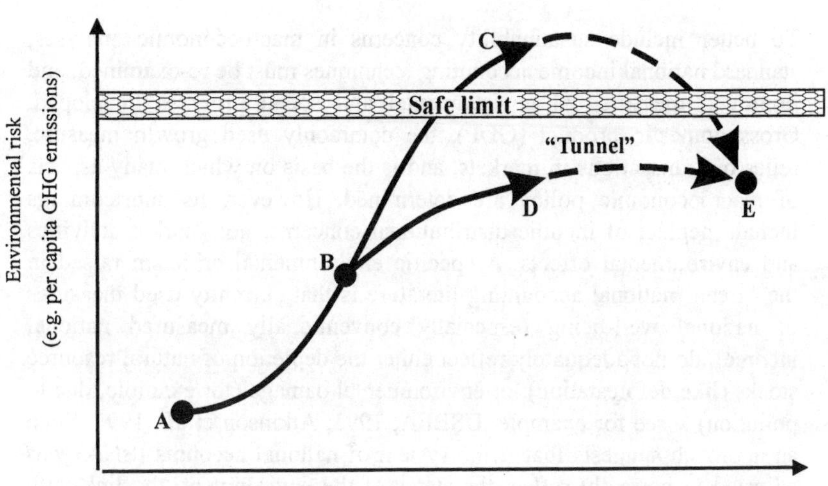

Source: Adapted from Munasinghe (1995).

Figure 2.4 Tunneling through to reduce environmental risk

The earlier discussions suggest that there are several actions that might help decision-makers in finding such a 'tunnel':

1. Actively seeking 'win–win' policies that simultaneously yield both economically and environmentally (and socially) sustainable paths – especially in the context of economywide liberalization and market-based reforms.
2. Pre-empting excessive environmental (and social) harm through a variety of measures including ex ante environmental (and social) assessment of projects and policies, promptly introducing remedies that eliminate imperfections (like policy distortions, market failures and institutional constraints), and strengthening the capacity for environmental regulation and enforcement of standards.
3. Critically examining the effects of growth-inducing economywide policies, and considering the fine-tuning of such policies (for example, altering their timing and sequencing) – especially in cases where severe environmental (and social) damage could be anticipated.

Macroeconomic Performance Measurement Issues

To better include sustainability concerns in macroeconomic analyses, standard national income accounting techniques must be re-examined, and improved measures of environmental and social progress developed. Gross domestic product (GDP), the commonly used growth measure, relies on transactions in markets, and is the basis on which many aspects of macroeconomic policy are determined. However, its shortcomings include neglect of income distributional concerns, non-market activities and environmental effects. A specific environmental criticism raised in the 'green' national accounting literature is that currently used measures of national well-being (especially conventionally measured national income), do not adequately reflect either the depletion of natural resource stocks (like deforestation), or environmental damage (for example, due to pollution) – see for example, USBEA, 1995; Atkinson et al., 1997. Such an approach suggests that if the system of national accounts (SNA) was adjusted to correctly reflect the status of the environment, the link with macroeconomic policies would become more apparent.

Currently, several countries are exploring different types of environmental adjustments to the conventional system of national accounts (SNA). Several measures of assessing national product and wealth are being considered, including *natural resource (stock) accounts*, *resource and pollutant flow accounts*, *environmental expenditure accounts*, and *alternative national accounts aggregates*, are described in Atkinson et al., (1997). However, no countries have definitely altered their standard national accounts to reflect resources and the environment, beyond what is in the 1993 revision to the SNA (United Nations Statistical Office, 1993).

The United Nations integrated system of environmental and economic accounting (SEEA) has taken the first step towards standardizing the various accounting approaches (United Nations, 1993). The SEEA is designed to be a *satellite* account to the conventional system of national accounts (SNA), that is, it is an adjunct to (rather than a modification of), the core accounts. It is highly complex, involving disaggregation of the standard accounts to highlight environmental relationships, linked physical and monetary accounting, imputations of environmental costs and extensions of the production boundary of the SNA. A comprehensive framework like the SEEA may be used to estimate various national accounts aggregates such as 'green GNP' – which are adjusted downward to reflect the costs of net resource depletion and environmental pollution. At the same time, the selection of a specific green accounting aggregate turns out to be important. For example, it may be argued that obtaining measures of Hicks–Lindahl or sustainable income, that is, a 'green NNP', is intrinsically important. However, this is not the same thing as saying that green measures of income have direct relevance with regard to formulating policies for sustainable development.

One issue is that producing a new figure for the *level* of national income does not readily translate into a policy signal about the sustainability of development. Green NNP basically measures *potentially* sustainable income. It does not in itself answer the question of whether the rate of saving is sufficient to maintain this income indefinitely. There is the additional difficulty that green NNP represents the amount that could be consumed while leaving the rate of change of utility *instantaneously* constant. Therefore, green NNP is not fully satisfactory as an aggregate sustainability indicator, because it typically does not measure the amount that could be consumed if the economy were actually on a constant-utility path. A recently proposed measure involving 'genuine savings' is being studied by development agencies like the World Bank.

Total wealth per capita becomes a useful indicator of sustainability, if the greening of national accounts includes the expansion of the measure of national wealth – including the value of stocks of not only manufactured capital, but also living and non-living resources. If the former ratio is non-decreasing, then development is sustainable (or *weakly* sustainable – since it is assumed that produced assets are highly substitutable for natural assets). That is, for total wealth W and population P, the sustainability criterion is:

$$S = [\mathrm{d}(W/P)/\mathrm{d}t]/[W/P] \geq 0$$

This index has several desirable properties, including the possibility of separately accounting for the changes in the level of natural assets for which substitution possibilities are low.

To summarize, while trends in national income per capita (using green or traditional measures) may say something about economic performance in the short run, measuring trends in wealth per capita gives a clearer picture of how the wealth creation and population growth influences the potential for future income per capita.

The foregoing discussion highlights the distinction between conventional income per capita as an indicator of development, and a more complex set of measures that might better capture the essence of sustainable development. For example, as discussed earlier (see Figure 1.1) sustainable development has been defined in terms of three key elements – economic, social and environmental. Some researchers have sought to compute a composite index of human welfare and show that the relationship between 'true' welfare and conventional income per capita is positive in the early stages of development, but becomes negative later on – in contrast to the EKC effect (see for example, Daly and Cobb, 1989; Max-Neef, 1995). They estimate that one such measure based on the Index of Sustainable Economic Welfare (ISEW), has already peaked in the 1970s or 1980s and is now declining for the US, UK, Germany, Austria and Netherlands. Thus, recent work is seeking to expand the social accounting matrix (SAM) to include the distributional impacts of environmental damage across income groups (Munasinghe, 2002b).

2.5 CONCLUDING REMARKS

Overview

The papers reproduced in this volume trace the evolution of ideas that interlink macroeconomics and the environment. Current thinking on the subject recognizes that a wide range of economywide policy reform programs has been undertaken to address macroeconomic and sectoral problems. Although these policies are not directed explicitly towards addressing sustainability issues, they often have significant environmental and social impacts. While such impacts are often too diverse to be comprehensively traced with precision, many key economywide reforms have specific, identifiable impacts on high priority environmental and social problems. Some of these impacts may be intuitively obvious, and many of them may be traceable on the basis of country-specific analysis.

From a policy perspective, even modest progress in this regard is helpful because the proper recognition of the environmental and social benefits of countrywide policies will help to design better economic reforms. At the same time, broader recognition of the underlying economic and policy causes of environmental and social problems can enhance support for sustainable development initiatives.

Analytical Findings

The stylized results reviewed in this introduction (based on both empirical case studies and theoretical models), indicate that macroeconomic reforms, including removal of price distortions, promotion of market incentives and relaxation of other constraints, could contribute simultaneously to economic, social and environmental gains. However, unintended adverse side effects occur in many cases – when such reforms are undertaken while other neglected policy, market or institutional imperfections persist. The remedy does not generally require reversal of the original economywide reforms, but rather the implementation of additional complementary measures (both economic and non-economic) that remove such policy, market and institutional difficulties. Introducing such remedial measures ex ante, before broad reforms are undertaken, is the most desirable approach.

Measures aimed at restoring macroeconomic stability also will generally yield economic, social and environmental benefits. However, the stabilization process may have unforeseen adverse short-term impacts on sustainability issues. Once again, specific complementary measures designed to address the possible adverse environmental and social consequences of stabilization policies would be justified.

Economywide policies will have additional (and often unpredictable) longer term effects on the environment through employment and income distribution changes. Often, adjustment-induced changes generate new economic opportunities and sources of livelihood, thereby alleviating poverty and reducing pressures on the environment due to over-exploitation of fragile resources by the unemployed. However, while growth is an essential element of sustainable development, it will necessarily intensify pressures on environmental resources. Increasing efficiency, reducing waste and properly valuing resources, will help reshape the structure of growth and reduce undesirable environmental impacts.

Policy Implications

In general, most past economywide reforms have been implemented without adequate consideration of their environmental and social, as well as economic impacts. In the case of structural adjustment policies implemented to address the debt crisis faced by many developing countries in the 1980s, partial or piecemeal reforms often pressured countries to adopt methods of increasing economic production that were not only socially harmful, but also environmentally damaging. Nevertheless, despite short-term sacrifices, properly managed adjustment facilitates long-term growth without which environmental damage could be worse. More specifically, non-growth scenarios tend to give rise to worse results than growth situations, because of the linkages between poverty and both environmental and social unsustainability.

Hence, the best approach seems to be the successful implementation of sound economic policies aimed at the recovery or maintenance of growth, combined with the adoption of specific remedial environmental and social programs. The availability of appropriate sustainability indicators is a crucial prerequisite for improving all such development decisions. Most importantly, sustainable development strategies must be devised on a country by country basis, with due regard for local conditions, resource endowments and social needs.

The analytical process will be strengthened by developing a more systematic framework based on the concept of an action impact matrix (AIM), which clearly identifies a country's environmental problems in relation to its program of economywide policy reforms and major projects. Such a stepwise approach focuses initially on the links among a relatively small sub-set of priority environmental and social concerns and a few key economic policy reforms. In subsequent stages, the analysis may be made much more comprehensive.

The process for avoiding environmental (and social) damage may be summarized as follows:

1. The AIM-based analysis may be used to identify, prioritize and analyze the most serious economic–sustainability linkages.
2. Ideally it would be desirable to devise specific ex ante complementary measures to limit environmental and social harm, whenever economywide reforms are contemplated.

3. Where data and resource constraints preclude the accurate tracing of such links (ex ante), the preliminary screening and prioritization of environmental and social issues could be followed by establishing contingency plans and carefully monitoring these sustainability problems to deal with them if they worsen ex post.
4. In cases involving more severe environmental and social harm (especially where ex ante analysis has carefully prepared the ground), decision makers might wish to consider orchestrating the timing and sequencing of various economywide policies and complementary measures, to minimize environmental and social damage.

These findings, based on both empirical and theoretical evidence, also suggest that developing countries seeking sustainable development paths might be well advised to learn from the experience of the industrialized countries, in order to avoid repeating the same mistakes. Economic imperfections that make private decisions deviate from socially optimal ones tend to exacerbate environmental damage along an EKC growth path. Tunneling through the EKC is possible, by adopting 'win–win' policies that provide simultaneous economic, environmental and social gains; using complementary measures to address harmful impacts on sustainability; and even reshaping economywide policies in cases where the threat to sustainability was serious enough.

There are many problems associated with the measurement of both environmental damage and economic development. Nevertheless, important policy insights may be gained by using currently available environmentally adjusted measures of national income.

Areas for Further Work

More in-depth work is required in tracing the sustainability implications of economywide policies, which will help to relate comprehensive packages of countrywide policy reforms to a range of priority environmental and social concerns in different countries. Exploring the sustainability of long-run growth is important, especially in the context of worsening natural resource scarcities, including degradation of the global environment. Some areas of current interest such as trade reform and privatization policies should receive early attention. At the same time, there ought to be more emphasis on developing more practical models and analytical tools that can be applied in a variety of situations, and are based on approaches that are more familiar to practising macroeconomists (for example, extended IS–LM framework).

Distributional, political economy, and institutional issues also need to be addressed in future work. The nature of environmental and social problems is heavily dependent on the allocation of political and institutional power, and policy reforms may have substantial implications for redistributing income and wealth. Thus, there are obvious obstacles to overcoming what might be very powerful vested interests when environmental and social reforms are recommended, and implementation problems such as asymmetries in the incidence of costs and benefits, and the timing of reforms, will have to be studied. The cross-linkage between environmental and social impacts of economywide policies needs to be further explored.

More systematic ways of monitoring the sustainability impacts of policies and projects require that better environmental and social indicators should be developed. Thus far, the more successful attempts to value environmental impacts in the macroeconomic context have been based on their effects on conventional economic output, which are priced in the marketplace (supplemented sometimes with shadow pricing corrections). This approach may be linked up more easily with commonly used market measures of aggregate output like GNP).

Some environmentally and socially crucial impacts (for example, loss of biodiversity or human health hazards) are often important, and may require the extension or adaptation of conventional economic techniques. One step would be to improve environmental valuation by using a wider range of methods that employ both market and non-market information to estimate indirectly the economic value of environmental assets (for example, travel cost or contingent valuation methods). Such techniques have been used quite widely in project level applications in the industrial countries (Freeman, 1993). There is a growing body of case studies on the environmental valuation of project impacts in the developing countries (Munasinghe, 1992). However, considerable work is required to extend this experience to cover economywide impacts.

Other (non-economic) indicators of environmental and social well-being (both micro and macro) also would be helpful in decision making, especially in cases where economic valuation of environmental and social impacts was difficult (Munasinghe and Shearer, 1995). Techniques such as multi-criteria analysis (MCA) may be used to trade off among different economic, social and environmental indicators, as a supplement to conventional cost–benefit analysis. The essential point is that even when valuation of environmental and social impacts is not possible, techniques like MCA exist that will help to better prioritize such impacts, thereby improving development actions (Munasinghe, 1996, Chapter 8).

Severe data constraints are likely to limit the applicability of certain methods, in many developing countries. Therefore, 'short-cut' methods need to be developed. For example, easily applicable rules-of-thumb (calibrated by well-chosen national studies) could be used to devise baseline estimates of national wealth in the form of natural resources, human capital and produced assets (Atkinson et al., 1997). Environmental indicators of land use, soil, water and air quality could supplement economic measures, in the same way as social indicators – such as education and health status.

PART II

Brazil Case Study

3. Production, consumption and the environment in Brazil

3.1 INTRODUCTION

The industrialization process and growth in income per capita achieved by Brazil during the past four decades has been accompanied by persistent social inequalities and increasing environmental degradation. Until the early 1980s, the Brazilian model of development was based on industrialization through import substitution. Protectionism, development of state companies and ambitious fiscal and credit incentives transformed the previous agrarian economy into a highly industrialized society within a time span of 30 years. During the most dynamic period, the 1970s, Brazil grew at an average annual rate of 8.7 percent (IBGE, National Accounts) while the percentage of the population living in urban areas increased from 30 percent to 70 percent (IBGE, Population Censuses).

Nonetheless, the distribution of this economic prosperity was not spread evenly across the population. Approximately 40 percent of the households were below the poverty line by the end of the 1970s and the Gini coefficient was 0.60 in 1979, one of the poorest income distributions in the world (Barros, Henriques and Mendonça, 2000). Low investments in primary and secondary education induced a perpetuation of high-income concentrations. In addition, the lack of land reform policies caused land to be owned mainly by the rich. Moreover, during the 1970s, the government substituted the needed land reform policy for a colonization process in the Amazon which led to severe consequences on the pattern of deforestation in the region.

The social inequalities were exacerbated by the oil and debt crises of the late 1970s that generated fiscal imbalances slowing investment capacity and leading to a long recession in the following decade. Unemployment rates increased and inefficient industrial and agricultural structures were unable to sustain a dynamic growth process. Furthermore, during the 1980s and the beginning of the 1990s, high inflationary pressures jeopardized Brazil's opportunities for growth, and increased social conflicts. An acute fiscal crisis created a continuous threat of hyperinflation that reached levels over 2000 percent per annum during the

1990s.

Since 1988 several structural reforms have been implemented. Growth promoting market oriented policies related to trade and capital liberalization; privatization and deregulation have been introduced. As a result, between 1991 and 1997, foreign direct investment increased by US$ 14.7 billion and labor productivity in the manufacturing sector increased by 8.7 percent (Bonelli, 1998).

In conjunction with the previous policies, restrictive macroeconomic reforms were implemented during the 1990s. The most important was the Real Plan, introduced in 1994, which applied a successful monetary stabilization policy that reduced the monthly inflation rate from 80 percent to 1 percent. The control of inflation created a reliable environment for private investors, but also generated an immediate redistribution effect through the reduction of the inflationary tax. The Gini coefficient decreased from 0.58 in 1993 to 0.57 in 1995 (Rocha, 2000). Subsequently, this redistribution faded out with the increase in unemployment. Table 3.1demonstrates this trend through inequality coefficient estimates by Ramos and Vieira (1997).

Table 3.1 Theil t statistics for income inequality in Brazil, 1992–97

Years	Theil t
1992	0.563
1993	0.677
1995	0.599
1996	0.586
1997	0.595

Source: Ramos and Vieira (2000).

Unlike macroeconomic policies, social and environmental policies have not been as successful in achieving their goals. Although the accumulated growth rate in the period 1990–98 reached 24 percent, the growth perspective in the short run is difficult to forecast, especially with the current fiscal crisis. Although social care programs for the poor in urban and rural areas have been continuously extended, they have not been efficient in reducing overall poverty and decreasing inequality. According to Barros, Henriques and Mendonça (2000), Brazil is still one of the most unequal countries in the world. The Gini coefficient during the 1990s was around 0.60 and the fraction of 10 percent richest households to the 40 percent poorer households was approximately 24 (while it is below 10 in most countries). A similar degree of inequality is indicated for land tenure where small farms (with less than 10 ha) cover less than 3 percent of the total farming area while the share of big farms (with more than 10 000 ha) is above 40 percent. In rural areas, land taxation has recently been modified in order to discourage land concentration, causing dramatic increases in tax brackets for idle land.[1] Agrarian reform programs have received a large share of the budget and ambitious targets have been set. Nonetheless, rural poverty has not decreased significantly and remains a serious problem, especially in the northeast of Brazil. In 1996, 63 percent of poor households were concentrated in the Northeast region, of which almost 50 percent lived in rural areas.

Furthermore, rural areas are suffering from serious environmental problems associated with water pollution, soil degradation, deforestation and biodiversity loss. Urban regions also suffer from increasing environmental degradation through air and water pollution, lack of sewage facilities for poorer households, and increasing solid waste generation. These increasing environmental problems could impose restrictions on future growth possibilities. Nonetheless, a substantial portion of government and the population do not understand that environmental degradation can affect long -run growth possibilities. As such, environmental degradation is seen as an unavoidable outcome of rapid growth.

A public opinion poll[2] carried out by the Ministry of the Environment has shown that only 47 percent of Brazilians agree with the idea that the environment should take priority over economic growth. Moreover, there is an increasing acceptance to diminish environmental quality in exchange for growth among the lower income classes. Deforestation and burning were singled out as the main national environmental problems by 45 percent of the interviewees. Environmental problems related to urban regions such as water pollution, sanitation and solid waste correspond to 34 percent of indications while air pollution is only 12 percent. Results from the same survey directed at 90 opinion makers (experts, public officials, congressman and businessman) indicate a highest policy priority for urban issues (59 percent) followed by deforestation (36 percent) and water concerns (33 percent).

The current political agenda in Brazil is, without doubt, to resume growth, strengthen the country's share in the global economy, reduce social gaps and protect the environment. These national priorities are widely recognized by all political parties and accepted by the general public. Nonetheless, they are hard to achieve simultaneously, as some policies involve trade-offs which are not well understood. This study will attempt to analyze this trade-off and the environmental consequences of economic growth that occurred during the last decade in Brazil. The following areas will be explored: industrial growth and pollution; consumption patterns, environment and income classes; and causes of deforestation in the Amazon.

3.2 INDUSTRIAL PRODUCTION PATTERNS AND POLLUTION

The Brazilian economy has experienced successive policy changes to alleviate the pressure on the balance of payments caused by an external debt crisis. In the early 1980s, many incentives were given to increase exports in order to improve the external debt situation. The expansion of the export sector was a key element in the structural adjustment strategy carried out with the approval of the IMF and the World Bank. This change in the orientation of the industrial policy, which is dedicated to import-substitution, has affected the Brazilian industrial structure considerably. As a result, export-oriented industries performed much better relative to the traditional, domestic market-oriented industries.

In the late 1980s and, even more in the 1990s, the economy went through a stop-and-go cycle characterized by the expansion of imports, following trade liberalization policies which were adopted more aggressively by each successive government in the period. This trend of import expansion was particularly accentuated with the exchange rate overvaluation after the Real stabilization program in 1994. As a result, there was a large increase in the use of imported inputs in many production chains, and a subsequent decrease in the use of domestic materials.

During the same period, there is evidence that the pollution problem has increased in Brazil. The Brazilian Statistical Office (IBGE) has created an index of industrial growth according to a classification of potential pollution, following the methodology proposed by Carvalho and Ferreira (1992). The index combines output data from IBGE's monthly industrial survey, classified according to the air and water pollution potential of each product, as adopted by the State of Rio de Janeiro environmental agency (FEEMA). It is important to highlight that FEEMA's classification is based on the potential hazard to the air or water quality from producing the good, assuming that no mitigation measures are taken. Therefore, this index does not consider the existence of abatement processes, which may reduce or even eliminate the pollution impact. In other words, it is an estimate of potential rather than actual industrial pollution.

Figure 3.1 shows that the industries with high pollution potential grew at higher rates than the average polluting Brazilian industry. The conclusion is that the dynamics of industrial growth in the Brazilian industry since the 1980s has been positively associated with the level of potential pollution in a way that industrial growth has been diverted towards the potentially polluting industries. (Note that the output of industrial sectors classified with high pollution potential grew faster than the average of the industry during the period 1981–99).

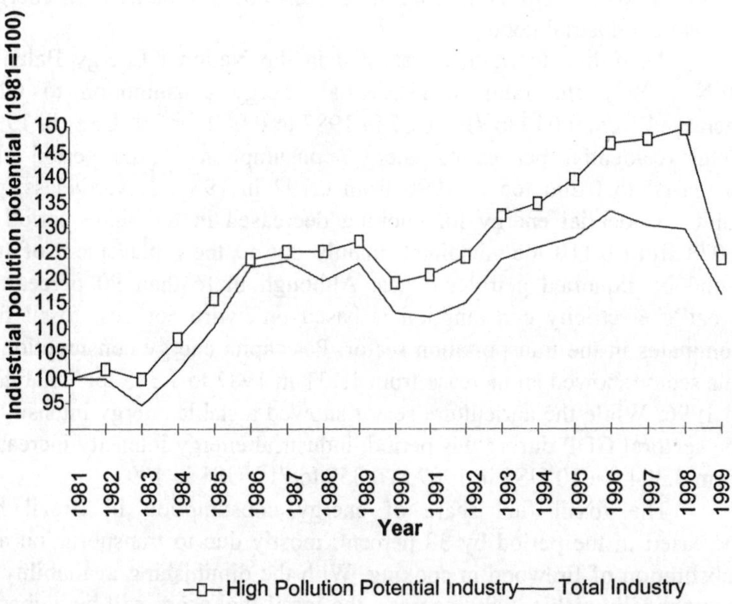

Source: IBGE/DPE/Industry Department

Figure 3.1 Evolution of the Brazilian industry according to its potential pollution (1981 = 100)

3.3 URBAN CONSUMPTION PATTERNS AND THEIR COSTS

Recent surveys on household expenditures in Brazil have shown significant changes in consumption patterns in the period 1987–96. The percentage increases in ownership of durable goods among households exceeded the percentage increase in population of 15 percent. In Table 3.2 we present the growth in ownership of domestic electric appliances by income groups. The average ownership across all income groups exhibit large increases for drier machines (173 percent), freezers (211 percent) and dishwasher machines (275 percent). Compared to averages of all income groups, some of the lower income groups have substantially higher increases in ownership levels of these appliances. The increase in appliance ownership is leading to a consumption pattern of energy-intensive industrial goods.

According to figures presented in the National Energy Balance, BEN (1997), the ratio of residential energy consumption to GDP increased from 0.049 toe/10^3 US$ in 1987 to 0.060 toe/10^3 US$ in 1996. Total residential per capita energy consumption in the period also increased to 0.206 toe in 1996 from 0.192 in 1987. Nevertheless, per capita residential energy for cooking decreased in the same period to 0.078 from 0.110 toe/inhabitant, mainly due to the replacement of fuel wood by liquefied petroleum gas. Although more than 90 percent of Brazil's electricity consumption is based on hydro sources, fossil fuel dominates in the transportation sector. Per capita energy consumption in this sector showed an increase from 1.131 in 1987 to 1.348 toe/inhabitant in 1996. While the agriculture sector showed a stable energy intensity in the sectoral GDP during this period, industrial energy intensity increased from 0.304 toe/10^3US$ in 1987 to 0.359 toe/10^3US$ in 1997.

The fossil fuel share of energy consumption in Brazil has increased in the period by 38 percent, mostly due to transportation and substitution of firewood in cooking. With the diminishing availability of economically viable hydro sources, the fossil fuel share will be higher in the future.

Table 3.2 Durable good ownership in Brazil, 1996–87

Goods	Income class groups										
	All %	0—2 %	2—3 %	3—5 %	5—6 %	6—8 %	8—10 %	10—15 %	15—20 %	20—30 %	30—+ %
Air conditioning	54	6	234	133	72	41	198	59	68	60	29
Vacuum cleaner	10	−22	120	2	−2	23	9	19	−2	−5	18
Automobile	22	43	112	26	69	31	24	31	11	8	21
One automobile	24	35	110	25	65	33	21	27	11	17	20
Two automobiles or more	17	–	–	43	191	3	54	68	14	−19	21
Churn	27	78	80	39	41	31	37	36	8	14	21
Bike	53	171	102	55	74	53	40	50	35	43	35
Hi-Fi set	59	178	242	83	74	74	51	37	35	30	39
Pressing iron	16	59	36	10	16	14	7	8	8	6	22
Cooker	14	42	31	6	16	14	6	7	7	5	22
Freezer	211	1262	816	677	756	477	491	420	272	193	96
Refrigerator	18	57	48	17	24	16	10	9	6	4	21
Tape-recorder	4	260	69	50	19	24	−4	−15	−29	−26	−10
Liquidizer	15	59	47	10	16	14	8	8	7	3	19
Washing machine	81	207	351	210	216	144	103	95	57	32	42

Dish washer machine	275	–	–	310	727	436	776	208	429	249	240
Drier machine	173	–	277	361	367	196	156	350	148	86	139
Table radio	3	9	13	6	6	13	−14	7	−8	−12	13
Hairdryer	3	75	30	14	7	−5	−7	−5	−6	−7	18
Television	64	288	281	148	125	91	50	37	25	15	24
Pick-up Phonograph	6	12	−23	−38	−42	−27	−32	8	28	26	88
Toaster	9	96	−45	−41	10	−10	−2	25	9	3	19
Ventilator	40	109	68	43	35	36	28	40	23	14	44

Note: i) % = (1996 value − 1987 value) / 1987 value.
ii) Income class groups: minimum wages.

Source: IBGE – Pesquisa de Orçamentos Familiares (POF).

Data from the national household sample survey, PNAD (1998), indicates that treated water supply service in urban areas is provided to 91 percent of the households. Sewage collection systems and septic tanks have increased and today supply 50 percent and 25 percent of the urban households respectively. According to Seroa da Motta (1996) less than 20 per cent of sewage generated is treated. Waste collection services are offered to 80 percent of urban households but less than 45 percent is adequately disposed.

As in any growing urban and industrial society, consumption patterns in Brazil is shifting towards environmentally intensive goods and services, thereby increasing pressure on the environment and ecosystems. Although the literature on the environmental impacts of economic growth typically emphasize deforestation, pollution effects tend to be more relevant in countries where a greater share of the population is located in dense urban areas.

Urban pollution is a severe problem in many Brazilian cities, but does not affect all people equally. Since the poor cannot afford to mitigate the impacts of pollution, the poor tend to suffer most by the effects of degradation. Seroa da Motta and Rezende (1999) analyzed the relationship between the six most common waterborne diseases[3] and child death incidence. They used an econometric model correlating child death incidence rates with variables of sanitation services available to poor urban households, such as: publicly treated water supply, sewage collection system and sewage treatment system for the period 1980–90. The results indicate the number of children who would probably be saved if the sanitation services were expanded to 1 percent of the population of the families earning less than five minimum wages.

Increasing the provision of public water supply to another 1 percent of the population not yet served, without any improvement in other sanitation services, would reduce the number of mortality cases of children under 14 years of age associated with waterborne diseases by 2.5 percent (462 lives). For a 1 percent increase in sewage collection and treatment, the equivalent reductions would be 1.6 percent (298 lives) and 2.1 percent (395 lives) respectively. If all three services provided, there would be a 6.1 percent (1139 lives) reduction in mortality. The importance of water supply is confirmed by the higher level of mortality reduction resulting from an initial 1 percent increase in service expansion.

The investment required to save one life when accomplishing the 1 percent increase in the served population is determined by the total investment necessary to increase the served population by 1 percent for each sanitation service, divided by the total lives saved by that increase.

Costs are estimated according to average per capita investment costs of the conventional sanitation services projects undertaken by the sanitation companies in Brazil. The costs of saving each life by increasing access to public water supply, sewage treatment and sewage collection are US$ 115 102, US$ 175 207 and US$ 214 562, respectively. To expand all three services jointly by 1 percent, the Brazilian society needs to invest US$ 164 385.

These estimates for the costs of each life saved may be taken as the value of life for mortality cases associated with waterborne diseases in Brazil. (i.e., how much the Brazilian society values the possibility of saving one poor child's life.) Considering that sanitation facilities last for more than 50 years and operational and maintenance costs are equivalent to 10 percent of capital costs, the annualized value of a saved life would be, for the joint alternative (involving increasing access to water supply, sewage treatment and sewage collection), around US$ 18 000, which is more than four times the Brazilian per capita income. Although the value of life may seem to be intangible, these figures indicate that the impacts of water pollution on human health are significant and mitigation costs are very high.

Another outcome of economic growth is air pollution. The social cost of air pollution is estimated in Seroa da Motta and Fernandes Mendes (1996), where health costs are estimated by a function of mortality rates caused by respiratory diseases with meteorological parameters (humidity and temperature), pollution concentration data (particulate and SO_2) and socio-economic data (medical care, education level, etc.) for the period 1980–89. This regression was composed of 395 observations for the districts and sub-districts in the Municipality of São Paulo using data from 11 air quality monitoring stations. The study indicates that a variation of $10 \mu g/m^3$ of particulate matter changes the mortality rate by 1.62 percent. This result is close to the upper confidence levels found in the literature mentioned by Ostro (1992) and confirms that particulate matter concentrations harm human health.

Using the estimated elasticity, the authors projected the proportion of reduced deaths due to pollution control in São Paulo. For instance, a reduction of 44 per cent pollution in the region would result in the air quality concentration level of $50 \mu g/m^3$, which reflects the legal primary ambient standard, and could avoid the death of 6.4 percent of patients who died of respiratory diseases in the region in 1991. Costs of these respiratory diseases may be estimated from hospital diagnosis and treatment costs, and the value of foregone output resulting from missed work days and premature death. The estimates indicate that air pollution costs in the study area would be around US$ 1.7–2.2 million.

The previously calculated pollution costs are due to increasing urbanization and its changes in consumption patterns occurring together with a very unequal income distribution. Degradation can be very severe from consumption patterns of high-income groups who have high consumption of energy and water and generate large amounts of sewage and solid waste, while owning large amounts of durable goods.

However, income restrictions drastically reduce the capacity of the poor to expend on defensive expenditures against negative effects of degradation, such as medical care and a better housing environment. In other words, the burden of environmental costs is falling disproportionately on the poor.

3.4 PRODUCTION PATTERNS AND DEFORESTATION IN THE BRAZILIAN AMAZON

The Brazilian Amazon is regarded as one of the most important ecosystems in the world boasting almost 50 percent of the known biodiversity in the planet. It comprises an area of nearly 5 million square kilometers, of which approximately 70 percent is continuous forest domain. The extent of deforestation has grown significantly during the past twenty years. Approximately 400 000 km^2 of tropical forest was cleared between 1978 and 1998 according to satellite image estimates.[4]

Coinciding with such a deforestation trend, the region had a substantial growth in income per capita. Economic growth was achieved in the Amazon through the establishment of colonization projects in the region and massive infrastructure investment and credit concessions. Average GDP in the Amazon region grew by an average of 15 percent per year from 1970 to 1980 while per capita income more than doubled. The leading sector in this boom was the industrial sector, which had an average growth rate of 26 percent per year motivated by the creation of the Manaus Free Export Processing Zone. The share of industry in local production increased from 15 percent in 1970 to an impressive 40 percent in 1980 (Reis and Blanco, 1996).

During the 1980s and 1990s, though growth was maintained, there was a substantial difference among states. Industrial growth was not widespread and in some states agricultural activities were the main factor motivating growth. Table 3.3 shows the average and the cumulative GDP growth for each state of the Legal Amazon from 1985 to 1997. We also include the agriculture GDP growth as a means of comparison. The first important observation is that the most industrialized state, Amazonas, has a low average growth rate while other states such as Acre and Rondônia that depend mostly on agriculture, cattle and extraction had average growth rates over 4 percent. We also observe that the states with the highest economic growth rates, Roraima and Amapá, also had high agriculture GDP growth rates indicating that their growth is based on agriculture and cattle ranching, both of which have been identified as causes of deforestation. Indeed, these states exhibited the highest agricultural GDP growth and high deforestation rates in the Amazon between 1988 and 1998 (Table 3.4).

Table 3.3 GDP growth rates in the Amazon region states between 1985 and 1997

State	GDP average growth rate	Cumulated GDP growth rate	Agriculture average growth rate	Cumulated agriculture GDP growth rate
Acre	4.86	58.31	0.31	3.71
Amapá	6.72	80.65	11.02	132.20
Amazonas	0.56	6.77	0.50	6.06
Maranhão	1.05	12.56	0.94	11.24
Mato Grosso	2.91	34.96	2.68	32.13
Pará	2.68		32.17	61.65
Rondônia	4.01		48.11	54.85
Roraima	7.20		86.34	203.82
Tocantins	2.53		30.41	2.65
Amazon region	3.61			

Source: Silva and Medina (1999).

Despite the high levels of deforestation in some states, the expansion of deforestation for the whole Amazon region decreased during 1988–1998 when compared to 1978–1988. Nonetheless, in the cases of the states of Amapá, Mato Grosso and Roraima, the extent of deforestation increased during the 1990s, whereas in Acre and Rondônia it remained relatively stable.

Table 3.4 The extent of deforestation in the Brazilian Amazon, 1978, 1988 and 1998 (km²)

State	1978	1988	1998	% growth in deforested area 1978–88	% growth in deforested area 1988–98
Acre	2 500	8 900	14 714	256.0	65.3
Amapá	200	800	1 962	300.0	145.3
Amazonas	1 700	19 700	28 866	1 058.8	46.5
Maranhão	63 900	90 800	100 590	42.1	10.8
Mato Grosso	20 000	71 500	131 808	257.5	84.3
Pará	56 400	131 500	188 372	133.2	43.2
Rondônia	4 200	30 000	53 275	614.3	77.6
Roraima	100	2 700	5 791	2 600.0	114.5
Tocantins	3 200	21 600	26 404	575.0	22.2
Total	154 178	379 488	553 780	146.1	45.9

Source: INPE (2000).

Most of the deforested areas have been converted to pasture land. Table 3.5 presents data from the 1985 and 1996 Agriculture Censuses. Decomposing the major land uses and comparing their evolution, it was established that approximately 145837 km² of land clearing occurred between 1985 and 1995/96 (this is close to the value of 174292 obtained if we subtract the extension of deforestation in 1998 from the value in 1988).[5] The area of planted pasture increased from 298423 km² in 1985 to 477272 km² in 1996, representing an increase of approximately 60 percent in ten years. On the other hand, the area used for crops did not change significantly and although the area of planted forests increased considerably, it still accounts for a small share of land use in the Amazon.[6] Therefore, results from the agriculture census indicate that the conversion of forest into planted pasture is still the main source of deforestation in the Brazilian Amazon.

Logging is considered a significant source of deforestation. Although it is hard to measure the exact amount of extracted timber due to illegal and unreported logging, Table 3.6 presents the volume of timber extracted in the Brazilian Amazon for the years 1980, 1985, 1990 and 1995, as estimated by the Brazilian Statistical Office (IBGE). The volume of timber extraction increased by 345 percent between 1980 and 1995, although the rate of growth declined during the 1990s.[7]

Table 3.5 Land use in the Brazilian Amazon: 1985 and 1996 (area in km²)

Land use	1985	1996
Perennial crops	10 183.27	10 788.24
Annual crops	79 735.44	70 604.42
Planted forest	3 031.78	5 800.30
Planted pasture	298 423.46	477 273.20
Fallow land	43 517.64	29 030.27
Productive land not used	114 754.61	74 275.44
Total cleared area	1 378 194.56	1 524 032.00

Source: IBGE agriculture census 1985 and 1995. The Brazilian Amazon considered here includes the state of Maranhão and the state of Goiás.

Table 3.6 Timber extraction in the Brazilian Amazon (1000 m³)

Year	Volume of timber logs extracted
1980	11 720.7
1985	23 960.0
1990	46 310.3
1995	52 285.6

Source: IBGE Extraction Survey.

Despite the significant growth in GDP in many regions of the Amazon, inequality of income and land is strongly present in the region. The Gini coefficient for land in the northern region of Brazil decreased from 0.86 in 1975 to 0.79 in 1985 (Schneider, 1995), but is still one of the highest in the world. In addition, environmental and land degradation and the lack of rural development have led to large scale migration to urban areas creating additional problems. The urban population in the Amazon region increased considerably during the 1990s. In 1991, 44 percent of the population in the Amazon was rural. In 2000, the preliminary results from the census indicate that this proportion decreased to 32 percent. Moreover, the urban population in the Amazon region increased by an average of 5.9 percent per year while for Brazil as a whole the urban population increased by an average of 2.7 percent per year. An important point is that the largest growth in urban population occurred in Amapá and Roraima, states which are both agriculture based. This could be an indication of a rural–urban migration process that may be occurring due to the unsustainable pattern of agriculture production and poor living conditions in remote rural areas.

3.5 COSTS OF DEFORESTATION IN THE BRAZILIAN AMAZON

Deforestation and environmental degradation in the Amazon introduces social costs to local economic agents as well as affecting citizens outside its borders. The current unsustainable deforestation process can have significant effects on future growth possibilities in the region. The conversion of forest into pastureland and crop area is almost irreversible since soil nutrients are exhausted, leaving the soil in extremely poor condition. Seroa da Motta and Ferraz (2000) estimated the user cost associated with timber extraction in the Amazon. They demonstrate that logging, following the process of land conversion to agriculture, does not reflect scarcity and depletion costs. The deforestation process harms other activities as well. The possibilities of future income from sustainable forestry, use of biodiversity, eco-tourism, carbon sequestration and other environmental services, decrease considerably with the current deforestation rate.

One of the main consequences of deforestation is the loss of biodiversity. In 1997, of the 228 faunal species in danger of extinction in Brazil, approximately 90 species were from the Amazon (IBAMA, 1997). Although calculation of the value of biodiversity in the region is difficult, it is commonly agreed that the Amazon encompasses several unique ecosystems and species, some that could have pharmaceutical value and others that may have high existence values for non-residents.

In addition to the problems associated with biodiversity loss from deforestation, the predatory logging process can also cause extinction of valuable commercial tree species such as mahogany. Martini et al. (1994) categorized 305 species of trees into three groups according to commercial interests and ecological parameters. They found that 45 species are strongly susceptible to timber extraction in terms of population reduction.

The deforestation process in the Amazon also contributes to climate change through release of CO_2 to the atmosphere. Between 1970 and 1985, Andersen and Reis (2000) estimated average carbon emissions attributed to deforestation from the Legal Amazon to be 168 million tons per year or approximately 95 tons of carbon per hectare cleared.

Deforestation and logging also increases the risk of fires in the region. With its humid microclimate, the tropical forest helps control fires. Both selective logging and land clearing increase the probability of fire dispersion significantly. This occurs as a result of damages wreaked by logging, particularly because logging opens the forest canopy, by up to 50 percent, allowing the sun's heat to reach the earth, drying out leaf litter and other material that may become combustible. Therefore, deforestation increases the potential for massive ecological and economic losses through accidental fires. With an increase in the frequency and intensity of El Niño events, it will become more common for forests to dry out sufficiently that they become flammable (Nepstad et al., 1999).

NOTES

1. Although in the case of forestland, the tax level has actually been reduced.
2. See Crespo et al. (1998).
3. Intestinal infections, cholera, typhoid fever, poliomyelitis, amoebic dysentery, schistosomiasis and shigellosis. Vector-borne disease, such as malaria, was not considered because of the difficulty in ascribing causality to water quality rather than other environmental and health factors. It should also be noted that, of the cases analyzed, the occurrence and geographical distribution of morbidity due to the different diseases vary.
4. Those estimates are based on INPE (2000) subtracting the estimated forest cover in 1998 from the estimated forest cover in 1978.
5. Although there are some problems of comparability between both censuses, a general trend can be inferred by comparing their results. For a description of the change of methodology that was undertaken by IBGE for the 1995/96 census and its possible consequences, see Helfand (1999).
6. It is important to note that the area devoted to agriculture is underestimated due to the change in the date for which the 1995/96 census was undertaken.
7. These results are highly controversial. Veríssimo et al. (2000), based on a field survey undertaken by the Amazon Institute of People and the Environment applied in a sample of sawmills throughout the Amazon, estimated an extraction of 27.8 millions of m^3 for the period 1997/96. This is substantially lower than the IBGE figures presented in Table 3.6. According to this study, the surveys' estimates of timber extraction output is, in general, very weakly correlated to the Census's data.

4. Trade and the environment: linkages between competitiveness and the industrial pollution in Brazil

4.1 INTRODUCTION

The basis of Brazilian trade policies in the last decade has been greater openness, both in commercial and financial terms. Some of the arguments in favor of these market-oriented policy reforms state that economic liberalization reduces static inefficiencies arising from resource misallocation and that economic liberalization enhances learning, technological change and economic growth. The objective is to extend modernization and competitiveness of the production sectors, in order to increase their participation in global markets.

Nevertheless, there are intense criticisms of the way these policies are being implemented in Brazil. The most conventional arguments are related to the concerns with deindustrialization and return to the phase of dependence on natural resource-based activities. The reversal of the trade balance and massive unemployment in the industrial sector, observed in the mid-1990s, are usually pointed out as negative consequences of the accelerated trade liberalization program. This issue is complex, and is receiving considerable attention by researchers.

Another crucial point has not thus penetrated far into the trade liberalization discussions in Brazil: the environmental consequences associated with freer trade. The theoretical debate over trade and environment is not new, but its importance increased substantially with the trade liberalization processes that have been taking place around the world. The hypothesis over the trade and environment link can be divided in two groups. From one side, there exists a possibility that countries with lower environmental standards would develop a comparative advantage in dirty industries. This is associated with the so-called pollution haven hypothesis.[1] From another perspective, there exists the possibility that by imposing environmental control and regulation in order to avoid the pollution-intensive specialization, a country would create additional costs and thus lose competitiveness in world markets.

The main focus of this research is: if economic growth is recovered with a strong component of export-led activities (as expected by policy in the government and in the international agencies), what are the long-term consequences of this strategy? Is it compatible to expand Brazilian exports (and production as a whole) without worsening pollution problems? On the other hand, what would be the economic costs of improving pollution control and other mitigation measures?

The study will be divided into two parts. The first part will deal with the consequences of rising industrial output (particularly those associated with exports) on urban pollution. This section will examine the impact of greater openness of trade – proxied here by industrial exports – on the level of urban pollution. The methodology will be based on the use of input–output modeling techniques, whereby pollution emission coefficients are linked with industrial activities. The aim is to estimate the total amount of emissions required to obtain a specified industrial export volume (exogenously determined).

The second part of the study will emphasize the consequences of pollution control/mitigation costs for export competitiveness. This section will be an extension of the previous one. Given the impact of industrial exports on urban pollution, what would the impact of adoption of pollution controls be on external competitiveness? The analyses will combine various (estimated) mitigation costs and price elasticities of demand for industrial exports, while also considering chain effects through input–output modeling. An attempt will be made to estimate employment impacts of pollution abatement expenditures.

4.2 TRADE AND THE ENVIRONMENT IN BRAZIL: A HISTORICAL PERSPECTIVE

The strong doubts by the environmentalist movement about the consequences of increasing openness is strongly related to the role played by foreign markets in Brazilian history. The last 500 years, since the arrival of the Portuguese in Brazil (22 April 1500), have seen extensive environmental degradation, directly or indirectly caused by trade relations. The early occupation of the colony was already determined by trade. Even the country was named after a commodity: the once abundant pau-brasil tree (*Caesalpinia echinata*), which was in high demand in European markets as a source of red tincture used to color fabrics. The depletion was so extensive that, in less than 60 years after discovery, the best reserves could only be found 20 km away from the shore (Bueno,

1998). During the first century after its discovery, an estimated 2 million trees were cut down and shipped to Europe. The mounting scarcity led the Portuguese Crown, in 1605, to take action against unplanned logging, resulting in forest rangers being dispersed along the Brazilian coast (Bueno, 1998). Not surprisingly, the pau-brasil tree became almost extinct in Brazilian native forests.

The other economic cycles during colonial times were dominated by the overexploitation of natural resources in order to provide goods for export – the main purpose of the colony was to profit via trading commodities based on the abundant natural resources (Furtado, 1959). The sugar cane cycle in the northeast and southeast, which took place during the first two centuries of Portuguese settlement, was the first wave of massive destruction of the Atlantic rainforest (Mata Atlântica). The main reasons why forests were endangered was due to the demand for timber, fuel wood and agricultural land – the technological pattern used by the Portuguese (and the Dutch, during their brief occupation of the sugar cane plantations in the northeast) in the processing of sugar was not very different from that which resulted in the total depletion of native forests on the Madeira island.[2]

In the seventeenth and eighteenth centuries, the gold cycle in Minas Gerais and other interior parts of the country resulted not only in the quick exhaustion of reserves (which lasted less than two centuries), but also in considerable damage to the environment due to mining techniques. Changing the natural courses of rivers became a common practice to search for gold, and an even more harmful technique was to deviate the river flow against its margins, 'washing' the embankments to reveal the precious ore (Dean, 1995). Cattle raising was not directly connected to trade relations with Europe, but was indirectly encouraged by them. The rising demand for meat in the mining areas established cattle migration routes and increased the pressure for overgrazing, seriously damaging natural pasture areas, particularly in the interior of the northeast.

Another crucial element in the economic formation of Brazil was slavery. The development of international trade routes, followed by the Industrial Revolution, cannot be dissociated from the triangular trade between Europe, Africa and the Americas – even though this issue is usually neglected in the current debate, which tends to forget this tragic consequence of the development of international trade routes in the past. Brazil received the largest number of Africans, and almost four centuries of slavery has produced scars that are yet to be healed, including the deepest social inequality in the Western world. Slaves were an essential part of the sugar cane production, gold and other precious ore mining, and almost any other commodities produced for foreign markets (such as tobacco and cotton).

Independence presented no change in this pattern, and coffee plantations mainly drove the Imperial economy. This new commodity was again destined for foreign markets (this time without the interference of the metropolis, with the increasing importance of the British Empire and the United States as trade partners) and the rising exports were obtained through the massive destruction of the Mata Atlântica. The State of Rio de Janeiro was the first to suffer with the invasion of coffee plantations: Dean (1995) estimated that around 18 percent of the total area of the state was cleared for coffee plantations, employing around 140000 slaves. However, unsustainable practices led to the fast decline of production causing its complete eradication. Nowadays, most of these areas in the State of Rio de Janeiro are used for cattle raising with very low productivity.

Slavery was only abolished in 1888 and, not by coincidence, one year after the Republic was proclaimed. However, the expansion of coffee exports at the expense of clearing native rainforests was not altered by this change. Using migrants from Southern Europe (mainly Italians), coffee remained the main economic factor in Brazil until the world recession during the 1930s. More appropriate soils in the State of São Paulo (Terra Roxa) and less erosive practices have resulted in more permanent cultivation, but the clearing of forest areas remained the main result of output expansion. The wave of forest clearing has also migrated to the states of Paraná and (Southern) Minas Gerais. The final result of this and other forest-consuming activities (such as charcoal production in Minas Gerais, pulp and paper production in Paraná and Santa Catarina) is the reduction of the Mata Atlântica to less than 7 percent of its original domain.

The natural rubber boom in the Amazon in the late nineteenth century and early twentieth century was an exception to this trend. This was an important economic cycle directed to foreign markets that was based on extractivism practices causing little harm to the environment (as trees are not destroyed during latex extraction). Unfortunately, this sustainable activity could not face the competition of rubber tree plantations in Southeastern Asia (which have had important deforestation consequences in these regions). The decline in production has resulted in the paradoxical situation of Brazil currently being a net importer of natural rubber.

The 1930s' crisis presented an important change in policy making in Brazil. Until then, all major economic relations were driven towards foreign markets, and there was little integration of activities aiming at domestic markets. Even the spatial distribution within the country was created according to the proximity to export ports. The economic dependence on export of natural commodities had resulted in a cycle of crises, caused by falling prices in external markets when supply increased over demand, which usually happened after a period of boom when prices had previously gone up. Therefore, in the 1940s and mainly in the 1950s, a new strategy of growth was adopted, based on the idea that Brazil (as other developing countries) would have to increase its participation in the global markets as a supplier of industrialized goods, or else it would become permanently relegated to a second-class position. This strategy was heavily influenced by the so-called Latin American Structuralist school, following the pioneer studies of Raúl Prebisch, which have shown that an outward-oriented economy based on primary goods (and, therefore, not incorporating the benefits of technical progress) would never develop to its full potential.[3] A new pattern of development was required, in which industrialization became the main objective.

The golden age of industrialization in Brazil (1950s, 1960s and 1970s) has resulted in fast economic growth and structural changes in the productive structure. Nevertheless, the social and environmental consequences of this process were far from desirable. A fair number of studies on the social exclusion in the Brazilian industrialization process have been conducted, but the consequences to the environment are yet to be researched in detail. The expansion of industrial activities were not followed by the establishment of pollution control authorities: the first environmental agency (FEEMA, in the State of Rio de Janeiro) was created only in 1977, when the industrialization process was already losing its momentum and the rates of investment and output growth rates were declining from their historical averages. The first effective national environmental law was created in 1981. The consequences of this lack of standards and mitigation procedures on pollution were dramatic, as exemplified by the tragedy of the Cubatão industrial area (in the state of São Paulo).[4] The shift towards a more inward-oriented development has not resulted in improvements in environmental issues.

One point that is usually misunderstood is that, during the import-substitution process, export-oriented policies were not important. Exports played a major role for financing the industrialization process, which relied heavily on imports, particularly machinery and intermediate inputs. For instance, the Second National Development Program (1975–79), a crucial stage to complete the industrial structure, targeted the expansion of export capacity in intermediate goods, such as metallurgy, petrochemicals and pulp and paper. Providing fiscal and credit incentives to these sectors, which are characterized by their high consumption of energy and other natural resources, has created a pattern of high-emitting activities, considerably affecting the Brazilian industrial export capacity. The environmental consequences of this shift in the export structure towards more energy- (and pollution-) intensive goods are discussed in this study.

An important shift towards trade liberalization and privatization occurred in the 1990s. Import barriers were lifted, and legal changes were made in order to ease foreign investment and the process of economic integration within the South American free trade agreement (Mercosul) gained speed. The impact of these measures was concentrated mainly in deregulation and increasing imports, particularly due to the overvaluation of the exchange rate after the real economic plan (1994). Measured in terms of proportion of the GDP, there was no significant improvement in export quantities, or the sum of exports and imports. However, other changes can be more easily identified such as the increase in industrial output and fall in industrial employment. The environmental changes associated with these transformations are analyzed in the next sections.

In summary, the environmentalist's position is strongly influenced by the past and present consequences of international trade in Brazilian history, which demonstrates plenty of instances when natural resources depletion and degradation were a hidden cost of increasing exports. Therefore, environmentalists tend to be very skeptical about the argument that the future is not necessarily a reproduction of the past and that, under certain ideal conditions (implementation of property rights, in order to solve market failures, and the correction of public policies that encourage the overexploitation of natural resources), improvements in trade relations will not represent an additional threat to the environment. Indeed, they tend to consider that it is unrealistic to implement these policy reforms under the social and political structure of Brazil, or, even worse, they would result in further harm to the environment – since the economic groups that tend to benefit from trade expansion are not concerned with the social and environmental damage. Nevertheless, their refusal to accept both the outward-looking model imposed by globalization, and the inward-looking economic growth experienced in the industrialization period (also harmful to the environment), has not yet been accompanied by feasible policy suggestions.

4.3 THE ENVIRONMENT DEBATE IN THE ECONOMIC LITERATURE

The environmentalist movement (and NGOs in general) has argued that trade has negative consequences on the environment because of ideological positions (mostly motivated by historical events). However, part of the economic literature on the subject tends to present the opposite vision. The principle argument presented by those who defend the positive environmental aspects of international trade is that higher competition would close down companies operating with old and inefficient equipment. These are companies with a higher probability of being environmentally harmful, either because of old machinery/technology, or are wasteful in their production processes. A more competitive atmosphere would force them to adopt modern ways of production, which tend to be more efficient in all aspects including the environment (in terms of emission avoidance and raw materials savings).

Eliminating subsidies or other incentives for energy-intensive sectors would help to reduce energy consumption and, therefore, emissions and pollution. These sectors also tend to be capital-intensive, and according to the theory of comparative advantages, free trade policies would favor a shift in developing countries towards labor-intensive activities, which tend to be less polluting.

The reduction of trade barriers would favor imports of modern, state-of-the-art equipment. Since this machinery is developed to follow the tough environmental standards of developed countries, use of such equipment would result in an overall improvement of the environmental performance of the importing country.

Consumers in developed countries are showing growing concern about the environmental standards of products bought, thus forcing the adoption of environmentally friendly production patterns, certified by green labels, for those exporting to these markets. The demonstration effect has led to producers aiming at domestic markets to adopt similar practices, as local consumers become more aware of the environmental implications of production and consumption of the products they buy.

To understand the difference between those who complain against trade, and those who do not, it is crucial to bear in mind that most of these analytical studies are not based on historical analysis, but are deeply rooted in theoretical arguments derived from idealized models of reality (which, again, are strongly related to ideological positions). The recent document issued by the World Trade Organization (Nordström and Vaughan 1999) is a good example of the belief that, under 'ideal' circumstances, promoting free market is always the best policy: 'In the best of all worlds, governments would use proper environmental policies to "internalize" the full environmental costs of production and consumption – the "Polluter Pays Principle". In this idealized world, trade liberalization would unambiguously raise welfare' (Nordström and Vaughan 1999, p. 2).

Hence, the 'conclusion' of this argument is simply a consequence of the fact that problems are eliminated by construction in any idealized world according to the beliefs of whatever ideology – including the ideology of a free market. The 'ideal world' is considered to be perfect because it is the best application of that set of beliefs.[5] Nevertheless, this kind of argument is repeatedly used by governments and multilateral development agencies in their justification to deepen reforms towards more openness (for a critical analysis of the environmental consequences of adjustment policies, see Young, 1997). Once problems with the implementation of reform policies are identified, it is usually considered not a fault of the policy itself but a 'failure' of the real economy, in the sense that it does not behave according to the 'perfect' world proposed by theory. The solution would need even more reforms to make the real world 'more perfect' – that is, closer to the idealized theoretical model.

Nevertheless, once more realistic assumptions are considered, even neoclassical theoretical models present results showing that improving trade relations may result in damages to the environment. Two counter-arguments are commonly used to justify a change in the current regulatory framework concerning international trade that disallowed restrictions based on environmental issues (Nordström and Vaughan, 1999):

1. The legal argument: the existing rules provide legal cover for foreign countries to challenge domestic environmental policies that interfere with their trading rights.
2. The political economy argument: the competitive pressure from the world market sometimes makes it impossible to forge the necessary political support at home to upgrade environmental standards.
3. The market failure argument: in the existing institutional conditions of developing countries, international trade may magnify the effects of poor environmental policies in the world (increasing the tendencies of overexploitation of natural resources). Or, in more general terms, that economic growth driven by trade may speed up the process of environmental degradation unless environmental safeguards are put in place.

The basic assumption of these arguments is that environmental standards are weaker in developing countries, stimulating the migration of pollution-intensive industries to such countries (for a review of these arguments, see Leonard, 1988 and Weil et al., 1990). Empirical evidence shows that polluting industries have in fact expanded faster in developing countries than the average rate for all industries (Lucas et al., 1992; Low and Yeats, 1992). However, the evidence is not clear about the existence of a migration process of dirtier industries from developed countries. Using trade and investment figures for US-based industries, Leonard (1988) concludes that, in aggregate, the years immediately following the emergence of stringent environmental regulations in the US did not witness widespread reallocation of pollution-intensive industries to countries with lower regulatory requirements. Pollution abatement and control expenditures do not seem to have significant effects on competitiveness of most industries, since they are small in comparison with total costs. Other reasons include (Low, 1992), fear of liability in the event of an accident; reputation damages in the originating countries if an accident happens; the costs of 'unbundling' technology; potential claims of environmentally-concerned consumers in export markets; expectations of more stringent local environmental standards in the future; and the relatively high costs of retrofitting aging capital equipment instead of starting up with 'top of the line' equipment. It has been observed empirically that open developing economies became less pollution-intensive than closed economies in the 1970s and 1980s (Lucas et al., 1992; Birdsall and Wheeler, 1992).

This lack of a definitive answer to these opposing arguments is consistent with the results of recent surveys of theoretical models:

> The literature has been timely in that the issue (the link between environmental policy and international trade) has been one of considerable public debate, and the literature has been well placed to address some of the issues raised by that debate, since the literature has focused on imperfect competition and the potential scope for governments to manipulate environmental policy for strategic reasons. I have shown that this recent analysis is capable of providing starkly different predictions of environmental policy under liberalized trade regimes from those derived from the traditional literature, but there is a severe problem of non-robustness of results. This is especially problematic when it comes to trying to draw policy conclusions from this new literature, although the analysis does not support some of the policy prescription discussed in popular debates. (Ulph, 1998, pp. 237–8)

The need for empirical findings are common ground in all studies that reject a priori statements such as 'trade is good' or 'trade is bad' for the environment – there is a strong need to improve our understanding of these links in the economy. The objective of the following sections is to provide a systematic empirical analysis of the link between international trade (more precisely, industrial exports) and the environment in the past decades in Brazil, in order to provide guidance to policy making in the future.

The overall conclusion is that both sides of the debate are partially correct, in that they have considered only part of the whole process: trade reforms may, at the same time, improve and worsen environmental conditions. The main message for public policy making is, therefore, that neither blocking trade relations, nor laissez-faire policies are appropriate for improving environmental conditions in developing countries (or, at least, in Brazil). Trade is an important source of effective demand and employment generation, but there are important failures to be considered and corrected. One tendency to specialize in resource-intensive activities, empirically observed in Latin America for a long time (and supported by structuralists arguments), results in higher than average emission coefficients in the export sector. A second counter-trend arises from the pressures imposed for environmental standards by some OECD consumer markets, plus a more environmentally friendly behavior by multinational companies, which leads to dissemination of environmental innovations.

The question is how to reduce the first trend and accelerate the second one. The encouragement and diffusion of environmental innovations and a wider comprehension of the social dimensions of the pollution problem, coupled with the elimination of policy failures that encourage the establishment of pollution-intensive industries (an issue particularly important in the recent 'fiscal war' between Brazilian states, which offer all kinds of subsidies and incentives to attract investments) are amongst the policy options to be pursued.

4.4 INDUSTRIAL EMISSION MODEL

Input–Output Model

The objective of the input–output model is to describe the interdependence of the economy, given the current levels of production and consumption. Assuming that all sectors (n) of an economy keep a constant share in the market of each product, and that the production processes of all these sectors are technologically interdependent and characterized by a linear relation between the amount of inputs required and the final output of each sector, it is possible to obtain a system containing *n* equations relating the output of every sector to the output of all other sectors. The model also considers an autonomous sector (final demand), which is determined exogenously to the model. The sales of each sector should be equal to autonomous consumption (related to the categories of final demand) plus the amount of production destined for the intermediate consumption of all the other sectors (Dorfman, 1954).

In formal terms:

$$x_i = \sum_{i=1}^{n} x_{ij} + C_i + I + G_i + E_i - M_i \tag{4.1}$$

where x_{ij} is the amount of output from sector *i* demanded as intermediate consumption to sector *j*, and C_i, I_i, G_i, E_i, M_i and x_i are, respectively, the private consumption, investment, public administration consumption, exports, imports and domestic production of sector *i* (Prado, 1981).

The basic assumption is that the intermediate consumption is a fixed proportion of the total output of each product:

$$x_i = \sum_{j=1}^{n} a_{ij} \cdot x_j + d_i \tag{4.2}$$

where a_{ij} is the technical coefficient determining the amount of product of sector *i* required for the production of one unit of product in sector *j*, and d_i is the amount of final demand for products from sector *i* ($d_i = C_i + I_i + G_i + E_i - M_i$). In matrix terms, this is expressed by:

$$x = Ax + d \tag{4.3}$$

Where *x* is an $n \times 1$ vector with the total product of each sector, *d* is an $n \times 1$ vector with sector final demand, and *A* is an $n \times n$ matrix with the technical coefficients of production.

Since the final demand is exogenously determined, the intermediate consumption can be obtained by the following equation:

$$x = (I - A)^{-1} d \tag{4.4}$$

Where $(I - A)^{-1}$ is the $n \times n$ matrix containing the input–output coefficients for the relationship between sectors.

The same formula is valid for calculating the direct and indirect effects of exports or any other component of the final demand, instead of its aggregate:

$$x_f = (I - A)^{-1} d_f \tag{4.5}$$

Where x_f is the $n \times 1$ vector containing the total production per sector necessary to obtain the $n \times 1$ vector of the f-category of final demand (d_f). Therefore, the input–output model determines the level of economic activity in each productive sector as a function of the final demand for each product.

Introducing Emission Coefficients

The use of extended input–output tables to estimate emissions and other residual discharges has become an important instrument in assessing environmental problems at the macroeconomic level (for a review, see Førsund, 1985; the methodology adopted in this section is based on Pedersen, 1993). It is assumed that emissions are linearly related to the gross output of each sector, in a way that each industry generates residuals in fixed proportions to the sector output. The emission coefficient of pollutant h by sector i (ef_{hi}) can be obtained by dividing the total emission of a sector (em_{hi}) by the total output of the same sector (x_i):

$$ef_{hi} = \frac{em_{hi}}{x_i} \tag{4.6}$$

Given this assumption, it is possible to obtain the total emission caused by the f-category of final demand through the use of emission coefficients for each sector. In formal terms, this is expressed by:

$$z_{hf} = diag(ef_h) \cdot x_f = diag(ef_h) \cdot (I - A)^{-1} d_f \tag{4.7}$$

Where z_{hf} is the $n \times 1$ vector containing the total emission of pollutant h per sector associated to the f-category of final demand, and $diag(ef_h)$ is the $n \times n$ matrix containing in its principal diagonal the emission factors of pollutant h for each sector, and zeros elsewhere (Pedersen, 1993).

Measuring the Composition Effect

It is possible to disaggregate the changes in the emission pattern of the industry into three different effects:

1. Scale effect: refers to changes in emissions caused by the changes in the overall output level due to the expansion (or retraction) of activities associated with more exposure to the world economy.
2. Composition effect: refers to changes in emissions caused by the industrial restructuring that takes place because of higher exposure to the world market. In other words, the composition effect considers the change in emission because some sectors have their share increased in the economy's total output, while others have it reduced.
3. Technology (or technique) effect: refers to changes in emissions caused by innovations introduced because of the openness of the economy.

The input–output model allows the identification of the scale and composition effects, but the technology effect cannot be captured because of the use of fixed emission coefficients. In analytical terms, the argument of specialization in 'dirty' activities is usually associated with the composition effect. The composition effect occurs when the proportion of emissions directly or indirectly associated with exports in relation to the total emissions exceeds the ratio between the value of production associated with exports and the total value of production of the economy. In formal terms:

$$\frac{[1]_{1\times n}(I-A)^{-1}d_x}{[1]_{1\times n}(I-A)^{-1}d} < \frac{[1]_{1\times n}diag(e_h).(I-A)^{-1}d_x}{[1]_{1\times n}diag(e_h).(I-A)^{-1}d} \qquad (4.8)$$

where:

$[1]_{1\times n}$ is a line-vector with the number 1 in every cell; n is the number of sectors in the economy;
$(I-A)^{-1}$ is the $n \times n$ Leontief inverse matrix;
$diag(e_h)$ is the $n \times n$ diagonal matrix containing the emission factors of pollutant h for each sector, and zeros elsewhere (obtained in equation);
d_x is the vector containing the exports of each of the n sectors;
d is the vector containing the final demand of each of the n sectors.

The left side of expression (4.8) represents the proportion of the output directly and indirectly required by the exports compared with the total output, while the right side represents the emissions of pollutant *h* directly or indirectly caused by exports divided by the total emissions of the pollutant. If the right side is bigger than the left, the composition of goods destined to foreign markets is more intensive in emissions of pollutant *h* than the average of the economy.

4.5 APPLICATION TO BRAZIL

This section describes the procedures used to estimate equation (4.7) for the Brazilian economy, combining the input–output tables (42 × 42 activities) prepared by the Brazilian Institute of Geography and Statistics (IBGE) and four different sets of emission coefficients, for local and global pollutants. The objective is to empirically test the hypothesis of a composition effect taking into account that Brazilian industrial exports are relatively dirty activities when compared with the production destined for domestic markets.

The IPEA Emission Coefficients (Local Pollutants)

The first set of emission coefficients (for local pollutants) was calculated using the results from empirical studies carried out by the Environmental Economics Research Division at IPEA (Seroa da Motta et al., 1993; Mendes, 1994; Seroa da Motta, 1993a, 1993b, 1996). These studies estimated the effectiveness of abatement policy and the status of current industrial water and air pollution in Brazil based on indicators of water and air quality for 13 states where systematic monitoring was undertaken.[6] This database was built using pollution emission and abatement estimates for the year 1988 according to a World Bank funded project, PRONACOP (Brazilian National Program of Pollution Control), covering 12 states, plus similar information for the state of São Paulo for the year 1991, using data from the state's environmental agency (CETESB). The parameters considered for water pollution were biochemical oxygen demand (BOD) and heavy metals, and for air pollution, particulate matter, sulfur dioxide (SO_2), nitrogen oxides (NO_x), and hydrocarbons (HC).

The estimates of potential emissions were obtained by multiplying the potential output of every industry registered at the respective state environmental agency by emission parameters obtained from the technical literature (mostly taken from the World Health Organization). These potential pollution emissions were considered as a measure of pollutant emitted by the industrial establishment without any treatment.

The second stage was to estimate the level of remaining emissions (potential emissions minus abatement capacity), which is a better proxy for the level of industrial emissions. The pollution treatment capacity of every industrial unit was calculated according to the potential for emission treatment at the source points (that is, every industrial establishment registered in the database). The indicators of (remaining) emissions were then divided by the value added of the respective industrial sectors, at the state level, in order to calculate the emission intensity coefficients (for more details, see Mendes, 1994).[7] Tables 4.1 and 4.2 portray the average value for the 13 states.

Table 4.3 shows the results of associating the above coefficients into input–output tables, as stated in equation (4.7), in order to obtain (remaining) emission coefficients for each category of final demand.

Table 4.1 Water pollution: potential and remaining emission intensity coefficients, by industrial sector (g/US$ of value added), IPEA

Industrial sector	Biochem. oxygen demand		Heavy metals	
	Potential	Remaining	Potential	Remaining
Metallurgy	1.12	0.04	1.73	0.85
Mechanical	0.73	0.60	0.16	0.07
Transport equipment	0.49	0.18	0.13	0.05
Wood products	19.83	8.82	0.00	0.00
Paper & cellulose	37.35	12.91	0.00	0.00
Chemicals	86.85	16.15	0.03	0.03
Drugs & medicine	2.25	1.47	0.00	0.00
Cosmetics & soap	7.02	4.58	0.00	0.00
Textiles	7.11	4.40	0.00	0.00
Leather & footwear	45.36	21.69	1.84	0.76
Food products	27.96	11.31	0.00	0.00
Beverages	105.11	40.98	0.00	0.00

Source: Mendes (1994).

Table 4.2 Air pollution: potential and remaining emission intensity coefficients, by industrial sector (g/US$ of value added), IPEA

	Partic. matter		SO_2		NO_X		HC	
Sectors	Potential	Remaining	Potential	Remaining	Potential	Remaining	Potential	Remaining
Non-metallic minerals	689.1	261.4	51.2	51.0	10.9	10.9	0.2	0.2
Metallurgy	247.0	111.4	50.7	50.7	17.2	17.2	6.2	6.2
Mechanics	5.8	1.1	1.3	1.3	0.1	0.1	2.0	2.0
Electric materials	0.4	0.1	0.2	0.2	0.0	0.0	2.2	1.6
Transport equip.	0.4	0.1	0.2	0.1	0.0	0.0	0.6	0.5
Wood products	42.2	42.1	2.5	2.5	9.7	9.7	2.9	2.9
Paper & cellulose	133.8	28.2	16.0	15.8	32.5	32.5	0.7	0.7
Rubber products	0.4	0.4	3.3	3.3	0.5	0.5	0.1	0.1
Chemicals	41.4	18.3	61.4	59.9	45.7	45.6	38.8	18.4
Drugs & medicine	0.4	0.4	2.0	1.9	5.5	5.5	0.1	0.1
Domestics & soap	8.8	4.5	32.3	32.3	2.9	2.9	0.1	0.1
Textiles	26.4	24.3	13.8	13.4	11.2	11.2	0.4	0.3
Leather & footwear	1.0	0.9	5.5	5.5	0.7	0.7	0.7	0.7
Food products	27.5	21.8	72.5	72.5	8.8	8.8	0.2	0.2
Beverages	68.1	58.2	35.7	35.7	17.4	17.4	0.4	0.4

Source: Seroa da Motta et al. (1993)

For all pollutants analyzed, the emissions from producing one unit of export-related output exceeds the average of the economy. Indeed, the intensity of pollution is higher in export-related activities than in any other group for all but one parameter (particulates, in which exports are the second highest). In other words, exports are more pollution-intensive than the average of the economy.

It is clear that only a few sectors produce most of the industrial water and air pollution. These 'dirty' industries are usually related directly or indirectly to export-oriented activities, such as metallurgy (input for the automobile industry and other industrial export goods), paper, cellulose and footwear (leather products). The most polluting industries are: chemicals, food products, paper and cellulose for BOD; metallurgy for heavy metals; non-metallic minerals and metallurgy for particulate matter; chemicals, metallurgy and non-metallic minerals for SO_2; chemicals, metallurgy, paper and cellulose and food products for NO_X; and chemicals for HC.

Table 4.3 Pollution intensity per unit of output (kg/US$ million)

Parameter/ Year	Investment*	Exports	Public consumption	Private consumption	Total
BOD					
1985	569	1420	361	1298	1043
1990	436	1292	277	1243	936
1995	453	1370	288	1116	861
Metals (water)					
1985	31	44	3	14	21
1990	24	50	3	13	17
1995	24	47	2	10	15
Particulates (air)					
1985	9364	7760	1296	4118	5553
1990	9390	8497	1041	3938	5035
1995	8232	8549	1034	3398	4441
SO_2					
1985	4146	6957	1134	4268	4278
1990	3520	6441	884	3983	3652
1995	3356	6442	855	3528	3298
NO_X					
1985	1878	3243	860	2011	2029
1990	1613	2969	646	1918	1763
1995	1574	3029	666	1672	1603
HC					
1985	674	1105	188	585	636
1990	575	974	148	554	537
1995	566	880	138	430	448
CO					
1985	40265	51294	4525	14781	24792
1990	32104	58715	3519	13318	20030
1995	31445	55460	3113	10899	17855

Note: * Investment includes changes in stocks.

If the (fixed) emission coefficients estimated by IPEA with data for the Brazilian industry (for the 1988/91 period) are applied to a time series up to 1995, there is a clear decreasing trend in average intensity of emissions per unit of output for all parameters considered, suggesting that the composition of the Brazilian industrial output has changed towards less (potentially) polluting activities. However, the emission intensity of metals, particulates and CO would have increased, showing an increase in the dependence of Brazilian industrial exports in (potentially) dirty activities.

Nevertheless, there are many limitations to this approach. Firstly, the emission estimates for water and air quality were not obtained directly at emission points but indirectly from specifications of the industrial plants surveyed. The environmental impact of a specific pollutant is affected by many other variables that were not considered in the exercise.[8] Secondly, a linear relationship is assumed between value added and the level of emissions – it is possible that this relationship is far more complex. Third, only establishments that were registered with the environmental agencies were considered. It is possible that the total emissions were underestimated. This point would be important in the case of sectors where a very large number of marginally polluting establishments (not registered with the environmental agencies) are responsible for a considerable amount of the total emission.

IPPS Emission Coefficients (Local Pollutants)

Production and emission data from 200 000 factories in the United States (1987) was combined to obtain estimates of sector pollution intensity (pollution per unit of activity), and used by the World Bank as the basis for the Industrial Pollution Projection System (IPPS). Although the estimates based on the IPPS are not actual emissions, they are useful as a guideline in order to rank industrial sectors in terms of potential emissions.[9]

The IPPS index expresses the pollutant output intensity for six types of air pollutants (SO_2, NO_2, CO, VOC, PM_{10}, TP), three types of water pollution (BOD, TSS and metals) and metals disposed in landfills.[10] Pollution intensity is expressed as pollutant output divided by total manufacturing activity. The total manufacturing activity can be measured by numerous variables, but the main choice is between the value of output and the output quantity. Only industrial activities are covered.

The IPPS provides emission coefficients based on the value of production (*shipment value*), value added or employment. Since the input–output coefficients usually refer to the first of these categories, the coefficients used in this exercise refer to emissions divided by the value of production. Additionally, it is important to point out that the EPA data used to calculate the IPPS coefficients only cover facilities releasing pollutants over the threshold level of emissions. As a result, pollution intensities based on this data may be biased. In this study, it was decided that the *lower bound* coefficients were more appropriate to estimate the Brazilian industry's environmental performance. These coefficients assume that non-reporting facilities had no emissions (that is, they were assigned with zero emissions). Hence, there is an underestimation in the calculation of Brazilian emissions using these coefficients.[11]

The use of IPPS coefficients to estimate Brazilian industrial emissions also assumes that there were no significant technical differences between the production sectors of both countries (at least in terms of average emission per unit of output). Therefore, since the effective degree of emission treatment in Brazil is unknown, it is very likely that errors result from the application of the IPPS coefficients. Moreover, since the denominator is expressed in monetary terms (value of production), we need to assume that the relative price structures in both countries are the same, which is not likely. Finally, translating the classification of IPPS coefficients to the IBGE input–output classification is problematic. The aggregation level of IPPS is the International Standard Industrial Classification (ISIC) level 4, which is more detailed than the classification level 80 adopted in the input–output tables of IBGE. Non-equivalence in the translation of classifications, such as the lack of IPPS emission coefficients for the coffee industry (coffee industry emission coefficients were thus considered to be zero) and alcohol processing (included under sugar processing in the IPPS, but included under chemical elements in the IBGE), is also a problem.

In summary, the results obtained through these coefficients (see Tables 4.4 to 4.12) must be examined with extreme caution because of the methodological problems described above and can only be considered as *potential* indicators of actual emissions (which are, in fact, unknown).

Despite the difference in the source of the coefficients from the previous exercise, the conclusions tend to be very similar: the emission intensity of the export sector is higher than the average emission intensity of the economy.

Table 4.4 Emission intensities: BOD, kg/US$ million (1987), IPPS coefficients

Year	Consumption	Investment	Exports	Total
1985	310	130	195	252
1990	315	126	245	265
1991	316	130	242	268
1992	316	118	235	265
1993	299	121	227	253
1994	287	117	244	246
1995	283	113	285	248
1996	285	125	276	253

Table 4.5 Emission intensities: total suspended solids, kg/US$ million, IPPS coefficients

Year	Consumption	Investment	Exports	Total
1985	3713	9587	11726	6368
1990	3771	8405	14368	6091
1991	3502	8095	14973	6094
1992	3354	8407	13893	6216
1993	3314	8599	13786	6158
1994	3520	8969	13187	6131
1995	3488	8428	12976	5781
1996	3507	8765	13202	5792

Table 4.6 Emission intensities: SO_2, kg/US$ million, IPPS coefficients

Year	Consumption	Investment	Exports	Total
1985	1904	2871	3492	2389
1990	1977	2724	3817	2368
1991	1944	2762	3654	2356
1992	1915	2712	3498	2352
1993	1876	2758	3459	2322
1994	1884	2704	3538	2308
1995	1850	2558	3704	2244
1996	1853	2735	3678	2263

Table 4.7 Emission intensities: NO_2, kg/US$ million, IPPS coefficients

Year	Consumption	Investment	Exports	Total
1985	1142	1339	1726	1287
1990	1210	1327	1663	1292
1991	1195	1354	1576	1283
1992	1197	1352	1536	1288
1993	1163	1343	1515	1259
1994	1159	1300	1543	1247
1995	1131	1217	1616	1213
1996	1127	1304	1562	1218

Table 4.8 Emission intensities: CO, kg/US$ million, IPPS coefficients

Year	Consumption	Investment	Exports	Total
1985	1743	2447	3152	2141
1990	1793	2280	3520	2114
1991	1757	2267	3520	2117
1992	1717	2285	3339	2118
1993	1685	2332	3329	2097
1994	1725	2344	3339	2102
1995	1671	2218	3388	2013
1996	1683	2347	3410	2037

Table 4.9 Emission intensities: VOC, kg/US$ million, IPPS coefficients

Year	Consumption	Investment	Exports	Total
1985	835	788	1176	885
1990	875	788	1076	881
1991	868	799	996	873
1992	864	787	991	873
1993	854	792	981	865
1994	852	781	1008	862
1995	828	742	1032	837
1996	825	781	1002	840

Table 4.10 Emission intensities: fine particulates, kg/US$ million, IPPS coefficients

Year	Consumption	Investment	Exports	Total
1985	264	753	546	417
1990	268	723	610	408
1991	264	756	584	408
1992	266	763	568	414
1993	256	755	578	406
1994	257	707	565	396
1995	264	662	585	390
1996	261	717	584	391

Table 4.11 Emission intensities: total particulates, kg/US$ million, IPPS coefficients

Year	Consumption	Investment	Exports	Total
1985	514	880	844	649
1990	519	849	904	638
1991	518	885	836	637
1992	523	882	832	647
1993	504	877	842	634
1994	503	825	855	623
1995	506	775	928	618
1996	501	839	907	619

Table 4.12 Emission intensities: metals – land, kg/US$ million, IPPS coefficients

Year	Consumption	Investment	Exports	Total
1985	138	331	363	219
1990	140	292	465	213
1991	132	289	470	212
1992	124	284	438	211
1993	124	298	434	211
1994	129	305	431	212
1995	128	291	439	203
1996	129	306	453	206

The average emission intensity of the economy for all parameters has declined between 1985 and 1996 (with the exception of BOD, which has remained almost the same); nevertheless, emission intensities in the export sector have increased for all but two parameters (NO_2 and VOCs).

Emission intensities estimated according to the IPPS coefficients are considerably lower than the values obtained using the IPEA coefficients, indicating that the environmental profile of the Brazilian industry in the late 1980s was considerably worse than the US.

These results demonstrate that exports are dependent on production chains that are potentially dirtier (according to the IPPS) than the average of the economy. Despite the methodological problems discussed previously, this is a strong indication of a composition effect in the direction of specialization in (potentially) contaminating industries.

IPEA-IE/UFRJ Emission Coefficients Inventory (Local Pollutants)

The third database used to estimate the emission of local pollutants by Brazilian industry was built specifically for this study using data from CETESB (the environmental agency for the State of São Paulo). The calculation of industrial emissions generated in São Paulo was based on the information given by local production units about their potential emissions and their capacity to abate them (obtaining, by residual, the level of remaining emissions) according to the CETESB inventory. Note that, yet again, this data does not give actual emissions, but is data given by the industries to the environmental agency (in that case, up to the end of 1996); therefore they are also 'theoretical' (rather than observed) emissions.

These figures were then divided by the value of production (or value added, or employment) for every industrial sector in the State of São Paulo, in order to generate the emission coefficients. Ideally, production data would have been obtained from the same local units surveyed by CETESB. However, since this comparison is not possible, the value of production of the São Paulo industry, by sector, was estimated using the Annual Industrial Survey (PIA/IBGE) for the year 1996. Once the coefficients were estimated, they were applied to the value of industrial production for the country as a whole (assuming that the environmental performance of industries in São Paulo reflect the average behavior of Brazilian industry).

Emission coefficients were obtained for inorganic and organic water pollutants, sulfur dioxide (SO_2) and total particulates. Table 4.13 presents the results using the emission coefficients estimated according to the CETESB inventory.

Table 4.13 Emission intensities, kg/US$ million, IPEA-IE/UFRJ coefficients

Pollutant/year	Consumption	Investment	Exports	Total
Organic				
1985	956	203	534	723
1990	937	203	590	736
1991	973	210	591	766
1992	972	199	623	764
1993	932	196	625	740
1994	925	184	647	732
1995	923	177	779	747
1996	903	190	744	744
Inorganic				
1985	7.7	7.6	8.8	7.9
1990	7.4	7.2	10.4	7.7
1991	6.9	7.2	10.5	7.5
1992	6.5	7.1	10.9	7.4
1993	6.8	7.4	11.4	7.7
1994	7.0	7.5	10.5	7.6
1995	6.8	7.3	10.5	7.4
1996	6.6	7.2	11.5	7.4
Particulates				
1985	2542	2839	2186	2542
1990	2378	2811	2384	2472
1991	2514	3019	2427	2601
1992	2617	3018	2470	2666
1993	2351	2974	2550	2503
1994	2445	2723	2843	2563
1995	2350	2549	3983	2608
1996	2388	2794	3667	2634
SO_2				
1985	928	1150	1026	992
1990	946	1158	943	991
1991	965	1232	894	1008
1992	977	1231	889	1009
1993	952	1220	890	991
1994	949	1129	919	981
1995	934	1058	945	962
1996	934	1151	939	976

These results are significantly different from the previous exercises. Firstly, emission coefficients are considerably smaller than the ones based on the IPEA data, yet higher than those from IPPS. Considering the estimates for 1995, the average intensity for organic matter (equivalent to BOD) based on the IPEA-IE/UFRJ coefficients is 747 kg/US$ million, in contrast to 861 kg/US$ million estimated with the IPEA coefficients, and 248 kg/US$ million using the IPPS. The intensity for particulates obtained from the IPEA-IE/UFRJ coefficients is 2608 kg/US$ million, while the same estimate using IPEA's coefficients is 4441 kg/US$ million and 618 kg/US$ million using the IPPS. The only exception is SO_2: the estimate of emission intensity based on the IPEA-IE/UFRJ coefficients (962 kg/US$ million) is smaller than the other two estimates (3298 kg/US$ million using IPEA, and 2244 kg/US$ million using IPPS). There has been a modest improvement in the environmental performance of Brazilian industry during the 1990s, even though it still emits more than US industry emitted a decade before (with the exception of SO_2).

Another important point is that the difference between the emission intensities of the export sector and the average of the economy is not so accentuated as in the previous cases. Indeed, the export sector intensity emits below the average intensity in some cases, particularly for SO_2. Nevertheless, in general terms, the conclusions are similar to the previous ones: the export sector tends to be more polluting than the rest of the economy (even though the difference from the other sectors is less accentuated).

Carbon Dioxide Emissions from Fossil Fuel Consumption (Global Pollutant)

A recent study by COPPE/UFRJ (1998) estimated carbon dioxide (CO_2) emissions from fossil fuel consumption in Brazil in the period 1990 to 1994. Data were obtained using the methodological procedures of the Intergovernmental Panel on Climate Change (IPCC) as they were used in the Brazilian official inventory of greenhouse gas emissions. Table 4.14 summarizes the main results.

Table 4.14 *CO_2 emissions from fossil fuel consumption, Brazil (1990 to 1994)*

Sector	1990		1991		1992		1993		1994	
	1 000t CO_2	%	1 000t CO_2	%	1 000t CO_2	%	1 000t CO_2	%	1 000t CO_2	%
Energy	13 226.3	7.3	11 875.2	6.3	12 462.4	6.5	13 471.4	6.7	13 954.0	6.6
Residential	13 767.5	7.6	14 140.6	7.4	14 650.2	7.6	15 184.1	7.5	15 188.4	7.2
Commercial & Public	2 546.4	1.4	2 428.0	1.3	2 458.0	1.3	2 411.6	1.2	3 523.9	1.7
Agriculture	9 997.8	5.5	10 425.5	5.5	10 726.2	5.6	11 851.1	5.9	12 516.4	5.9
Industrial	59 850.3	33.2	65 771.8	34.7	66 635.1	34.6	69 839.0	34.6	72 272.2	34.3
Transport	81 142.2	44.9	85 165.7	44.9	85 807.6	44.5	89 214.8	44.2	93 331.3	44.3
Total	180 530.5	100.0	189 806.9	100.0	192 739.5	100.0	201 972.1	100.0	210 786.2	100.0

Source: COPPE (1998).

Employing the same approach used in the other exercises, based on equation (4.7), Table 4.15 presents the intensity coefficients (CO_2 per unit of output) in each production chain.

Table 4.15 Emission intensity per unit of output (kg CO_2/R$ 1994)

Year	Exports	Consumption	Investment	Total	Annual change (%)
1990	0.634	0.264	0.275	0.302	
1991	0.702	0.270	0.316	0.324	7.1
1992	0.637	0.275	0.294	0.325	0.3
1993	0.607	0.279	0.283	0.320	-1.5
1994	0.635	0.281	0.303	0.326	1.7
Change 94/90 (%)	0.1	6.7	9.9	7.8	

The tables above clearly indicate that the relative contribution of the export sector to CO_2 emissions was constantly around twice the equivalent value of their contribution to total output. In other words, the production of export goods and respective inputs is considerably more emission-intensive than in the other chains. Even though the intensity of CO_2 per output unit in the export sector remained relatively stable (while it increased in the rest of the economy), export sector emission intensity is almost double that of the average intensity of the economy. This is a strong indication that the Brazilian export sector is comprised of 'dirty' activities.

In sector terms, most emissions are concentrated among a few 'dirty' activities, directly or indirectly related to exports: metallurgy, chemicals, agriculture (the high increase in agricultural emissions is a consequence of the mechanization process, resulting in more fuel consumption) and the transportation sector.

On the other hand, despite the accelerated growth in imported goods, the average emission intensity has increased (more emissions to produce the same output). Therefore, the empirical evidence contradicts the hypothesis that free trade and capital flows would lead to higher efficiency in environmental standards.

We conclude that despite all limitations (pollution estimates not directly observed; the environmental impact of a specific pollutant is affected by many other variables that were not considered in the exercise; linear relationships between output and emissions may not be realistic etc.), the results from these analyses consistently show the relatively high contribution of export oriented activities to air and water pollution problems in Brazil. The convergence of these results with other empirical studies on the same issue (Veiga et al., 1995; Torres et al., 1997), but with a less aggregate perspective, confirms the relative specialization in dirty industrial exports. Therefore, any expansion of export activities based on the existing set of parameters will lead to a greater increase in industrial emissions than would result from an expansion in domestic-oriented activities.

Nevertheless, it is crucial to note that only the composition effect was considered in these exercises. The argument that openness brings benefits to the environment is mainly based on another aspect – the technological effect. This issue is discussed later in Section 4.6.

4.6 IMPORTS AND EMISSION 'SAVINGS'

Estimating Emission Savings

An integrated analysis of the environmental impacts of international trade liberalization has to consider that importing goods may significantly reduce domestic pollution emission levels. Imports 'displace' emissions to the country where the good was manufactured – the idea is that, if no trade relations were kept, manufactured goods would have been produced domestically, increasing the level of emissions.

In this section, we examine the emission 'savings' caused by the fast growth of industrial imports in Brazil after the trade liberalization policies. Emission savings figures were estimated using a hypothetical increase in emissions if these imported goods were made in Brazil. This can be done using the same input–output and emission coefficient tables presented in the previous section, and by using the table of the supply and demand of *import* goods (Table 4 of the input–output matrix of IBGE), instead of the supply and demand tables of domestic products (Table 3 of the input–output matrix). Emission coefficients were obtained from the Industrial Pollution Projection System (IPPS) of the World Bank, as before.

The flagship of the liberalization process was automobile imports, which increased 1380 percent in the 1990–96 period. Other industrial sectors with very high rates in growth of imports included plastics (307 percent), textiles (286 percent), wood and furniture (248 percent), electronics (246 percent), other industries (220 percent), other metallurgic goods (200 percent), car components (200 percent), electrical equipment (199 percent) and vegetable oils (193 percent). The average increase in industrial imports was 148 percent. The sectors with the lowest rates of import growth were slaughtering (−41 percent), sugar production (73 percent), footwear (78 percent) and chemical elements (88 percent).

Table 4.16 shows the aggregate emission savings for each pollutant during 1990–96. The average change in the associated level of (potential) emissions was 46 percent. At first sight, this suggests relatively stable emissions from imports. However, a closer look suggests that there were considerable differences between pollutants. For example, in the case of metal emissions for water and BOD, the growth in domestic emission savings was below the average, revealing that the selection of imported goods were becoming less polluting with regard to water. On the other hand, imported goods producing high levels of air pollution (VOC, metals, SO_2 and NO_2) increased in the same period, indicating that the emission savings effect has grown for these parameters.

Table 4.16 Emission savings (tons), IPPS coefficients, 1990–96

Pollutant	1990	1996	Change %
BOD	6183.86	14262.22	131
Total suspended solids	175387.86	429782.33	145
SO_2	65818.26	167426.61	154
NO_2	32209.98	82996.04	158
CO	60391.33	150209.10	149
VOC	23963.26	63944.79	167
Fine particulates	7666.07	19514.42	155
Particulates (total)	12870.87	33092.61	157
Metals – air	13569.27	35060.37	158
Metals – land	28751.79	66923.65	133
Metals – water	2520.36	5344.16	112
Imports	20602.72	51017.03	148

Combining the emission savings in physical units with their output value, we can estimate the avoided emission intensity per unit of imports (Table 4.17). Following the same pattern described previously, there is an asymmetry between changes in water and air pollutants: while there was a decrease in emissions of water and land pollutants per unit of import, air pollutants were increasing.[7]

Table 4.17 Emission intensity per unit of imports (g/US$), IPPS coefficients, 1990–96

Pollutant	1990	1996	Change (%)
BOD	0.30	0.28	−6.86
Total suspended solids	8.51	8.42	−1.04
SO_2	3.19	3.28	2.73
NO_2	1.56	1.63	4.06
CO	2.93	2.94	0.45
VOC	1.16	1.25	7.76
Fine particulates	0.37	0.38	2.80
Particulates (total)	0.62	0.65	3.83
Metals – air	0.66	0.69	4.34
Metals – land	1.40	1.31	−6. 00
Metals – water	0.12	0.10	−14. 37

Comparing Export and Import Emission Intensities

The comparison between the import and export emission intensity coefficients is very important for policy analysis (Table 4.18). It is clear that for Brazil, the potential emissions per unit of exports is always greater than the potential emissions per unit of imports for all parameters considered. The reason behind this is that the composition of the production chain associated with Brazilian industrial exports tends to be concentrated in potentially dirty activities compared with the production chain that would be required if the imports were produced domestically. In other words, Brazil is a net 'exporter' of sustainability, in the sense that its participation in international markets is through the production of potentially polluting industrial goods, while it consumes products that are less harmful to the environment.

It is important to bear in mind that these results reflect the composition of exports and imports based on the hypothesis of fixed emission coefficients. One argument in favor of trade liberalization is the improvement in environmental performance of industries as capital goods can be easily imported, creating lower emissions (since they are designed for the more restrictive markets of developed countries). However, this cannot be empirically verified by using fixed emission coefficients, such as the ones used in this study. Improvement in data availability for effective environmental performance of the industry, instead of proxies based upon fixed emission coefficients, is important to better understand the connections between economic and environmental variables.

Table 4.18 Difference between export and import emission intensities (g/US$)

Pollutant	1990	1991	1992	1993	1994	1995	1996
BOD	0.03	0.03	−0.01	0.08	0.06	0.14	0.08
TSS	11.73	11.83	9.37	10.29	8.72	7.31	8.23
SO_2	2.10	1.83	1.24	1.64	1.56	1.31	1.50
NO_2	0.65	0.58	0.33	0.51	0.55	0.42	0.47
CO	1.93	1.84	1.29	1.63	1.41	1.16	1.33
VOC	0.28	0.18	0.04	0.14	0.18	0.04	0.10
Particulates	0.50	0.48	0.37	0.47	0.42	0.42	0.42
Fine particulates	0.67	0.61	0.45	0.63	0.60	0.63	0.63

We can conclude that the rapid expansion of imports in the 1990s in Brazil created a positive environmental effect by avoiding emissions associated with producing these goods. However, although growth in industrial imports was concentrated on relatively clean goods, the industrial exports sector continued to have high polluting industries. Therefore, the overall reduction in the (potential) emission of pollutants in the Brazilian industry caused by import growth was smaller than it would have been had imports been based on 'dirtier' activities.

4.7 BRAZILIAN COMPETITIVENESS AND THE CONTROL OF WATER POLLUTION

The previous sections demonstrated that the presence of emission-intensive products in Brazilian industrial exports is significant. This creates two kinds of problems: firstly, the welfare losses caused by pollution because of the lack of an environmental accounting system, are not included as external markets become more rigorous in terms of imposing environmental standards, and secondly, as treatment costs are high, the competitive advantage of lower production costs for being 'dirty' will turn out to be a disadvantage.

The first issue has already been analyzed by specialists who conclude that laisse-faire environmental policies may end up with higher social costs than benefits. This chapter discusses the second issue, which has received less attention from the literature: how much would it cost to clean up production, and what would be the trade losses from resulting increases in export prices?

Theoretical Model

The analysis in this chapter follows the approach by Pasurka (1984) to estimate the direct and indirect price effects caused by higher environmental protection costs. He suggests that Brazilian pollution control costs raise prices of various products and their respective inputs at the domestic level, but not the prices in international markets (assuming that Brazilian firms are price-takers). The price increases for inputs must be passed on to the outputs, generating a chain of inflation in the economy. In terms of the input–output approach, the final price increase can be represented by:

$$\Delta P = v\,(I - A)^{-1} - v^{*}\,(I - A^{*})^{-1} \tag{4.9}$$

Where ΔP is a vector of the absolute as well as proportionate price changes, V is the vector representing the sum of the costs of direct labor and capital services used in the production and pollution control activities, V^{*} is the v matrix only in respect of production activities, A^{*} is the matrix of direct intermediate input coefficients only in respect of production activities.

Assuming that the exchange rate is not affected, the cost of the good increases and its competitiveness is reduced. The degree of impact will depend on the demand price-elasticity of Brazilian export goods. This approach assumes that the intermediate consumption for the pollution abatement activity could not be included because of the lack of data (to fix this, the whole input–output table would have to be modified). Another assumption is that the costs of treating pollution do not affect the technical coefficients of the matrix. In addition, it is assumed that production factors necessary for the pollution control activities are not employed for other activities – or else it would have generated a reallocation of production factors incompatible with the existing composition of the aggregate value. Finally, since it refers to a short-term, partial equilibrium analysis, the impacts of pollution control over investment (and, consequently, economic growth) could not be considered. It is assumed that all costs associated with environmental protection are fully incorporated in prices (mark-up hypothesis), characterizing these markets as imperfect competition at the domestic level (despite the fact that export markets are considered as price takers).

Control Costs for Water Emissions from Industry

For the simulation exercise, emission control costs were obtained from simulations based on original parameters developed by Mendes (1994). Only the cost of controlling water emissions from industrial sources was considered, with respect to organic matter (BOD) and toxic metals, including investment costs.[12] The estimates were based on the emission volume calculated according to the IPEA coefficients, cost parameters developed by Mendes (1994) (which were partially derived from a World Bank study based on Brazilian data that estimated the costs for pollution control), and economic data for Brazilian industry from IBGE.

The costs of emission control was calculated for three different scenarios: removal of 50 percent, 75 percent or 100 percent of the pollutants. Each of these scenarios can be considered as different levels of requirement in pollution control legislation. As stated earlier, emission control costs were disseminated through the production chain according to the relative weight of each input to the overall production costs (Pasurka, 1984).

Table 4.19 presents the estimated increase in cost per sector. Overall, the increase in costs are not very large: 93 percent of the economic activities presented have cost increases between 0 percent to 3 percent of the value added. Even when the total removal is required (100 percent scenario), most sectors exhibited an increase in costs lower than 1 percent of the value added.[13]

As expected, sectors with higher (direct) control costs result in larger increases in total costs. Non-ferrous metallurgic, other metallurgic and footwear sectors have increases in costs greater than 3 percent in the three scenarios, indicating these industries may require certain complementary measures to ensure their competitiveness under more stringent environmental regulations.

The sectors with cost increases between 1 percent and 3 percent represent 26 percent of all sectors in the most exigent scenario (100 percent removal). However, the number of sectors experiencing such cost increases falls to less than 10 percent in the least controlling scenario (50 percent removal), and includes machinery and equipment, electric material, vehicle parts and other vehicles, and wood and furniture.

It is interesting to note that these low values are consistent with a survey conducted recently (BNDES/CNI/SEBRAE, 1998), showing that most of the Brazilian industries (65 percent) declared environmental costs to represent less than 5 percent of revenues. In any case, it is also important to highlight that the BNDES/CNI/SEBRAE survey asked about costs already faced by the industry, while the Mendes (1994) coefficients refer to the expenditures that are necessary to remove emissions, but have not yet been implemented.

Table 4.19 Proportion of direct and indirect costs for controlling industrial water emissions, as a proportion of the sector value added (%)

Activities	50%	75%	100%	50%	75%	100%
Agriculture	0.00	0.00	0.00	0.13	0.17	0.31
Mineral extraction	0.00	0.00	0.00	0.31	0.36	0.55
Oil and natural gas	0.00	0.00	0.00	0.27	0.31	0.47
Non-metallic minerals	0.00	0.00	0.00	0.28	0.33	0.51
Iron and steel	0.00	0.00	0.00	0.52	0.61	0.92
Non-ferrous metallurgic	5.30	6.18	8.99	7.71	9.00	13.15
Other metallurgic	5.30	6.18	8.,99	6.55	7.64	11.15
Machinery and equipment	0.00	0.00	0.00	1.10	1.28	1.89
Electric material	0.00	0.00	0.00	1.54	1.80	2.66
Electronic material	0.00	0.00	0.00	0.47	0.55	0.81
Motor vehicles	0.00	0.00	0.00	0.99	1.15	1.72
Vehicle parts and other vehicles	0.00	0.00	0.00	1.41	1.64	2.42
Wood and furniture	1.00	1. 06	1.37	1.56	1.70	2.34
Pulp, paper and paperboard	0.16	0.18	0.55	0.46	0.54	1.22
Rubber industry	0.00	0.,00	0.00	0.28	0.33	0.53
Chemical industry	0.39	0.57	1.19	0.62	0.84	1.63
Petroleum refineries	0.00	0.,00	0.00	0.17	0.20	0.32
Other chemical products	0.39	0.57	1.19	0.72	0.98	1.91
Pharmacy and veterinary products	0.03	0.03	0.06	0.28	0.34	0.59
Plastic products	0.00	0.00	0.00	0.20	0.24	0.39
Textiles	0.48	0.53	0.74	0.92	1.03	1.48
Wearing apparel	0.48	0.53	0.74	0.98	1.09	1.64
Footwear	5.01	5.96	16.01	6.42	7.64	20.24
Coffee industry	0.13	0.14	0.29	0.28	0.33	0.63
Other vegetable products	0.13	0.14	0.29	0.35	0.40	0.71
Meat industry	0.13	0.14	0.29	0.31	0.36	0.68
Dairy products	0.13	0.14	0.29	0.44	0.50	0.89
Sugar factories and refineries	0.13	0.14	0.29	0.43	0.50	0.87
Vegetable oils	0.13	0.14	0.29	0.48	0.55	0.95
Other food products	0.13	0.14	0.29	0.46	0.53	0.95

Activities	50%	75%	100%	50%	75%	100%
Other industries	0.00	0.00	0.00	0.53	0.62	0.95
Public utilities	0.00	0.00	0.00	0.14	0.16	0.25
Civil construction	0.00	0.00	0.00	0.75	0.87	1.28
Commerce	0.00	0.00	0.00	0.07	0.09	0.15
Transportation	0.00	0.00	0.00	0.17	0.20	0.31
Communications	0.00	0.00	0.00	0.13	0.15	0.24
Financial institutions	0.00	0.00	0.00	0.03	0.03	0.06
Services to households	0.00	0.00	0.00	0.25	0.29	0.46
Business services	0.00	0.00	0.00	0.07	0.08	0.16
Renting	0.00	0.00	0.00	0.11	0.12	0.18
Public administration	0.00	0.00	0.00	0.07	0.09	0.15
Non-mercantile private sectors	0.00	0.00	0.00	0.04	0.05	0.08

Source: Mendes (1994).

Impacts on Brazilian Exports

Potential impacts of emission control costs on the competitiveness of Brazilian exports were identified based on export data from CHELEM.[14] Three destination areas were considered: European Union, NAFTA countries and Latin America. Table 4.20 shows the importance of the three selected regions for Brazilian exports. The three selected areas account for most of the Brazilian exports. Trade within Latin America is the most dynamic, mainly because of the Mercosul integration process. Although there is an extensive diversification of exports, the export of basic and semi-manufactured goods still continues.

Table 4.20 Brazilian exports (US$ million, current prices)

Region	1980–84	1985–89	1990–94	1995–96
Latin America (excluding Mexico)	2993	3636	6655	10345
NAFTA	5581	8444	8757	9658
European Union	6390	8501	10774	12415
Total	22255	28911	36434	46429

Source: CHELEM.

In order to obtain trade deviation estimates, it is necessary to determine how much demand would vary if prices changed (the price-elasticity of demand for Brazilian export goods). A few empirical studies have been carried out, but almost none have been done at the sector level.[15] Another problem arises from changes in trade patterns and macroeconomic conditions, particularly changes in the exchange rates that affect relative prices, greatly impacting the evolution of exports.

In this report, values similar to the ones estimated by Cavalcanti et al. (1998) for the price-elasticity of the exports quantum were used – although they are aggregates, they were obtained during the same time period of the cost estimation. Cavalcanti et al. (1998) present two estimates of price elasticities, one for the semi-manufactured goods (−0.34) and another for the manufactured ones (−0.78). These values were then applied to the estimates of cost increases in each sector, from Table 4.20. Given the uncertainties in the exercise, a sensitivity analysis was carried out assuming a minimum and a maximum value for all sectors. Hence, the estimations of trade deviation are presented under two scenarios: optimistic (elasticity of −0.34) and pessimistic (elasticity of −0.78). Tables 4.21 and 4.22 present the results in US$, and Tables 4.23 and 4.24 as a percentage of the observed exports.

Table 4.21 Pessimistic scenario: export losses caused by emission control costs, US$ million (current); elasticity: −0.78

	1980–84	1985–89	1990–94	1995–96
Removal of 50% of emissions				
Total	154	255	366	467
Latin America	27	31	66	103
NAFTA	59	110	127	136
European Union	31	56	86	98
Removal of 75% of emissions				
Total	180	299	429	548
Latin America	32	36	77	120
NAFTA	69	129	150	161
European Union	36	66	101	115
Removal of 100% of emissions				
Total	333	555	790	982
Latin America	49	55	121	192
NAFTA	143	265	311	328
European Union	69	125	192	218

Table 4.22 Optimistic scenario: export losses caused by emission control costs, US$ million (current); elasticity: −0.34

	1980–84	1985–89	1990–94	1995–96
Removal of 50% of emissions				
Total	67	111	160	204
Latin America	12	13	29	45
NAFTA	26	48	55	59
European Union	13	24	37	43
Removal of 75% of emissions				
Total	79	131	187	239
Latin America	14	16	33	52
NAFTA	30	56	65	70
European Union	16	29	44	50
Removal of 100% of emissions				
Total	145	242	344	428
Latin America	22	24	53	84
NAFTA	62	115	136	143
European Union	30	54	84	95

Table 4.23 Pessimistic scenario: export losses caused by emission control costs, % of observed exports; elasticity: −0.78

	1980–84	1985–89	1990–94	1995–96
Removal of 50% of emissions				
Total	0.7	0.9	1.0	1.0
Latin America	0.9	0.8	1.0	1.0
NAFTA	1.1	1.3	1.5	1.4
European Union	0.5	0.7	0.8	0.8
Removal of 75% of emissions				
Total	0.8	1.0	1.2	1.2
Latin America	1.1	1.0	1.2	1.2
NAFTA	1.3	1.5	1.7	1.7
European Union	0.6	0.8	0.9	0.9
Removal of 100% of emissions				
Total	1.5	1.9	2.2	2.1
Latin America	1.7	1.5	1.8	1.9
NAFTA	2.6	3.1	3.6	3.4
European Union	1.1	1.5	1.8	1.8

Table 4.24 Optimistic scenario: export losses caused by emission control costs, % of observed exports; elasticity: −0.34

	1980–84	1985–89	1990–94	1995–96
Removal of 50% of emissions				
Total	0.3	0.4	0.4	0.4
Latin America	0.4	0.4	0.4	0.4
NAFTA	0.5	0.6	0.6	0.6
European Union	0.2	0.3	0.3	0.3
Removal of 75% of emissions				
Total	0.4	0.5	0.5	0.5
Latin America	0.5	0,4	0.5	0.5
NAFTA	0.5	0.7	0.7	0.7
European Union	0.2	0.3	0.4	0.4
Removal of 100% of emissions				
Total	0.7	0.8	0.9	0.9
Latin America	0.7	0.7	0.8	0.8
NAFTA	1.1	1.4	1.6	1.5
European Union	0.5	0.6	0.8	0.8

Some important conclusions can be drawn from these results. Given the relatively low cost of environmental control, the estimated loss of exports is not high. The total loss remains between 1 percent and 2 percent of the total value of exports. These figures are similar to those obtained by Repetto (1995) in his analysis of US industry, indicating that the costs of pollution abatement are not as high as argued by those who are against more effective environmental controls.

On the other hand, impacts may be very differentiated in terms of sectors and destination markets. Some industries are more problematic, and export losses may be sizeable in certain sectors. The most affected sectors are footwear (loss of up to 15.8 percent in the pessimistic case, assuming 100 percent removal), non-ferrous metallurgic (maximum loss of 10.3 percent) and other metallurgic (maximum loss of 8.7 percent). The larger concentration of exports of these goods in some markets where buyers are more environmentally conscious may lead to more important trade losses. A typical case is the European Union – fortunately, they purchase goods less dependent on production activities with environmental liabilities. On the other hand, NAFTA receives the biggest basket of goods that require more expenditure in environmental control. If trade barriers based on environmental claims were accepted, exports to North America would face significant restrictions.

Although the study did not consider the impact on imports, it is very likely that imports would increase if the similar domestic goods become more expensive. This condition is very difficult to estimate, but it is crucial to understand the potential impacts in terms of higher regional integration via Mercosul. The harmonizing of more rigorous emission standards in Brazil and the removal of trade barriers with its neighbors may lead to an increase in imports of the goods currently produced under worse environmental conditions. Even though the aggregate result may be relatively small, localized impacts in terms of regions and/or sectors may result from the disparity between the relatively more rigorous standards in Brazil and the lack of environmental control in other Mercosul countries.

It is important to highlight the problems and limitations of this study. The results discussed above are entirely dependent on the reliability of the information on direct control costs, in addition to all other assumptions that were necessary to estimate emissions. There are many problems associated with adequately evaluating the impacts of differentiation of environmental control costs. Control costs depend on the assimilative capacity of the environment (not considered in the exercise) as well as the level and composition of the economic activity. Moreover, only the end-of-pipe costs are usually available. Hence, these estimates may lead to unrealistic conclusions, as it overlooks the importance of investment in new technologies and modern equipment, which are, at the same time, cleaner and more efficient in economic terms.

This approach ignores the role of innovations, which systematically alters the relationship between production and environmental control costs. This so-called technological effect has not been considered in the analysis so far. The following section aims to take account of this point: once the dynamic process of environmental innovations is considered, the conclusions concerning trade and the environment may change completely.

4.8 ENVIRONMENTAL INNOVATION AND OPENNESS IN BRAZILIAN INDUSTRY[16]

The previous chapters have discussed the specialization of the export sector in 'dirty' activities emphasizing the so-called 'composition effect'. However, the input–output analysis that empirically supported this hypothesis is essentially a static approach as it does not consider the technological changes in time. Many favor the idea that openness has positive effects on the environment as better environmental performance is essential for keeping up competitiveness. This section discusses the issue of environmental innovation, trying to investigate if companies with global insertion (either because of capital ownership or trade flows) behave differently when compared with nationally owned, domestic oriented ones.

The empirical evidence is based on data for the state of São Paulo obtained using the PAEP/SEADE survey. The survey was conducted for 43 900 industrial companies from all sectors in 1996. The answers were voluntary, explaining the difference in the number of answers in each table.

The first hypothesis to be tested was that companies with global interests (at least part of its property is owned by foreigners) tend to adopt environmental innovations and perceive the environment as a business opportunity (thus with potential losses if inadequate environmental procedures are adopted) to a higher degree than other companies.[17]

In the PAEP/SEADE questionnaire, the following variables were chosen to test if firms are concerned with environmental issues:

- Business opportunities – if the answering company considered that the development of environmentally friendly products and processes is a means to increasing its business activity. Possible answers: yes/no.
- Environmental implications: market losses – if the answering company considered that its environment performance has resulted in the loss of markets, domestically or internationally. Possible answers: yes/no.
- Environmental implications: higher costs – if the answering company considered that the activities associated with its environmental performance have resulted in higher costs (investment in control measures, fines and levies, etc.). Possible answers: yes/no.

Tables 4.25 and 4.26 present survey results according to origin of capital ownership. Table 4.25 shows that, of the 843 companies with global interests (capital owned at least partially by foreigners), 52.4 percent believe that the development of products and processes less harmful to the environment may turn out to be a business opportunity. Of the companies that are solely owned by foreigners, 54.9 percent believe in the idea. Among the companies exclusively owned by nationals, the percentage drops to 29.2 percent. Therefore, this result confirms the hypothesis that firms with global interests are more inclined to foresee environmental concerns as business opportunities than nationally owned ones.

Table 4.25 Firms that consider the environment as a business opportunity, according to their ownership, 1996

Firm's capital ownership (as of 31 December)	Data	Business opportunity – environmentally friendly products and processes		
		1 = Yes (A)	2 = No (B)	Total (C)
1 = National	Number of Firms	11702	28367	40069
	Percentages A/C and B/C	29.2	70.8	
2 = Foreign	Number of Firms	322	264	586
	Percentages A/C and B/C	54.9	45.1	
3 = National and foreign	Number of Firms	120	137	257
	Percentages A/C and B/C	46.7	53.3	
	Total no. of firms	12144	28768	40912
	Percentages A/C and B/C	29.7	70.3	

Source: Fundação Sistema Estadual de Análise de Dados – SEADE; Pesquisa da Atividade Econômica Paulista – PAEP 1996.

Table 4.26 Firms that consider market losses caused by the environmental consequences of their actions, according to their ownership, 1996

Firm's capital ownership (in 31 December)	Data	Environmental consequences – market losses		
		1 = Yes (A)	2 = No (B)	Total (C)
1 = National	Number of firms	1721	38326	40047
	Percentages A/C and B/C	4.3	95.7	
2 = Foreign	Number of firms	72	511	583
	Percentages A/C and B/C	12.3	87.7	
3 = National and foreign	Number of firms	24	234	258
	Percentages A/C and B/C	9.3	90.7	
	Total no. of firms	1817	39072	40889
	Percentages A/C and B/C	4.4	95.6	

Source: Fundação Sistema Estadual de Análise de Dados – SEADE; Pesquisa da Atividade Econômica Paulista – PAEP 1996.

Nevertheless, only 11.4 percent of the companies with global interests admitted market losses because of the environmental effects of their activities. This falls to only 4.3 percent for nationally owned companies, and rises to 12.3 percent if the answers are restricted to the companies exclusively owned by foreigners. So, most of the answers (95.6 percent), regardless of the origin of capital, indicated that no losses were perceived in either domestic or international markets resulting from company impacts on the environment.

Table 4.27 shows that 41.1 percent of the companies with global interests considered that their costs were increased because of environmentally related activities. This is reduced to 14.8 percent for nationally owned companies. In total, 84.7 percent considered that there were no cost increases because of environmental concerns.

Table 4.27 Firms that identify rising costs due to environmental consequences of their actions, according to their ownership, 1996

Firm's capital ownership (as at 31 December)		Data	Environmental consequences – rising costs 1 = Yes (A)	2 = No (B)	Total (C)
1 =	National	Number of firms	5919	34131	40050
		Percentages A/C and B/C	14.8	85.2	
2 =	Foreign	Number of firms	242	341	583
		Percentages A/C and B/C	41.5	58.5	
3 =	National and foreign	Number of firms	104	155	259
		Percentages A/C and B/C	40.2	59.2	
		Total no. of firms	6265	34627	40892
		Percentages A/C and B/C	15.3	84.7	

Source: Fundação Sistema Estadual de Análise de Dados – SEADE; Pesquisa da Atividade Econômica Paulista – PAEP 1996.

In conclusion, the findings confirm the hypothesis that foreign owned companies are more environmentally conscious than nationally owned companies. However, most of the companies, both foreign and nationally owned, did not identify market losses as a consequence of undertaking environmental protection measures. A better definition of companies with global interests would have to consider the domestically owned companies that export a considerable share of its production; it is possible that with this new classification the differences between the two groups of companies would be even greater. The variables in the survey chosen to reflect the adoption of environmental innovations were:

1. Factors motivating the company to innovate (from 1994 to 1996): environmental preservation – indicates the degree of importance given by the answering company to the strategy of environmental preservation as a motivation factor to innovate. Possible answers: indifferent, less important, important, very important or crucial.
2. Investment: changes in the production process for environmental reasons (from 1994 to 1996). Possible answers: yes/no.

Table 4.28 shows the relationship between the first variable and the origin of capital. A majority (85.5 percent) of the firms with global interests consider environmental preservation as important, very important or crucial in motivating the company to innovate. For domestically owned companies this falls to 78.4 percent, illustrating that most companies are more inclined to innovate due to environmental concerns, and that this behavior is more evident in companies with global interests.

Table 4.28 Degree of importance of the environment protection strategy as a factor that motivated the firm to innovate, according to their ownership, 1996

Factors that motivated the firm to innovate – environment protection (94–96)	Data	Firm's capital ownership (as at 31 December) 1 = National	2 = Foreign	3 = National and foreign	Total
1 = Indifferent (A)	Number of firms	1 095	10	16	1 121
	Percentages A/F	14.7	3.3	14.8	
2 = Less important (B)	Number of firms	518	22	12	552
	Percentages B/F	6.9	7.2	11.1	
3 = Important (C)	Number of firms	2 361	113	22	2 496
	Percentages C/F	31.6	36.8	20.4	
4 = Very important (D)	Number of firms	2 458	109	41	2 608
	Percentages D/F	33.0	35.5	38.0	
5 = Crucial (E)	Number of firms	1 028	53	17	1 098
	Percentages E/F	13.8	17.3	15.7	
Total no. of firms (F)		7 460	307	108	7 875

Source: Fundação Sistema Estadual de Análise de Dados – SEADE; Pesquisa da Atividade Econômica Paulista – PAEP 1996.

Table 4.29 presents the companies that did or did not invest in changes in the production process to reduce environmental problems. Again, the 40.8 percent of the companies with global interests answered positively, compared to 18.3 percent of the domestically owned companies. Therefore, it can be concluded that companies with global interests tend to be more prone to adopt environmental innovations than domestically owned ones, even though most of the latter also consider the environment as a motivating factor for innovation.

Table 4.29 Firms that made investments in changes in their production processes for environmental reasons, according to their ownership, 1996

Investment – changes in production processes	Firm's capital ownership (as at 31 December)			
	1 = National	2 = Foreign	3 = National and foreign	Total
1 = YES (A)	7294	251	92	7636
Percentages A/C and B/C	18.3	43.1	35.5	18.7
2 = NO (B)	32674	331	167	33173
Percentages A/B and B/C	81.7	56.9	64.5	81.3
Total no. of firms (C)	39968	582	259	40809

Source: Fundação Sistema Estadual de Análise de Dados – SEADE; Pesquisa da Atividade Econômica Paulista – PAEP 1996.

Another possible hypothesis is that innovative firms are the ones that invest the most in R&D. In other words, companies who spend more resources on R&D are more inclined to adopt new innovations, including the environmental ones. The variable chosen to reflect R&D efforts was 'Internal sources for innovation activities, 1994 to 1996 – R&D department', which indicates the degree of importance of the internal department of R&D as an induction source of innovation development within the company. The possible answers were indifferent, less important, important, very important or crucial.

Table 4.30 shows the proportion of companies that invested in changing the production process in view of reducing environmental problems, according to the importance attributed to their internal R&D department. Companies that placed greater importance in R&D also invested more in modifying production processes to solve environmental problems. Thus, only 28 percent of the companies that declared indifference to their internal R&D department invested in changes in the production process. This proportion rises to 49 percent for the companies that declared that their own R&D departments were crucial for the innovation process within the firm.

Table 4.30 Firms that invested in changes in their production processes for environmental reasons, according to the degree of importance of their own R&D department, 1996

Investment – changes in the production processes	Data	Internal sources of innovative activities – R&D department (94–96)					
		1 = Indifferent	2 = Less important	3 = Important	4 = Very important	5 = Crucial	Total
1 = YES (A)	Number of firms	242	193	1277	789	380	2880
	Percentages A/C	27.8	38.3	39.6	42.6	49.0	39.9
2 = NO (B)	Number of firms	629	311	1945	1063	395	4343
	Percentages B/C	72.2	61.7	60.4	57.4	51.0	60.1
Total no. of firms (C)		871	504	3221	1852	775	7223

Source: Fundação Sistema Estadual de Análise de Dados – SEADE; Pesquisa da Atividade Econômica Paulista – PAEP 1996.

Table 4.31 shows the relationship between the degree of importance attributed to environmental protection as a motivation factor for innovation, and the degree of importance of the internal R&D department. The results demonstrate an increase in the proportion of companies that consider it important to invest in internal R&D activities according to the importance attributed to the environment as a motivation factor for innovations.

The results confirm that companies investing internally in R&D are more able to generate or adopt innovations, including ones that will help protect the environment. Companies attributing a higher degree of importance to their R&D departments are the ones with higher positive answers in terms of innovation in processes (carried out to reduce environmental damage), and environmental considerations as motivating factors in the innovation process.

Table 4.31 Degree of importance of the environment protection strategy as a factor that motivated the firm's innovation according to the degree of importance of their own R&D department, 1996

Factors that motivate innovation – environmental protection (94–96)	Internal sources of innovative activities – R&D department (94–96)					
	1 = Indifferent	2 = Less important	3 = Important	4 = Very important	5 = Crucial	Total
1 = Indifferent (A)	182	46	296	151	132	808
Percentages A/F	25.2	10.4	10.8	9.8	21.0	13.3
2 = Less important (B)	49	56	164	111	65	447
Percentages B/F	6.8	12.7	6.0	7.2	10.4	7.4
3 = Important (C)	221	157	933	337	137	1784
Percentages C/F	30.6	35.6	34.1	21.9	21.8	29.4
4 = Very important (D)	201	153	914	599	195	2062
Percentages D/F	27.8	34.7	33.4	38.9	31.0	34.0
5 = Crucial (E)	69	29	429	341	99	967
Percentages E/F	9.6	6.6	15.7	22.2	15.8	15.9
Total no. of firms (F)	722	441	2737	1539	628	6067

Sources: Fundação Sistema Estadual de Análise de Dados – SEADE; Pesquisa da Atividade Econômica Paulista – PAEP 1996.

Export-oriented Firms

In the previous section, we saw that foreign-owned firms are more environmentally concerned than nationally owned firms. The following section demonstrates that export-oriented companies, independent of their capital ownership, are more concerned environmentally than more domestically-oriented companies. In other words, the pressure for better environmental performance is perceived better in companies that are more exposed to the global economy.

According to Table 4.32, the companies that have declared the environment as a business opportunity (instead of a constraint) tend to display a higher level of exports. The contrast is more accentuated for domestic owned companies, but the better perception of the potential for 'green' business can be seen among foreign-owned companies.

Table 4.33 confirms the link between companies that admit the possibility of market losses because of environmental consequences of their activities and those that are more export-oriented – the average of those who answered yes is more than double those who answered no. The results of Table 4.33 also steer in the same direction, that is, the firms that spent on activities related to the environment have a higher proportion of exports.

If considering only domestic owned companies, the export average of those who answered positively (2.03 percent) is almost four times the average for those who do not spend (0.55 percent). This difference is also significant for foreign-owned companies.

Table 4.32 Average percent of exports over total sales, according to the origin of capital and the consideration of the environment as a business opportunity

		Environment as a business opportunity		
Origin of capital		Yes	No	Average % exports
Domestic	Average % exports	1.04	0.66	0.77
Foreign	Average % exports	9.40	8.94	9.19
National and foreign	Average % exports	7.39	5.99	6.64
Total		1.32	0.76	0.93

Source: SEADE/PAEP.

Table 4.33 Exports over total sales according to the origin of capital and the effect of losing markets because of the environmental consequences of their activities

		Environmental effects: market losses		
Origin of capital		Yes	No	Average % exports
Domestic	Average % exports	1.47	0.74	0.77
Foreign	Average % exports	15.21	8.20	9.07
National and foreign	Average % exports	11.35	6.20	6.69
Total average % exports		2.14	0.87	0.93

Source: SEADE/PAEP.

Table 4.34 Exports over total sales according to the origin of capital and the effect of increasing costs because of activities related to the environment

Origin of capital		Higher costs because of environmental activities		
		Yes	No	Average % exports
Domestic	Average % exports	2.03	0.55	0.77
Foreign	Average % exports	13.55	5.87	9.07
National and foreign	Average % exports	6.72	6.67	6.69
Total average % exports		2.55	0.63	0.93

Source: SEADE/PAEP.

Finally, it is important to analyze the differences among sectors. Table 4.35 shows, for each industry, the average exports according to selected variables: products and processes perceived as environmentally friendly; costs incurred due to environmental activities; investment in the contaminating input substitution; and investments in process modification in order to reduce environmental stress. The answers are not homogeneous in all sectors, but in most sectors there was a distinct relationship between higher concern for the environment and a greater importance played by exports in total sales. Some aspects that deserve attention include: the questions where there were differences in the answer patterns refering to costs already incurred in environmental issues in the sectors with large exports (footwear; motor vehicles; machinery and equipment; pulp and paper), there were considerable differences between the average export proportion of firms declaring concern with environmental issues and the ones declaring indifference – the principal exception to this pattern was in petroleum refineries and alcohol distilleries.

The survey confirmed the hypothesis that firms with global interests are the most likely to adopt environmental innovations, even though most nationally-owned companies or domestic-oriented ones would also be motivated to use new innovations to reduce environmental problems. This counterbalances the previous sections, in the sense that it shows that the process of opening the economy has some environmental advantages, as theoretically argued by many. Important policy recommendations drawn from these conclusions are discussed in the following chapter.

Table 4.35 Environmental perception and exports over total sales, by sector

	Environment as business opportunity		Higher costs because of environmental activities		Investment in the substitution of pollutant inputs		Investment in environmentally friendly processes	
Sectors	Yes	No	Yes	No	Yes	No	Yes	No
Mineral extraction	0.66	0.15	0.40	0.39	0.12	0.43	0.49	0.31
Refineries & alcohol dist.	3.40	3.80	3.05	4,.82	1.21	5.15	1.04	5.44
Chemical products	1.86	2.21	3.07	1.47	2.89	1.67	2.92	1.54
Rubber and plastic products	0.56	0.33	0.98	0.31	0.79	0.34	0.57	0.37
Non-metallic minerals	0.57	0.81	1.53	0.59	2.46	0.53	1.88	0.52
Metallurgy (basic)	1.38	0.37	1.57	0.45	1.18	0.53	0.94	0.59
Metallic products (excl. machinery and equipment)	0.72	0.44	1.38	0.34	1.31	0.38	1.15	0.35
Pulp and paper	1.45	0.54	2.50	0.50	3.19	0.38	2.67	0.42
Food and beverages	1.70	0.64	2.86	0.42	3.76	0.59	2.63	0.50
Textiles	1.46	0..50	1..54	0.56	1.93	0.54	1.70	0.55
Wearing apparel	0.04	0.13	0.15	0.11	0.09	0.11	0.05	0.12
Leatherware	5.53	2.23	16.40	1.64	8.22	2.25	12.81	1.86
Machinery and equipment	2.54	1.97	5.00	1.72	5.13	1.53	3.49	1.81
Machinery for offices/computers	0.00	0.84	10.87	0.10	4.71	0.11	6.92	0.11
Electric equipment	1.14	1.05	2.52	0.91	2.61	0.79	2.04	0.86
Electronic and communications material	2.62	0.90	2.92	1.26	3.04	1.13	1.92	1.36
Medical equip., optics, industrial automation	3.12	2.59	4.83	2.56	2.60	2.78	2.79	2.75
Motor vehicles	3.49	1.91	6.81	1.38	4.89	1.67	4.80	1.75
Other transportation equip.	1.06	2.84	6.97	1.42	4.96	1.95	2.25	2.39
Other industries	0.50	0.53	1.04	0.44	0.89	0.47	0.80	0.47
Total	1.32	0.76	2.55	0.63	2.49	0.67	2.00	0.68

Source: SEADE/PAEP.

4.9 CONCLUSIONS AND POLICY RECOMMENDATIONS

The debate about the environmental consequences of open trade cannot be summarized by simplistic answers such as trade-oriented policies are good (or bad) for the environment. The links between competitiveness and the environment are complex. The analyses above showed that there are empirically sound arguments for both issues.

In an input–output perspective, using constant coefficients for industrial emissions, it is clear that the production chain associated with Brazilian industrial exports is more emission-intensive than the production chains catering to domestic markets. This trend was observed for most of the pollution parameters analyzed, showing that Brazilian industry has specialized in the supply of potentially polluting goods to the international markets. This result is, thus, compatible with the hypothesis that developing countries tend to accommodate 'dirty' industries that are less competitive in developed countries due to tighter environmental controls.

This process was, nevertheless, counterbalanced by emissions 'savings' created by the fast expansion of imports in the 1990s. By importing goods, the emissions associated with the production of those goods are avoided as they are produced abroad. However, this counterbalancing effect was much attenuated by the composition of the import goods basket, compared with exports: the growth in industrial imports was concentrated in relatively clean activities, particularly those that were technology-intensive (electronics, for example), while industrial exports remained associated with more emission-intensive sectors. Therefore, the overall reduction in the (potential) emission of pollutants in the Brazilian industry caused by import growth was smaller than it could have been if these imports were concentrated in 'dirtier' activities (intermediate goods, for example).

Another important result was that the direct costs of introducing environmental control strategies are relatively low, considering the industry as a whole. The exercises carried out in Section 4.6 showed that the estimated loss of exports induced by higher production costs resulting from the control of water pollutants (BOD and heavy metals) would remain between 1 percent to 2 percent of the total value of Brazilian exports. In other words, the comparative advantage of being 'dirty' are not as high as argued by those who oppose effective environmental controls. However, the impacts of introducing pollution abatement measures may differ in terms of sectors and destination markets. The sectors facing the highest risks of losing markets are footwear, non-ferrous metallurgic and other metallurgic goods. However, currently highly polluting sectors risk future market losses in regions where consumers are becoming more environmentally conscious. For example, exports to the NAFTA region could involve higher expenditure on environmental control in the future.

Innovations also play a significant role as it changes the effective relationship between production and environmental control costs. The static nature of the input–output analyses does not capture the so-called technological effect, which is dynamic and very difficult to measure and model. Section 4.6 illustrates that, based on the answers from the PAEP survey, obtained from industries in the State of São Paulo, firms with international orientation tend to be more concerned about environmental issues and invest the most in 'cleaning' their production processes. Data demonstrated that export-oriented and/or foreign capital companies tend to consider the competitive advantages of environmental innovations more seriously than inward-oriented and/or domestic capital firms, due to the higher environmental standards and pressures in international markets. This is compatible with the hypothesis that trade and capital openness tend to encourage the adoption of environmentally sound practices and products.

These results have important implications for policy making. First of all, it is clear that the relatively high concentration of Brazilian industrial exports in pollution-intensive activities makes exports very sensitive to environmental barriers to trade. A change in the institutional framework regulating international trade towards the acceptance of an environmental criteria for import control, as advocated by many environmental organizations in developed countries, could lead to significant losses for Brazilian industrial exports. Two possible strategies to deal with this problem include:

1. adopt an aggressive position against the proposed changes in trade regulations, maintaining the status quo of limited environmental barriers in the international trade agreements; and/or
2. enhance the environmental performance of Brazilian industries, either improving local emission standards or changing the composition of industrial exports by becoming less dependent on exports associated with 'dirty' production chains.

Even though these strategies are not contradictory, they reflect different perspectives. Option (1) reflects a view that the claims for environmental restrictions in trade (and capital) flows are a short-term pressure that will not be approved in the future. However, one possible difficulty that may emerge in the forthcoming years is that, with the deepening of regional trade agreements such as Mercosul and possibly the American Free Trade Agreement, Brazilian producers could face competition from exports from neighboring countries who are subject to lower environmental standards – bear in mind that Brazil is a leader in

Latin America in terms of environmental controls. This would reverse the present situation, causing Brazilian producers to be the losers if no standardization of environmental controls are adopted.

Therefore, the second strategy would be more appropriate to deal with the problem in the long term. There is a smooth but consistent change in the perception of Brazilian policy makers towards the adoption of economic instruments in environmental management, based on the user/polluter-pays principle, and as a consequence some sectors may experience short-term losses in competitiveness. However, the results above show that this overall cost increase may be considerably less than is assumed (with the exception of some specific sectors, that could receive special compensation policies during the transition to cleaner production), and that many firms are already voluntarily searching for better environmental procedures. This is another significant feature of international trade that counterbalances the original problem of specialization in emission-intensive activities: the pressures of consumers in developed countries are 'reaching their target', in the sense that export-oriented and/or foreign-owned firms tend to see the potential gains from adopting environmental innovations in a different way from firms that are not exposed to these pressures.

However, this transition towards a more environmentally sound economy cannot rely on a laissez-faire principle that by exposing Brazilian firms to the market it will automatically move towards the desired situation. One important step is the push for economic instruments for environmental management, allowing flexible but efficient measures to improve environmental standards. This must be combined with industrial policies with the aim of spreading win–win environmental innovations (energy and other input savings; better access to markets, particularly in developed countries; higher quality and efficiency standards associated with changes in processes associated with environmentally friendly measures etc.). Some examples of these policies are:

1. support for the technological capacity for firms in environmentally related technologies;
2. better dissemination of new technology in the productive sector;
3. improvement of educational and technical skills of the labor force;
4. improvement in the quantity and quality of research centers, linking them to the productive sector interests;
5. specific programs aimed at reducing regional differences in environmental performance;

6. incentives for certification programs, including the process of public procurement; and
7. improvement of the domestic consumer's awareness and perception of the benefits of environmentally sound products and processes, creating a domestic market for 'green' products.

Finally, it must be highlighted that the results presented in this report have important limitations with regard to the methodology and hypotheses used, and that the quality of data is far from accurate. The improvement of data and environmental indicators are important to improve our understanding about the relationship between trade and competitiveness issues and the environment. Therefore, it is recommended that an effective system for gathering environmental information connected to economic indicators is implemented.

NOTES

1. See Low (1992) for a general discussion of trade and environment and Birdsall and Wheeler (1992) for a discussion on this issue for Latin America.
2. Again the original name given to the colony expresses a valuable natural resource that quickly became exhausted: *madeira* means wood in Portuguese.
3. There is extensive literature on the subject. A brief summary of thoughts is provided in Prebisch (1984).
4. In the mid-1980s, 320 sources (related to 116 industrial units) were emitting around 400 000 tons of pollutants annually in Cubatão. The consequences to human health were dramatic: Cubatão had the highest rate of child mortality in the state of São Paulo (72/1000) despite generating more than 3 percent of the country's GDP, and 18 percent of the local population was suffering from respiratory diseases. Villa Parisi, the village around the industrial complex, was nicknamed 'The Valley of Death'. However, it was the very high level of fetus malformation and other problems for newborns ('the children of pollution') that caught more attention from the public opinion (Almeida, 1997).
5. This is easily shown if one uses the argument of the 'idealized' world according to a theoretical model different from the proposed free market. For example, in an idealized world according to the Marxist–Leninist theory, any improvement towards more socialism (against almost all pro-market proposals) will unambiguously lead to raising welfare.
6. These 13 states combined were responsible for 96 percent of the Brazilian manufacturing industrial output according to the 1985 Industrial Census.
7. One adaptation was required because the above emission coefficients were based on the value added (VA) for each industrial sector. However, equation (4.6) refers to the total value of production (VP), including intermediate consumption. Therefore, the VA-based emission coefficients were multiplied by the VP/VA ratio for each industrial sector, in order to provide VP-based emission coefficients that could be applied to the direct and indirect effects of each category of final demand.
8. The primary data on water emissions were reviewed in the work by Mendes (1994), although the data on air emissions were not. The latter does not represents a significant difficulty for the exercise, because the most important problem identified in the primary data concerned the leather and footwear sector, which is not a major source of air emissions.

9. For more detail on the construction of the IPPS database see Hettige et. al. (1994).
10. The IPPS also provides aggregate estimates of toxicity; however, since the interpretation of these aggregates is not an easy task, they were not considered in this analysis.
11. On the other hand, the other option (*interquartile* coefficients), which consider the emissions of industries in the second and third quartiles, raisess even more complicated problems, including the lack of sufficient data for some sectors, and the difficulty of determining if the coefficients have an underestimation or an overestimation bias.
12. A similar exercise was carried out using emission control costs available in the IPPS; nevertheless, in this case, they refer to the average current costs of US industry in emission control for the year 1994. Hence, the results were considerably smaller than those obtained using the Mendes (1994) coefficients. In order to avoid further confusions (and because the underestimation was much more significant than in the case of emission estimates and these values more precarious), these results were left out of this report.
13. The result that cost increases are not very large is similar to the estimates of Pasurka (1984) and other studies for the US (such as Repetto et al., 1995).
14. Comptes Harmonisés sur les Échanges et l'Économie Mondiale – database on international trade organized by the Centre D'Études Prospectives et d'Informations Internationales (CEPII), Paris, France.
15. IPEA is currently working on estimating these sector elasticities, but there were no results available at the time of concluding this report. The use of these elasticities in the future will considerably improve the quality of these estimates.
16. This section draws heavily on Lustosa and Young (2000). It complements the previous analysis, since it discusses the issue of the technological effect that cannot be captured in the input–output analysis carried out earlier.
17. In the PAEP/SEADE survey, companies with global interests were considered as the ones with capital ownership classified as foreign (100 percent of the capital is owned by foreigners) and national and foreign (at least one of the controllers is a foreigner).

5. Consumption patterns, income distribution and the environment in Brazil

5.1 INTRODUCTION

Despite continuous growth, Brazil has been unable to reduce social inequalities at the same pace. Nevertheless, as in any growing urban and industrial society, consumption patterns in Brazil are changing towards environmental-intensive goods and services, increasing pressure on the environment and ecosystems.

The current political agenda in Brazil is, without doubt, to resume growth and reduce social gaps. These national priorities are widely recognized by all political parties and totally grasped by public opinion. Environmental concerns are relevant but they must be balanced against development and equity issues.

Can growth and the environment be reconciled? We know that each level of income gives rise to a certain level of degradation pressure. Nevertheless, higher income levels may allow for higher consumption of the clean environment that induces an endogenous technological path that reduces degradation per unit of consumption. When this intensity declines at a rate exceeding income growth rate, total degradation decreases despite consumption growth. In this case, one may expect that when average income exceeds a certain threshold level, economic activity may be decoupled from degradation. In other words, the income and environment relationship may follow an inverse U curve shape.[1]

Much has been said about this relationship among countries at distinct income stages in the environmental Kuznets curve literature[2]. However, little analysis has been done on degradation pressure arising from distinct income groups within a country,[3] although most environmental pressures arise from technological processes that indistinctly affect degradation intensity of all classes, and thereby reduce the possibility of the occurrence of such a threshold income. The pattern and magnitude of consumption vary in each income group and directly affect the degradation pressures from each class.

Degradation pressure from the rich tends to be higher due to their higher income levels. Nevertheless, they tend to consume less of their income, consequently reducing their degradation pressure. In other words, one may expect degradation intensity to change depending on income distribution and marginal propensity to consume rather than on technological factors. In this case the inverted U curve relationship may not be relevant. Therefore, knowledge of the trend and magnitude of this relationship becomes a key parameter when analyzing environmental equity issues that cannot be avoided when designing environmental policies, particularly in developing countries.

This study attempts to address the following questions in the context of the Brazilian economy:

- What are the levels of degradation generated by each income class?
- How concentrated are these levels among the income classes?
- What are the changes in these levels if income inequality is altered?

Although this subject should cover many degradation sources, data availability will limit our analysis to some urban-related environmental issues for the year 1995.

The marginal propensity to degrade was first calculated for each source. Based on these values we calculated degradation pressure per household and degradation concentration ratios for ten income groups among the Brazilian urban population.

Indicators of the environmental pressures from consumption patterns of distinct income groups and their respective concentration coefficients are estimated and presented in the following two sections. Lastly, an analysis is made of changes in pollution and natural resource use levels due to income transfers within the economy.

5.2 ENVIRONMENTAL EFFECTS OF CONSUMPTION PATTERNS

Knowledge of emissions or natural resource use is an essential step in any exercise dealing with the environmental impacts of consumption. The ability to analyze the links between different levels of personal consumption and potential environmental effects is crucial to assess future environmental problems. This chapter analyzes how consumption patterns exert pressure on the environment. Environmental pressures include pollution and natural resource use related to the production and direct consumption of the good.

Methodological Procedures

We apply the following methodology to analyze degradation pressure from distinct income groups in Brazil.

Per capita degradation pressure (E_i) generated by an individual i is given by the pollution intensity (p_i) multiplied by consumption level (C_i):

$$E_i = p_i\, C_i \tag{5.1}$$

C_i is the marginal propensity to consume with respect to income (c_i) multiplied by income level (Y_i). Thus, total pollution of individual i is:

$$E_i = p_i\, c_i\, Y_i \tag{5.2}$$

The marginal propensity to degrade (pollute or use natural resources) with respect to income of individual i will be:

$$\text{Pmg}_i = \delta E_i / \delta Y_i = p_i\, c_i \tag{5.3}$$

Note that Pmg will depend on p (a technological factor), and c (an income-related factor). Total degradation E_i will also capture income scale effects, since it depends on income levels too.

Pmg of individual i is given by the weighted sum of Pmg of the good or service j consumed by individual i. Thus:

$$p_i\, c_i = \Sigma_j\, p_{i,j}\, c_{i,j}\,.$$

In this case, $p_{i,j}$ is the degradation intensity of good j consumed by individual i. So Pmg captures technological effects in p and consumption composition effects in c for each good or service j.

If we know E_i for relevant pollutants and uses, it is possible to measure levels of environmental pressure by distinct consumption patterns. Furthermore, knowing Pmg_i will enable us to analyze how income changes within the economy will affect this pressure.

The following section looks at the measurement of Pmg and pollution and use levels for distinct consumption patterns. Based on these values, we analyze the relationship between income distribution and the environment in Brazil.

Estimation Procedures

In this section we calculate the parameters indicated in the previous section, namely: total per household degradation level E and the respective propensities to degrade Pmg. Since we cannot deal with individual consumption and degradation indicators, we have to assume a certain level of aggregation and take into account that all individuals in this level are homogeneous. This exercise will hence be based on the ten income groups that are usually used for household expenditure surveys in Brazil.

Each income household group is represented by i and pollution or use level per household is given by the total group level divided by the number of people in the group. Natural resource use and pollution result from the production of goods consumed by households as well as from the direct consumption of these goods.

Due to data limitations, our analysis will be limited to two production sources (industrial and agricultural) and three direct consumption sources (transportation, water and sewage) following these main environmental effects:[4]

1. industrial water pollution from organic and inorganic matter and air pollution from sulfur dioxide (SO_2) and particulates;
2. agricultural pollution from fertilizer use;
3. household transport pollution from atmospheric emissions of carbon monoxide (CO), hydrocarbons (HC) and nitrogen oxide (NO_x);
4. household water consumption;
5. household sewage discharge.

Our estimates will be concentrated on urban areas since most of our data is restricted to those areas and they represent more than 90 percent of national personal income. Estimates also will be related to the year 1995 to which the 1995/96 household expenditure data was used to split up the personal consumption vector of the 1995 input–output matrix into ten income classes.

Industrial Pollution

In order to capture all the industrial pollution generated from manufacturing a good, we need to account for downward and upward linkages. That is, to account for each emission flow related to the production of this good from the input production up to the assembling phase. Such an approach requires the application of an input–output model (I–O) which compares changes on personal consumption vectors of distinct income groups to potential industrial pollution levels, as described below.[5]

The gross output requirements in the Leontief model are given by:

$$X = AX + Y \tag{5.4}$$

Where Y is the final demand vector (divided into personal consumption, capital formation, government expenditure and exports), X is the vector of gross output and A is the matrix of direct intermediate input coefficients. If the elements of A are constant, then the gross output requirement for any bill of final demand Y can be obtained by:

$$X = (I - A)^{-1} Y \tag{5.5}$$

Where $(I-A)^{-1}$ is the matrix of direct and indirect input requirements.

In the case of industrial emissions, pollution coefficients of the production of consumed goods do not vary by income groups (that is, p_i is the same for all classes) since the production of the good can be assumed to be not class-specific.[6] Therefore, pollution emissions from personal consumption can be easily introduced in the I–O model. Let P be the matrix of pollution coefficients where p_j represents the pollution generated by output of industry j (amount of pollutant in physical unit/output of industry j in currency unit). Following the basic principles of the input–output model mentioned above, then:

$$E = P(I - A)^{-1} C \tag{5.6}$$

Where E is the total pollution or use level matrix, P is the pollution vector p, $(I - A)^{-1}$ is the Leontief matrix, given the matrix A of technical coefficients and C is the relevant income group consumption vector.

If C is split up into i vectors representing one monetary unit of consumption of every i income group, each of its cells will represent propensities to consume of income group i of good j (c_{ij}). Constructing C in this way, E is a matrix of Pmg vectors for each income group related to each good j, that is, a matrix where the cells represent Pmg_{ij}.

An input–output matrix for Brazil is available for several years and is disaggregated into 80 sectors, including 42 industrial sectors. However, the personal consumption vector is aggregated by the whole economy, and is therefore not split up by income classes.

To break down the aggregated consumption and estimate c_{ij} we need indicators of income group consumption levels from urban household expenditure surveys.[7] To estimate c_{ij} we first identify each industrial consumption good with its relevant matrix sector and classify consumption items accordingly. Ten personal consumption group vectors of the *C* matrix were constructed by adopting the ten POF income groups. The ten groups are classified by urban household income measured by minimum salaries[8] (MW), namely: 0–2; 2–3; 3–5; 5–6; 6–8; 8–10; 10–15; 15–30 and > 30.

Estimates of pollution intensities were based on actual emission data from São Paulo.[9] Previous studies (see Mendes, 1994) have estimated nationwide water pollution intensities for the Brazilian industrial sector for the year 1988 based on information taken from inventories of state environmental agencies. Recent revisions to these inventories are no longer available except for in a few states, for example, at the São Paulo EPA (CETESB), which is able to offer a user-friendly database.

The inventory is updated systematically and figures refer to scenarios from the previous year. We have had access to the database for the period 1995–97 from which we can estimate the '1996' sectoral emission charges and associate them to the respective sectoral production values presented in the 1996 Annual Industrial Survey, to determine sectoral coefficients of matrix *P*.

The CETESB inventory provides potential and residual emission levels. Potential emissions represent emission charges after abatement practices and, therefore, signify actual emissions. A comparison of Pmg values estimated with the emission indicators allows us to analyze how abatement investments are affecting consumption patterns.

The main setback of using CETESB data for nationwide purposes is evident. Apart from being specific for the represented state industrial structure, it only covers a selection of firms that are closely monitored by CETESB. Since information revealing the identity of selected firms cannot be disclosed we are unable to identify the firm's production or aggregate values. As a result, attempts to estimate p_{ij} have to be based on total state values, which may underestimate p_{ij} values.

Residual pollution coefficients, which are readily available from the World Bank's Industrial Pollution Projection System (IPPS), based on the US EPA database, could also be used. These values are estimated from a very large sample of industries and products, and therefore are more technologically consistent, making these coefficients more representative of the US industrial profile.[10]

Finally, since our c_{ij} values are taken from the POF sample, we need to estimate total and per household E_i for the whole population by multiplying Pmg_{ij} by group i total income and dividing the number of people of group i as given by the 1995 Demographic Household Survey (PNAD).[11]

Agricultural Pollution

The same I–O model was applied for fertilizer use in agriculture. As we only have one pollutant associated with this sector use, the matrix **E** is a vector with one single cell that represents the fertilizer intensity (p). This intensity was estimated as the ratio of total fertilizer consumption (ton) by agricultural value added in 1995/96 obtained from IBGE (1998).

Direct Consumption

For direct consumption, emission and use levels (given by p_i) may vary across income groups when direct consumption is dependent on the efficiency of the emitter or user. This is the case, for example, of different emission levels of car vintage owned by each income group. The same applies for sewage generation, where sewage collection services are distinctly offered depending on household income groups.

Three types of consumption effects were analyzed:

- household private transport emissions: carbon monoxide (CO), hydrocarbons (HC) and nitrogen oxide (NO_x);
- household water consumption;
- household sewage discharge.

For direct consumption we directly estimate the degradation level, instead of estimating p and c as was done for industrial sources. In order to do this, we have used the 1995–96 POF figures and the same income group brackets. Estimates of Pmg, however, are directly determined from pollution and use levels associated with household expenditures. As such:

- Household consumption levels are illustrated by per household expenditure divided by the consumed good price (transport fuel and water and sewage tariffs).
- Per household degradation level is given by multiplying the relevant consumption level by its respective emission or use factors.
- Estimates of Pmg_i will consist of emission or use levels, indirectly calculated as mentioned above, divided by the average household income of the class.

Transport Emissions

Transport emissions consist of pollutants generated by the use of private vehicles, buses and taxis, which are directly related to the fuel consumption, fuel economy and vehicle emission profiles. Private vehicle fuels include gasoline and ethanol. Annual average fuel prices for both fuels are presented in the Brazilian Energy Balance (BEN, 1997).

First we measure per household fuel consumption by dividing fuel expenditure by fuel price for each income group, by taking the same income classes used for industrial pollution. Secondly, we are able to calculate a proxy for per household emissions (E_i) by multiplying fuel consumption by fuel economy (liters/km) and by emission profile (g/km), thereby illustrating the technological dimension of p. Finally dividing E_i by average class income reveals the respective Pmg_i.

Ferraz and Seroa da Motta (1999) have determined annual average levels of fuel economy and emission profiles for vehicles in Brazil during the period 1992–97. Their findings demonstrated that, due to the application of stricter emission norms and tax differentials, emission levels of cars have radically declined in this period.

As data on car ownership related to household income was not available, we have made assumptions for emission profiles for each income group based on these emission parameters, assuming that lower income groups own cars that emit more.[12] In the absence of better judgment we assumed that: (1) 1992 emission levels of cars are a proxy for income levels below 5 MW and (2) subsequent year's parameters will be given by average emission levels of the following two emission years; and (3) the same level is applied for the last two richest classes. The same schedule was employed for fuel economy. This is not an accurate breakdown, but it may capture emission level differentiation, which can be expected among income groups.

Emissions from taxis and public transport by buses cannot be calculated using the same process as for private vehicles. Household expenditures on taxis and public transport are dependent on the mode. Therefore, no fuel consumption data is discriminated by mode. In the case of taxis, we are unable to differentiate the use of natural gas, ethanol and gasoline. In public transport, we know that buses depend heavily on diesel oil but we are not able to identify average emission levels from buses.

Therefore, in both cases we had to calculate per household emissions and Pmg based on a proportional relationship of gasoline emissions from private vehicles related to their emission shares calculated in the emission inventory of the Great Metropolitan Area of São Paulo published by CETESB (1998). Each class will be allocated a portion of taxi and bus emissions equivalent to its share of all classes' expenditure on taxi or bus.

Therefore, per household emissions and Pmg for each class *i*, for taxis and buses will be the product of gasoline per household emissions or Pmg of class *i* to the respective taxi or bus inventory share. This total emission is distributed among classes by multiplying total emissions to the share of the income group expenditure on the mode in relation to total expenditures of all groups. We assume that each group has the same per household emission contribution for all transportation modes.[13] Based on the estimates of each transportation mode, total transportation indicators are calculated.

Water Consumption and Sewage Generation

Following a similar procedure as for the estimation of private vehicle emissions, we divide the expenditures on treated water supplied by sanitation companies, by average water tariffs, to estimate the consumption of treated water. For sewage collected by sanitation services, we can estimate volumetric discharge of collected sewage in the same way. Following the method used for calculating the Pmg_i for transport emissions, we can estimate Pmg_i directly by dividing water consumption and sewage discharge by average income for each income group. Next we can adjust sewage generation estimates by average sanitation coverage in each income class.

Tariffs for water and sewage services are charged together in Brazil (on the same bill) and, consequently, POF expenditure items related to these direct consumptions are represented by one survey item. Therefore, in order to apply the same estimation procedures as for vehicle emissions, we have to determine the average tariff and expenditure share of each service.

A survey on sanitation services in Brazil published by PMSS (1996) shows that average national water and sewage tariffs are R$ 0.63. Sanitation rates have a fixed lower tariff for water consumption below 10 m^3 and increase in subsequent higher consumption brackets.

Based on survey data for the Paraná State, Andrade (1998) has shown that such fixed value for minimum consumption is, in fact, a regressive schedule resulting in higher average tariffs per unit of m^3 (up to 20 percent) for lower consumption brackets. In order to account for this regressive bias, we have adopted the relative differences of average bracket tariffs measured by Andrade (1998) to adjust our average tariff values according to each consumption class. Based on these price parameters we estimated the consumption of treated water and collected sewage provided by sanitation companies. Total water consumption and sewage discharge should account for non-treated water and non-collected sewage that will also change when income varies due to differences in coverage of sanitation services. The PNAD indicates the proportion of households in each income class that are covered by these sanitation services.

Based on these price parameters we estimated the consumption of treated water and collected sewage provided by sanitation companies. Total water consumption and sewage discharge should also account for the volume of non-treated water and non-collected sewage that will also change when income varies due to differences in coverage of sanitation services. The PNAD indicates the proportion of households in each income class that are covered by these sanitation services.[14]

The total values for water consumption and sewage discharge represent the sum of covered and non-covered quantities, assuming that water and sewage have the same volumetric level. The respective Pmg can be calculated by dividing consumption and discharge estimates by the average income of each group.

Therefore, for water and sewage we will have Pmg and per household parameters for total, treated and non-treated water consumption and total collected and non-collected sewage discharge. Note that total and non-treated water and total and non-collected sewage are equivalent to potential and residual industrial emissions mentioned above, respectively.

5.3 RESULTS

Our results of Pmg and *E* estimates are presented separately for each type of pollutant or use level in Tables 5.1 to 5.3, according to income groups.

Table 5.1 and Figures 5.1 to 5.10 clearly indicate that industrial and agricultural Pmg values, as expected, vary across income groups. However, although industrial and agricultural Pmg values do not vary monotonically, they tend, except for inorganic matter, to decrease with income. Comparing the lowest with the highest income group, Pmg variation reaches a reduction of almost 60 percent in residual organic matters and 70 percent in fertilizers.

The observed trends in inorganic Pmg, which increases in middle income brackets,[15] is expected since upper classes have a higher propensity to consume goods such as car parts, fuel and leather artifacts produced from heavy industrial activities involving inorganic pollution. For the other pollutants, emission levels do not differ substantially between income brackets.

Table 5.1 Estimates of propensity to degrade (g/10^3 R$) and per household degradation (g) for income groups in Brazil for industrial and agricultural sources, 1995

Indicators	Income Groups*										
	0—2	2—3	3—5	5—6	6—8	8—10	10—15	15—20	20—30	30—+	TOTAL
Production											
Industrial pollution											
Organic											
Potential Pmg	13249.1	13132.3	11644.0	11793.9	8981.1	7769.6	7851.9	6827.2	6500.7	4566.1	7542.1
Potential per household	1857.7	3459.3	4766.0	6664.9	6383.5	7114.9	9800.7	12080.0	16075.6	24435.6	6886.5
Residual Pmg	646.5	629.0	582.4	574.3	476.2	429.6	439.2	386.8	363.5	265.7	407.0
Residual per household	90.6	165.7	238.4	324.5	338.5	393.4	548.2	684.5	899.0	1422.0	371.3
Residual/potential ratio (%)	4.9	4.8	5.0	4.9	5.3	5.5	5.6	5.7	5.6	5.8	5.4
Inorganic											
Potential Pmg	11.9	11.6	12.2	13.6	11.6	11.1	12.2	11.5	10.8	9.7	11.1
Potential per household	1.7	3.1	5.0	7.7	8.2	10.2	15.2	20.3	26.7	51.9	10.1
Residual Pmg	3.0	2.9	3.1	3.5	3.0	2.9	3.2	3.1	2.9	2.5	2.9
Residual per household	0.4	0.8	1.3	2.0	2.1	2.6	4.0	5.5	7.2	13.6	2.7
Residual/potential ratio (%)	24.9	25.2	25.4	25.4	25.9	25.8	26.4	27.2	27.0	26.2	26.2
Particulates											
Potential Pmg	31808.5	31228.0	30344.6	32135.3	26813.9	25149.1	26724.6	24369.6	23907.8	18952.0	24618.8
Potential per household	4459.9	8225.9	12420.3	18160.1	19058.5	23029.8	33357.3	43119.3	59121.7	101423.0	22441.6
Residual Pmg	19090.6	18714.6	18150.0	19251.4	16045.2	15035.2	16004.5	14585.5	14325.8	11374.9	14747.8

Indicators	Income Groups*										
	0—2	2—3	3—5	5—6	6—8	8—10	10—15	15—20	20—30	30—+	TOTAL
Residual per household	2676.7	4929.7	7428.9	10879.2	11404.4	13768.2	19976.6	25807.5	35426.2	60873.6	13443.8
Residual/potential ratio (%)	60.0	59.9	59.8	59.9	59.8	59.8	59.9	59.9	59.9	60.0	59.9
Sulfur dioxide (SO_2)											
Potential Pmg	1166.3	1118.1	1060.9	1071.3	898.0	831.3	842.1	759.9	723.4	556.1	787.1
Potential per household	163.5	294.5	434.3	605.4	638.3	761.3	1051.2	1344.6	1788.8	2975.9	717.9
Residual Pmg	647.2	619.4	582.0	584.6	487.1	451.7	451.4	405.7	381.3	291.5	422.9
Residual per household	90.7	163.2	238.2	330.3	346.2	413.6	563.5	717.8	942.8	1560.0	385.7
Residual/potential ratio (%)	55.5	55.4	54.9	54.6	54.2	54.3	53.6	53.4	52.7	52.4	53.7
Agricultural pollution											
Fertilizer											
Pmg	36.8	36.7	32.1	30.4	24.7	21.4	20.6	17.2	17.5	10.6	19.8
Per household	5.2	9.7	13.1	17.2	17.6	19.6	25.7	30.4	43.3	56.7	18.1

Note: * Number of minimum wages (MW). MW = R$ 100.

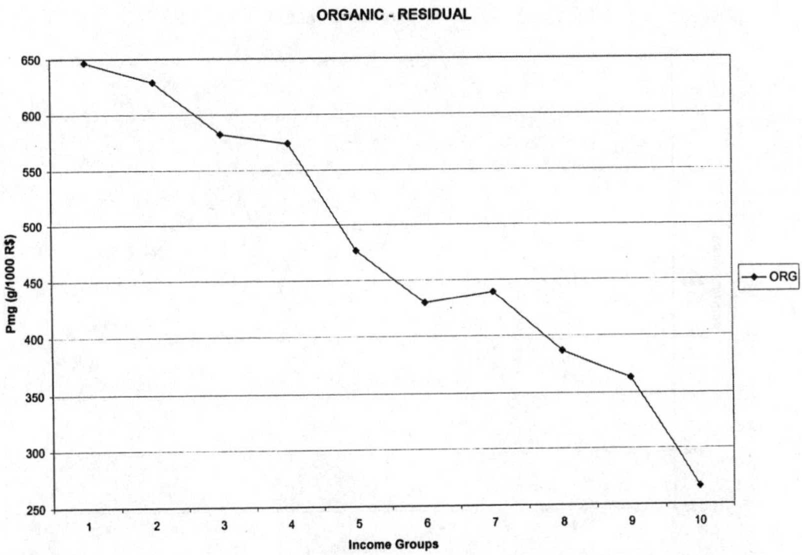

Figure 5.1

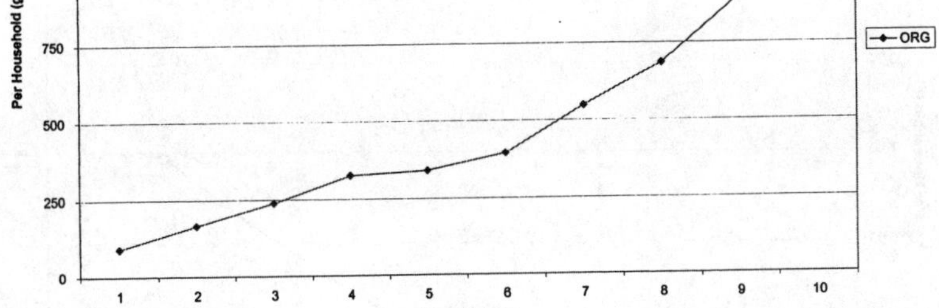

Figure 5.2

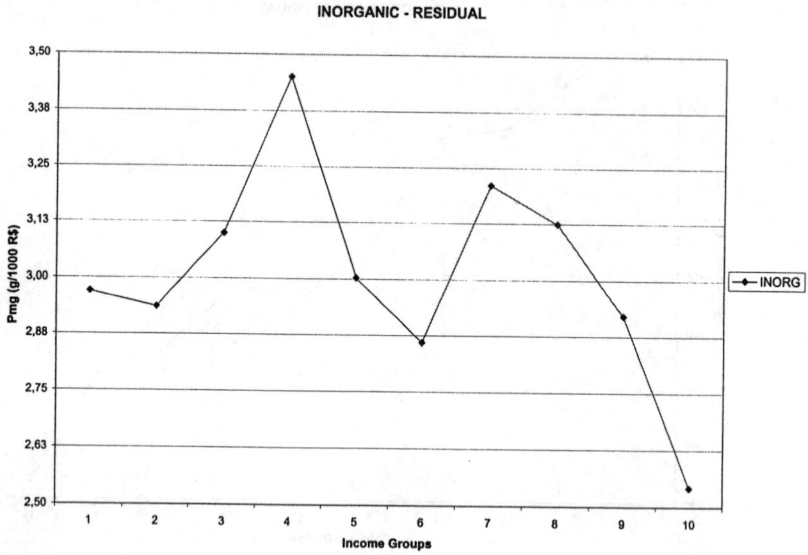

Figure 5.3

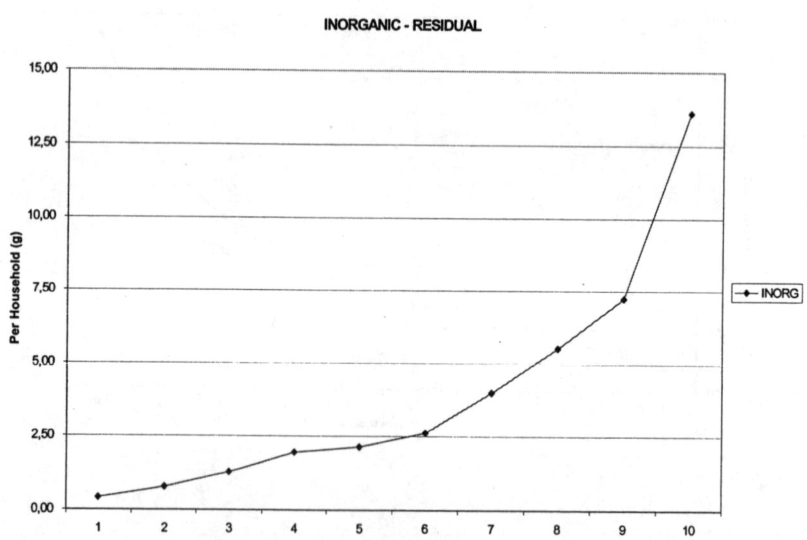

Figure 5.4

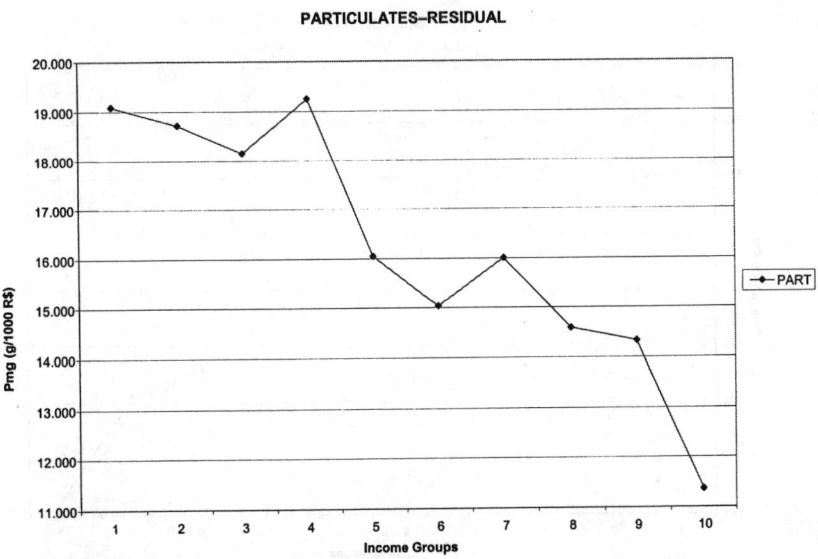

Figure 5.5

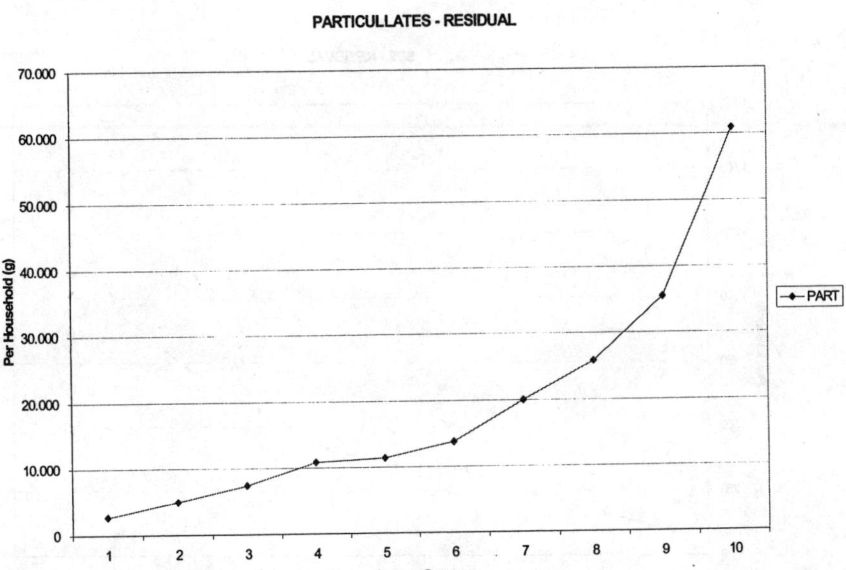

Figure 5.6

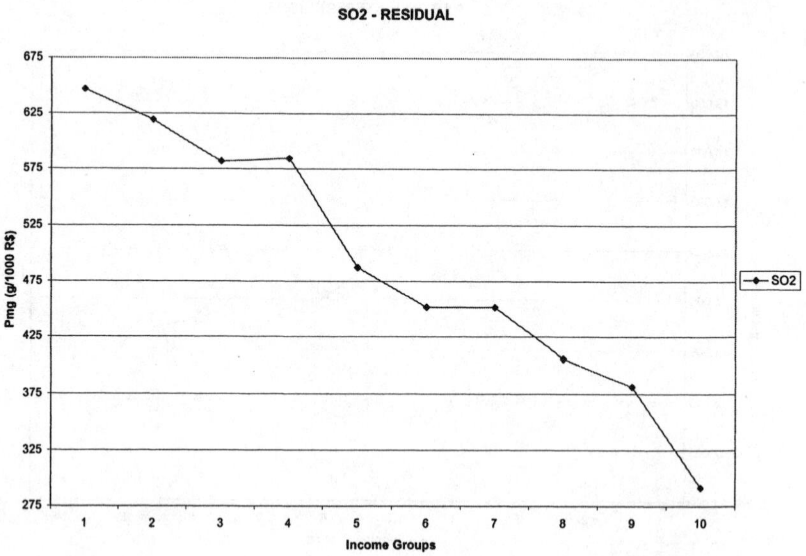

Figure 5.7

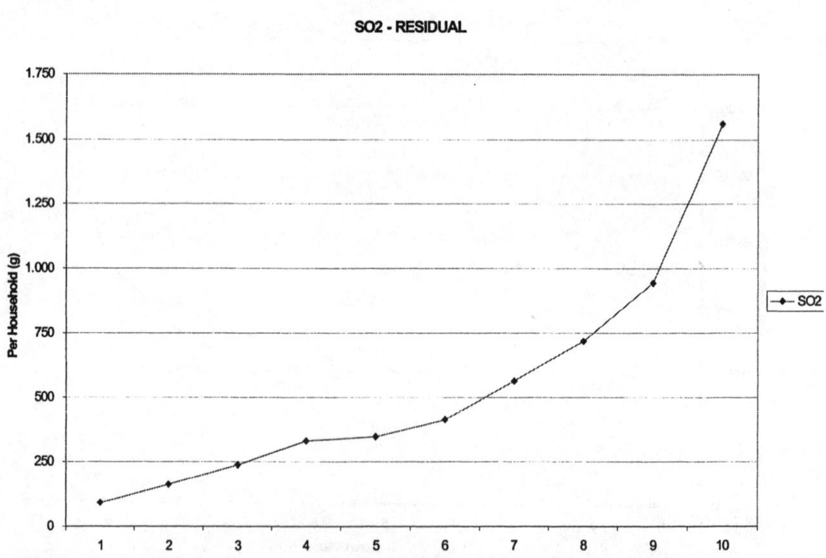

Figure 5.8

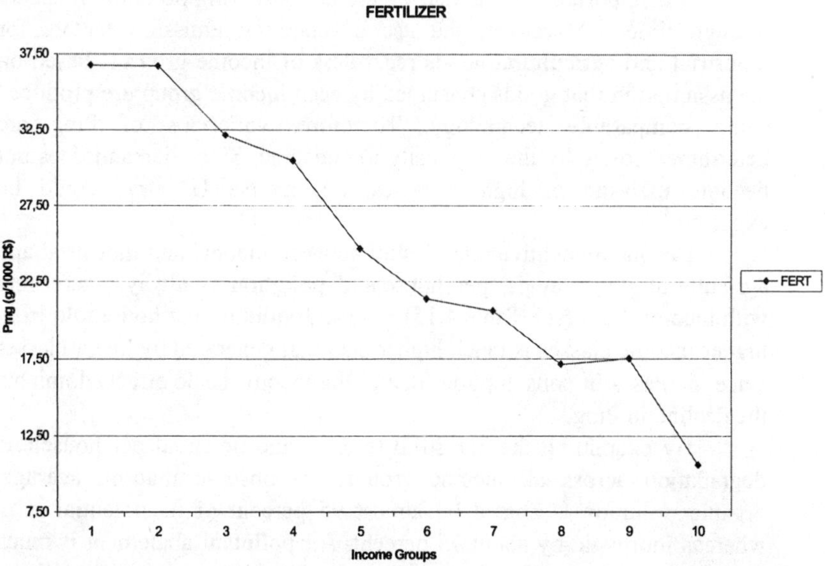

Figure 5.9

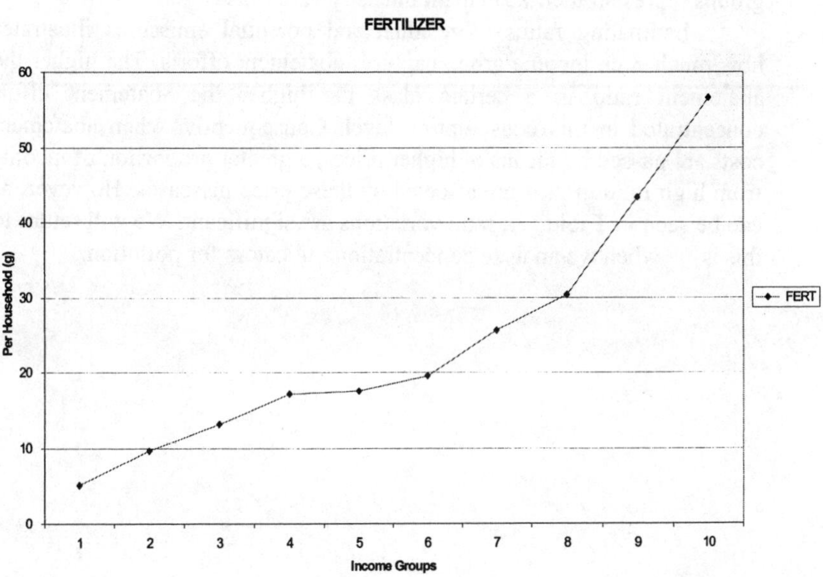

Figure 5.10

It is important to note that we are not observing pollution intensity through time. Moreover, the use of common emission factors for industrial and agricultural goods regardless of income group is based on the assumption that goods consumed by each income group are produced using comparable technology. Therefore, variations of Pmg are determined solely by the propensity to consume. Since demand does not become inelastic in higher classes, no inverse U curve could be expected.[16]

Despite a negative relationship between income and industrial and agricultural Pmg values, per household pollution is always increasing with income class (see Table 4.15). In fact, pollution per household from higher income classes is much higher than that generated by lower classes since increases in consumption (due to the income scale effect) dominate the decline in Pmg.

By examining the industrial residual and potential per household degradation across all income groups, we observe that on average, organic pollution is abated by almost 95 percent of its potential level whereas inorganic by about 75 percent. Air pollutant abatement is much less at around 40–45 percent. These values demonstrate significant abatement efforts. Differences in abatement percentages across income groups represent their abatement intensity variations.

Estimating ratios of residual and potential emissions illustrates how much each income group captures abatement efforts. The higher the abatement ratio in a certain class the higher the abatement effort concentrated in this consumption level. Consequently, when abatement costs are passed by means of higher prices, a greater proportion of income from high ratio groups are affected by these price increases. However, as can be seen in Table 5.4, ratio variations are significant. We will return to this issue when we analyze concentration indicators for pollution.

Table 5.2 Estimates of propensity to degrade (g /103 R$) and per household Degradation (g) for income groups in Brazil for Transportation Sources, 1995

Indicators	Income Groups*										
	0—2	2—3	3—5	5—6	6—8	8—10	10—15	15—20	20—30	30—+	TOTAL
End consumption											
Urban Transportation											
Carbon monoxide (CO)											
Pmg	1969.7	1869.5	2168.2	2136.4	2229.6	2009.6	1642.7	1722.4	1214.9	858.2	1524.9
Per household	276.2	492.4	887.4	1207.3	1584.7	1840.3	2050.4	3047.7	3004.3	4592.9	1389.8
Hydrocarbons (HC)											
Pmg	224.5	223.9	234.0	280.5	271.9	248.2	206.8	233.2	180.8	118.7	195.2
Per Household	31.5	59.0	95.8	158.5	193.2	227.3	258.1	412.6	447.2	635.1	177.9
Nitrogen oxide (NOx)											
Pmg	1072.9	1192.3	860.6	1585.4	1,055.1	1142.2	756.4	1078.5	719.2	314.4	776.1
Per household	150.4	314.1	352.2	895.9	750.0	1045.9	944.1	1908.4	1778.4	1682.7	707.3
Private vehicle pollution (alcohol)											
Carbon monoxide (CO)											
Pmg	148.4	145.3	263.8	71.8	250.5	130.0	112.3	138.6	168.5	108.7	147.1
Per Household	20.8	38.3	108.0	40.6	178.0	119.1	140.2	245.3	416.8	581.6	134.1
Hidrocarbons (HC)											
Pmg	22.4	21.9	39.8	11.1	41.0	21.8	23.0	28.3	34.8	22.5	27.1
Per Household	3.1	5.8	16.3	6.3	29.2	20.0	28.6	50.1	86.1	120.2	24.7
Nitrogen oxide (NOx)											
Pmg	22.4	21.9	39.8	7.6	32.4	19.6	20.5	25.3	41.8	26.9	27.7

Per household	3.1	5.8	16.3	4.3	23.0	18.0	25.6	44.8	103.3	144.2	25.3
Private vehicle pollution (gasoline)											
Carbon monoxide (CO)											
Pmg	1,338.1	1,174.7	1,568.3	1,278.4	1,523.9	1,347.0	1,209.3	1,049.7	717.0	613.3	1,028.2
Per household	187.6	309.4	641.9	722.4	1,083.1	1,233.5	1,509.5	1,857.3	1,773.1	3,282.0	937.1
Hydrocarbons (HC)											
Pmg	111.5	97.9	130.7	122.3	144.9	126.8	124.0	107.7	87.4	74.8	104.4
Per household	15.6	25.8	53.5	69.1	103.0	116.1	154.8	190.5	216.2	400.2	95.2
Nitrogenn oxide (NOx)											
Pmg	170.7	149.8	200.0	154.3	184.1	158.5	159.5	138.4	139.9	119.7	148.5
Per household	23.9	39.5	81.9	87.2	130.9	145.1	199.1	244.9	346.0	640.4	135.3
Urban Transportation pollution (bus)											
Carbon monoxide (CO)											
Pmg	454.8	528.4	321.2	735.4	433.9	498.1	297.6	470.3	275.1	83.2	308.5
Per household	63.8	139.2	131.5	415.6	308.4	456.1	371.4	832.1	680.2	445.1	281.1
Hydrocarbons (HC)											
Pmg	87.8	102.0	62.0	141.9	83.7	96.1	57.4	90.7	53.1	16.0	59.5
Per household	12.3	26.9	25.4	80.2	59.5	88.0	71.7	160.6	131.2	85.9	54.2
Nitrogen oxide (NOx)											
Pmg	875.8	1,017.5	618.6	1,416.1	835.6	959.1	573.0	905.6	529.6	160.2	593.9
Per household	122.8	268.0	253.2	800.2	593.9	878.3	715.2	1,602.3	1,309.7	857.1	541.3

Note: * Number of minimum wages (MW). MW = R$ 100,00.

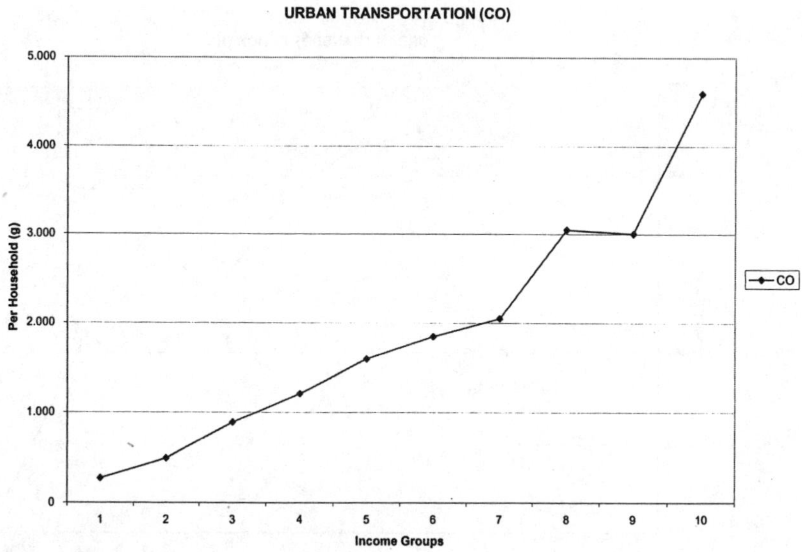

Figure 5.11

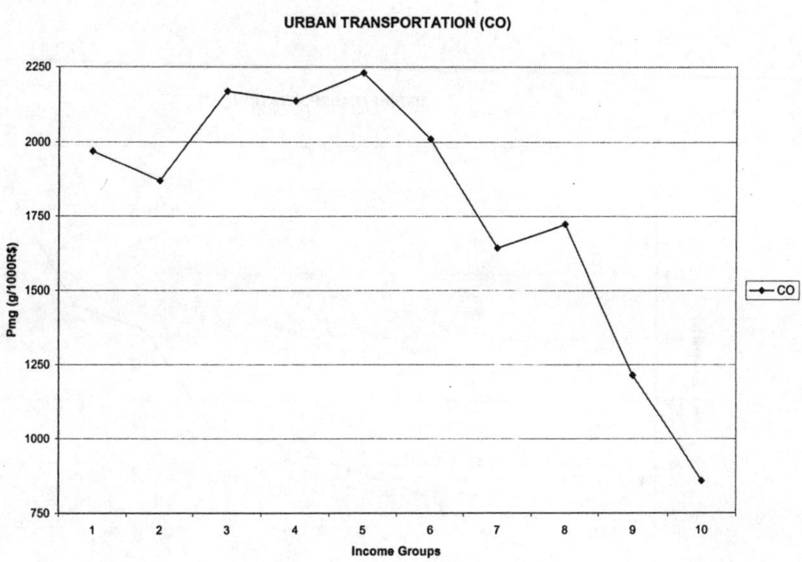

Figure 5.12

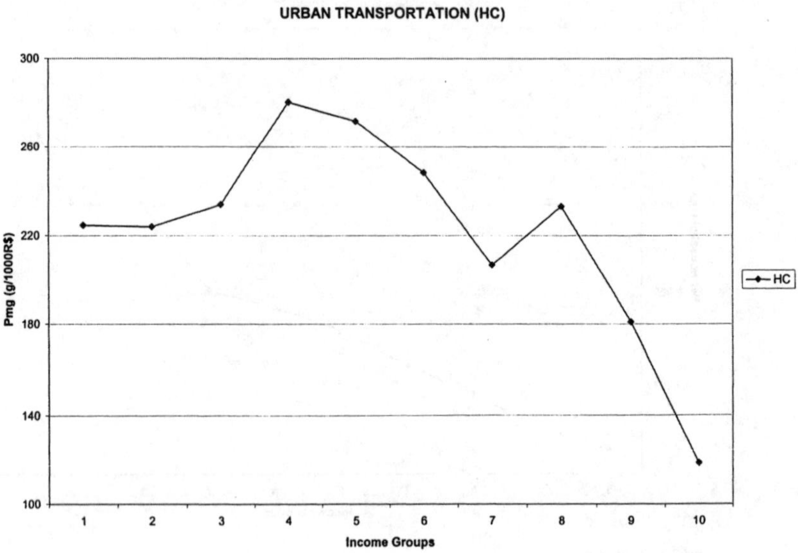

Figure 5.13

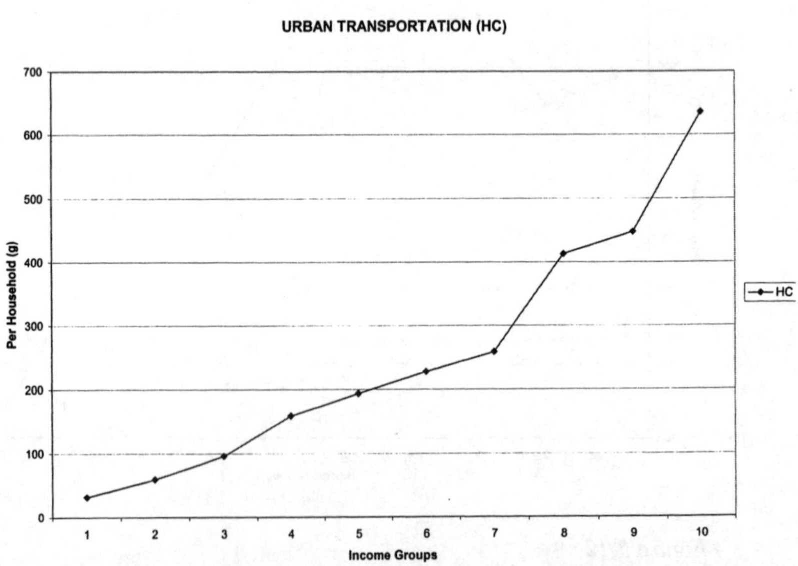

Figure 5.14

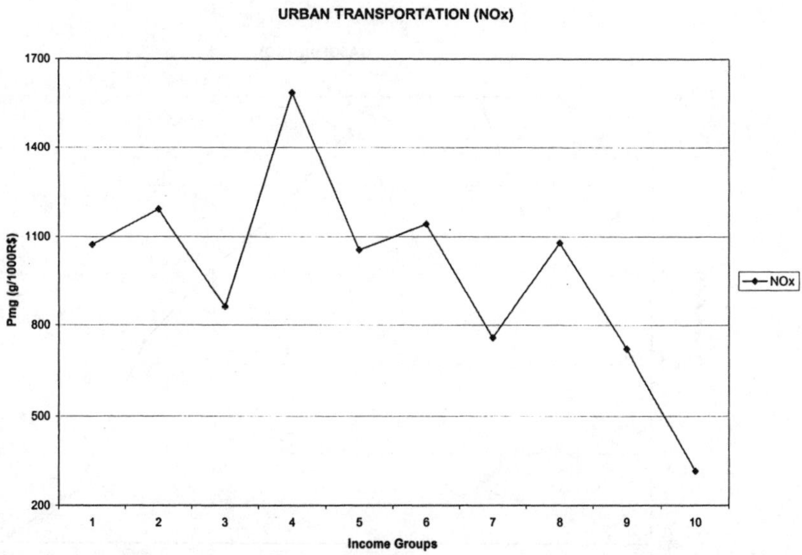

Figure 5.15

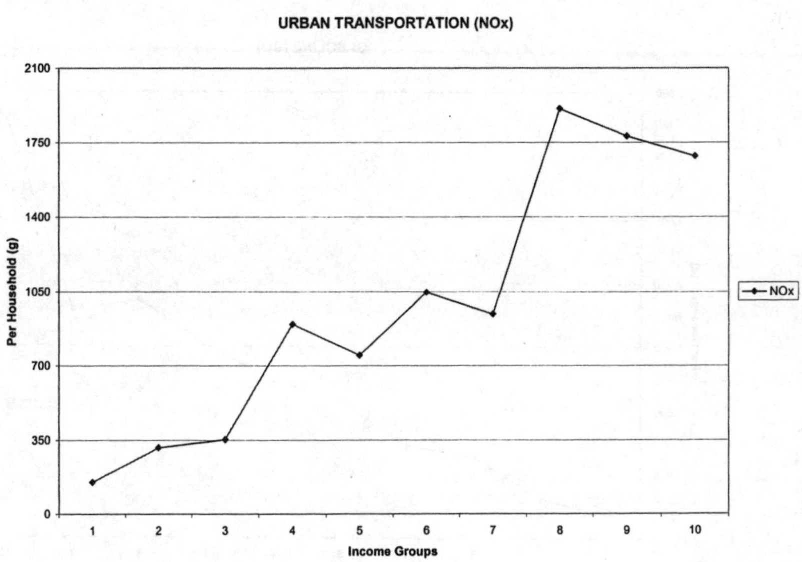

Figure 5.16

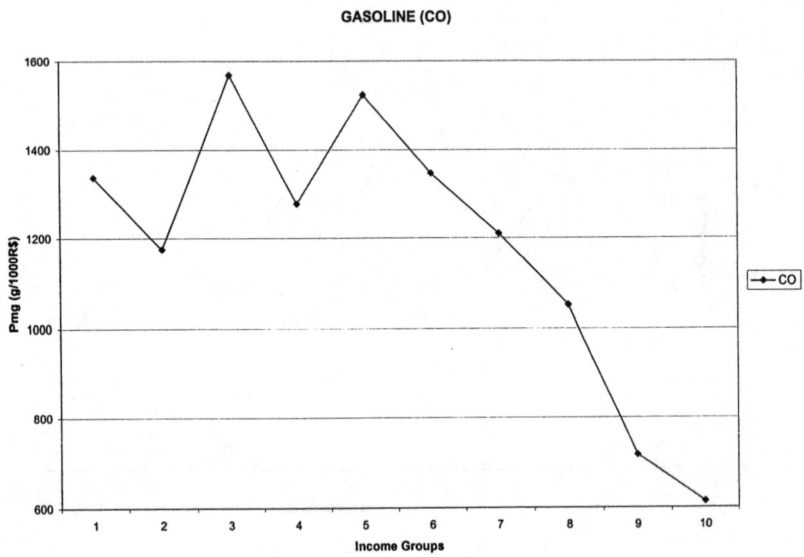

Figure 5.17

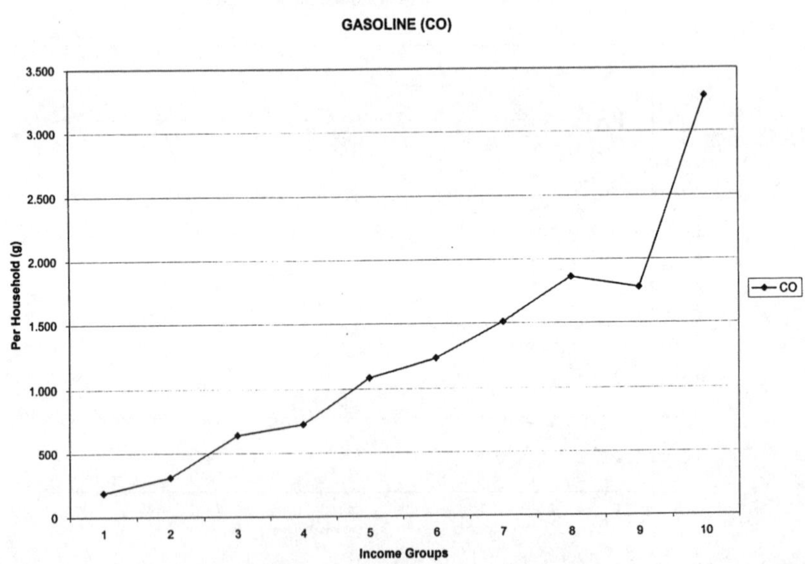

Figure 5.18

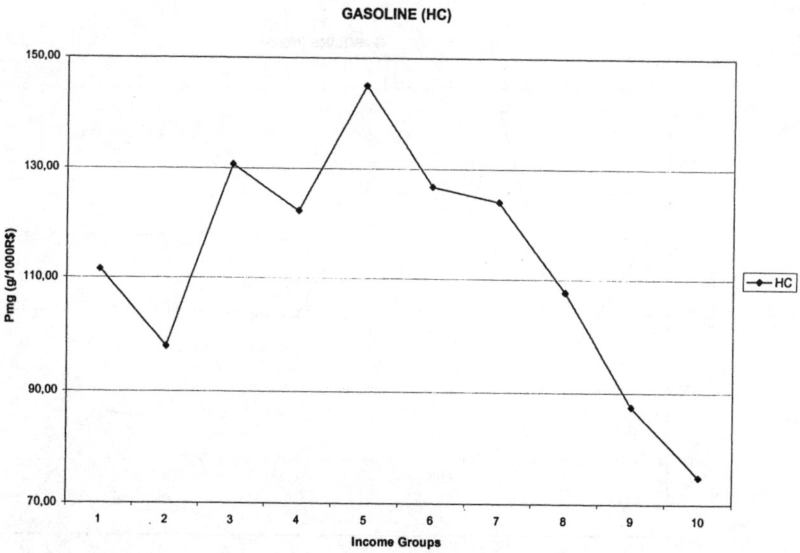

Figure 5.19

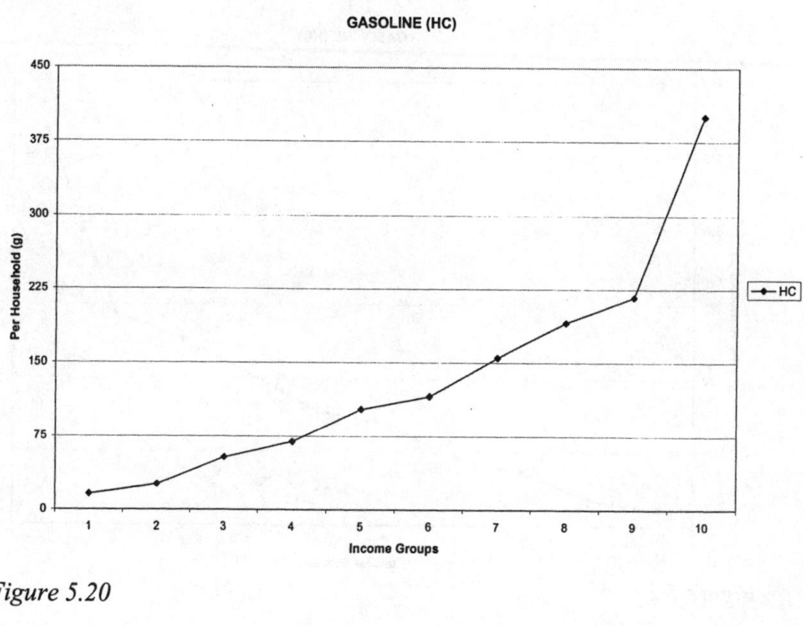

Figure 5.20

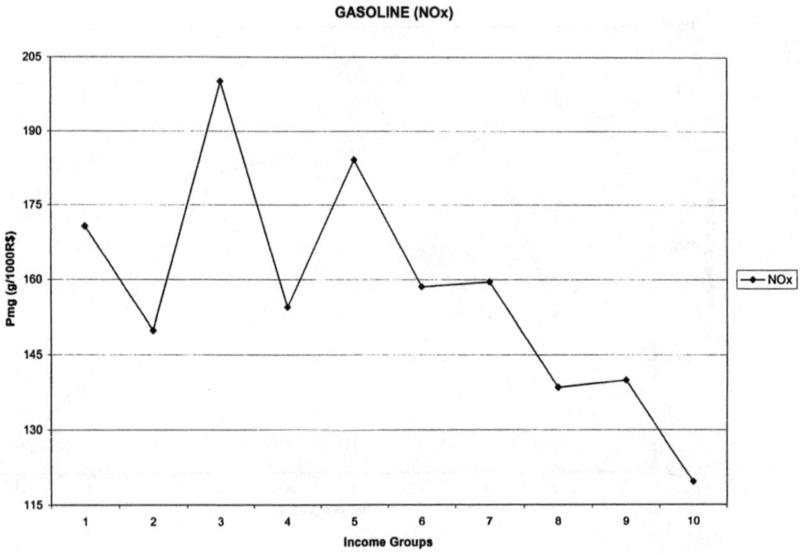

Figure 5.21

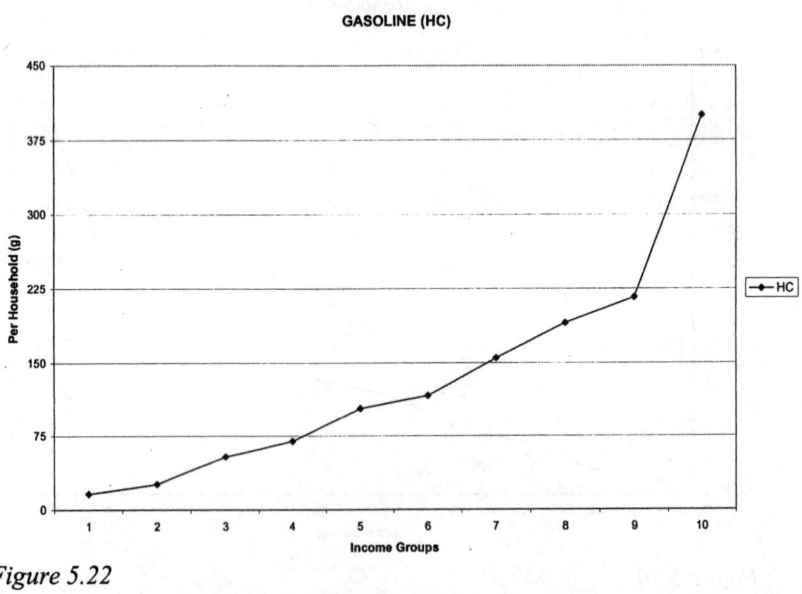

Figure 5.22

For urban transport emissions (Table 5.2 and Figures 5.11 to 5.22) we have introduced emission factor differentials across groups that use private vehicles by assuming that richer people own newer cars which emit less than older ones run by poor households. As a result, Pmg, as can be seen in the supra-mentioned graphs, increases and decreases in lower income groups (particularly due to our *ad hoc* allocation of car vintage[17]) and fall substantially in upper classes, (for example: from 6–8 MW bracket onwards in the case of gasoline). This trend clearly suggests a type of inverse U shape for Pmg, since private vehicle emissions are significant in total transport emissions and car ownership is highly concentrated in the upper classes with car use being particularly income elastic.[18]

There is no clear quadratic relationship between income and per household pollution for transport Pmg. Again, scale effects are so significant that all emissions show a positive relationship with income.

In the case of total water consumption and sewage discharge, Pmg values are negatively correlated with income, reflecting the declining propensity to consume water when income increases[19] (Table 5.3 and Figures 5.23 and 5.27). Once again, income level disparities among classes cancelled out this trend and per household water consumption and sewage discharge increased with income level (Figures 5.24 and 5.28). An exception to this is the 15–20 MW bracket, which may be biased due to our water pricing procedures used when measuring consumption from expenditure figures.

Figures 5.25 and 5.29, for non-treated water and non-collected sewage, illustrate the same Pmg relationship due to the fact that coverage of sanitation services are also increasing with income. Therefore, in the case of per household consumption of non-treated water and non-collected sewage discharges (Figures 5.26 and 5.30) we identify somewhat of an inverse U curve for Pmg, respectively, at classes 6–8 MW and 2–3 MW. However, this results from changes in *p*, which is given by the lack of sanitation services.

In sum, the observed positive relationships between per household degradation and income suggest that degradation pressure in Brazil can be also concentrated in high income levels. This will be analyzed in the next section.

Table 5.3 *Estimates of propensity to degrade ($m^3/10^3$ R$) and per household degradation (g) for income groups in Brazil for Sanitation Sources, 1995*

Indicators	Income groups*										
	0—2	2—3	3—5	5—6	6—8	8—10	10—15	15—20	20—30	30—+	Total
End consumption											
Household water consumption											
Total											
Pmg	45.1	37.3	27.7	23.3	21.5	18.1	14.0	11.2	6.6	3.2	13.9
Per household	6.3	9.8	11.4	13.2	15.3	16.6	17.5	19.8	16.3	16.9	12.6
Non-treated											
Pmg	2.6	2.3	1.5	1.1	1.1	0.7	0.5	0.3	0.2	0.1	0.6
Per household	0.4	0.6	0.6	0.6	0.7	0.7	0.6	0.5	0.4	0.4	0.6
Non-treated/Total ratio	0.1	0.1	0.1	0.0	0.0	0.0	0.0	0.0	0.0	0.0	0.0
Household sewage generation											
Total											
Pmg	45.1	37.3	27.7	23.3	21.5	18.1	14.0	11.2	6.6	3.2	13.9
Per household	6.3	9.8	11.4	13.2	15.3	16.6	17.5	19.8	16.3	16.9	12.6
Non-collected											
Pmg	20.4	14.7	8.3	5.5	4.2	3.0	1.8	1.0	0.4	0.1	3.1
Per household	2.9	3.9	3.4	3.1	3.0	2.8	2.2	1.8	1.1	0.7	2.8
Non-collected/Total ratio	0.5	0.4	0.3	0.2	0.2	0.2	0.1	0.1	0.1	0.0	0.2

Note: *Number of minimum wages (MW). MW = R$ 100.00.

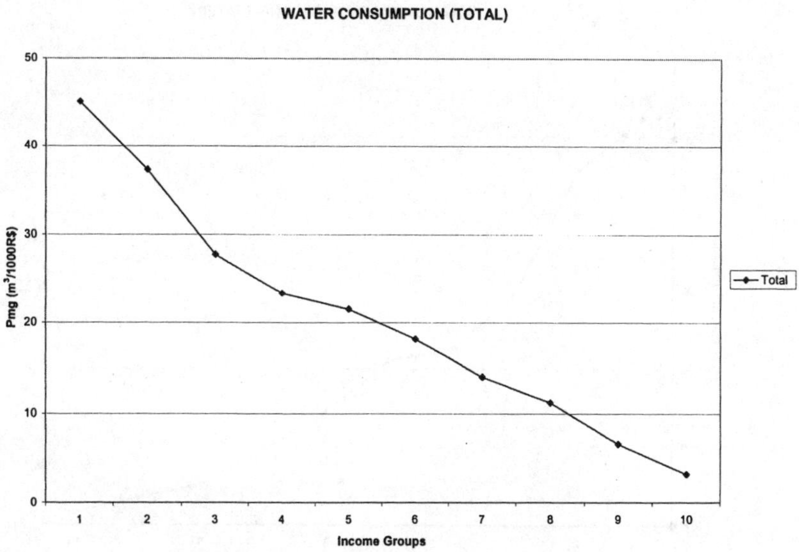

Figure 5.23

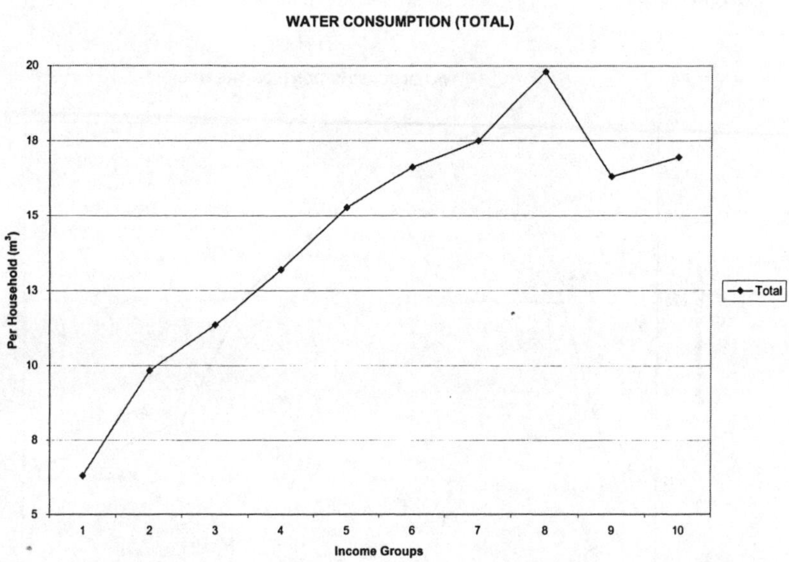

Figure 5.24

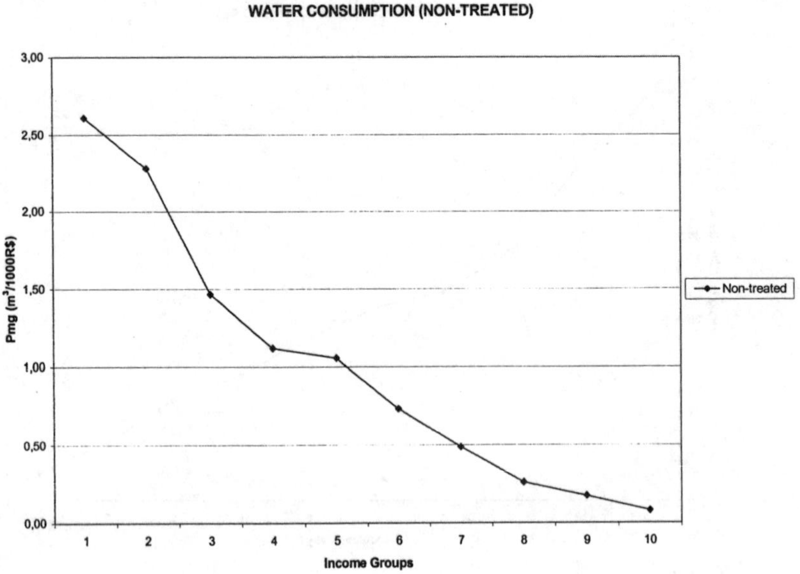

Figure 5.25

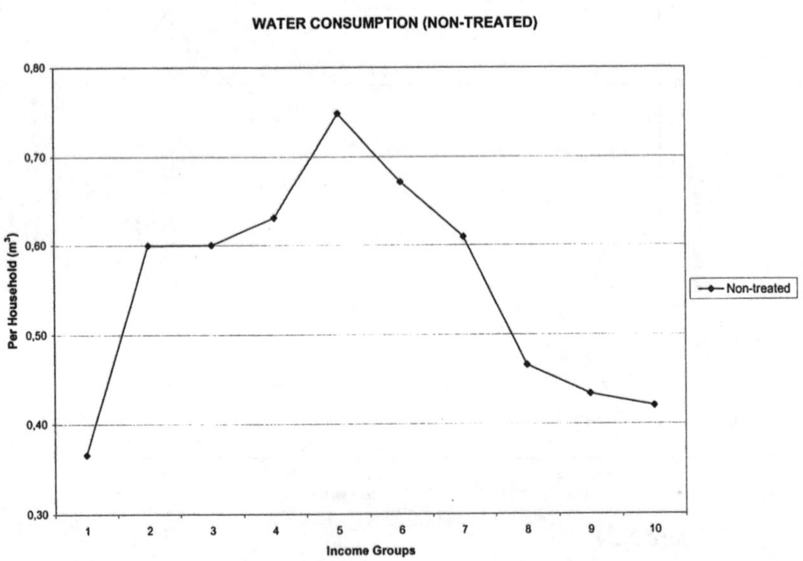

Figure 5.26

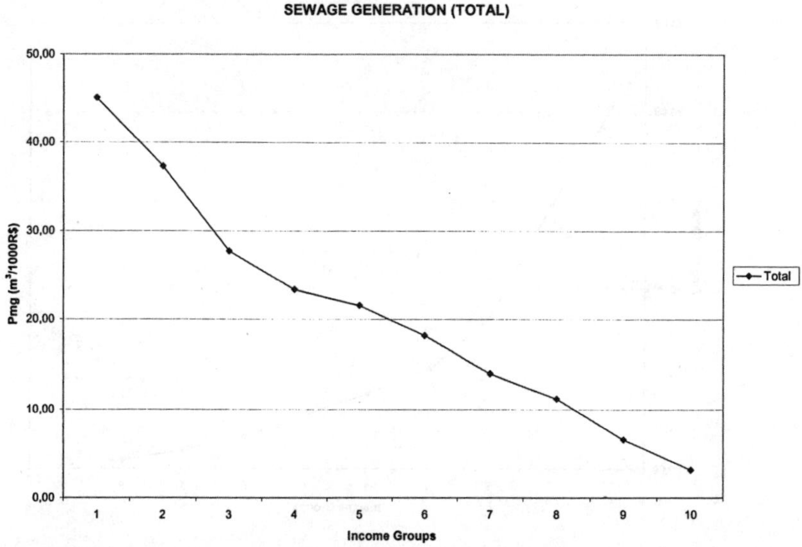

Figure 5.27

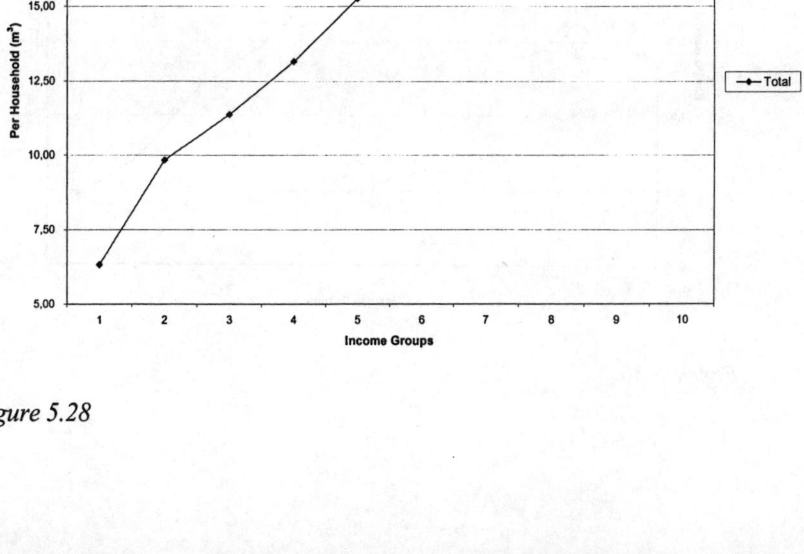

Figure 5.28

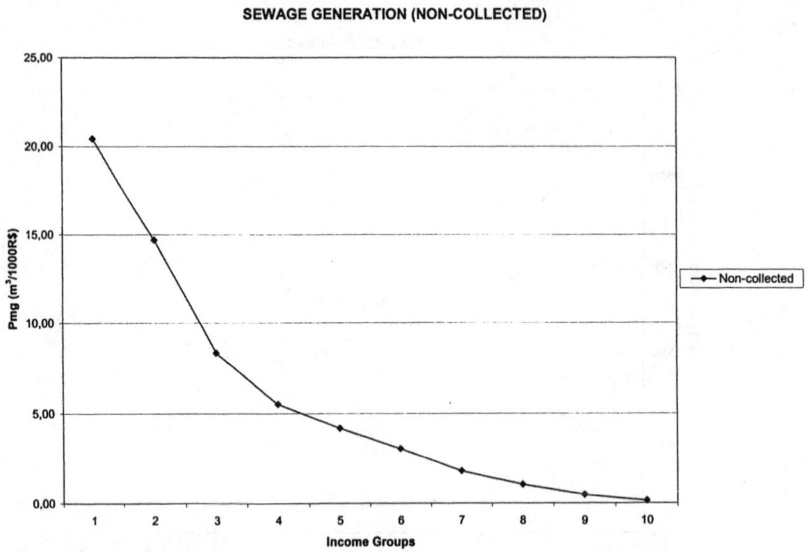

Figure 5.29

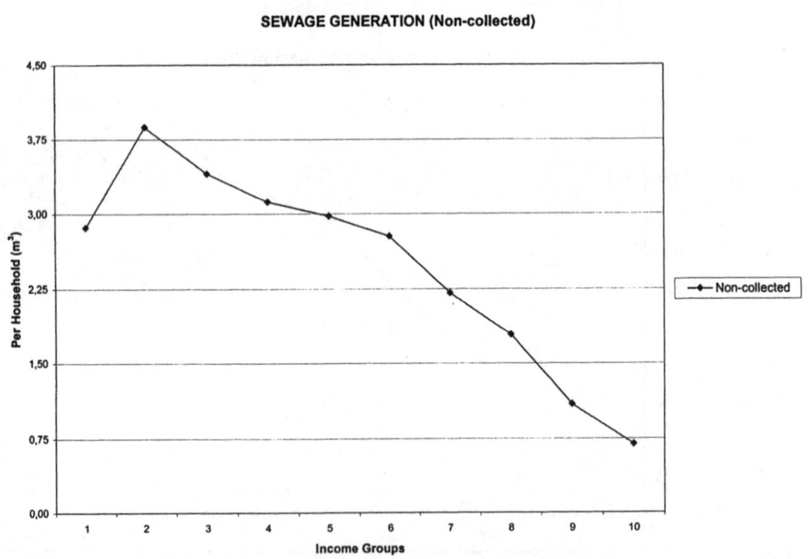

Figure 5.30

5.4 POLLUTION CONCENTRATION IN BRAZIL

In the following section we analyze how concentrated by income is degradation in Brazil, given the previously estimated degradation indicators. We first calculate total degradation (product of Pmg for total urban income) by income group. We then estimate the respective concentration indicators as the ratio of total pollution or use levels of the 10 percent richest urban families to the 50 percent poorest ones. Following our income bracket classification, this is equivalent to the ratio of the total levels of the two highest income brackets (> 20 MW) to the first three poorest ones (up to 5 MW) added to one-seventh of the fourth class (5–6 MW).[20]

Using the income information in Table 5.4, we can calculate the income concentration ratio (of the 10 percent richest urban families to the 50 percent poorest ones) and compare it to the degradation ratio. These results will allow us to put forward several equity issues, namely:

1. If pollution is equally distributed according to the number of families, the pollution concentration ratio should be equal to 0.2. Consequently, if the ratio is higher than 0.2, we can say that a rich household (that is, a household belonging to the richest 10 percent) is imposing greater pressure on the environment than a poor one (that is, a household belonging to the poorest 50 percent). In view of the fact that, as mentioned in Section 5.3, impacts of degradation tend to be borne primarily by the poor who cannot afford defensive expenditures, at ratios over 0.2 poor people are affected by degradation pressure above its own population share.
2. In the case of industrial sources, water consumption and sewage discharge, where concentration ratios for potential and residual pollution indicators are measured, differences indicate that costs of abatement efforts already in place, when passed through prices and tariffs, are captured differently by the poor and the rich.
3. When degradation ratios are lower than income ratios, the degradation intensity of income is lower for richer classes than poorer classes. In other words, units of income related to the consumption of goods and services by the poor are associated with higher degradation intensities. As a result, if prices of consumed goods and services increase due to increasing degradation control levels, total disposable income of the poor may be more affected than the rich since they will spend more on control costs per unit of income.[21]

Table 5.4 shows that, apart from non-treated water and non-collected sewage, the analyzed cases show concentration ratios exceeding 0.2. Degradation pressure is particularly concentrated in industrial residual pollution where ratios vary between 1.3 to 2.3, followed by transportation with the range of 1.2 to 1.6. A more equitable degradation distribution is observed for total water consumption and sewage discharge. As mentioned previously, ratios over 0.2 indicate that poor individuals are bearing degradation costs above their own per household contribution.

In the case of industrial sources (Table 5.4) water pollution (organic and inorganic matter) has residual concentration ratios higher than potential ones, whereas for air pollution these differences are not significant. This may be due to the fact that water sources bear a much higher level of control than air sources. However, the significant upward difference in concentration ratios, particularly for organic matter, indicates that consumption by the poor is generating proportionally less pollution than that of the rich. Consequently, the poor are paying proportionally more, in relation to their consumption levels, for abatement costs that are passed through prices.

The bias of sanitation service coverage towards richer households is confirmed by concentration ratios of treated water and collected sewage above its respective residual indicators, particularly, for the case of non-collected sewage. However, this pattern can be explained further by public investment choices rather than consumer's choices.

Accordingly, degradation control is a relevant distributive mechanism as it will reduce the unequal burden of degradation costs on the poor. However, such actions also affect equity in other ways when control costs are passed through prices.

It is important to note that income distribution in Brazil (Table 5.4), as mentioned in the Introduction, is very unequal. Our ratio of 2.6 is saying that the richest 10 percent perceive almost three times more income than the poorest 50 percent of the people.[22]

Table 5.4 Changes in concentration ratios and degradation pressures for income distribution scenarios in Brazil, 1995

Indicators	Income Distribution, 1995		Progressive Scenario			Regressive Scenario		
	Concentration ratio	Degradation pressure	Concentration ratio	Degradation pressure	Variation* %	Concentration ratio	Degradation pressure	Variation* %
Income	2.6	–	2.1	–	2.9	2.9	–	1.0
Industrial pollution (ton)								
Organic								
Potential	1.1	209 349.2	0.9	215 349.3	2.9	1.2	207 199.2	−1.0
Residual	1.3	11 286.1	1.0	11 547.8	2.3	1.4	11 192.5	−0.8
Inorganic								
Potential	2.2	307.9	1.7	309.6	0.5	2.4	307.3	−0.2
Residual	2.3	80.7	1.8	81.0	0.4	2.5	80.6	−0.1
Particulates								
Potential	1.8	682 225.2	1.4	691 026.2	1.3	1.9	679 121.5	−0.5
Residual	1.8	408 692.6	1.4	413 949.6	1.3	1.9	406 834.5	−0.5
Sulfur dioxide (SO_2)								
Potential	1.5	21 823.5	1.2	22 237.5	1.9	1.6	21 675.1	−0.7
Residual	1.4	11 724.8	1.1	11 966.1	2.1	1.5	11 638.1	−0.7
Agricultural pollution (ton)								
Fertilizer	1.0	549.1	0.8	567.1	3.3	1.1	542.7	−1.2
End consumption								
Urban transportation (ton)								
Carbon monoxide (CO)	1.2	42 249.2	1.0	43 157.9	2.2	1.4	41 949.3	−0.7
Hydrocarbons (HC)	1.6	5 409.3	1.2	5 487.1	1.4	1.7	5 383.3	−0.5
Nitrogen oxide (NO_x)	1.2	21 503.2	0.9	21 962.8	2.1	1.3	21 334.2	−0.8

Indicators	Income Distribution, 1995		Progressive Scenario			Regressive Scenario		
	Concentration ratio	Degradation pressure	Concentration ratio	Degradation pressure	Variation* %	Concentration ratio	Degradation pressure	Variation* %
Household water consumption ($106 \times m^3$)								
Total	0.3	384.2	0.3	409.5	6.6	0.4	374.5	−2.5
Treated	0.4	367.4	0.3	391.1	6.5	0.4	358.2	−2.5
Non-treated	0.2	16.9	0.1	18.4	9.0	0.2	16.3	−3.5
Household sewage generation ($106 \times m^3$)								
Total	0.3	384.2	0.3	409.5	6.6	0.4	374.5	−2.5
Collected	0.5	298.9	0.4	313.5	4.9	0.6	293.6	−1.8
Non-collected	0.1	85.3	0.0	96.0	12.5	0.1	80.9	−5.2

Note: *for income (total transferred income/total income); for degradation (degradation pressure before transfer – degradation pressure after transfer)/degradation pressure before transfer.

Environmental concentration ratios other than those for industrial inorganic matter show lower values than income distribution ratios, indicating that a lower marginal propensity to degrade at higher incomes has helped reduce the environmental impacts of increased consumption.

These results allow us to illustrate the conflict between equity and environmental control and derive relevant policy issues, namely:

1. When degradation is less concentrated in the population than income, future efforts to control pollution, which are passed through prices of consumed goods, may affect the disposable income of the poor more than the rich. This trend is illustrated from comparisons between actual industrial potential and residual emissions. Although several studies have shown that abatement costs are not always significant and decrease through time,[23] this is relevant if the current trend of the Brazilian industrial sector is considered to improve environmental performance related to trade competitiveness. Consequently, short-run effects on industrial prices, due to increasing industrial abatement efforts, can bring about important distribution issues.
2. The same applies to consumption of treated water and collection of sewage discharge. Significant investments by Brazilian sanitation companies to increase the current low treatment levels of sewage will result in higher tariffs for consumers. Such trend also brings about distribution concerns considering the estimated concentration ratio of this direct consumption. In addition, non-treated water and non-collected sewage concentration ratio values are much lower than 1, indicating that poor people, at current sanitation service coverage levels, consume much more non-treated water and live with more non-collected sewage than rich households. Accordingly, expanded coverage of water supply and sewage collection has to be targeted at the poor.
3. Transport emission patterns show the converse. Since the rich people's consumption is the main source of emission, control efforts will not be regressive as in the previous cases.

The discussion above is not postulated as a case against tougher environmental control. The aim is to draw attention to short-run equity problems associated with improving environmental control. Although the reduction of degradation is justified on equity grounds when one looks at the concentrated negative effects of degradation impacts on the poor, opposition to the improvement of the environmental performance of the economy is often manipulated by concerns about the cost-raising impacts from the internalization of environmental control costs that will affect prices paid by the poor.

A welfare analysis of negative effects of degradation and positive effects of control for each income group would be challenging. Such a cost–benefit approach is beyond the scope of our study. We limit ourselves to revealing that there are equity concerns for the internalization of control costs and, consequently, environmental policies need to consider equity. On the other hand, policy design must account for equity costs and propose compensation policies. Balancing compensation measures with efficiency remains, however, the most crucial challenge.

Finally, we must focus our attention on changes in degradation pressures arising from income distribution policies. The negative correlation between urban income and degradation intensity reflected in the Pmg values and urban income classes suggest that, given an equivalent income increase in all groups, richer households will create less pollution than poor ones. That is to say, marginal increases in income will generate more pollution or higher natural resource use levels when consumed by the poor. This is crucial when analyzing income distribution and the environment in the next section.

5.5 INCOME DISTRIBUTION AND ENVIRONMENTAL DEGRADATION PRESSURE[24]

How much degradation pressure would have been generated if income distribution was different in Brazil? Transfer of income within an economy changes both income and degradation distribution. If income distribution changes in the economy without a change in total income, there will be transfers of monetary units from one individual to another. Therefore, a change in degradation pressure (EC) in the economy will be given by the difference between the Pmg of the donor (*id*) and the beneficiary (*ib*), that is:

$$EC = Pmg_{id} - Pmg_{ib} \tag{5.7}$$

If $Pmg_{id} > Pmg_{ib}$ the value of EC is negative, meaning that income transfer reduces degradation. If $Pmg_{id} < Pmg_{ib}$, total degradation increases.

Assuming a total income transfer of T is made out of distinct shares of several donor individuals (s_{id}) and captured in distinct shares by several beneficiary ones (s_{ib}). Then individual transfers (T_i) will be:[25]

$$T_{id} = -s_{id}T \tag{5.8}$$

and

$$T_{ib} = s_{ib}T \tag{5.9}$$

And total transfer T,

$$T = -\Sigma T_{id} = \Sigma T_{ib} \tag{5.10}$$

So with a transfer of T_i, changes in pollution levels or natural resource use in any i is:

$$\text{EC}_i = \text{Pmg}_i T_i \tag{5.11}$$

Then total degradation change due to transfer T is:

$$\text{EC} = \Sigma \text{Pmg}_{id} T_{id} + \Sigma \text{Pmg}_{ib} T_{ib} \tag{5.12}$$

The EC magnitude will then depend on the differences of Pmg of the affected individuals and the level of transfer (T_i). Since Pmg values tend to decrease with income, we can expect higher levels of degradation pressure for progressive transfers, from rich to poor, and lower levels for regressive transfers, from poor to rich.

In order to illustrate changes in degradation pressure if income distribution would have changed in Brazil, we have created scenario that assumes either progressive and regressive transfer schedules as follows:

1. We use our estimates of Pmg previously presented, and take i as an income group in which we assume that all individuals within the group have the same Pmg.
2. Concentration will be reduced or increased by transferring T from donor to beneficiary groups.
3. T_{ib} is such that beneficiary group i will receive the average household income of the group, in addition to the transfer, reaching four-fifths of its upper limit in MW.
4. T_{id} is such that average household income of donor classes will not exceed four-fifths of its lower limit of MW.[26]

The two scenarios are:

progressive: where ib = three lowest income classes and id = two richest classes;
regressive: where ib = two richest classes and id = three lowest income classes.

Our scenario does not consider changes in class consumption patterns given by income increases, which could move a family to a higher income group. This assumption on distribution schedule could be easily captured from our scenario if one understands part of the beneficiary group share of *T* as income increase due to this upward movement.

Progressive Scenario

In the progressive scenario, these *ad hoc* rules signified positive transfers equivalent to 34 percent, 11 percent and 18 percent of income of the first, second and third poorest classes (0–2, 2–3 and 3–5 MW), respectively. This also resulted in a negative transfer of richest classes equivalent to around 6 percent of household income of the second richest class (20–30 MW) and 8 percent of the richest class (> 30 MW) or an average reduction of 7 percent on the 10 percent richest families. Such reductions are very significant in relative values and represent, in absolute values, a transfer of US$ 10 billion (at 1995 exchange rates) or 3 percent of total urban income in Brazil in the year 1995.

The results of the progressive scenario are presented in Table 5.4. The table demonstrates that the adopted transfer schedule made a substantial reduction in income concentration ratio to 2.1 from 2.6, signifying a reduction of about 25 percent. Consequently, equivalent reductions also occurred in all ratios of degradation sources.

When comparing the share of 3 percent of transferred income with the variations of degradation in Table 5.4, we observe that industrial and transport pollution varied by less than 3 percent. To be precise, income transfer did not increase degradation at the same proportion. Even agricultural sources were just above (3.3 percent). Sanitation sources, due to their low coverage of poor households, changed considerably as a result of the income transfer by 6.5 percent for water and 12.5 percent for sewage.

Regressive Scenario

In the regressive scenario, income distribution ratios increase by 12 percent – from 2.6 to 2.9. This transfer schedule also made equivalent increases in all ratios of degradation sources (Table 5.4).

These ad hoc scenario rules represented a positive transfer equivalent to 1.9 and 2.6 percent of the first and second richest classes (> 30 and 20–30 MW), respectively. The two classes received, on average, a 2.4 percent increase in income.

However, this resulted in a transfer equivalent of 6.6 percent of household income of the three poorest classes. While the third and second classes transferred 3.0 and 3.6 percent, respectively, of their total urban income, the poorest classes lost about 20 percent, thereby illustrating a very radical regressive case.

In absolute values, a transfer of US$ 3.7 billion (at the 1995 exchange rate) or about 1 percent of total urban income in Brazil, was made in 1995.

As expected, all degradation pressures are reduced – with greater reductions for water and sewage. In the progressive scenario, variations of total degradation pressures are much lower than the corresponding increase in income concentration.

Although these findings are exclusively associated with specific distribution scenarios and should not be generalized, they demonstrate that income distribution changes are not greatly affected by significant changes in degradation pressures, thereby raising some interesting issues about the relationship between income distribution and the environment in Brazil.

5.6 FINAL COMMENTS

Each level of income gives rise to a certain level of degradation pressure. Higher income levels uses cleaner technologies, thereby inducing an endogenous technological path and reducing degradation intensity. When this intensity declines at rates greater than income growth, total degradation decreases despite consumption growth.

In this event, it is expected that when average income exceeds a certain threshold level, economic activity may be decoupled from degradation. In other words, the income–environment relationship may result in an inverse U curve.

Although confirmation of this relationship continues to be controversial and tested in case-specific degradation sources, if this relationship exists when examining an economy through time, an inverse U curve could not arise from in-country analysis of income group consumption patterns.

Within an economy, technological innovations are likely to be equally adopted by all groups or used for product differentiation. Consequently, the dominant parameter of degradation pressure is the propensity to consume the service or good. Even when adoption of cleaner technology increases with income, increasing levels of consumption can result in increasing degradation intensity.

In order to analyze consumption patterns for urban income groups in Brazil, we estimated marginal propensity to degrade for several degradation sources and ten urban income classes, as the product of degradation intensity of propensity to consume. Household degradation for each income group is estimated by the product of its propensity to degrade and the average household income of each class.

Our results show that, in the case of Brazil, there is no evidence of an inverse U curve shape for levels of degradation pressure and income groups, since per household degradation pressure, except that from industrial inorganic pollution and non-collected sewage, tends to increase with income.

Propensities to degrade from transportation have, however, showed this inverse U shape for urban transportation, particularly due to the great reduction on emission levels of new cars usually owned by rich people. Even in this case, a continuous positive relationship to income was identified for degradation pressure. That is, the great concentration of income was always enough to compensate for variations in propensity to degrade consume and, when it applied also for variations in technological factors.

Secondly, using our estimates of propensity to degrade for each pollution source and income class, we measured concentration ratios for degradation pressure by dividing total degradation pressure estimates of the richest 10 percent by the poorest 50 percent of the population. Apart from for non-treated water and non-collected sewage whose services are concentrated in rich households, every source we examined exhibited ratios above 0.4, indicating that rich people tend to degrade more than their population share.

Lastly, we analyzed how degradation pressure would change if income distribution was altered in Brazil. We developed two scenarios based on income transfer among groups to measure changes in total degradation pressure. A progressive scenario assumed transfer from rich to poor and the regressive scenario from poor to rich.

As expected, regressive transfers increased degradation and progressive ones decreased degradation. In both cases, however, we found that industrial and transport sources encompassed an inelastic relationship between income distribution and total degradation pressure in which the transferred income share is bigger than the resulting degradation pressure.

The high concentration of degradation pressure from rich people's consumption pattern adds another regressive aspect for unequal income distribution in Brazil. Overall, our results bring about serious distributive issues for environmental policy in Brazil:

- Although the consumption level of poor people is not the main source of degradation, they tend to bear most of the degradation costs due their low capacity to incur defensive expenditures.
- As degradation pressure is mainly due to high income groups' consumption patterns, any attempt to avoid stricter degradation controls that affect consumption decisions will create a subsidy for the rich people's consumption at the expense of the poor.

However, as degradation concentration ratios are lower than the respective income ratios, when degradation control becomes more stringent, poor people will tend to pay more for environmental control per unit of consumption if these costs are passed through prices.

In fact, this might be already happening with control costs for industrial water pollution, which present the highest control levels for industrial sources. The comparison of potential and residual (after control) emissions illustrates that concentration ratios for residual levels are higher than potential ones, indicating that a greater part of reduction was done at the poor consumption level.

Our analysis can be further developed to include other degradation sources and incorporate multiplier effects on income transfer scenarios.

The implications of environmental control on income distribution are crucial for environmental policies aimed at reducing degradation pressure in Brazil. If this regressive aspect is to be mitigated, policy instruments have to allow for compensatory measures. In this view, the use of environmental taxation may be a good candidate as it reduces social control costs and generates revenue that can be recycled into the economy to create room for compensatory policies towards the poor.

NOTES

1. That is, degradation and income would follow a quadratic relationship.
2. Cross-country analysis may not capture the temporal evolution of the relationship between degradation and income. See, for example, Opschoor (2001) and Panayotou (1997) for an extensive review on this issue.
3. Kahn (2000) has show this expected inverse U shape relationship between cans emissions and income level for the US.
4. Generation and disposal of solid waste is also a very important direct consumption, but it was not covered in this study due to the lack of data related to class income. For example, payments for waste collection is not charged directly to households but as part

of other municipal taxes.

5. Following the seminal work of Leontief (1970), environmental issues have been applied in I–O models, for example, Vaughan and Pasurka (1995); Breuil (1992) and Førsund (1985).
6. This may not hold for some goods, although pollution from class-specific goods may also not be class-specific.
7. The latest Household Expenditure Surveys (POF) for Brazil are for the years 1995/96.
8. It is the 1996 legal monthly minimum wage equivalent to R$ 112 or about US$ 113 at the prevailing average 1996 exchange rate to American dollar.
9. See Young's study previously presented for a detail discussion of these parameters.
10. A simple exercise calculating total Brazilian pollution by multiplying residual CETESB and IPPS coefficients to total production in Brazil, show that CETESB total pollution is lower in organic and higher in particulate and SO_2 and almost the same in inorganic. Such a result is expected since, as pointed out by Seroa da Motta (1993); water pollution control in Brazil dominates air pollution and it is based mostly on organic matter that is easier to notice and monitor. Nevertheless, the application of US coefficients should not be recommended for Brazil.
11. Both surveys are based on an equivalent urban sample.
12. Khan (2000) has accessed such income-related car ownership databases for the US and has proved this expected inverse U shape relationship between car emissions and income level.
13. Since rich people tend to use more comfortable buses with lower carrying capacity than the poor, their emissions per trip tend to be higher. This is a bias toward upper classes' contributions and can be compensated for the fact that buses serving the poor are older and tend to emit more than those serving the rich.
14. These estimates are only valid if we assume that opportunity costs of deriving water from other sources, rather than the public system, is equivalent to the tariff levels. This is not a totally implausible assumption since several studies in Brazil on willingness-to-pay (WTP) measurements of water supply has shown that WTP estimates exceed current tariffs, see Ardila et al. (1998). Discharged sewage is directly related to volumetric water consumption.
15. That is, it does not follow a quadratic form, as an inverse U shape would suggest.
16. Note that environmental Kuznets curves are expected from both p and c variations, which are supposed to occur through time and not in a single year as assumed here.
17. We have also applied different schedules of year-class, assuming that poor people use old cars, and all results have not shown any significant change in curve shapes for E and Pmg.
18. Kahn (2000) has observed such an environmental Kuznets curve for private vehicle use in the US depending on the estimated use level. In our case, since we have used actual fuel consumption, we can say that this inverse U shape does not apply for Brazil.
19. Water demand is expected to be inelastic since basic water requirements are not supposed to vary much among classes, although it is highly dependent on household size.
20. It was included linearly according to this share.
21. Of course, this depends on supply and demand price elasticity effects as well and, therefore, consumer surplus measures would be more appropriate for welfare analysis. Here we are only concerned with actual disposable income.
22. This ratio increases slightly to about 3.1 when rural income is considered.
23. See, for example, a recent survey by Neumayer (2000).
24. Another interesting way to look at distribution issues is by introducing abatement costs into this model and estimating changes in resulting consumption levels. We have not been able to pursue this approach due to data restrictions. See, for example, Ketkar (1983), for an application to the US economy.
25. That is, multiplier effects are captured.
26. This is only bidding for the second richest class since the first one has an open upper limit.

6. Agriculture expansion and deforestation in the Brazilian Amazon, 1980–95

6.1 INTRODUCTION

The Brazilian Amazon is regarded as one of the most essential ecosystems in the world containing nearly 50 percent of the known biodiversity on the planet. It comprises an area of nearly 5 million km^2, of which approximately 70 percent is continuous forest domain. Due to its vast unclaimed territory, it has attracted migrants from other regions of the country searching for agricultural land. Nonetheless, it still remains a frontier region. Due to the great distances from main centers and due to dense forest areas, almost 85 percent of the original forest cover is still intact.

Figure 6.1 Map of the Brazilian Amazon

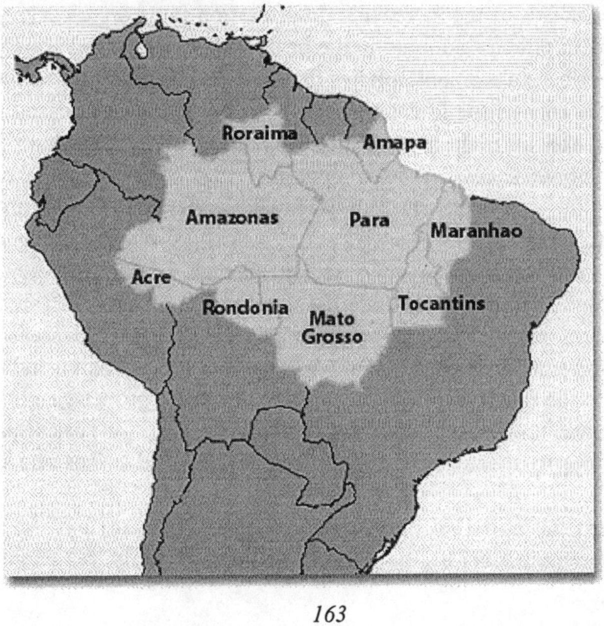

Several attempts at development have been undertaken by the Brazilian government since the beginning of the 1960s. In order to integrate the northern region to the rest of the country a series of highways were constructed starting with the Belém-Brasília, followed by the Cuiabá-Santarém and the Tranzamazônica (Mahar, 1988; Moran, 1996). Additionally numerous settlement projects were undertaken in regions near the new highways in order to compensate for the lack of agrarian reform and relieve demand for land in other regions of the country (Ozorio de Almeida and Campari, 1995). Large amounts of subsidized credit were given for agriculture and cattle ranching activities and huge development projects such as the Carajás project were undertaken (Reis, 1996). Nonetheless, these efforts were not successful in generating a sustainable growth process in the region. Although the regional GDP has grown substantially in the last 20 years, poverty and inequality in income and land distribution are evident in the region. Moreover the pattern of growth is generating an unsustainable deforestation process that can jeopardize future economic potentials.

The extent of deforestation has grown significantly during the past 20 years. Approximately 400 000 km^2 of tropical forest were cleared between 1978 and 1998 according to satellite image estimates.[1] Moreover, the increasing forest fires and selective logging activities, which are not captured by satellite images, could imply that the extent of the deforested area is even larger.[2]

The causes of the increasing deforestation trend are closely related to government policies adopted in the past. Mahar (1988) and Binswanger (1991) describe government policies that have induced and aggravated the economic incentives for forest clearing. Among others, subsidized credit, tax breaks for agriculture and cattle ranching activities, land titling processes in open access areas and construction of highways, have created incentives for the clearing of forested lands for agriculture and settlements.

The macroeconomic environment generated additional incentives for deforestation through high interest rates and uncertainty derived from high inflation rates. The prevailing high price of land decreased the incentive for smaller farmers to buy land and increased the incentives for migrating to the forest frontier – generating a race for property rights. This movement was undertaken not only for acquiring land for agriculture, but also as a way to speculate on future rises in the land prices and capital gains.[3]

Since the mid-1980s, several government policies have changed. Agriculture credit subsidies have decreased considerably, tax exemptions have been reduced drastically, direct colonization settlements have been terminated and large infrastructure projects have been phased out. Nevertheless, deforestation has not slowed down.

The building of new roads and the paving of existing roads are regarded to be among the main factors driving the continuing deforestation process. In some cases, roads facilitate the development of new settlements in frontier regions. More often, however, they drastically reduce transportation costs in earlier settled areas, thus increasing the profitability of agro-pastoral activities and hence encouraging their expansion into the Amazon. Alves (1999) estimates that between 1991 and 1996, more than 75 percent of the total cleared area near the three major road networks occurred within a 50 km distance from the roads.[4] The clearing and appropriation of open access areas adjacent to paved roads, particularly those constructed for logging purposes, also contribute to a substantial amount of deforestation. Additional incentives for deforestation were created by the contradictory policies of government agencies such as the Brazilian Renewable Resource Institute (IBAMA) and the Agrarian Reform Institute (INCRA). While the IBAMA obliges all properties in the Amazon to retain 80 percent of their forest area, the INCRA will often consider a property that follows this rule as unproductive and thus susceptible to expropriation (Alston, et al., 2000).

The macroeconomic policies adopted during the 1990s may have exacerbated the prevailing institutional failures. Stabilizing policies may have increased incentives for deforestation through high interest rates and low credit availability, which could have had a significant impact on the choice for land clearing, although theoretically, the impact of interest rates on deforestation is ambiguous. An increase in interest rates makes a large owner postpone investment in agriculture and cattle ranching and tends to decrease new land clearing. On the other hand, for small owners and agents living in the frontier, an increase in interest rates increases the cost of capital, generating a negative income effect that could increase frontier settlement. This is an important effect for smallholders and could help explain why deforestation by smallholders increased in the Amazon during the 1990s.

The objective of this chapter is to analyze the causes of frontier expansion and deforestation in the Brazilian Amazon in recent decades. The analysis uses annual data, from 1980 to 1995, for eight states of the region[5] to explain the expansion of crop areas and cattle herds. Based upon a simple theoretical model the chapter undertakes panel data estimation of the causes of deforestation using, as explanatory variables, output and input prices, government credit and road extension.

Previous econometric studies of tropical deforestation in the Amazon used cross-section (Reis and Guzmán, 1993) or panel data models, based upon municipal data from the Brazilian Agricultural Census published every five years except for 1990 when the census survey was not undertaken (Reis, 1996; Andersen and Reis, 1997; Young, 1997). Another approach was undertaken by Reis and Margulis (1991), combining agricultural census data with satellite image data for 1978 and 1988. None of the previously mentioned empirical analyses, however, went beyond the mid-1980s. Moreover, to incorporate the 1995/96 Agricultural Census data is not an easy task because of methodological changes that created problems of comparison with the previous 1985 census.[6]

The chapter uses a new database, which combines state level data from two annual agricultural surveys undertaken by IBGE (Pesquisa Agrícola Municipal – PAM and Pesquisa Pecuária Municipal – PPM) and data on agricultural credit and roads from other government sources with FGV (Fundação Getúlio Vargas) data on crop and factor prices in agriculture, thus making it possible to update the analysis of deforestation process in the Amazon up to the mid-1990s. An additional contribution of the chapter is the improved specification of the dynamics and causation of the deforestation process allowed by the use of annual data, notwithstanding the fact that the time span of the sample – 15 years – is still very short. A disadvantage of using the PAM and PPM is that the data on cropped areas and cattle herds are less precise estimators of deforestation compared with the consistent land use categories of the Agricultural Census. Cropped areas do not necessarily lead to clearing and deforestation, since fallow lands could be available for use. The same is true for pasture areas. However, for cattle raising, even pasture areas will have to be inferred from the size of herds, the only information available. To do this, it is necessary to assume a stable relation between herds and pasture areas or intensity of grazing.

The theoretical background model used is based upon Deacon (1995) and Barbier (1999). The land clearing process is simply modeled as an interaction of demand and supply of cleared land for agriculture and a reduced form for the demand of cleared agriculture land is obtained. Although this model does not take into account important dynamic issues such as land speculation, we believe it is simple enough to motivate the economic determinants of deforestation in the Amazon.

The reduced form demand equation is taken from the data using as dependent variables the density of agriculture cleared area and the density of cattle herd. This econometric model is closely related to other applications of panel data to deforestation estimations such as Young (1997); Andersen and Reis (1997); Cropper and Griffiths (1999) and Foster et al. (forthcoming).

6.2 EVOLUTION OF THE CAUSES OF DEFORESTATION IN THE BRAZILIAN AMAZON

The economic literature on deforestation, summarized by Kaimowitz and Angelsen (1998), separates the variables affecting the land clearing process into three levels: underlying causes, immediate causes and sources. Underlying causes are related to macro level variables and are generally thought of as income, population and macroeconomic policies.

Underlying Causes

In this level, increasing rural population density and GDP per capita are usually blamed as the most important factors driving the deforestation dynamics (Cropper and Griffiths, 1994). Nevertheless, the evidence is somewhat mixed once other important variables are included in the econometric analysis (Angelsen and Kaimowitz, 1999). Existing evidence for the Brazilian Amazon seems to support the hypothesis of rural population migrations having a large effect only in opening new frontier areas. Once the area is occupied, Pfaff (1999) found that increasing population density, controlling for other variables, has a negligible effect on land clearing expansion. It is important to note that population is actually an endogenous variable and migrations occur as a response to economic incentives. An alternative model is used by Andersen and Reis (1997) who explain migration based on a set of economic variables. Nonetheless, after controlling for other characteristics including neighbor change in clearing rural population density it is not found to be statistically significant.

From the macro perspective, the deforestation process is closely associated with the colonization of the Amazon forest as a frontier region. Table 6.1 demonstrates the evolution of rural population in the states that comprise the Legal Amazon. In Roraima, Rondônia, Mato Grosso and Pará, the growth in rural population decreased considerably when we compare the 1991–2000 period with the 1980–91 period. Moreover, for Pará and Mato Grosso there is a reduction in rural population probably as a consequence of migration to new frontier areas or to villages and cities.

Table 6.1 Rural population, 1980, 1991 and 2000[a]

State	1980	1991	2000	% growth 1980–91	% growth 1991–2000
Acre (AC)	169 134	159 198	187 541	−5.9	17.8
Amapá (AP)	71 522	55 266	52 262	−22.7	−5.4
Amazonas (AM)	573 472	600 489	732 411	4.7	22.0
Maranhão (MA)	2,741 248	2 957 832	2 282 804	7.9	−22.8
Mato Grosso (MT)	483 739	542 121	515 181	12.1	−5.0
Pará (PA)	1 736 035	2 353 672	2 072 911	35.6	−11.9
Rondônia (RO)	262 530	473 365	494 744	80.3	4.5
Roraima (RR)	30 425	76 765	77 420	152.3	0.9
Goiasa (GO)	1 458 111	1 160 454	902 652	−20.4	−22.2

Note: [a] For 1991 and 1996 the population of the State of Goias includes the population of the State of Tocantins which was created out of the territory of Goias in 1988.

Source: IBGE.

Allied with the population trend, the region had a substantial growth in income per capita. Economic growth was acheived in the Amazon through the establishment of colonization projects in the region and the massive infrastructure investment and credit concessions. Average GDP in the Amazon region grew by an average of 15 percent per year from 1970 to 1980 and income per capita more than doubled. The industrial sector showed the highest growth with an average growth rate of 26 percent per year motivated by the creation of the Manaus Free Export Processing Zone. The share of industry in local production increased from 15 percent in 1970 to an impressive 40 percent in 1980 (Reis and Blanco, 1996).

During the 1980s and 1990s, the growth was maintained, but there was a substantial difference among states. Industrial growth was not widespread and in some states agricultural activities were the main factor motivating growth. Table 6.2 demonstrates the average and cumulative GDP growth for each state of the Legal Amazon from 1985 to 1997. We also include the agriculture GDP growth as a means of comparison. The first important observation is that the most industrialized state, Amazonas, has a low average growth rate while other states such as Acre and Rondônia which depend mostly on agriculture, cattle and extraction, had average growth rates over 4 percent. We also observe that the states with the highest growth rates, Roraima and Amapá, also had the highest agriculture GDP growth rates, indicating that their growth is based on agriculture and cattle ranching, both activities that induce deforestation. This pattern seems to be confirmed when, as shown in Table 6.2, these states presented the two highest agriculture GDP growth rates together with the highest deforestation growth rates between 1988 and 1998.

Table 6.2 GDP growth rates in the Amazon region states between 1985 and 1997

State	GDP average growth rate	Cumulated GDP growth rate	Agriculture GDP average growth rate	Cumulated agriculture GDP growth rate
Acre	4.86	58.31	0.31	3.71
Amapá	6.72	80.65	11.02	132.20
Amazonas	0.56	6.77	0.50	6.06
Maranhão	1.05	12.56	0.94	11.24
Mato Grosso	2.91	34.96	2.68	32.13
Pará	2.68	32.17	5.14	61.65
Rondônia	4.01	48.11	4.57	54.85
Roraima	7.20	86.34	16.98	203.82
Tocantins	2.53	30.41	0.22	2.65
Amazon region	3.61		4.71	

Source: Silva and Medina (1999).

Immediate Causes of Deforestation: Prices, Credit and Roads

Macro variables affect proximate causes, which can be described as parameters that shape economic agents' decisions. These parameters are related to institutions (property rights), markets, governments and technology. Both levels are important for the Brazilian case and are closely related. Government policies have had an impact on both the deforestation process and the microeconomic relations through an institutional context of land inequality, insecure tenure rights and market imperfections that have contributed to intensifying regional policy failures.

Migration processes and property right allocations are closely linked to deforestation. Poorly defined property right structures are known to be one of the main determinants of land clearing processes in tropical forests. The colonization projects introduced in the Amazon during the

1970s attracted a huge amount of farmers to the frontier, motivated by property right claims. Ozorio de Almeida and Campari (1995); Schneider (1995) and Alston et al. (1996) have found a strong relationship between incentives for land clearing and insecure property right regimes.

Evidences from the Agriculture Census show that land titling has been active in the Amazon region. Table 6.3 shows the proportion of land area that was used or cultivated without formal title compared with the total land use for each state in 1980, 1985 and 1996. The percentage of land cultivated without property rights decreased considerably from 1980 to 1985 for all states except Amapá and Acre, which are predomoninantly frontier areas. Between 1985 and 1996, the decrease in percentage of land in all states cultivated without land ownership could be explained by an increasing land titling process combined with decreasing occupation of frontier areas.[7] Hence, these results could suggest that deforestation is mainly occurring on private land rather than on open access areas in frontier forests. Deforestation of these recently claimed private lands is consistent with Alves' (1999) findings that most deforestation takes place in early settlements. Additionally, we may interpret these numbers as showing some evidence that the movements along the frontier motivated by the search for property rights (Schneider, 1995) have slowed down as a consequence of the reduction in land speculation due to the declining price of land since 1986 and the increasing trend for agrarian reform in other areas of the Brazilian territory.

Table 6.3 Percentage of the area occupied without land ownership

State	1980	1985	1996
Acre	0.26	0.35	0.18
Amapá	0.10	0.24	0.04
Amazonas	0.35	0.26	0.10
Goiás	0.07	0.02	0.02
Maranhão	0.06	0.05	0.05
Mato Grosso	0.05	0.02	0.01
Pará	0.15	0.11	0.04
Rondônia	0.46	0.17	0.05
Roraima	0.64	0.12	0.09

Source: IBGE Agriculture Census, 1980, 1985, 1996.

Immediate causes of deforestation are closely linked to economic incentives. Imperfect markets for crops, labor and land have induced land-clearing processes. Among these factors, land speculation has been one of the driving aspects inducing deforestation processes in the region. The open access characteristic of the Amazon forest induced a race for property rights, both as direct government strategy and as a market response to the possibility of obtaining land titles. Subsidized rural credit for pasture conversion and cattle ranching created an additional pressure on land prices through the demand for large amounts of land.[8] Additionally, the great uncertainty generated by high inflationary processes contributed to the use of land as a secure asset.

Therefore, the relationship between changes in the price of land and the demand for cleared land is quite complex. An increase in the price of land raises the cost of acquiring or renting land and tends to decrease the demand for cleared land as an input. Nevertheless, in dynamic terms, an increase in the price of land generates expected future gains and could increase the demand for land for speculative motives. Additionally, cattle and land serve as secure assets in periods of high inflation.

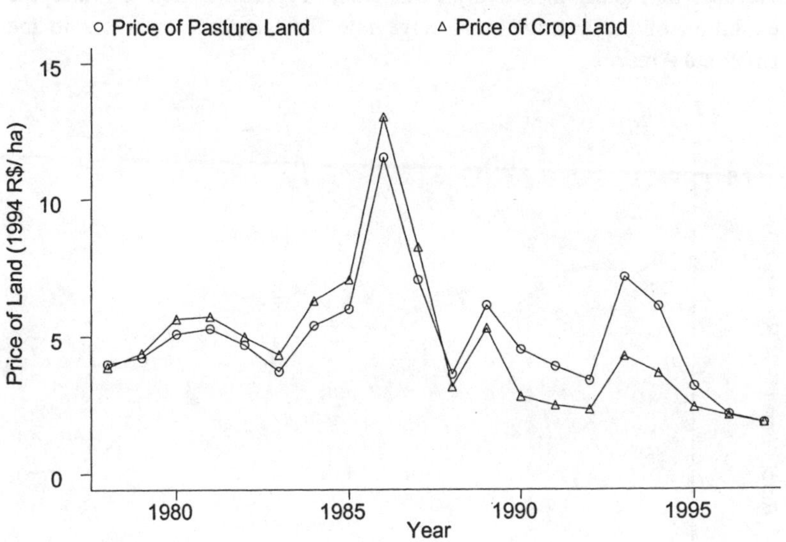

Figure 6.2 Average price of land in the Brazilian Amazon

In Figure 6.2 we present the evolution of the price of land in the Amazon region. From the early 1980s until the real plan in 1994 the price of land was greatly determined by macroeconomic variables, especially inflation and interest rates. The increase in the real price of land that occurred in the 1970s until the mid-1980s created an additional incentive for deforestation through smaller farmers. Since high land prices limited the possibility of smaller farmers to buy land, it created incentives for migration and frontier settlements, generating further forest conversion (Schneider, 1995). After a peak in 1986 the price of land has decreased considerably, and since 1994 reduced inflation rates associated with restrictive macroeconomic policies on credit and consumption brought down definitively the price of land for both crop areas and pastureland as we observe in Figure 6.2. The price of pastureland is, on average, higher than the price of crop land, although over time their behavior is almost identical.

Deforestation in the Amazon is closely linked to the rural labor market as well. The opportunity cost of migrating to the frontier is given, in part, by the rural wage, which could be obtained by working on a farm. Low rural wages imply low opportunity cost of migration inducing higher land clearing. Moreover, the demand for additional land is also related to the cost of inputs, inclusively rural labor. Figure 6.3 demonstrates the evolution of the average rural wage rate for temporary workers in the Brazilian Amazon.

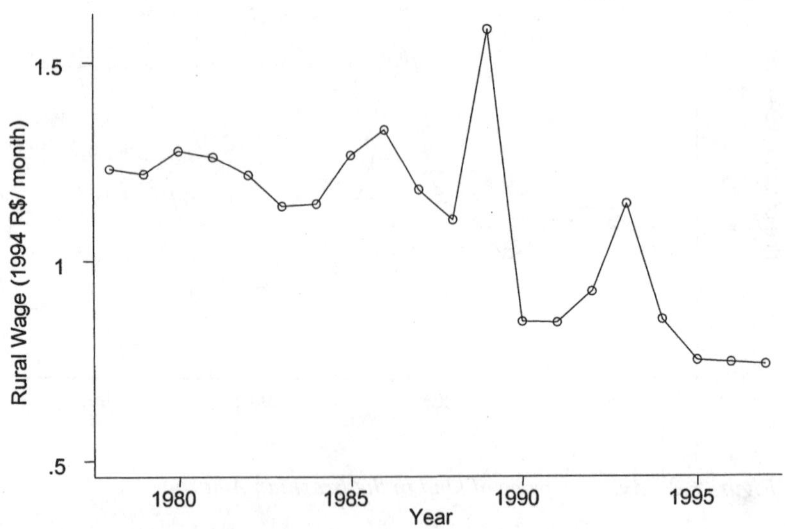

Figure 6.3 Average rural wage in the Brazilian Amazon

Except for peaks in 1989 and 1993, the rural wage has been declining since 1978. This decline creates incentives for hiring labor for clearing activities and, at the same time, decreases the opportunity cost of migration, creating incentives for movements along the frontier in search of open access land.

Land price dynamics and wage rate movements in the Amazon are closely related to infrastructure building, especially road constructions (Binswanger, 1991). Since the 1970s the Brazilian government undertook a massive colonization effort through road building. The availability of roads decreased transport costs, enabling large pastures and agriculture areas to become financially viable.

An extensive network of paved and unpaved roads was built in the Amazon during 1980–95 as illustrated in Table 6.4. The extension of paved roads increased by more than 100 percent during 1980–95 and unpaved roads increased by approximately 460 percent. On average, 16 000 km of additional unpaved roads were built between 1980 and 1995. Although paved roads are generally related to new frontier areas, small, unpaved roads opened by logging companies also generate further occupation.

Table 6.4 Extension of road network in the Brazilian Amazon (km)

State	1980		1985		1990		1995	
	Paved	Unpaved	Paved	Unpaved	Paved	Unpaved	Paved	Unpaved
Acre	151	1 174	224	1 853	222	1 881	315	1 881
Amazonas	1188	1 754	1 995	3 377	1 954	3 619	2 028	4 660
Amapá	20	1 124	134	1 869	205	2 123	224	1 765
Goiás	4 288	18 805	6 959	98 783	8 391	98 732	9 139	102 186
Maranhão	2 396	4 505	2 843	46 456	3 471	48 122	4 016	48 607
Mato Grosso	895	13 726	2 732	37 933	3 926	76 419	3 970	78 999
Pará	2 122	8 152	2 422	19 209	3 385	30 930	3 418	30 926
Rondônia	119	2 378	764	8 524	1 056	8 945	1 397	20 960
Roraima	26	2 225	40	3 161	64	3 110	409	4 458
Total	11 205	53 843	18 113	221 165	22 674	273 881	24 916	294 442

Source: Anuário Estatístico dos Transportes GEIPOT, several years.

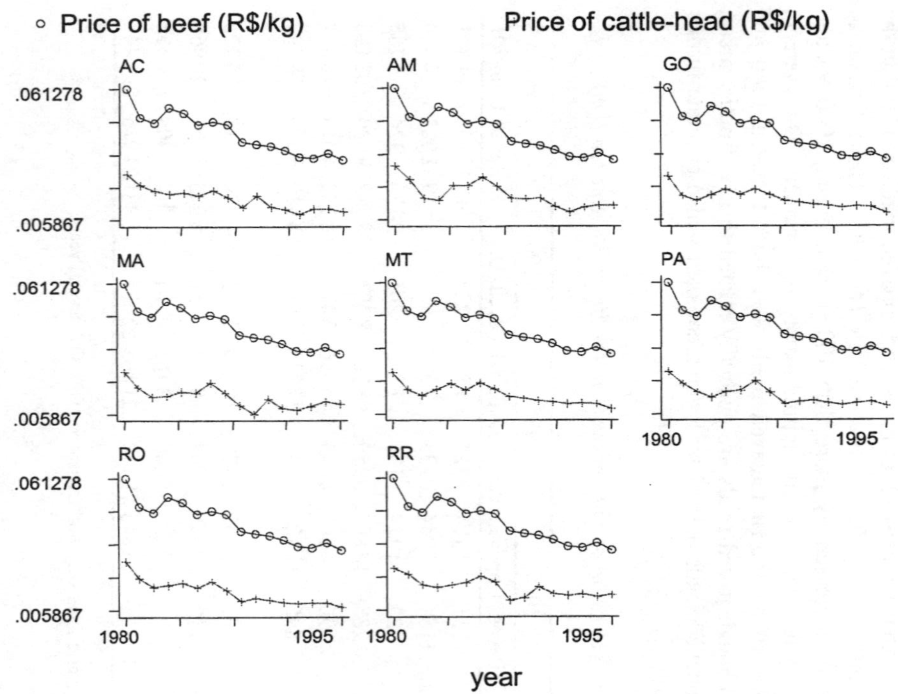

Figure 6.4 Price of cattle-head and price of beef, 1980–95

A fraction of the deforestation process is undertaken by smallholders who clear land for subsistence consumption. Another substantial portion is carried out by commercial crop and cattle ranching activities. Since cattle ranching activities are generally oriented towards the market, we would expect the price of output to determine the expansion of commercial agriculture and cattle ranching in the Amazon region.

Figure 6.4 demonstrates the evolution of the average price of commercialized cattle in the Amazon from 1978 to 1997 for all eight states being analyzed compared with the evolution of beef prices in São Paulo (the most important market). Despite some short-term fluctuations, both prices show a declining trend. Moreover, the price of beef seems to be closely correlated to the price of cattle in the medium run.

Although the price of output (beef) has been declining in real terms since the early 1980s, the price of one of the main inputs of cattle ranching (cattle) has also been felt. Schneider et al. (2000) estimates a low internal rate of return for the cattle activity in the Amazon, suggesting that additional explanations are needed in order to elucidate on the massive growth of cattle in the region. Walker et al. (2000) suggest that even though beef prices fell in real terms, the relative price of beef with respect to crops such as rice, beans and black pepper have increased, making cattle ranching profitable even for small farmers. Additionally it is important to take into account that there are additional returns to the cattle activity such as the establishment of property rights and protection against high inflation. Another possible explanation for the increasing cattle-herd is history dependence and important cultural and institutional aspects, especially due to past government incentives.

It is widely agreed that government credit, through subsidies and tax break incentives, was one of the most important factors that drove the agriculture frontier expansion in the Amazon (Biswanger, 1991; Schneider, 1995; Andersen and Reis, 1997). Agriculture and cattle ranching credit decreased considerably during the economic crisis of the early 1980s. Nonetheless, from 1984 to 1989 there was a substantial growth in government credit especially for agriculture activities. A substantial reduction occurred in 1990, but government credit increased for both agriculture and cattle ranching activities since 1991 (Figure 6.5).

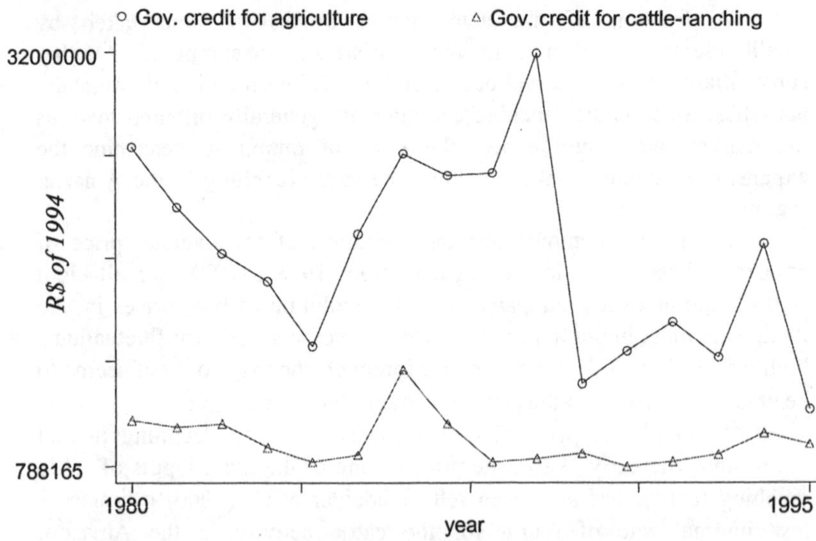

Figure 6.5 Government credit in the Amazon (R$ of 1994)

Source of Deforestation

The sources of deforestation are defined as land use options, which include cropped areas, pasture and timber extraction. This distinction is not only important conceptually, but helps in building the right model and including the right variables in estimating equations. Moreover, in the Brazilian case, the different sources of deforestation have a strong synergy. Timber extraction in the Amazon takes advantage of the legal land clearing for agriculture, which gives right to deforestation. Timber sale based on this license at that time is an opportunity for making up-front capital for full clearing afterwards and to bear later costs of securing property rights. Therefore, timber exploitation, in fact, acts in some areas as an inducing factor for land conversion.

Most of the deforested areas have been converted to pastureland. Table 6.5 presents data from the 1985 and 1996 Agriculture Censuses. Decomposing the major land uses and comparing their evolution, it is found that approximately 145 837 km^2 of land clearing occurred between 1985 and 1995/96 (this is close to the value of 174 292 obtained if we subtract the extension of deforestation in 1998 from the value in 1988).[9] The area of planted pasture increased from 298 423 km^2 in 1985 to 477 272 km^2 in 1996, representing an increase of approximately 60 percent in ten years. On the other hand, the area used for crops did not change significantly and although the area of planted forests increased considerably, it still accounts for a small share of land use in the Amazon.[10] Therefore, results from the Agriculture Census seem to indicate that the conversion of forest into planted pasture is still the main source of deforestation in the Brazilian Amazon.

Table 6.5 Land use in the Brazilian Amazon, 1985 and 1996 (area in km^2)

Land use	1985	1996
Perennial crops	10 183.27	10 788.24
Annual crops	79 735.44	70 604.42
Planted forest	3 031.78	5 800.30
Planted pasture	298 423.46	477 273.20
Fallow land	43 517.64	29 030.27
Productive land not used	114 754.61	74 275.44
Total cleared area	1 378 194.56	1 524 032.00

Source: IBGE Agriculture Census 1985 and 1995. The Brazilian Amazon considered here includes the state of Maranhão and the state of Goiás.

6.3 EMPIRICAL MODEL AND ECONOMETRIC SPECIFICATION

Constructing a simple model to describe the pattern of deforestation in the Brazilian Amazon is not an easy task, as the Amazon is a heterogeneous region where several institutional settings coexist. In some parts of the region, especially in the first frontier areas such as parts of Maranhão, Mato Grosso, Tocantins and Pará, there are developed lands and labor markets. Conversely, in areas beyond the frontier, markets are weakly developed and open access areas prevail. Further differences arise from economic agents clearing the forest, which range from small subsistence agrarian peasants to large cattle landholders.

In order to simplify our analysis and study the specific variables that are likely to influence the evolution of cleared land, we will assume that we can represent the process of deforestation by a simple demand and supply model. Instead of developing a dynamic framework, we opt for presenting a simple static model (e.g., based on Reis and Guzman (1993) and Barbier (1999) with some dynamic features found in Angelsen (1999)). We hope to use this model to isolate the variables we consider important to explain the Brazilian deforestation process.

We follow Cropper and Griffiths (1999) in breaking up the deforestation process into two steps: at each price level, economic agents chose the amount of land that is cleared. Separately, at prevailing prices, farmers chose the amount of land, which would be used for cropping. Although farmers may clear their own land and farm it, this two-step framework allows us to model the effects of agriculture decisions on the deforestation process separately.

One drawback of the previously cited papers is that they do not take into account the possibility of gaining access to new land through clearing to obtain property rights. As it is well known (Schneider, 1995), this is a process that is important to explain deforestation motives in the Brazilian Amazon. Barbier (1999) attempts to introduce institutional characteristics associated with open access by presenting a model similar to Cropper and Griffiths (1999), but assuming that if there is a market for cleared land and this land is an open access resource, then in equilibrium, the price of land will equal the average cost of conversion and no surplus would be generated. Nonetheless, his model does not incorporate the possibility of frontier expansion due to the existence of land titling. A dynamic model presented in Mueller (1997) models the evolution of the frontier with capital gains from property right acquisition through deforestation, but does not derive the demand for land explicitly.

We opted for characterizing the deforestation with a simple model that merges the ideas in Cropper and Griffiths (1999) and Barbier (1999) with the Von Thunen type of model presented in Angelsen (1999). Hence, instead of assuming that economic agents simply equal the average clearing cost with the shadow price of cleared land, we use the Angelsen (1999) model in order to derive the amount of cleared land as a function of economic and geographical variables. This strategy allows clearing to depend not only on the current land price, but also on the expected land price. The formal model is derived in Ferraz (2001). The reduced form equation of cleared land obtained depends on the factors affecting the demand for cleared land, but also on factors affecting the supply of deforested land. Thus, the equilibrium amount of cleared land, X^e, is given by:

$$X^e = X(p,\rho,w,r,g,e,x,\lambda,\beta,q). \tag{6.1}$$

Equation (6.1) implies that the reduced form equilibrium amount of cleared land depends on the output price (p), the cleared land (or rental price) (ρ), the rural wage (w), the rental rate of capital (r), the expected growth in the value of land (g), agro-ecological characteristics (e), the land productivity (x), the probability of losing the land (λ), the discount rate (β) and the transport cost (q).

Following the model summarized by equation (6.1), our objective is to estimate the main determinants of the evolution of agriculture land and cattle-head in the Brazilian Amazon. Our approach will consist in estimating a separate independent regression for each source using a panel-data approach.[11] According to our model, the area of cleared land for agriculture and the number of cattle-heads, in state i at period t, are determined by three types of factors: market incentives, geographical factors and agro-ecological characteristics. We estimate a first-order linear approximation to equation (6.1) relating the variation of agriculture land density and cattle-head density to output prices, input prices (land price and rural wage), road extensions (paved and unpaved roads), rural credit, distance to federal capital and soil quality. Although equation (6.1) incorporates other interesting and important features such as property rights, we are not able to find a complete series of data that could be used for estimation purposes. Therefore, the reduced form estimated equation could be written as:

$$\begin{aligned} \ln y_{it} = \alpha + \beta \ln pa_{it} + \delta \ln pl_{it} + \gamma \ln w_{it} + \lambda\ \ln crd_{it} + \\ \gamma \ln prd_{it} + \varphi \ln nprd_{it} + \rho \ln dist_{i} + \zeta \ln sd_{i} + f_{i} + \varepsilon_{it} \end{aligned} \tag{6.2}$$

where y_{it} is the fraction of cleared land in the agriculture estimation and the density of cattle-head in the pasture estimation; pa_{it} is the price of output (agriculture products for agriculture and the price of cattle-head for cut in the cattle equation); pl_{it} is the price of land (differentiated by crop land and pastureland according to the dependent variable); w_{it} is the rural wage rate; crd_{it} is the rural credit density (differentiated by agriculture and cattle raising credit for each equation, credit/state area); prd_{it} is the density of paved roads (paved roads/state area); $nprd_{it}$ is the density of unpaved roads (unpaved roads/state area); $dist_i$ is the distance from the state capital to the federal capital; sd_i is the proportion of high quality soil; f_i is a specific effect for each state and ε_{it} is the contemporaneous error term.

Since the extension of cleared land for agriculture and the number of cattle-head per state are likely to vary with the size, omitting size from equation (6.2) causes a spurious correlation between cleared agriculture area and size with varying variables such as roads and credit.[12] This is not a problem in the fixed effect estimation since size will disappear once we take first differences, but in the random effect estimation we control for different state sizes by dividing the dependent variable and size varying factors such as roads and credit by the size of the state area.[13]

Although equation (6.2) represents a simple model, its estimation raises several important econometric issues. There are significant fixed effects even when we take into account state specific variables such as soil quality and distance from main markets. Several other factors such as state inherent population ability, rainfall, climate, vegetation cover, slopes, public infrastructure and other factors could explain different crop area and cattle-head density. Since these omitted factors are likely to be correlated with included variables such as rural credit, roads and land prices, the omission of any of these variables would generate biased coefficients under OLS estimation. The advantage of working with panel data is that such fixed effects can be wiped out using first differences generating more precise estimates of the causes of land clearing expansion. The disadvantage of using a fixed effect model is that we cannot estimate directly the effect of soil quality and distance to main markets on the planted area and cattle density.[14] Our approach undertakes both fixed effect and random effect estimations and uses the Hausman test to check the importance of fixed effects.

Another important point in the estimation procedure is related to the price of land. It is hard to assume that perfect functioning land markets exist in the whole Amazon. Some regions have weak markets and sometimes no markets (open access). This is exactly one of the causes of deforestation. Therefore, introducing the market land price seems like a strong assumption based on our model. Nonetheless, in regions where land markets are developed, an increase in the price of land would induce a reduction in the demand for land as a factor of production and consequently a decrease in land clearing. If land is just used as a production factor in a static context, then a negative relationship between the land price and the amount of cleared land is expected. Nevertheless, our model indicates that a higher expected value of land will generate further land clearing.[15] The first effect occurs through the demand for cleared land while the latter occurs through the supply of deforested land. That is, by privatizing the land, prices will increase from zero (open access) to some positive value. Hence an increase in the price of land can be a signal for increasing clearing and supplying additional deforested land. Hence, we cannot assume a priori a specific sign for the relationship between cleared land and land price.

Another difficulty in the estimation procedure is related to simultaneity. Since we are estimating an assumed reduced form of a demand and supply system of agriculture cleared land, the price of land could be correlated with the error term.[16] In order to identify our reduced form demand equation, we would need a cost-shifting variable that can serve as an instrument for land price. As is well known, this variable has to be correlated with land price and not correlated with the error term. Nevertheless, in practice, finding a suitable instrument is not an easy task.[17] To diminish this problem, we use the lagged value of the land price as an explanatory variable for the cleared land and cattle-head. Thus, in our model, farmers are assumed to decide how much crop land would be used in the beginning of the period and if they decide to use more land, they would make the purchase decision at the beginning of the period depending on previous period prices.

Using current rural wages could also cause simultaneity problems. An increase in the planted area is likely to generate an additional demand for rural labor, which would increase the rural wage rate. A solution would be to find a valid instrumental variable for rural wage as well, as in the case of the land price, such an instrumental variable is not available. We choose the same strategy using the rural wage from the last period as an explanatory variable for current planted area.

The problem of simultaneity is also important for the other variables such as credit and roads. It is hard to define the right causality between credit and crop area since more rural credit creates incentives for increasing the crop area, but usually land is used as collateral and a higher proportion of crop area would induce a larger amount of rural credit. The same is true for roads since the demand for new roads could be generated in places where the crop area is large and there is a necessity for a distribution network. In order to avoid reversal causality effects and simultaneity we prefer to include both credit and road variables using one period lag.

6.4 DATA

In order to analyze the causes of land clearing expansion in the Brazilian Amazon we use state level data from 1980 to 1995 for eight states considered part of the Amazon ecosystem: Acre, Amazonas, Goiás, Maranhão, Mato Grosso, Pará, Rondônia and Roraima. The State of Amapá, although part of the Amazon, is not included in our analysis due to the lack of complete data on land prices, cattle prices and wages. On the other hand, the States of Maranhão and Goiás are completely included, although only part of them is considered to be on the Amazon ecosystem. Moreover, the State of Goiás, which was separated into the States of Goiás and Tocantins in 1988, is also included entirely since it was not possible to obtain data for some variables for Tocantins alone prior to 1988. For the years after 1988, we combined the data for Goiás and Tocantins.

Our aim is to estimate the causes of the expansion of the deforestation. Since the data on the extent of deforestation measured by satellite, for all states of the Amazon, is only available after 1988, we approximate the agro-pastoral frontier evolution by analyzing the change in the proportion of crop area and the density of cattle-head through time. It is important to note that this is a different approach from the methodology undertaken by Reis (1996) and Andersen et al. (1996), which used census data at the municipality level and estimated the cleared area as cropland plus pastureland and planted forest. Since the Agriculture Census is not available yearly, we opted to use annual data, but losing information on the extension of pastureland. Our study also differs from Andersen et al. (1997) who estimated the probability of forest land being converted into crop area or pastureland.

Each indirect deforestation source is analyzed in a separate regression. Data for crop area was obtained from the Pesquisa Agrícola Municipal (PAM) and the data for cattle-head was taken from the Pesquisa Pecuaria Municipal (PPM), both surveys are undertaken yearly by the IBGE at the municipal level. Nevertheless, since economic variables such as prices, wages, credit and roads are only available annually, we aggregated the municipal information. There are substantial differences between the results reported by the PAM and PPM when compared with the Agriculture Census. Since the census is a more detailed survey we will expect it to be more precise with respect to estimated crop area. Nevertheless the PAM and the PPM are the only annual agriculture surveys available, and although we observe its limitations and interpret the results obtained here with caution, it is the best source available.

The price of agriculture products was calculated using a moving base Laspeyres index. Two types of indices were constructed: one using all products and another using only the five most important products for each state.[18] The price of each product was obtained implicitly from the PAM by dividing the reported value of production by the quantity produced of each crop. The indexes were then deflated by the general price index (IGP-OG) with a 1994 = 100 base.

Land prices were obtained from the Fundação Getulio Vargas (FGV) for crop area and pastureland. Prices are available by semester and an average was calculated in order to obtain annual figures. The price of land given in real per hectare were then deflated and expressed in 1994 currency. Rural wages for permanent workers were also obtained from the FGV database.[19] Monthly wages were averaged to get annual figures and then deflated in order to obtain real wages in terms of 1994 currency.

For both land prices and rural wages we are missing variables for five observations. Two alternatives were used to complete the series. First, a linear interpolation was used between the years for which data was available. Second, we analyzed the evolution of the missing variables in neighbor states and assumed that the variables behaved as an average of the change in neighbor states. We undertook a simple comparison of both strategies for years where data was available and found that the second methodology yielded more accurate estimations.

The extension of paved and unpaved roads was obtained from the Geipot statistical yearbook. The yearbook provides data on the extension of paved and unpaved roads in kilometers for all Brazilian states. For 1994, the data was not available for some states and we undertook a linear interpolation between 1993 and 1995. It is important to note that due to depreciation and lack of investment the extension of roads decreased in some periods.

Data on soil quality was obtained from soil maps available from the IBGE tabulated in the DESMAT dataset.[20] The soil quality variable was calculated as the percentage area of each state that have soils considered of high quality. This variable is imperfectly measured due to the aggregation of soil types that made it impossible to separate medium quality soils from high quality soils. Another important variable is the distance from the main market that is used as a proxy for transportation costs. The distance of each state capital to the national capital Brasilia was calculated.

Finally, government agriculture and livestock credit was obtained from the Central Bank Rural Credit Annual Yearbook. It includes total rural credit that was granted by government institutions for rural activities. Two adjustments were undertaken on total rural credit figures. For agriculture credit, we subtracted credit given for extractive activities which we think do not influence the crop choice. For livestock credit, we subtracted all credit granted for other activities other than cattle ranching. Both credit variables were then converted to 1994 currency and deflated by the IGP-OG.

6.5 RESULTS

We estimate two versions of equation (6.2): one using the density of cattle-head as the dependent variable and another using the proportion of crop area as the dependent variable. Both equations are estimated independently. Although it is widely agreed that deforestation agents first use the land for temporary crops and then introduce cattle, it was not possible to introduce a structural approach due to the difference in the type of our data (we do not have the area devoted to cattle, only the number of cattle-heads).

We estimate both equations by fixed effects and random effects and use the Hausman test to decide which estimator is more accurate. A drawback from using a fixed effect estimator is that we lose the variables, that do not vary over time such as the soil quality and distance to federal capital. Therefore, we present both results. Additionally, in order to correct possible mis-specifications due to heteroscedasticity and serial correlation, we estimate a GLS model which accounts for the existence of heteroscedasticity and serial correlation.

The estimations were undertaken in linear and log form, in order to decrease the effect of outliers. The logarithmic specification resulted in a better fit according to expected signs of coefficients and significance. Therefore, we only present the estimated equations in logarithmic form, which yields a direct elasticity estimate. Estimated results for cattle-head density and crop density are presented in Tables 6.6 and 6.7 respectively. Both equations are estimated as a function of four types of variables: output prices and input prices, government subsidized credit, road availability, distance to the market and the proportion of high quality soil. Of course, variables that do not vary over time (distance and high quality soil) drop out when we estimate the fixed effect model. For each equation, we estimate two alternative specifications: one with all the available explanatory variables and another excluding the non-significant variables. As mentioned before, some deforestation econometric models use the rural population density as an explanatory variable. We expect its effects on land use decisions to be captured in wages and land prices. Nonetheless, we include rural population density together with price variables in order to test for its significance.

Estimated Values for Density of Cattle

The results for the regression on the behavior of cattle-head density are reported in Table 6.6. The dependent variable is the density of cattle-head (number of cattle-heads divided by the state area) and the independent variables used are the price of pastureland, the price of cattle-head, rural wage, government credit, paved and unpaved roads, distance to federal capital and the proportion of high quality soil.

Table 6.6 Determinants of cattle-head density in the Brazilian Amazon, 1980–95

Independent variables	Alternative Models		
	(1) Fixed effects	(2) Random effects	(3) GLS-AR
ln (price of cattle-head lagged) $_{it}$	−0.398	−0.377	−0.240
	(0.095)*	(0.106)*	(0.092)*
ln (price of pastureland lagged) $_{it}$	−0.046	−0.080	−0.037
	(0.076)	(0.082)	(0.058)
ln (cattle credit density lagged) $_{it}$	0.034	0.062	0.060
	0.024	(0.026)*	(0.019)*
ln (paved road density lagged) $_{it}$	0.307	0.261	0.174
	(0.063)*	(0.064)*	(0.058)*
ln (unpaved road density lagged) $_{it}$	0.104	0.210	0.404
	(0.049)*	(0.051)*	(0.046)*
ln (distance to federal capital) $_{i}$	—	−0.799	−0.676
		(0.149)*	(0.100)*
Constant	3.221	9.168	8.655797
	(0.454)*	(1.037)*	(0.640)*
F-test all $f_i = 0$	30.26		
Breusch-Pagan LM test for $f_i = 0$,		X^2 (1) = 45.66 *Prob* > chi^2 = 0.0	
Hausman test	X^2 (5) = 0 *Prob* > chi^2 = 1.0		
N	128	128	128
R^2	0.58		
Log-likelihood			5.144

Note: Dependent variable: ln (cattle-head density)
Standard errors are in parentheses. * Indicates variables significant at 5% level. States included in the regression are AC, AM, MA, MT, PA, RO, RR.

Although the price of beef is an important variable, it is not available for individual states in the Amazon. We include this variable varying through time, but not between states. The other variables are the same as used for explaining the evolution of agriculture land density, except that we add the price of cattle, which is an input to the cattle-head activity instead of rural wage since cattle ranching is not a labor-intensive activity. The price of land used refers to pastureland and the credit variable consists of government credit given to cattle ranching activities. It is important to note that as we have no data for cattle ranching land use, we use cattle-head density as a proxy for pastureland expansion.[21]

The result for the three regressions are as follows. A fixed effect regression (1) that is compared with a random effect regression (2) and for which the Hausman test was undertaken. The random effect regression takes into account the variables that do not vary over time: distance to federal capital. Since all variables are lagged, there is a high chance of a shock in one period propagating into the next one. The dynamics in our model are likely to be mis-specified in our estimation due to serial correlation. Therefore, the last column estimates a GLS model assuming an auto-regressive AR(1) process.

First, if we look at columns (1) and (2) we find quite similar results except for the significance in the credit variable. The price of beef was not found to be significant in any of the regressions undertaken, and is thus not included in the reported results. The same was true with rural wage, although this was already expected for the cattle ranching activity. The price of pastureland has the expected negative sign, but it is not found to be statistically significant in any of our specifications. On the other hand, the price of cattle has the expected negative sign and it is significant at a 5 percent level in all three specifications. This result could be an indication that in choosing the inputs for the cattle activity, land and cattle, farmers are more sensitive to changes in the price of cattle. The estimates imply that the elasticity of cattle density to the price of cattle varies between 0.24 and 0.39 depending on the specification chosen.

The density of government credit for agriculture has the expected positive sign in all three regressions, although it is not statistically significant in the fixed effect estimation. In the other two specifications the elasticity is quite similar varying between 0.60 and 0.62. This result was expected and confirms the historical importance of government credit subsidies in the Amazon region. The other expected positive signs are on paved and unpaved roads. It is widely known that roads induce higher deforestation because they decrease transport costs, increasing profitability and open frontier areas. In all three specifications, paved and unpaved roads are found to be significant with a positive sign, although their impact varies across equations. The fixed effect estimation seems to overestimate the paved road coefficient and underestimate the unpaved road coefficient while the third model that takes into account serial correlation does exactly the opposite. The elasticity of cattle-head density with respect to paved roads varies between 0.17 and 0.30 while the elasticity of unpaved roads varies between 0.10 and 0.40. In the random effect estimation, paved and unpaved roads seem to have quite similar effects on the expansion of cattle.

Finally, we introduce the distance to the federal capital in the last two estimations. The expected negative sign is found, implying that states that are far away in the frontier, controlling for other variables, have a lower cattle-head density. This effect can be capturing precipitation levels, which are quite important for a profitable cattle activity and it is not included in our model. States localized further away in the north have higher average precipitation rates and a lower probability of succeeding with cattle activities (Chomitz and Thomas, 2000).

The Hausman test cannot reject the hypothesis that the coefficients from the fixed effect and random effect estimations are the same. Therefore, we are able to assume that the repressors are not correlated with the error term that only varies in the cross-section. In this way, theory would say that the random effect estimation would be more efficient. We opted for presenting the fixed effect estimation as well because it would be hard to believe that no correlation exists between repressors and other types of fixed effects, which are not included in the random effect estimation. Additionally, other types of mis-specifications could result from the lack of a dynamic model introducing the possibility of serial correlation. We treat this problem by estimating a GLS model assuming that the error term follows an AR(1) process over time. In general, the estimated coefficients are similar to the results obtained from the random effects model. Nonetheless, if serial correlation is present, this model would be more efficient in generating our estimators. We observe that once we model the serial correlation, the coefficient on the lag of the price of cattle decreases considerably, while the coefficient on unpaved roads increased substantially.

Estimation Values for Agricultural Cleared Area

For the agriculture cleared land density, the output price used is a Laspeyres index calculated with the five most important products in each state. Similar to what was done for the cattle-head density, Table 6.7 presents three specifications. The agriculture estimation uses data on wages and the proportion of high quality soil, together with similar variables used in the cattle-head equation such as credit, paved roads and unpaved roads and open frontier areas. Additionally, we would expect the price of land to play a crucial role in determining the crop area. It is important to note that due to data restrictions, the price index of agriculture output uses data from 1980 until 1994.

Table 6.7 Determinants of cultivated area in the Brazilian Amazon, 1980–95

Independent variables	Alternative specifications		
	Fixed effects (1)	Random effects (2)	GLS AR (3)
ln (price of agriculture products lagged)	– 0.007	0.250	0.117
	(0.053)	(0.084)*	(0.057)*
ln (price of crop land lagged)	– 0.046	– 0.048	– 0.129
	(0.053)	(0.087)	(0.059)*
ln (rural wage lagged)	–0.198	–0.302	–0.149
	(0.115)**	(0.234)	(0.115)
ln (agriculture credit density lagged)	0.060	0.247	0.148
	(0.0266)*	(0.039)*	(0.034)*
ln (paved road density lagged)	0.273	0.494	0.425
	0.068*	(0.056)*	(0.066)*
ln (unpaved road density lagged)	0.052	0.373	0.216
	(0.046)	(0.047)*	(0.051)*
ln (distance to federal capital)	—	0.246	–0.220
		(0.114)*	(0.137)
ln (proportion of high quality soil)	—	0.269	0.390
		(0.035)*	(0.051)*
Constant	1.902	2.568	6.056
	(0.331)*	(0.914)*	(0.954)*
F-test all $fi = 0$	42.71		89.65
Breusch-Pagan LM test for $fi = 0$		X^2 (1) = 108.60 *Prob > chi*^{2} = 0.0	
Hausman test	X^2 (6)= 19.86 *Prob > chi*^{2} = 0.0029		
N	120	120	120
Log-likelihood R^2	0.34		2.69

Note: Dependent variable: ln (proportion of crop area)
Standard errors are in parentheses. * Indicates variables significant at 5 percent level and ** indicates variables significant at the 1 percent level. States included in the regression are AC, AM, MA, MT, PA, RO, RR.

In contrast to the equation of cattle-head, the result from the Hausman test rejects the hypothesis that the coefficients from the fixed effect and random effect estimations are the same. Therefore, the random effect estimation yields biased coefficients given that regressors are not orthogonal to the fixed-effect error term. Nevertheless, as we did for the cattle-head equation, we also undertake an estimation using GLS, assuming an AR(1) serial correlation pattern in the error term. Moreover, in the models presented in columns (2) and (3) the price of output has the expected positive sign. A higher price of output creates incentives for increasing the crop area. Nevertheless, once we control for fixed effects this relationship disappears. This could be due to the importance of the price of output for large farms and commercial agriculture, but not for family farms and subsistence peasants. This lack of response of agriculture clearing to output prices was also found by Cropper and Griffiths (1999) in Thailand, who tested the effect of the prices of rice and other crops such as cassava and maize on land clearing expansion and did not find any evidence of incentives for deforestation created by agriculture output price variation.

This result could indicate that shifting cultivation, which does not have access to major markets, could be responsible for an important part of agriculture clearing in the Brazilian Amazon. Another important point relates to the motive for clearing the land. If land is cleared mainly as a frontier process, the pattern of deforestation would be dominated by the race for property rights and we would not expect agriculture price variations to have a significant effect on deforestation.

Rural wage is also found to be significant with the expected negative sign in the first specification. A higher rural wage, keeping everything else constant, increases the cost of clearing and reduces the pressure on agriculture land conversion. On the other hand, a higher rural wage could also mean that the farmer would substitute labor for land, therefore generating a positive relationship between wage and land clearing. In our results, rural wage is not found to be significant in models (2) and (3).

The price of land is expected to play a dual role in deforestation incentives. Higher prices decrease the demand for land as an input and therefore decrease the incentives for agriculture land clearing. In contrast, a higher price for land creates a wealth for deforestation agents by increasing expected prices, generating sustained speculative processes. This effect can only be picked up in models which include time series variables since price change dynamics are not incorporated in cross-section spatial models such as Chomitz and Gray (1996) and Pfaff (1999). The price of land is only found to be significant in explaining the proportion of crop area once we take into account serial correlation. The negative sign indicates that a higher price of land would reduce the demand for additional crop areas. Nonetheless, once we control for fixed effects the importance of the price of land seems to disappear. This could be a result of the lack of formal land markets in several regions in the Amazon due to large open access areas and a high cost of investment to obtain property rights.

The effect of government credit on agricultural land clearing is also complex. We assume that credit affects the way in which the farmer allocates inputs by facilitating the acquiring of more land, the incorporation of more capital (tractors) and purchase of more seeds as well as other infrastructure necessities. Therefore, we would expect that, keeping everything else constant, more subsidized credit from the government would induce additional land clearing. Nevertheless, it is important to take into account possible simultaneity. Usually land is used as collateral for credit. Therefore, states with a larger share of cleared land are more likely to receive a major proportion of credit. In order to avoid simultaneity problems we used a lagged credit variable in order to explain current crop area density.

Rural agriculture credit has a positive sign and is highly significant for all three specifications. Although rural government credit disbursements have been reduced for the Amazon region during the last decade, it still constitutes an important incentive for cropping in many areas. This result is related to previous work of Andersen and Reis (1997), which found a significant effect of credit in deforestation incentives.

The other variables related to government policies include roads. Paved road density expansion is considered as a main reason for deforestation in the Amazon. Our estimates confirm this result, as paved road density is highly significant and has the expected positive coefficient. Our results confirm the hypothesis that roads are among the main determinants driving the deforestation process in the Brazilian Amazon. Conversely, unpaved roads are not found to be significant once we take into account fixed effects. Nevertheless, the coefficient has a positive sign different from the previous result obtained by Pfaff (1999).

The variables are found to be significant with the expected signs in all three models, except unpaved roads, which are not significant once we control for fixed effects. Moreover, the paved road coefficient decreases considerably when compared with the other models once fixed effects are controlled. The same effect occurs with credit that has the expected positive sign in all three specifications, but its coefficient is much lower in the fixed effects estimation.

The goodness of fit of the model is acceptable, although including property right structures, different agriculture technology, productivity and other agro-ecological factors as well as other infrastructure variables, could help explain the deforestation dynamics better.

Although based on our tests heteroscedasticity does not seem to be a problem, the time structure of our data would suggest the presence of serial correlation. This is likely to happen due to mis-specification. Although we are estimating a static panel data model, a dynamic model would seem to represent a more precise indication of the process driving deforestation. Due to several complications that arise in estimating parameters with fixed effects and dynamic models, we leave this for future applications.

6.6 FINAL COMMENTS AND POLICY RECOMMENDATIONS

Deforestation in the Brazilian Amazon is a complex phenomenon. The forest conversion process is undertaken by several economic agents such as family farmers, large cattle ranchers, frontier settlers, land speculators and logging companies. Moreover, markets as well as institutions and government policies influence the process. Therefore, modeling its dynamics is not an easy task.

We use a simple model of the cleared land market in order to obtain a reduced form equation. We advanced beyond previous studies by using annual panel data at the state level in order to measure the causes of agriculture land clearing in the Brazilian Amazon. Moreover, previous econometric studies of the causes of deforestation had only used data until 1985.

The conversion of forest into pastureland is still the main source of deforestation in the region. This is found both by analyzing the land use pattern comparing the Agriculture Census of 1985 and 1996 and by observing the evolution of the cattle-herd in the Amazon. Nevertheless, such an observation does not explain why cattle formation has been increasing. Cattle ranching is the main source of forest conversion in the Brazilian Amazon. Nonetheless, it is not easy to understand its dynamics only in terms of economic returns. With an average of 0.3 animals per hectare in the whole region (Chomitz and Thomas, 2000) and with an internal rate of return for the activity that varies from 4 percent to 14 percent (Schneider et al., 2000), additional incentives must exist in order to generate such a massive investment in cattle ranching. Part of this process is explained by large government subsidies and the need to use the land for acquiring property rights.

Based on our estimates, we find that there are two types of factors driving the increasing cattle-head density. On the one side decreasing prices of land and cattle had allowed farmers to increase their stock. Nonetheless, our econometric results suggest that the decreasing price of cattle is more important than the change in the price of land. On the other hand, government policies, especially credit and road construction, are directly related to cattle-head expansion in the region. Both paved and unpaved roads have an important effect on pasture conversion. The lack of importance of the decrease in the price of beef is surprising, but could have been compensated by the decreasing price of inputs. The decrease in the price of pastureland has helped small and large owners to obtain land through markets and develop cattle-related activity. Walker et al. (2000) have found evidence that smaller farmers are responsible for a substantial portion of deforestation in the Amazon by adopting pasture and cattle ranching activities.

The construction of a paved road network has created access to potential markets and decreased transport costs. Nevertheless, our estimates present evidence that unpaved roads are also responsible for a substantial portion of cattle-head expansion, probably more associated with smaller farmers activities.

The expansion of crop area density, although a smaller source of deforestation in the Amazon, is also important since part of the land conversion process is undertaken through nutrient mining. Farmers first convert forest into crop area, use the soil as much as they can and then, when productivity has been sufficiently reduced by nutrient mining, the area is converted to pasture.

Changes in the demand for agriculture-cleared area seem to be more affected by economic variables. Output prices are found to be significant in two of our specifications. Surprisingly, land prices are not found to be significant in explaining agriculture land clearing, except when serial correlation is taken into account. This could be due to the lack of dynamics in our model, which generates mis-specification problems.

Rural wages are found to be significant in the fixed effect model, indicating that reductions in the real rural wage decreases the opportunity cost of going into the frontier and, at the same time, reduces the cost of hiring temporary labor for land clearing activities. Similar to what was found in cattle ranching, government agriculture credit is found to be significant in explaining agricultural land clearing.

Paved roads, as expected, are also found to cause agricultural land clearing. Road construction decreases transportation costs of inputs and outputs and creates networks for production distribution. Roads also facilitate the migration process and integrate rural labor markets, thereby increasing incentives for land clearing. Additionally, unpaved roads are also significant in explaining the evolution of crop area. This result is important due to the growing timber logging activities in the Amazon, which open small unpaved roads to extract timber creating the possibility for new peasant movement to the frontier.

Although the current study generates important insights on the deforestation process of the Brazilian Amazon, there are several data and methodological limitations. A better comprehension of the deforestation process could be obtained with more desegregated data, such as at the municipal level, or even household units. Such data would enable the application of spatial econometric techniques, which are crucial in understanding spatial deforestation distribution. Nevertheless, another important component of the deforestation process is dynamics. A dynamic model is needed in order to fully understand the effects of land prices, speculation and history dependence of previous settlements

Another point is related to the proxies used for deforestation. It would be important to combine as undertaken by Pfaff (1999) local census data with satellite images in order to analyze both the spatial and dynamic distribution of deforestation. Nevertheless, this type of data is not available yet under a large time-series with sufficient spatial distribution

Another important point is related to the contribution of logging to deforestation, especially in the 1990s. A reliable database is needed in order to access the contribution of logging to deforestation and create environmental policies that are related to the sources of deforestation in the region. Institutional factors are also important, and the incorporation of property rights in econometric models should be undertaken in the future. The dynamics of the frontier can only be fully understood once such institutional effects are introduced in the model. Technology adoption and technical change are other important features to be studied. An increase in technological change could either increase or decrease deforestation depending on the factors used and the type of technological change introduced. Therefore, understanding the effect of agriculture R&D on deforestation is crucial for sustainable policy formulations.

Finally, the results found here emphasize the importance of paved roads in driving both cattle ranching and crop area expansion. The Brazilian government is proposing under the Avança Brasil,[22] the construction of a network of paved roads in order to foster growth and development in the Amazon region. The possible effect of such infrastructure building, given the prevailing incentives and institutional background, are likely to accelerate deforestation while imposing serious doubts on the sustainable and equitable economic growth in the region.

NOTES

1. These estimates are based on INPE (2000) subtracting the estimated cleared area in 1998 from the estimated cleared area in 1978.
2. See Fearnside (1996) for a comparison of deforestation estimates.
3. For a description and analysis of this process see Alston et al. (1995) and Schneider (1995).
4. Moreover, Alves (1999) also seems to indicate that major deforestation processes are taking place near pioneer settlement areas opened up in the 1980s.
5. The region defined as the Legal Amazon comprises the states of Acre, Amapá, Amazonas, Maranhão (west of the 44° W), Mato Grosso, Pará, Rondônia, Roraima and Tocantins. Nevertheless, data on the state of Amapá was not available for the whole analyzed period.
6. See Helfand (1999) for a comparison of the 1995 census results with the PAM.
7. Nonetheless, another explanation for the change from 1985 to 1996 could be the different date in which the census was undertaken.
8. See Brandão (1988) for an analysis of the determinants of the price of land in Brazil.
9. Although there are some problems of comparability between both censuses, a general trend can be inferred by comparing their results. For a description of the change of methodology that was undertaken by IBGE for the 1995/96 census and its possible consequences see Helfand (1999).
10. It is important to note that the area devoted to agriculture is underestimated due to the change in the date for which the 1995/96 census was undertaken.
11. Although it would be desirable to estimate a structural model linking both sources, we do not undertake such a task due to data restrictions: the area for agriculture cannot be directly linked with the data for cattle-head. Only the use of census data would permit such a task.
12. See Granger and Hyung (1997) for possible problems of spurious correlation that occur when omitting size variables.
13. Of course, it would be more precise to divide it by the size of the potential agricultural area. Nevertheless, such figures are not available.
14. There are indirect methods of retrieving such estimates.
15. Moreover, an increase in the price of land diminishes the possibility of poorer farmers to buy land, creating incentives for penetration into open access areas.
16. One exception for this problem would be if the demand and supply are undertaken by the same economic agent as occurs in some regions of the Amazon.
17. For the Amazonian context, a variable that reflects the property right structure could be used as an instrument. We would expect property right structure to affect the behavior of land clearing, but not the demand for agriculture land. In a reduced form estimation, the property right structure would only affect the equilibrium amount of cleared land through its effect on the price of land. Although such a variable is available from the Agriculture Census, it is not available for all the years we are using.
18. The most important products were ranked according to crop area and production. Both categorizations yielded approximately the same results.
19. Similar calculations were undertaken for temporary workers, but did not introduce any significant changes in our results.
20. For a description of the DESMAT data set see Andersen and Reis (1997).

21. Although we know this is a far from perfect proxy due to the intensification of the cattle ranching activity in some states of the Amazon, we hope to obtain an approximate answer for the pattern of deforestation dynamics driven by the cattle ranching activity. Similar analysis was undertaken by Barbier and Burgess (1995).
22. See Nepstad et al. (2000) for an overview of the Avança Brasil project.

7. Summary of main findings in Brazil

7.1 TRADE, COMPETITIVENESS AND INDUSTRIAL POLLUTION IN BRAZIL

This study attempts to analyze the environmental profile of the Brazilian industrial sector using input–output modeling and describing results of environmental management indicators from a survey in the State of São Paulo.

In order to capture all industrial pollution generated in the whole industrial processing of a manufactured good we need to account for all emission flows from the input production up to the assembling phase. Such an approach requires the application of an input–output model (I–O) relating changes on demand vectors to potential industrial pollution levels.

The exercises were carried out using the I–O matrices of the Brazilian Statistical Office (IBGE). Four different sets of emission coefficients were used. The first one was estimated using pollution emission and abatement estimates for Brazilian industry for the year 1988 according to a World Bank-funded project denominated PRONACOP (Brazilian National Program of Pollution Control). The second one was the Industrial Pollution Projection System (IPPS), developed by the World Bank using data from the US industry for the year 1987. The third set of emission coefficients were calculated using emission data of industrial plants in São Paulo (estimated in the inventory of the state EPA, CETESB) related to industrial surveys' data on value added, for the year 1996. The fourth group of coefficients refers to carbon dioxide emissions from fossil fuel consumption in Brazil in the period 1990–94, estimated by COPPE/UFRJ.

The environmental management indicators were taken from the 1996 field survey ('PAEP') conducted by the statistical office of the State of São Paulo investigating, among other things, firms' decisions on environmental investments.

The results of these input–output exercises, using constant coefficients for industrial emissions, showed that the production chain associated with Brazilian industrial exports is more intensive in emissions than the production chains oriented towards domestic markets. This trend was observed for most of the pollution parameters analyzed, despite the diversity of sources for the emission coefficients, suggesting that the Brazilian industry has been relatively specialized in the supply of potentially polluting goods to international markets. This result is, thus, compatible with the hypothesis that developing countries tend to concentrate on 'dirty' industries that become less competitive in developed countries because of tighter environmental controls.

This process was, nevertheless, counterbalanced by the emissions 'savings' created by fast expansion of imports during the 1990s. The avoidance of emissions associated with the import goods, however, could have been greater if rising industrial imports were not concentrated in relatively clean activities, particularly those with higher intensity in technology (electronics, for example), while the structure of industrial exports remained associated with more emission-intensive sectors (mainly semi-manufactured and intermediate goods).

Another important result was that the direct costs of introducing environmental control strategies are relatively low, considering the industry as a whole. However, since these costs vary widely among sectors and destination markets, the impacts of introducing pollution abatement measures may be considerable in some specific industries, damaging their competitiveness. The industries with the highest risks of losing markets include footwear, non-ferrous metallurgic and other metallurgic industries and, in regional terms, the exports destined to the NAFTA region.

The static nature of input–output exercises, however, does not allow capturing the so-called technological effect, which is essentially dynamic and very difficult to measure and model. The PAEP survey, obtained from industries in the State of São Paulo, showed that firms with international insertion tend to be more concerned with environmental issues, to invest more in 'cleaning' their production processes, and to perceive the competitive advantages of environmental innovations. This is associated with higher environmental standards and pressures in international markets, thus being compatible with the hypothesis that the trade and capital openness process tends to encourage the adoption of environmentally sound practices and products.

These results have important implications for policy making. First of all, it is clear that the relatively high concentration of Brazilian industrial exports in pollution-intensive activities makes these exports very sensitive to the issue of environmental barriers to trade. If there is a change in the institutional framework regulating international trade towards the acceptance of environmental criteria for imports control, as advocated by many environmentalist organizations in developed countries, there could be important losses to Brazilian industrial exports. There are two possible strategies to deal with this problem:

1. to adopt an aggressive position against the proposed changes in trade regulations, maintaining the status quo of none/very restricted environmental barriers in the international trade agreements; and/or
2. to enhance the environmental performance of Brazilian industries, either improving local emission standards or changing the composition of industrial exports, becoming less dependent on exports associated with 'dirty' production chains.

Even though these strategies are not contradictory, they reflect different perspectives. Option (1) reflects a view that the claims for environmental restrictions in trade (and capital) flows are a short-term pressure, which will not be approved in the future. However, one possible problem that may emerge in the forthcoming years is that, with the deepening of regional trade agreements such as Mercosul and possibly the American Free Trade Agreement, Brazilian producers could face competition from the exports from neighbor countries that are subject to much less environmental controls, since Brazil is a leader in Latin America in terms of environmental controls. This would be a reversal of the present situation, and in that case the Brazilian producers could be the losers if no standardization of environmental controls are adopted.

Therefore, the second strategy seems to be a better way to deal with the problem in the long term. There is a smooth but consistent change in the perception of Brazilian policy makers towards the adoption of economic instruments in environmental management, based on the user/polluter-pays principle, and as a consequence some sectors may present short-term losses in their competitiveness. But the good news the results above show are that this overall cost increase may be considerably less than usually thought (with the exception of some specific sectors, which could receive special compensation policies during the transition to cleaner production), and that many firms are already searching voluntarily for better environmental procedures. This is another important feature of international trade that counterbalances the original problem of specialization in emission-intensive activities: the pressures of consumers in developed countries are 'reaching their target', in the sense that export-oriented and/or foreign-owned firms tend to see the potential gains from adopting environmental innovations in a different way from firms that are not exposed to these pressures.

However, this transition towards a more environmentally sound economy cannot rely on a laissez-faire belief that the simple exposition of Brazilian firms to the market will be a move towards the desired situation. One important step is the already referred push for economic instruments for environmental management, allowing flexible but efficient measures to improve environmental standards. This must be combined with industrial policies aiming the spread of win–win environmental innovations (energy and other inputs savings; better access to markets, particularly in developed countries; higher quality and efficiency standards associated with changes in processes associated with environmentally-friendly measures etc.). Some examples of these policies are the strengthening of the firm to absorb and generate environmentally-related technologies; investment in human capital at the basic and professional levels; reduction in the regional differences in environmental performance; and incentives to certification and domestic consumers' perception of the benefits of environmentally sound products and processes, creating a domestic market for 'green' products.

A final comment refers to the limitations of the empirical exercises because of data quality and methodological problems. This indicates the urgent need for improvements in the gathering and systematization of environmental indicators and statistics concerning industrial pollution.

7.2 CONSUMPTION PATTERN, INCOME DISTRIBUTION AND THE ENVIRONMENT IN BRAZIL

To analyze consumption patterns for urban income groups in Brazil, we have estimated household degradation level (E) for each income class estimated by the product of its propensity to degrade to the average household income of each class. In turn, propensity to degrade (Pmg) is estimated as the propensity to consume weighted by the pollution intensity of each consumption item.

Note that Pmg will be related to the cross-effect of the pollution intensity, a technological factor, and income elasticity of demand captured by the propensity to consume that, in turn, is an income composition factor. Total degradation E, on the other hand, will also capture income scale effects since it will be also dependent on income levels.

If we know E for relevant pollutants and environmental uses, it is possible to measure environmental pressure levels by distinct consumption patterns. Furthermore, knowing Pmg_i we will be able to analyze how income changes within the economy will affect this pressure.

Transfer of income within an economy changes degradation pressures that will be given by the difference between the Pmg of the donor individual and the beneficiary one. In order to produce an exercise on changes in degradation we have created illustrative scenarios assuming progressive and regressive transfer schedules.

The progressive scenario represented a transfer of richest classes equivalent to 7 percent of their income or in absolute values, a transfer of US$ 10 billion (at 1995 exchange rate) or 3 percent of total urban income in Brazil in the year 1995.

In the regressive scenario, the poorest classes lost about 20 percent of their total income. So this scenario can be seen as a very radical regressive case. In absolute values this represented a transfer of US$ 3.7 billion (at 1995 exchange rate) or about 1 percent of total urban income in Brazil in the year 1995.

Due to data availability for pollution intensity indicators, our analysis will be limited to two production sources (industrial and agricultural) and three direct consumption sources (transportation, water and sewage) following these main environmental effects:

1. industrial water pollution from organic and inorganic matters and air pollution from sulfur dioxide (SO_2) and particulate;
2. agricultural pollution from fertilizer use;
3. household transportation pollution from atmospheric emissions from carbon monoxide (CO), hydrocarbons (HC) and nitrogen oxide (NO_x);
4. household water consumption;
5. household sewage discharge.

We will concentrate our estimates to urban areas since most of our consumption pattern data is restricted to that and they represent more than 90 percent of national personal income. Estimates also will be related to the year 1995 to which the latest data on income group expenditures is available.

Industrial pollution is estimated based on input–output modeling, as mentioned in the previous study, and therefore accounts for each emission flow related to the production of this good from the input production up to the assembling phase. Degradation from direct consumption is measured based on quantum indicators.

Although this exercise is exclusively associated with specific distribution scenarios and should not be generalized, they illustrate that income distribution changes are not highly affected by significant changes in degradation pressures, which raises some interesting issues on the relationship between income distribution and the environment in Brazil.

Our results show that there is a negative relationship between income and Pmg. The poor tend, mainly due to their high propensity to consume, to degrade more per unit of consumption. However, no evidence of an inverse U curve shape is found in our estimates of degradation pressure levels by income groups. In most cases, the richest class can generate as much as 10 to 20 times the degradation of the lowest income group.

In sum, the great concentration of income was always enough to compensate for variations in propensity to consume and, when it applied, also for variations in technological factors among income groups. For example, propensities to degrade from transportation have showed this inverse U shape for urban transportation, particularly due to the great reduction on emission levels of new cars usually owned by rich people. Even in this case, a continuous positive relationship to income was identified for degradation pressure. That is, even observing the inverse U shape for transport Pmg, we cannot see any quadratic relationship between income and per household pollution. Again scale effects are so significant that all emissions show a positive relationship with income.

Secondly, using our estimates of propensity to degrade for each source and income class, we measured concentration ratios for degradation pressure by dividing total degradation pressure estimates of the 10 percent richest people by the 50 percent poorest ones. Except for non-treated water and non-collected sewage, which do not apply to rich households, for every source we found ratios above 0.4, showing that rich people tend to degrade more than their population share.

Lastly, we analyze how degradation pressure would vary if income distribution was changed in Brazil. As expected, regressive transfer increases degradation and the progressive one decreases. In both cases, however, we found that industrial and transport sources show an inelastic relationship between income distribution and total degradation pressure in which the transferred income share is bigger than the resultant share on degradation pressure.

The high concentration of degradation pressure from rich people's consumption patterns adds another regressive aspect for unequal income distribution in Brazil. In sum, our results bring about serious distributive issues for environmental policy in Brazil, namely:

- Although poor people's consumption level is not the primary source of degradation, they tend to bear most of the degradation impacts due to their low capacity spend on defensive expenditures.
- As degradation pressure is mainly due to high income groups' consumption pattern, any attempt to avoid stricter degradation controls that affect consumption decisions will create a subsidy for the rich people's consumption at the expense of the poor.

However, as degradation concentration ratios are lower than the respective income ratios, when degradation control becomes more stringent, poor people will tend to pay more for environmental control per unit of consumption if these costs are passed through prices.

In fact, this might be already happening for already incurred control costs in the cases of industrial water pollution, which presents the highest control levels for industrial sources. We have been able to compare potential and residual (after control) emissions and from this comparison we observed that concentration ratios for residual levels are higher than potential ones, meaning that the greater part of reduction was done on the poor consumption level.

The implications of our analysis of environmental control on income distribution are crucial for environmental policies aiming at the reduction of degradation pressure in Brazil. If this regressive aspect is to be mitigated, policy instruments have to allow for compensatory measures. In this perspective, the use of environmental taxation may turn out to be a good candidate to account for this since it reduces social control costs and generate revenue that can be recycled in the economy to create room for compensatory policies towards the poor.

7.3 ECONOMIC INCENTIVES AND DEFORESTATION IN THE BRAZILIAN AMAZON

Deforestation in the Brazilian Amazon is a complex phenomenon. The forest conversion process is undertaken by several economic agents such as family farmers, large cattle ranchers, frontier settlers, land speculators and logging companies. Moreover, markets as well as institutions and government policies influence the process. Therefore, modeling its dynamics is not an easy task.

We use a simple model of the cleared land market in order to obtain a reduced form equation that is taken to the data. We advanced beyond previous studies in using an annual panel data at the state level in order to measure the causes of agriculture land clearing and cattle-head expansion in the Brazilian Amazon.

The conversion of forest into pastureland is still the main source of deforestation in the region. This is found both by analyzing the land use pattern, comparing the agriculture censuses of 1985 and 1996 and by observing the evolution of the cattle herd in the Amazon. Nevertheless, such an observation does not explain why cattle formation has been increasing.

We estimate a panel data model for eight states of the Amazon from 1980 to 1995. Based on our estimations, we find that there are two type of factors driving the increasing cattle-head density. On the one side, decreasing prices of land and cattle had allowed farmers to increase their stock. Nonetheless, our econometric results suggest that the decreasing price of cattle is more important than the change in the price of land. On the other side, government policies, especially credit and road construction; are directly related to cattle-head expansion in the region. Both paved and unpaved roads have an important effect on pasture conversion. The lack of importance of the decrease in the price of beef is surprising, but could have been compensated by the decreasing price of inputs. The decrease in the price of pastureland has helped small and large owners to obtain land through markets and develop a cattle-related activity. Walker et al. (2000) have found evidence that smaller farmers are responsible for a substantial portion of deforestation in the Amazon adopting pasture and cattle ranching activities.

The construction of a paved road network has created the access to potential markets and decreased transport costs. Nevertheless, our estimations present evidence that unpaved roads are also responsible for a substantial portion of cattle-head expansion, probably more associated with smaller farmers' activities.

The expansion of crop area density, although a smaller source of deforestation in the Amazon, is also important since part of the land conversion process is undertaken through nutrient mining. Farmers first convert forest into crop area, use the soil as much as they can and then, when productivity has been sufficiently reduced by nutrient mining, the area is converted to pasture.

Changes in the demand for agriculture-cleared area seem to be more affected by economic variables. Output prices are found to be significant in two of our specifications. Surprisingly, land prices are not found to be significant in explaining agriculture land clearing, except when we take into account the possibility of serial correlation. The result could be due to the lack of dynamics in our model, which generates mis-specification problems.

Rural wages are found to be significant in the fixed effect model showing that reductions in the real rural wage decrease the opportunity cost of going into the frontier and, at the same time, reduces the cost of hiring temporary labor for land clearing activities. Similar to what was found in cattle ranching, government agriculture credit is found to be significant in explaining agriculture land clearing.

Paved roads, as expected, are also found to generate agriculture land clearing. Road construction decreases the transportation costs of inputs and outputs and creates networks for production distribution. Roads also facilitate the migration process and integrate rural labor markets. All this increases incentives for land clearing. Additionally, unpaved roads are also significant in explaining the evolution of crop area. This result is important due to the growing timber logging activities in the Amazon, which open small unpaved roads to extract timber, creating the possibility for new peasant movements in the frontier.

Finally, the results found emphasize the importance of paved roads in driving both cattle ranching activity and crop area expansion. The Brazilian government is proposing, under Avança Brasil,[1] the construction of a network of paved roads in order to foster growth and development in the Amazon region. The possible effect of such infrastructure expansion, given the prevailing incentives and institutional background, is likely to generate a boom in the deforestation process while restricting the possibilities of sustainable and equitable economic growth in the region

NOTE

1. See Nepstad et al. (2000) for an overview of the Avança Brasil project.

PART III

Chile Case Study

8. Introduction to computable general equilibrium (CGE) models

Achieving economic growth has been an important issue for over half a century. In recent times developed countries have understood the necessity of a more equitable and environmentally balanced growth. Considering the complexity of modeling an economy with all its interrelations, agents and sectors, common practice has led to the study of the economic, social and environmental policies in isolated form, as a partial equilibrium. Unfortunately, many measures that affect the environment also impact economic growth, poverty, employment and income distribution. Thus, to fully understand the effects of either macroeconomic policies on the environment or the impact of environmental or welfare approaches on macroeconomic policies we need to use models that incorporate the complex interrelations between the diverse sectors and agents of the economy. The last 50 years have seen developments in conceptual areas as well as in the analytic and computational tools that allow the implementation of such models.

During the 1960s, growth and economic development were the central objectives of 'economic planning'. In 1966, Kuznets emphasized that to achieve modern economic growth and to industrialize the developing countries, it would be necessary to introduce drastic and systematic changes in the productive structures along with changes in the demand, employment, investment and international trade. He indicated the relevance of carefully examining the speed and schedule for these changes. Accordingly, carefully planning the growth process, with a relevant level of detail and disaggregation, was deemed fundamental.

The systematic and structural nature of the intended economic changes, and the great velocity with which these were applied, generated consequences that revealed crudely that the productive sectors, trade structures, different markets and their participating agents could not be considered, analyzed or intervened in independently. Productive bottle-necks, excesses in sectoral supply, unsatisfied demand, inefficient resource allocations, in addition to the dependence of national policies and their structural adjustments to international events, increased the necessity to develop multi-sectoral models with increasing disaggregation. These should provide a useful framework to understand and plan structural changes, stressing the interrelations and interdependencies among productive sectors, markets, agents, etc., in setting a general equilibrium.

8.1 FRAMEWORK TO ANALYZE ENVIRONMENTAL, SOCIAL AND ECONOMIC POLICIES[1]

Since the 1960s, input–output models have been the main tools for determining economic policies. However, these models suffer from serious limitations such as their inability to incorporate market mechanisms and processes of optimization, their fixed coefficients and the absence of social and environmental variables. In spite of this, they allow the generation of simple production relationships in the general equilibrium context, and were thus used for these purposes, taking advantage of the incipient development of computer sciences.

In the 1970s, the exclusive concern about growth and development goals began to be perceived as insufficient. The debate about the need to balance economic growth and environmental impacts began with force in 1972 when the Club of Rome published the study 'The Limits to Growth'. Those in charge of generating social and economic policies in addition to all economic agents had to prepare for the incorporation of new relevant variables into their decision processes. The changes in productive structures and the patterns of growth increased their complexity and well-planned development strategies became even more necessary.

In 1987 the Brundtland Commission defined 'sustainable development' as the development that 'allows achieving the needs of the present generations without endangering those of future generations'. In practice, this definition implies that a developing society must meet economic, environmental and social objectives simultaneously (Pearce and Turner, 1990). As a result, current evaluation models take into account a wider diversity of objectives associated to sustainable development. The economic objectives consider the need of economic growth, more equity and efficiency, leaving behind the narrow notion of economic growth used before. The environmental objectives include concerns about systems integrity, biodiversity, ecological thresholds and capacity of assimilation and global topics. Finally, the social objectives include issues on participation, social mobility, cultural identity and institutional development, among others.

Debate over development has continued with more or less conflicting positions, incorporating and trying to integrate economic and environmental variables in the most appropriate way (*The Economist*, 1997; Dasgupta and Mäler, 1998; Kneese, 1998). Evaluations are carried out in a context of partial equilibrium, thereby hindering the analysis of simultaneous implications of equity and the efficiency of measures to protect the environment. In addition, the prevailing economic paradigm, not particularly prone to the 'planning' processes, further highlighted the shortcomings of input–output models when failing to incorporate market mechanisms.

At present, the complexity of direct and indirect interrelations among economic, environmental and social variables calls for models that allow generation of priorities for policies leading to sustainable development. At the same time, these models must take into account market mechanisms and optimizing behaviors, which determine the decisions of the economic agents and impact on the effectiveness of public policies and on the achievement of envisioned productive changes. It requires the progressive generation of more sophisticated analytical tools, which overcome the limitations of the early models. Finally, these models should capture, in commensurable form, the complex concept of sustainability, analyzing in a systemic context the evolution of its three macro-objectives (economic growth, equity and environmental sustainability). Also, it was deemed necessary that these tools could evaluate alternative actions when facing different scenarios, which has become increasingly easier with the exponential development of information processing capacity.

Since the late 1970s and especially in the 1980s, applications based on computable general equilibrium (CGE) models have flourished. These multi-sectoral models solve the limitations of the input–output models as evaluation instruments, representing in a more realistic way the economy of a country by incorporating market mechanisms in the allocation of resources. Also, they have proved to be a useful instrument to describe the main macroeconomic relationships and to evaluate quantitatively ex ante the effects of different economic, social and environmental policies, as well as the indirect effects, which, in many cases, evade the intuition.

Figure 8.1 schematically presents the relationships that can be modeled by means of CGE, based on the circular flow of the economy. It includes the main agents (firms, households and government), flows of goods and services, payments to factors, international trade and relationships with the environment. Each agent is modeled according to certain behavioral assumptions; in particular it is common to assume optimizing producers and consumers. Additionally, each market is modeled according to the specific reality of the economy, for instance, as a competitive or non-competitive market; or in the case of the labor market, with or without full employment. These models reach equilibrium according to the Walras law, that is, by balancing demand and supply at all markets, thus determining prices and quantities. As in input–output models, a fundamental characteristic of the productive sector is that it incorporates the demand for intermediate inputs, not just for capital and labor. However, they differ from the input–output models by allowing the substitution among production inputs. This characteristic furnishes equilibrium, which takes into account the transmission of effects through all the relevant markets. Additionally, the role of the government is included through modeling taxes, subsidies and transfers.

Finally, it must be noted that a CGE model integrates the short-term and long-term analysis, allowing the study of development strategies and growth paths,[2] as well as the assessment of contingent situations and stabilization policies,[3] without losing a sectoral perspective related to technological or investment processes.[4]

8.2 ORIGINS OF THE CGE MODEL

Computable general equilibrium models (CGE), or applied general equilibrium models, are multi-sectoral models that 'try to represent an economy in a realistic way, thus becoming a powerful tool for the quantitative ex-ante evaluation of the effects of a given policy' (de Haan, 1994).

The theoretical origin of the CGE models, and especially those of the neoclassic variety, resides in the theory of general equilibrium of the creation and flow of capital, developed by Walras in *Eléments d'Economie Politique Pure* (1954).[5] Later, this work has stood in contrast to the Marshallian analytic framework based on partial analysis. The neoclassic approach to general equilibrium was elaborated by Debreu (1959) in rigorous form and later on by Arrow and Hahn (1971). The first work, in spite of being mathematically very meticulous, was not devised to be a realistic description of the existing economic systems, but instead constituted a proof of the existence of Pareto-optimal equilibria in a competitive economy under multiple restrictions.

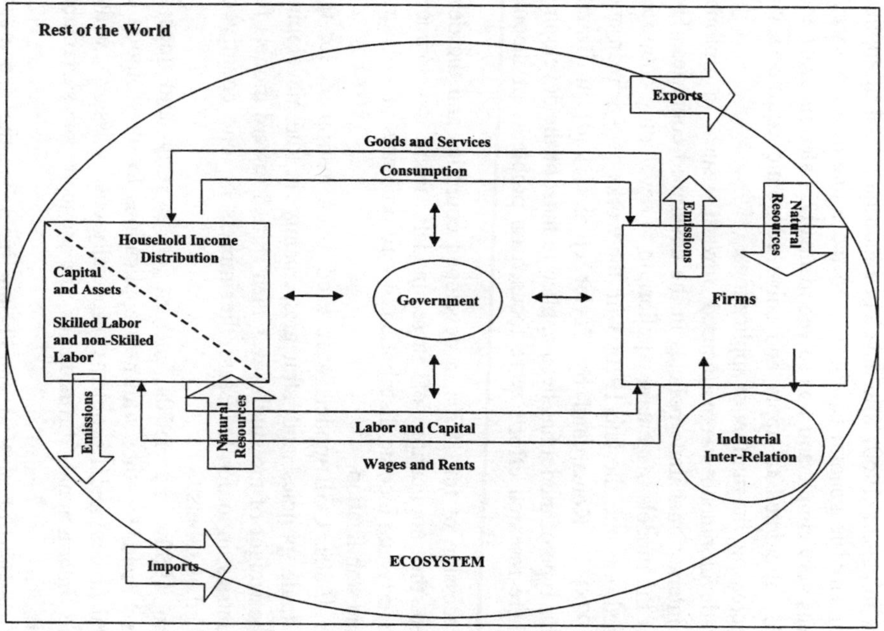

Source: Authors.

Figure 8.1 Economy circular flow

Practical applications were developed based on these theoretical foundations. Thus, Shoven and Whalley (1984) define the CGE model in the following way: 'A computable general equilibrium model represents the evolution of the structure of a Walrasian general equilibrium depicting the economy in abstract form, toward its realistic representation'. On the other hand, Dervis et al. (1982) stress the formalization and mathematical solution in their definition of a general equilibrium model: 'Mathematical Models incorporating the fundamental relationships of general equilibrium between the production structure, the entry of several groups, and the patterns of demand'.

The first practical intent of combining theory and practice was carried out by Johansen (1960) who developed the first model of applied computable or empiric general equilibrium to the economy of Norway. This model was very simple and was solved manually. Later on Scarf and Hansen (1973) attempted to apply and solve economic equilibria via computers, increasing the number of applications.

Later developments were focused toward issues in optimal taxation and international trade policies in the developed countries. The application of the models of general equilibrium to developing countries was not carried out until the late 1970s with the works of Adelman and Robinson (1978) in Korea, and by Taylor et al. (1980) in Brazil. Thereafter, this type of model has been applied to most of the developing countries, where research efforts were focused on problems of income distribution.

The recession of the 1970s in developed countries and the debt crises shifted the application of these models from development strategies, poverty and income distribution toward problems of structural adjustment and stabilization.

In the 1980s, CGE models were used as an instrument for the analysis of trade policies and strategies, mainly in the developing countries. The weight of the studies was then shifted toward models for multiple countries in order to assess the impacts on one country of policies applied by others.

In the 1960s and 1970s, interest on poverty and income distribution returned, together with new applications for the solution of environmental or ecological problems (especially energy issues), which followed the international diffusion of the concept of sustainable development.

Thus, models of general equilibrium have become a standard method for the analysis of a wide variety of policies, including trade, taxation, structural change, foreign exchange and social and environmental issues. Also, the application of optimal control methods to develop economic policies (which was of great interest in the 1960s), found a useful vehicle in CGE modeling based on dynamic optimization.

8.3 EVOLUTION OF THE INTERNATIONAL APPLICATIONS

After the first application of a CGE model, performed for Norway by Johansen (1960), there has been an exponential growth in number and diversity of topics, making it impossible to carry out an exhaustive summary of all of them.[6] As mentioned, first applications were focused on problems of optimal taxation and trade policies in the developed countries (1970s). Adelman and Robinson (1978) and Taylor et al. (1980) carried out the first applications in developing countries. Throughout the 1980s, as a result of the debt crisis, applications in developing[7] countries evolved from the issues of poverty, income distribution and development strategies toward policies of structural adjustment and stabilization. By the end of that decade, the analysis of trade policies and strategies reappeared. In the 1990s, together with recapturing the focus on poverty and income distribution, applications began to target environmental and ecological problems. Devarajan (1997) made a summary and explanation of the evolution and characteristics of the CGE models applied in developing countries with special emphasis on environmental applications.

With regard to income distribution, this new methodological framework allows a better perspective for analysis, given the flexibility assigned to relative prices. In fact, the above-mentioned models for Korea and Brazil dealt mainly with problems of income distribution. With these works emerged an interesting debate on the effects the theoretical perspective underlying in the model could have on the results. It was noticed that the neoclassic pattern generated insensibility in income distribution for a large number of policy simulations in these countries. As will be demonstrated later on, developing countries were not well represented by this theoretical framework and structural rigidities were included in the applications.

The analysis of trade policy is another area where these models showed substantial development. Up to 1990, most of the CGE models applied to the analysis of trade aspects assume perfect competition and constant returns to scale. Therefore, agents are price-takers, which is not realistic in some occasions. Relevant theoretical works in international trade suggest that the international low level of productive specialization is not caused by specific characteristics of the countries but by the existence of economies of scale and imperfect competition (Krugman, 1979). As a result, there were a new generation of CGE models which included imperfect competition (Cox and Harris, 1991; Sobarzo, 1991; Brown et al., 1991) and increasing returns to scale. Under these assumptions, trade liberalization would allow increasing competition in the economies, eliminating monopolistic behaviors. This would result in price reductions, and not necessarily in a gross product slump (rather on the contrary, given the existence of growing yields and the generation of a larger demand from the external markets).

In single country models, domestic relative prices and real exchange rates are determined by the equilibrium of the markets of goods and factors, subject to the fulfillment of the restriction of trade balance. In global and multi-country models, world relative prices are obtained by emptying the world market of tradable products, while real exchange rates derive from satisfying every country's budgetary restriction. As mentioned in the previous section, products are usually differentiated following the Armington assumption.

Finally, models for developing countries depart further from the Walrasian orthodoxy, since these economies present structural rigidities such as fixed wages, absence of factors mobility, etc.[8]

8.4 APPLICATIONS OF CGE MODELS IN CHILE

The applications of CGE models for Chile are few. Early applications tried to analyze the effects of alternative taxation policies on the rest of the economy. Ruiz and Yarur (1990) analyzed the effects on the economy of a change in taxation policies by using a recursive dynamic small and open economy (SOE) model. This study uses data from the I/O 1977, to analyzing the effects on the economy of the change in different taxes. In general, more recent applications have been dedicated to analyze the effect of changes in tariff policies, arising from the debate on trade agreements between Chile and MERCOSUR, NAFTA, European Union, United States of America and Asia-Pacific. Coeymans and Larraín (1994) carried out a study of the consequences of Chile joining NAFTA. The model is set up for SOE, and includes six productive sectors and three regions that trade with each other (Chile, US, Rest of the World or ROW). Data used for this study comes mainly from the I/O table of 1986. The results indicate that an agreement between Chile and the US would generate a new pattern of trade composition with the US and that; in general, a series of benefits would follow the agreement. On the other hand, Harrison et al. (1997) built a model that uses the database of the GTAP program (Global Trade Analysis Project).[9] This multi-regional model, with 11 regions and 24 productive sectors, is used to analyze the entry of Chile into MERCOSUR, NAFTA, European Community and the Rest of South America (RSA), and the effects of trade re-routing. The results of the study are interesting since they indicate that such free trade agreements are sometimes beneficial to Chile, and sometimes not. Harrison et al. (2002) applied the same model to assess the Chilean process of sequentially negotiating bilateral free trade agreements. The article focuses on the importance of market access and lowering tariffs.

The work of Bussolo et al. (1998) tries to analyze the effects of trade agreements focusing on the labor market. The model includes 24 productive sectors and seven occupational categories that are based on the updating of the SAM from 1986 to 1992. The article analyzes the effects of two different tariff reforms. In the first place, a competitive labor market is assumed, and later this assumption is relaxed by introducing certain rigidities (changes in salary negotiation and minimum wages).

Holland et al. (2002) applied a CGE to analyze the impacts of agricultural reforms consisting on price band removal and on eliminating all tariffs on agricultural and food commodities in Chile. Urban employment, rural–urban migration and welfare effects are addressed.

Among the CGE models applied to environmental issues is the model by Beghin et al. (1996a) – an application of the TEQUILA model developed by the OECD Development Centre. This study endeavors to analyze the environmental impact of carrying out environmental policy, trade liberalization and trade agreements by means of a dynamic CGE model. For this purpose, they built a multi-regional model that includes 26 regions and 72 productive sectors/activities. The model determined the emissions related to the estimated economic activity at the national level and re-scaled for Santiago. Using a linear dispersion model for Santiago, they estimated the concentration of pollutants in the air. Lastly, this concentration was translated into indexes of mortality and morbidity through dose-response functions. The results indicate that particulate material as well as SO_2 and NO_2 are complementary in the economic activity, and that their abatement produces a larger effect in the reduction of mortality and morbidity. On the other hand, the analysis of an eventual entry of Chile into NAFTA appears to be beneficial for the environment, whereas the entry to MERCOSUR or a unilateral drop in tariffs will not. The substitutes of the above-mentioned pollutants are toxic and bio-accumulative gases, whose emissions and concentration increase upon their eventual taxation, causing a negative net effect in the mortality and morbidity indexes. Beghin and Dessus (1999) applied a static version of the same model to assess the issue of double dividend, in the sense of substituting trade distortions for environmental taxes.

8.5 THE ENVIRONMENT IN GENERAL EQUILIBRIUM MODELS: THEORETICAL ASPECTS

This section will focus on the ways of modeling the environmental variables in a CGE model, with special attention to pollution-related issues. It is possible to classify the environmental CGE models according to how the polluting activities are modeled and evaluated. A first group would be classified based on the standard CGE model structure, in which pollution would be estimated by using fixed factors of emission intensity. That is to say, either pollution or emissions stand as a fraction of the final sectoral product or of the intermediate inputs. These models modify the level of pollution through changes in the level of taxes or prices, which result from changes in the environmental regulations. In these models, intermediate inputs, including energy, enter in the sphere of production as an aggregate intermediate input whose substitution is imperfect. Most of the models for developing countries follow this methodology to overcome the lack of accurate environmental data and information on abatement options. The application of this type of model to energy problems is not desirable in the absence of possibilities for substitution among different types of energy or with any other input.

The second type of environmental CGE model, used mainly for determining energy prices, incorporates the environmental variables in a different way. Lewis (1993) presents a model that incorporates substitution possibilities among a group of energy inputs that are divided into clean (natural gas, diesel, kerosene) and dirty fuels (gasoline, coal, fuel-oil, etc.). The use of each group of inputs (clean or dirty) is associated with different emission levels of different types of pollutants (CO_2, NO_x, SO_x, VOCs, PM10, etc.). In most simulations of this type investment remains constant, and the saving–investment equality is achieved by means of the government's net transfer adjustments .

Jorgenson and Wilcoxen (1990) incorporate the costs of controlling emissions in the sectoral production functions. Increasingly sophisticated models incorporate damage functions and the effects of pollution on productivity (Bergman, 1990) while others consider the effects of pollution on mortality and morbility (Beghin et al., 1996a and Beghin et al., 2002a). Models where the effects on consumption stem from pollution and abatement activities have been incorporated in the utility function. Robinson (1990) includes this effect by means of a Stone–Geary utility function. Piggot et al. (1992) include the benefits of reducing emissions in the utility functions; Perroni and Wigle (1994) and Tsigas et al. (1997) reflect variations of environmental quality in the utility function.

Despite the fact that most models consider these modifications on the production functions, and some on the utility functions, there are not many examples where the abatement options or the technological changes toward cleaner technologies are modeled. Robinson et al. (1993) identify technologies with different levels of pollution for different activities. To estimate the levels of abatement for each technology, the marginal abatement costs are set constant and equal to the unit cost of the inputs required by the abatement technology. Nestor and Pasurka (1994 and 1995) model the abatement activities in an input–output context, representing the processes of abatement and taxes based on input–output coefficients.

Xie (1995) developed a standard CGE economic model, which was modified to include 14 environmental equations to evaluate abatement activities in China. The model is specified using data on abatement that had been incorporated into an environmentally extended social accounting matrix. Pinto and Harrison (2003) develop a model for multilateral negotiations on climatic change, which is based on the IIAM (International Impact Assessment Model). They analyze optimal policies for the abatement of CO_2, assessing welfare impacts on each country.

8.6 THE ENVIRONMENT IN GENERAL EQUILIBRIUM MODELS: APPLICATIONS

Computable general equilibrium models that include environmental variables are becoming more and more widespread. The concern about addressing the environmental externalities of economic policies, the effects of environmental policies on prices, on volumes and on the socioeconomic structure, and the direct and indirect impacts of every policy on the three spheres of sustainable development, requires a wide analytical framework, which covers all the interrelations. Therefore, on top of the traditional applications assessing environmental impacts from economic policies, it is becoming more and more relevant to analyze the impacts on the economy of applying an environmental policy in a context of general equilibrium (Bergman, 1991).

Although the first environmental CGE models appeared in the late 1980s with the accomplishments of Førsund and Storm (1988) and Dufournaud et al. (1988), recent literature includes applications in many major areas. The bibliographical survey shows several environmental topics where the application of CGE models is highlighted:

1. Models used to evaluate the effects of trade policies or international trade agreements on the environment (Lucas et al., 1992; Grossman and Krueger 1993; Beghin et al., 1996; Madrid-Aris, 1998; or diverse applications in the area of the Global Trade Analysis Program, GTAP).
2. Models used to evaluate climatic change or global warming (Bergman, 1991; Jorgenson and Wilcoxsen, 1993; Li and Rose, 1995 or Rose et al., 1998) usually focus on the stabilization of CO_2, NO_x and SO_x emissions.
3. Models focused on energy issues (Piggot et al., 1992; Goulder 1993; Rose et al., 1995). They usually apply energy taxation or pricing to evaluate the impacts of changes in the price of energy on pollution or on control costs.
4. Models on natural resources allocation or management (Robinson and Gelhar, 1995; Mukherjee, 1996). The objective is usually the efficient inter-regional or inter-sectoral allocation of multi-use natural resources, for example, allocation of water resources between agriculture, mining, industry, tourism, human consumption and ecological watersheds.
5. Models focused on the evaluation of the economic impacts of specific environmental regulations such as the Clean Air Bill in the USA or of environmental instruments (Jorgenson and Wilcoxen, 1990; Hazilla and Koop, 1990). The assessment of economic costs of implementing international environmental protocols are also relevant, as is the case in Kiuila, 2003 in relation to the Second Sulfur Protocol (SSP) in Poland.

Chile presents problems and challenges in all the five previous topics, opening clear opportunities for the application of analytical tools such as CGE modeling. The first environmental CGE model applied in Chile (Beghin et al., 1996) was described above. O'Ryan et al. (2003) developed a version of it, named ECOGEM-Chile, to analyze the macroeconomic, sectoral, distributive and environmental effects of imposing environmental taxes on PM-10 as well as taxes on fuels.

8.7 ENVIRONMENTAL TAXES AND THEIR ROLE IN ENVIRONMENTAL CGE MODELS

The concept of environmental taxes has a long history since Pigou, in the 1920s, outlined a tax to incorporate the externalities into the private cost functions in order to correct them (Pigou, 1932). Nevertheless, this concept is subject to several restrictions. In the first place, it requires the fulfillment of the assumption of perfect competition in the reference market. In a situation of monopoly, it cannot guarantee the same result because of two problems, the monopoly and the environmental externality cannot be corrected with just one instrument – the tax. In such a case, one can easily arrive at a situation where the social optimum is obtained from applying a subsidy to production instead of a tax. The second assumption is not as strong as the first one, but is important from an operative point of view. To guarantee the achievement of a social optimum, it is essential to know both the function of marginal costs associated with the externality and the function of social marginal benefits (or the demand curve). In any case, this assumption can be relaxed if we accept that an iterative exercise of trial and error allows arriving at the optimal tax.

With regard to optimal taxation in the presence of externalities, the theory says that the optimal tax is the tax that internalizes the externality. In this sense, Pigou (Auerbach, 1985) ascertained that in the presence of existing distorting taxes, the social optimum would be reached with an additional tax to the good that generates the externality, equal to its associated costs (benefits). In general, the theory on optimal taxation has found evidence that the optimal tax in presence of other distorting taxes is lower than the estimates by Pigou. Bovenberg and De Mooij (1994) find that the optimal tax in presence of other distorting taxes is lower than the social damage produced by pollution. On the other hand, Bovenberg and Goulder (1996) find that the optimal tax should be the environmental marginal damage (EMD) divided by the marginal cost of public funds (MCPF).[10] When previously distorting taxes exist, this can even lead to negative environmental taxes. The reasoning behind this result is that incorporating a tax to a 'dirty' good raises its production costs, which drives to substitution in its consumption, thus eroding the tributary base, and therefore blocking a reduction of the distorting tax in addition to increasing the cost of living. In any case, Jaeger (1999) arrived at different results, finding that the optimal tax should in fact be larger than the Pigouvian tax.

Another important issue is that empirical studies (Bovenberg and Goulder, 1996) show that sub-optimal tax systems (from the point of view of minimizing the social loss) lead to an optimal environmental tax even smaller than the theoretical prediction. Also, the viability of using emission taxes is subject to discussion. Fullerton and West (1999), in a very interesting application, find that for the case of motorized vehicles, emission taxes can be replicated by means of several other instruments (a gasoline tax, a tax related to the type of engine and age, and a subsidy to abatement technologies). This result is extremely important since, upon finding evidence that an emission tax improves welfare even when it is not applicable, alternative ways can be devised to arrive to the same results.

8.8 CGE MODELS AND THE DEBATE ON THE DOUBLE ENVIRONMENTAL DIVIDENDS[11]

The concept of double dividend arises from the possibility of obtaining additional benefits from the introduction of environmental taxes in the economy in order to improve the environment. In theory, other benefits of the introduction of environmental taxes should appear, such as: improvement in individual welfare, solution to unemployment problems, improvements in income distribution, increase of gross product or higher growth, etc.

The mechanism that generates this second dividend or 'secondary' benefit is to be found in changes in the tax burden. When introducing environmental taxes, they can replace other taxes that are 'more' distorting, resulting in efficiency progress and generating other benefits in addition to the environmental improvement, that is to say a 'second' dividend. In practice, there are two conceptual mainstreams that have analyzed the existence of double dividend.

Tax Distortions

The first group of studies analyzes tax distortions, focusing primarily on individual welfare and on its improvements. At this point, two forms of double dividend are defined: weak and strong (Goulder, 1994). The weak form of double dividend refers to the fact that replacing distorting taxes by an environmental tax results in lower related costs than in the case of refunding the amount collected by the environmental tax as a lump sum transfer. Therefore, when introducing a new environmental tax, larger benefits are obtained when it is offset by lowering another distorting tax, which generates a second dividend.

On the other hand, 'strong' double dividend considers that, when replacing a distorting tax by an environmental tax, a second dividend is obtained in terms of a reduction in the tributary costs. What is meant is that the introduction of a 'green' tax, instead of another distorting tax, has negative net costs. That is to say, when carrying out the tax reform, existing distortions are corrected in the system, lowering the costs of taxation. This concept is in fact much more interesting because it allows achieving environmental improvements and economic efficiency by means of a tributary reform. Repetto et al. (1992) show that 'green' tax reforms can improve the welfare in the economy by recycling the revenues in order to reduce other more distorting taxes.

There is a noticeable criticism about the existence of a strong double dividend (the weak double dividend is generally accepted).[12] The discussion has taken place mainly in the US and Europe regarding the potential incorporation of taxes to CO_2[13] emissions. Most critics arise from the fact that including new taxes also has costs and generates other distortions in the market, which in general results in a lack of a second dividend (at least in the strong sense). This takes special emphasis when distorting taxes exist in the previous situation. The simplest models (Bovenberg and De Mooij, 1994) include two goods, one 'clean' and one 'dirty', in addition to a single productive factor, labor, subject initially to a labor tax. To carry out a tax reform toward taxing 'dirty' goods – keeping government's revenues constant – has two outcomes. Firstly, labor tax is reduced, increasing the net wage of the workers. At the same time, the tax on the 'dirty' good pushes its price up, and therefore: a) its demand decreases and b) the price index increases, reducing the worker's real wage. These side effects are not small according to the authors and generate a substitution toward leisure by the consumers, overcoming the impact of the initial reduction of labor taxes. It leads to discarding strong double dividend. Other authors have expanded this line with more complicated models (Bovenberg and Goulder, 1996 include intermediate inputs, Goulder, 1995 introduces dynamics in the model by including a second productive factor, capital), but in general they arrive at similar results, theoretically as well as empirically. In the empiric studies there is evidence that the effects can be even larger due to the fact that the previous distorting taxes are not 'optimal' from the collection point of view.[14]

On the other hand, Koskela et al. (1999) find that for the case of a small open economy with high unemployment (it refers to a European country), a moderate environmental tax reform can increase employment and the competitiveness of the country. The main difference with the studies of Bovenberg and De Mooij (1994) and Bovenberg and Goulder (1996) is the incorporation of clean and dirty factors instead of goods. In this case the polluting factor, energy, is imported, therefore a tax to its use is in a certain way equivalent to a tariff. Additionally, this tax generates the substitution of energy by the other factor (labor), which results in an employment boom. It is not difficult to see that, in this model, the unemployment assumption is the key for the existence of double dividend, confirming the thesis of Bosello et al. (1998) that, in general equilibrium modeling, assumptions influence the outcome of the studies.

In a different line, Bento and Rajkumar (1998) indicate that assumptions of the previous studies (that is, Bovenberg and De Mooij, 1994; Goulder, 1995; Bovenberg and Goulder, 1996) in general are important when the results are evaluated. According to them, the four assumptions a) the 'dirty' good as a substitute for leisure, b) environmental quality separable from the rest of the arguments in the utility function, c) linear production function or with constant returns to scale, and d) non-existing capital taxes, and therefore labor tax and the tax on 'dirty' goods are the only instruments of fiscal collection, hinder the generation of double dividend. Once these assumptions are relaxed a double dividend could exist. In particular they demonstrate that a positive second dividend is possible by relaxing the assumption of constant returns to scale.[15]

Parry and Bento (1999) find positively strong evidence of double dividend when replacing environmental taxes by labor taxes if the model includes the possibility of deducting a fraction of individual consumption from the labor tax. This study also includes other instruments of environmental regulation. This way, it analyzes the possibility of using a system of tradable permits. In this sense there are similar results in the case of a system where the permits are auctioned. A double dividend would not exist if permits are granted for free.

In any case the discussion is not yet over. Jaeger (1999) finds that the previous works on optimal taxation and double dividend, particularly those of Bovenberg and De Mooij (1994) and Bovenberg and Goulder (1996) do not compare appropriately the results. In essence, Jaeger sustains that in those models the effect of the environmental marginal damage normalized by gross income is compared with the individual welfare gain normalized by net income, which results in an optimal tax smaller than the Pigouvian tax. Compensating for this effect, Jaeger finds that, in fact, the tax is not smaller than the Pigouvian tax but larger. This fact opens up the possibility that a double dividend exists. As for the numeric models, Jaeger posits that the same error occurs in expressing the results in gross terms (the marginal environmental damage) and comparing them to the pollutant tax rate paid for with the taxpayers net income.

Other studies show indirect evidence of double dividend. In Europe, the implications of taxes on carbon (carbon taxes) have been recently discussed. There have been arguments against unilateral taxes because there will be substitution of emissions toward other countries and a loss of competitiveness in the country where the tax reform is carried out. Welsch (1996) finds that this should not necessarily be this way, depending on the destination of the revenues. In particular, the country will not confront a loss of competitiveness if revenues are used to reduce other more distorting taxes. Babiker et al. (2003) use the EPPA model (Emissions and Public Policy Analysis) to illustrate that the weak double dividend linked to reductions of carbon emissions is not reached by several European countries. They conclude that the effects of the interaction between carbon control policies and pre-existing taxation differ notoriously among countries.

Improvements in Macroeconomic Variables

The second group of studies related to double dividend focus on improvements in macroeconomic variables (employment, product, equity, etc.) with emphasis on the solution of unemployment problems.[16] This conceptual stream is due to high unemployment rates in countries of the European Union and the search for alternative solutions. The basic assumption of this thesis is that including environmental taxes may decrease labor tax rates, reducing the cost of labor and thus increasing employment.

It must be noted that most empiric studies regarding the existence of double dividend have been carried out in the USA and in countries of the EU,[17] although there are some examples in developing countries. The only study that analyzes the Chilean case is that of Beghin and Dessus (1999), who found double dividends when reducing tariffs and applying an environmental tax (emission tax). Two static simulations were carried out in this study. Firstly, a tax was applied to particulate material, resulting in welfare gains for consumers, but at the same time, there is also an increase in contamination by toxic bio-accumulative pollutants.

Secondly, a tax is applied to all the pollutants to prevent any increment, also showing evidence of a double dividend, but smaller than in the previous case. Nugent and Sarma (2002) apply a CGE model with environmental features to India. They simulate the introduction of new green taxes, the development of structural reforms in line with environmental taxation and the elimination of environmentally harmful subsidies, showing that it is possible to develop public policies to improve efficiency, equality and environmental protection simultaneously.

In any case, it is necessary to clarify that the assumptions in the models can have significant implications on the results. In the first place, a homogeneous labor market as well as a representative consumer are defined in most studies (for example, Bovenberg and De Mooij, 1994; Bovenberg and Goulder, 1996; Goulder, 1995; Parry and Oates, 1998; Fullerton and Metcalf, 1997 etc.). Therefore, it can be possible that more laxity in these assumptions favors the existence of a double dividend. On the other hand, there are still few empirical studies and, in general, models that study North American or European economies are not applicable to other countries with different tributary burdens. In Chile, labor tax is not significant, therefore it is not possible to generalize the results. Consequently, more applied studies that include indirect effects in the economy should be undertaken to obtain a wider scope on double dividend issues and a grasp of the different interactions taking place at the sectoral level and in the aggregate economy.

Another important criticism of the double dividend thesis is that there are no studies that incorporate the possibility of using abatement technologies for the reduction of emissions, through changes in the production structure and in tax payments by pollutant agents. Thus, models do not consider that there is a margin for reductions in emissions that will not be developed through the tax mechanism but by abatement possibilities, which will result in a smaller fiscal collection than expected.

On the other hand, when models include dynamics, it is expected that fiscal collection related to environmental taxation will decrease in time. If it is assumed that, in general, the most modern technologies are less polluting as well as efficient, in the long term it can be expected that firms will look for more economic ways of facing the regulations; for example, the implementation of environmentally friendly technologies. In this sense one can hope that new technologies will help firms emit less, thereby reducing tax payments and revenue for the government. It will provoke the necessity to increase the environmental tax rate to maintain a certain level of collection, which may not be politically viable.[18] In this sense, even when a priori second dividend is derived from the change in the tributary structure, it may dissipate over the time, which – in a long-term perspective – suggests that relaxing the tributary burden is not the best policy.

Even so, the incorporation of 'green' taxes can be beneficial for the sole existence of the first dividend: the improvement in environmental quality and correction of the associated externalities. This policy would be interesting to study, especially considering that there are other instruments that derive similar results (for example tradable emission rights), and may undoubtedly shed light on prospective impacts. Fullerton and Metcalf (1997) conclude that each reform should be evaluated separately, and consequently the a priori existence of double dividend cannot be granted. With this in mind, it is necessary to add that each country has different tributary structures as well as different labor markets. Therefore, it would be an error to posit a priori that a reform that is beneficial in a particular country should be so in another and vice versa. Parry and Oates (1998) agree that the results of the studies performed should not discard the use of economic instruments, but provide incentives for new studies, as it cannot be concluded that an environmental tributary reform is positive nor can we be certain that it is not so. In this sense we need to be cautious of partial equilibriums that do not consider the systematic effects between diverse taxes and the different sectors.

NOTES

1. The following is based on O'Ryan et al. (2000).
2. Approach that included input–output models, national accounts (especially social accounting matrices) and real economic variables, usually made use by Ministries of Planning and Economy.
3. More akin with macroeconomic models and balances of nominal flows, characteristic of Central Banks or Ministries of Economy and Treasury.
4. Subject of study of other line ministries in charge of key economic sectors.
5. The models of computable general balance that are habitually developed can be classified as neoclassic due to their theoretical and ideological conception and the characteristics of their balancing conditions; although there are different theoretical approaches which are seldom used. The balancing conditions that characterize a model can be decisive in their results; therefore any application should be analyzed in detail. For more information see De Miguel and Miller (1998).
6. Gunning and Keyser (1993) made a survey on applications with computable general equilibrium models in developing countries, summarizing more than 140 applications.
7. In this respect, the numerous works of Dervis and Robinson about Turkey are significant.

8. For a detailed revision of models and structuralism applications see Taylor (1990).
9. Project developed at Purdue University for the analysis of world trade, which has generated a global CGE model incorporating homogeneous SAMs for all the countries/regions.
10. This study incorporates a tax on a 'dirty' good by means of which CO_2 emissions are reduced in a static context. This way, for damages lower than 50 dollars per ton of CO_2 the environmental tax can even be negative. Goulder (1995) expands this model to a dynamic context and finds in turn that the optimal tax is lower than the Pigouvian tax.
11. For a more complete revision of the literature of double dividend see Goulder (1994); Fullerton and Metcalf (1997) and Bosello et al. (1998).
12. Hansen (1998) shows that when facing powerful groups, revenues from a 'green' tax are used to compensate the pollutants, which in turn dissipates welfare gains and therefore sheds doubts about the existence of weak double dividend.
13. The implicit problem is that, in the case of CO_2 emissions, there is no consensus about the fact that global warming is a problem. Therefore, under this perspective, taxing CO_2 emissions can still be beneficial, despite the uncertainty about the benefits associated to the first dividend, when the second benefit exists. But if the second dividend does not exist, since the first dividend is uncertain, it is not clear that incorporating this tax is helpful.
14. In general, authors find that, if taxes were optimal from the revenue point of view (minimizing the social loss), this result could be reverted, but even then double dividend would not necessarily exist. This would depend on the magnitude of the tax. Thus, for low levels of environmental taxes one could have a double dividend or at least a neutral situation.
15. According to the authors, the reason to relax this hypothesis is that in general carbon taxes are imposed on goods whose production is intensive in non-renewable resources, thus not subject to constant returns to scale.
16. For a more complete revision of the literature on employment double dividend see Bosello et al. (1998).
17. It is in these countries that environmental issues have raised a deeper concern; therefore the works on these issues are still incipient in the rest of the countries. It is also necessary to emphasize that precisely these countries have already applied different instruments, such as 'green' taxes, to deal with environmental issues and consequently the discussion of the existence of double dividend has been more relevant.
18. In Chile, as in many other countries, modifying a tax rate has to be approved by Congress. Therefore, to modify the rates can result in a very frustrating process, sluggish, and even impossible to complete.

9. The ECOGEM general equilibrium model for Chile

9.1 CHARACTERISTICS OF THE MODEL

The CGE model developed for Chile is static, characterized by multiple sectors and factors of production, differentiation of labor by occupational categories, of households by quintiles of income and of trade partners and pollutants, among other features.[1] It is basically a savings-driven neoclassic model, that incorporates energy-input substitution to reduce emissions of pollutants. Emissions are related to the use of different inputs and not only to production levels as it is commonly dealt with. Although not all the equations in the model are shown herein, the most significant will be included, in particular, those associated to environmental variables. The indexes *i*, *j* represent productive sectors or activities.

<u>*Production*</u> Production is modeled by the CES/CET nested functions (that is, constant elasticity of substitution – transformation). If constant returns to scale are assumed, each sector produces while minimizing costs:

$$\min PKEL_i KEL_i + PABND_i ABND_i$$

$$\text{s.t.}$$

$$XP_i = \left[a_{kel,i} KEL_i^{\rho_i^p} + a_{abnd,i} ABND_i^{\rho_i^p} \right]^{1/\rho_i^p}$$

The production function can be represented by a tree shape.[2] In the first level of the tree, a CES function allows the optimum choice between non-energy-producing intermediate input basket and a factor (capital and labor) and energy-producing inputs (KEL) composite basket. A Leontief-type function determines the non-energy-producing intermediate input basket. On the factors' side, the capital–energy basket and labor are split through a new CES function; then, energy is separated from capital, always assuming CES functions for substitution both between and within factors (types of labor, energy and capital).

Income distribution Income is allocated to the domestic economy, the government and financial institutions in the form of wages, capital returns and taxes.

Consumption Households distribute their income between saving and consumption through an ELES utility function (extended linear expenditure system).[3] This function also incorporates the minimum subsistence consumption as independent of the level of income:

$$\max\ U = \sum_{i=1}^{n} \mu_i \ln(C_i - \theta_i) + \mu_s \ln\left(\frac{S}{cpi}\right)$$

$$\text{subject to}\ \sum_{i=1}^{n} PC_i C_i + S = YD$$

$$\text{and}\ \sum_{i=1}^{n} \mu_i + \mu_s = 1$$

Where U stands for the consumer's utility; C_i is the consumption of good i; θ is the subsistence consumption; S, saving; cpi, the price of savings; and μ the consumption marginal propensity for each good and to save.

Other final demands Once the intermediate demands and household demands are defined, the model includes the rest of the components of the final demand, that is, investment, government expenditures and trade margins. Other final demands for each activity are defined as a fixed share of total final demand.

Public finances There are different types of taxes and transfers. The model includes several direct taxes: labor tax (differentiated by occupational categories), taxes on firms or corporate taxes and households income taxes (differentiated by quintile). Import tariffs and subsidies, export taxes and subsidies (by sector) and a value added tax VAT (for domestic and imported goods, and by sector) are also defined.

As a closure condition for public finances, the model allows two alternatives: first, government spending is fixed and defined as equal to the original level, prior to any simulation, allowing the adjustment through some tax/subsidy or government transfer. Second, government spending is allowed to vary, while taxes and transfers are kept constant. The first option was chosen for the simulations in this study.

Foreign sector The Armington assumption is used to break down goods by place of origin, allowing imperfect substitution between domestic and imported goods and services. As with production, there is a CES function that allows substitution between the imported and domestic basket. In turn, the domestic supply is treated similarly to demand, now including a CET function to distinguish domestic market from exports. For imports:

$$\min PDXD + PMXM$$

$$\text{subject to } \; XA = \left[a_d XD_\rho + a_m XM_\rho\right]^{1/\rho}$$

where *PD* and *PM* are the prices of domestic and imported goods, while *XD* and *XM* are the respective amounts. *XA* stands for the good made up of both or the 'Armington good'. Parameter ρ is the substitution elasticity between both goods. For exports:

$$\max PD\,XD + PE\,ES$$

$$\text{subject to } \; XP = \left[\gamma_d XD + \gamma_e ES_\lambda\right]^{1/\lambda}$$

where *PE* is the price of the exported good and *ES* is the respective amount. *XP* is the sector's total production. Parameter λ is the substitution elasticity between both goods.

Factor market equilibrium conditions To achieve labor market equilibrium, labor supply and demand are made equal for each occupational category, where supply is determined on the basis of real wages. As for the capital market, a single type of capital is assumed to exist in the model, which may or may not have sector mobility depending in the imposed elasticity. No capital mobility between sectors is assumed.

It is worth noting that long-term elasticities have been assumed in the CES production function for substitution between the factor nest and non-energy-producing inputs, as well as between capital–energy and labor, between capital and energy and among the various energy-producing sectors. Although this assumption allows for greater substitution between factors it is more realistic from a medium-term viewpoint.

Closure conditions The closure condition for the public sector has already been anticipated. Also, as is common in these models, the value of the demand for private investment must equal the net aggregate saving (from firms, households, government and net flows from abroad) of the economy. The last closing rule refers to balance of payment equilibrium. This equation will be introduced into the model through the Walras Law.

9.2 EMISSION REDUCTION IN THE MODEL

The model allows three possibilities to reduce emissions of pollutants in the economy. All of them come from introducing some kind of tax or policy that alters the decisions of the economic players in their profit or benefit maximizing processes. The first is the most traditional and common in general equilibrium models: the reduction in production of the most pollutant sectors. The second alternative is oriented to discourage the use of energy-producing inputs that discharge emissions into the environment whenever they are used in the productive process or in consumption. It allows the substitution of more polluting energy inputs for those emitting less. The last possibility is determined by the ability to reduce emissions through the use of 'end-of-pipe' technologies (for example, filters, treatment plants, etc.). This possibility is in an experimental stage and will not be included in the results of the simulations presented in this study.

Not included in the model is the possibility of technological change, based on investment processes driven by relative returns, which brings less polluting processes of production. Although it is possible to change substitution elasticities to simulate more flexible technologies bringing less polluting processes, it would be necessary to use a dynamic model to incorporate technological change accurately. The introduction of the environmental quality in the utility function as a good for which there is a willingness to pay is also part of the future research. It would alter decisions on goods and services consumption and their equilibrium prices.

Reduction of production In this case, introducing a tax on emissions generates an increase in production costs, which in turn causes – ceteris paribus – an increase in the price of the good produced by the polluting industry (that pays for the tax). Thus, it becomes less competitive at both the national and international levels, the demand for this good decreases and therefore its production declines (at least in the long run). In the case of an environmental regulation that sets a limit for emissions, the company will be forced to reduce its level of production to fulfill it.

Basically, in a general equilibrium model this process comes from making prices endogenous and the possibility of reallocating factors and resources among different productive sectors, substituting goods in the final demand and substituting between domestic and foreign markets (CES/ELES/CET–Armington functions, respectively).

Substitution between inputs The use of each type of input in either production or final demand consumption causes a certain level of emissions independent of the production process. Therefore, another way to reduce emissions is to substitute less polluting inputs for the more polluting ones. In the case of a tax on emissions, the costs associated with the use of that input are being indirectly increased, and thus their relative use is being made costlier and its substitution encouraged.

In the case of a new regulation on emission, a constraint is introduced into the optimization process of households and firms. In this case, maintaining the use of the same volume of polluting inputs leads to a sub-optimal situation, which will converge towards an optimum to the extent that substitution occurs towards less or non-contaminating inputs.

The model differentiates between energy-producing and non-energy-producing inputs. Non-energy-producing inputs are used in the production function assuming fixed coefficients. Substitution between energy-producing inputs or between these and other productive factors (capital and labor) is determined by CES functions, nested within the production function. Energy-producing inputs (that is, coal, PetrøGas, PetrøRef, Electricity and Gas) are associated to the emission of 13 types of pollutants (not all of them discharged by the energy-producing inputs) through emission factors. Those factors link the use of each monetary unit spent on the input with the amount of emissions of each pollutant in physical units. Total volume of emissions in the economy for each type of pollutant is therefore determined by:

$$E_p = \sum_i \upsilon_i^p \cdot XP_i + \sum_i \pi_i^p \left(\sum_j XAp_{ij} + \sum_h XAc_{ih} + \sum_f XAFD_f^i \right)$$

that is, by the sum of all the emissions of the pollutant '*p*' caused by all the productive sectors '*i,j*' included in the input–output matrix, generated either in their productive processes per se (independently of the emissions associated to the use of polluting inputs), or derived from the use of polluting intermediate inputs[4] in the productive processes and in the consumption by households '*h*' and by other components of the final demand '*f*'.

End-of-pipe technologies In order to incorporate the reduction in emissions through the implementation of end-of-pipe technologies, it is necessary to include a new productive sector that lets the others reduce their emissions when they consume the abatement products of the first. This sector then becomes the abatement technology sector.[5] For this, a CES function must be included to allow substitution between the abatement sector and the rest of the intermediate non-energy-producing input sectors. The result will be reflected in the following equations:

$$AB_j = \alpha_{AB\,j} \cdot \left[\frac{P_{ABND\,j}}{P_{AB\,j}} \right]^{\sigma^j_{ABND}} \cdot ABND_j$$

$$ND_j = \alpha_{ND\,j} \cdot \left[\frac{P_{ABND\,j}}{P_{ND\,j}} \right]^{\sigma^j_{ABND}} \cdot ABND_j$$

$$P_{ABND\,j} = \left[\alpha_{AB_j} \cdot \left(P_{AB\,j}\right)^{1-\sigma^j_{ABND}} + \alpha_{ND_j} \cdot \left(P_{ND\,j}\right)^{1-\sigma^l_{ABND}} \right]^{\frac{1}{1-\sigma^j_{ABND}}}$$

where *AB* stands for the abatement expenditure, *ND* is the expense in the rest of non-energy-producing inputs, and *ABND* is the nest that includes both. Parameters α_{AB} and α_{ND} are the shares used of each input, and σ_{ABND} is the substitution elasticity between both types of inputs. P_{AB}, P_{ND}, and P_{ABND} stand for the respective prices of each input and the price of the compounded input.

Total emissions in the economy will now be also determined by the existing expense on abatement. The coefficients that determine emissions are now weighted by the reduction factor associated to the abatement technologies used:

$$E_p = \sum_i \upsilon*^p_i \cdot XP_i + \sum_j \sum_i \pi*^p_i \cdot X_{ij} + \sum_i \pi^p_i \left(\sum_h XAc_{ih} + \sum_f XAFD^i_f \right)$$

Where for each sector and each pollutant:

$$\pi^* = \pi - \left(\frac{G_{AB}}{\theta}\right)^{\frac{1}{\omega}} \cdot \frac{1}{\sum_i X_{ij}}$$

$$\upsilon^* = \upsilon \cdot \frac{\pi^*}{\pi}$$

where G_{AB} is the sector's expenditure in abatement technologies, X_{ij} is sector j's intermediate demand for sector i, and θ and ω are parameters from the emission cost reduction functions, while υ and π are the emission coefficients associated to the production and use of intermediate inputs, respectively.

To introduce this mechanism in the model it is necessary to disaggregate the data for the abatement sector, and to figure out parameters θ and ω for each sector. Finally, it is necessary to create their market. The demand will then be made up of the sum of the demands of each and every sector in the input–output matrix, while the supply will be determined by a new sector generated from the sectors that produce the abatement technologies, or by a proportion thereof.

9.3 DATA

Economic Data

As in any general equilibrium model, the main source of information is the social accounting matrix (SAM). The matrix for Chile was built on the available input–output matrix for the year 1986 with information from the Chilean Central Bank (Venegas, 1995) and Alonso and Roland-Holst (1995). This matrix contains 74 sectors and was updated up to 1992. A new matrix will cover up to 1996.

The SAM for Chile was aggregated in order to enable a better mathematical convergence, without diminishing its capacity to analyze relevant political scenarios. The model has 18 economic sectors,[6] divides the labor factor into skilled and unskilled, includes the foreign sector, disaggregates the income of households by quintiles, and incorporates the new abatement sector (in the matrix presented herein, this sector has only been formally disaggregated). The matrix is measured in billions of pesos of 1992 purchasing power, although in this type of exercise, units of measures and amounts are not so relevant as the variables' ratio accuracy (relative weight).

As for the income, substitution and other elasticities, it is possible to choose long-term elasticities from the relevant international literature, providing more flexibility to the adjustment process and more realistic results. However, as the model is static, investment and capital accumulation processes cannot be incorporated and long-term elasticities only minimize this flaw.

Databases to Calculate Emissions

Energy-producing inputs

For the Chilean case, the input–output matrix considers the following set of energy-producing inputs/activities:

- Production of oil and natural gas (PetrGas). A priori, it considers the extraction of petroleum and natural gas in their mining phase.
- Coal mining.
- Oil refinery (PetrRef). This sector groups all the production of heavy petroleum, gasoline and kerosene.
- Electricity.
- Gas. Gas production and distribution.
- Water (Hydraulic). Hydraulic and sanitary operations sector.

Because the SAM updating to 1992 is based on the input–output matrix of 1986, the gas sector is undervalued – gas pipelines coming from Argentina were developed in 1996/97. This will affect the impacts of environmental policies on sectoral production as substitutions towards a more environmentally friendly energy (that is, gas) is limited. With the coal sector subsidized in those days, the reverse occurs. Section 11.4 presents a simulation that attempts to duplicate the current situation of this latter sector and the economy.

Emission Coefficients

There are two types of emission coefficients. One comes from the use of different inputs and the other is related to the productive processes per se. In the simulations, five types of air pollutants are presented, namely: SO_2, NO_2, VOC (volatile organic compounds), CO and PM10.

The emission coefficients of each of the aforesaid pollutants, associated with the use of inputs, are obtained from econometric regressions whose endogenous variable is the pollutant and the exogenous variables are the 15 sectors chosen as the main generators of pollution emissions in the United States. Observations are associated to all the sectors/activities of the SAM in that country that use each of the 15 inputs. The minimum limit for degrees of freedom is 70 (85 sectors using at least one of the 15 inputs minus 15 types of input-exogenous variables). No constants are used and the maximum number of activities/sectors is 345. Once the coefficients associated to the use of inputs have been calculated, dummy variables are included for those sectors that cause emissions of some pollutant independent to the type of input used. Thus, the emission factors associated to production are obtained, independently of the inputs used. Data is extrapolated to Chile through the SAM, thereby obtaining the levels of emissions on the basis of the inputs used in value terms.[7]

ANNEX 9A

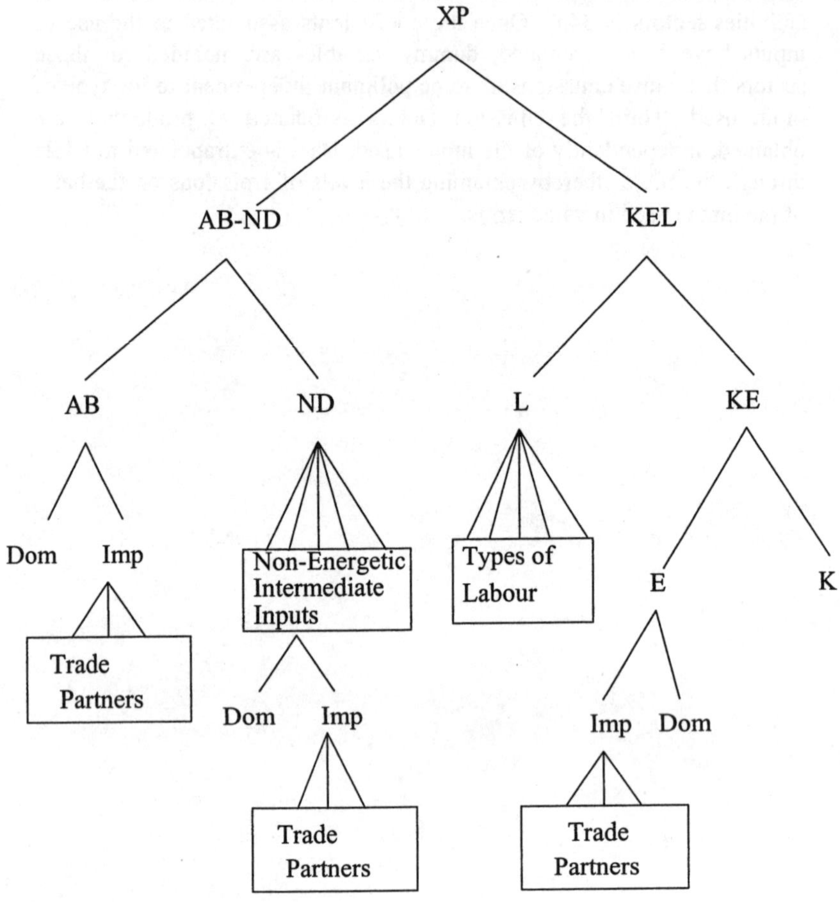

Figure 9A.1 Production nesting

Table 9A.1 Sectors used

Sectors	Reference to 1986 SAM	Description
Renewable	1–6	Agriculture, Fruit, Livestock, Agriculture Serv., Forestry, Fisheries
NonRenew	7, 8, 11	Copper, Iron, Other Minerals
OilExtract	9	Extraction of Oil and Gas
Coal	10	Coal
FoodInd	12–23	Slaughter, Dairy, Conserves, Sea Food, Oils, Bakery, Sugar, Other Foods, Feedstock, Drinks, Wine and Liquor, Tobacco
Textile	24–27	Textile, Clothes, Leather, Shoes
WoodInd	28–30	Wood Products, Furniture, Pulp and Paper
Chemicals	31–33, 35–38	Printing, Chemicals, Other Chemicals, Rubber, Plastics, Pottery, Glass
Refinery	34	Refinery
Machinery	39–46	Non-metallic Minerals, Basic Metals, Metal-mechanics, Non-electric Machinery, Electric Machinery, Transport Materials, Professional Equipment, Other Manufactures
Electricity	47	Electricity
Gas	48	Gas
Water	49	Hydraulic
Construction	50	Construction
Commerce	51-53	Commerce, Restaurants, Hotels
RoadTransp	55, 56	Load Transport, Passenger Transport
OtherTransp	54, 57–59	Railways, Sea Transp., Air Transp., Other Transport
Services	60–74	Communications, Banks, Insurance, Rents, Serv. to Firms, House Prop., Public and Private Education, Public and Private Health, Entertainment, Other Entertainment, Repair, Other Services, Public Adm.

NOTES

1. The model presented herein, ECOGEM-Chile, has been developed by the authors at the University of Chile, based on the one generated at the OECD by Beghin, Dessus, Roland-Holst and van der Mensbrugghe (1996, 2002).

2. See Annex 9A, to see the way the nest is built.
3. The way in which savings are included (divided by a price index of the other goods) partially neutralizes the substitution between consumption and savings, because the savings' price is a weighted price of all the other goods. In this sense, savings represent future consumption.
4. Not only energy-producing.
5. Abatement technology is the current expenditure on technology to comply with some green regulation or to avoid paying some environmental tax.
6. The specific sectors are described in Annex 9A.
7. To examine the procedure followed to calculate emissions as well as the results of the estimations, see Dessus et al. (1994).

10. Economic, social and environmental status in Chile

10.1 ECONOMIC STRUCTURE AND OVERALL ECONOMIC PERFORMANCE

During the 1980s, Chile engaged in trade liberalization and extensive privatization programs, promoting exports and free markets as the main engines for growth. This trend continued during the 1990s, albeit less strongly. Prices, with the exception of public transport and some public utilities and port charges, are not set by government. Import tariffs applied to countries without free trade agreements are basically uniform, and currently stand at 6 percent. Regulatory policies, though limited, have been improved in areas such as utilities, the banking sector, security markets and pension funds.

The main effort in this period, however, has been in maintaining macroeconomic stability, improving infrastructure provision, and focusing resources to reduce many of Chile's unsolved social problems. Legislation is now in place to privatize ports, water and sewage, and will probably be pushed during the next few years. The main reforms implemented in the last decade include privatization of public utilities; promotion of private investment in infrastructure, telecommunications, electricity and air transport; trade liberalization and trade agreement expansion; and reform of the educational system.

The policies applied have been very successful, resulting in Chile's economic performance during the 1990s being the best in the last century. The country grew at an impressive 8 percent per year between 1989 and 1998. The 1997/98 Asian Crisis also shocked the Chilean economy, which experienced a small recession in 1999.[1] Despite adverse international events (slowdown of the international economy, uncertainty after September 11 terrorist attacks, the Argentinean crisis, low commodity prices such as copper, fishmeal and cellulose, and a higher oil price, etc.), economic growth in 2000 achieved a remarkable 4.5 percent and decreased to 3.4 percent in 2001. It is estimated that in 2004 it will reach 5 percent. Clearly, Chilean economic performance far exceeds others in the region, which exhibit poor growth (between 0 percent and 1 percent).

Per capita GDP is currently 4500 US$ at current prices.

The real exchange rate has been key to this performance. It peaked in 1990 at almost double the value of a decade earlier, resulting in a significant increase in total exports that doubled relative to 1980. However, during the 1990s it fell to about 75 percent of the 1990 real exchange rate. Even so, exports have grown at an impressive 10 percent over the period. In 1999, Chile adopted a floating exchange rate regime, eliminating a price band for the dollar. To improve the competitiveness of the Chilean financial sector during the decade, the Central Bank followed a liberalization process of foreign exchange regulations, reducing restrictions on foreign exchange outflows and eliminating the capital inflow reserve requirement, while simplifying the foreign exchange regime.

Relevant variables (inflation, current account deficit, reserves, etc.) have been kept within acceptable limits.[2] Since the beginning of the 1990s, the Central Bank posts an inflation target for the year, which resulted in a fall in inflation from 27 percent in 1990, to 1.1 percent in 2003. Government spending has been prudent, permitting fiscal surpluses each year up to 1999. Notwithstanding, when the country suffers from an international situation that impacts negatively on unemployment rates, fiscal expansion has been moderate and the deficit is easily balanced in the following years. The current account has been in deficit most of the decade (currently, it stands below 1 percent of GDP), but has been easily financed by substantial foreign capital inflows, since Chile's performance has made the country very attractive for investment. External debt composition has changed from 30 percent private debt in 1990, to 85 percent in 2002 and it is mainly medium and long-term debt (83 percent). Currently, external debt (US$ 38.989 millions) reaches only 58 percent of GDP.

Gross internal investment has increased significantly in the period, reaching 27 percent of GDP in 1998, a very significant increment compared with the 16 percent average of the 1980s. However, internal savings have not grown much in the decade, and most of the increase in investment has been financed through foreign savings. After 1998, investment slowed down to around 23 percent of the GDP, paralleling a reduction in foreign savings.

As a result of this performance, real wages increased during the 1990s at an average rate of 3.2 percent. Unemployment fell from an average of 18 percent in the 1980s to 6 percent in the 1990s. However, since 1999 unemployment has jumped to 10 percent and, despite government efforts and sustained growth. it still remains at 9 percent.

Accordingly, poverty continued to decline falling from the 45 percent of total households in 1987 to 21 percent in 2000 although important regional differences remain, indicating a very significant reduction in a fairly short period of time. Income distribution is Chile's weak spot. The minimum wage, although increasing at a higher real rate than average wages, was only 160 US$ per month in 2002 (or just around twice the value defined as the poverty line). The richest 20 percent of households received more than 15 times the income of the poorest 20 percent in 2000; the Gini coefficient was close to 0.58. This situation has remained largely unchanged since the 1960s.

Historically, Chile's growth has been based on its natural resources, both renewable and non-renewable. Chile is the world's leading copper and iodine producer and a growing source of gold, lithium and other non-metallic minerals. Copper is by far the main export product, accounting for almost 40 percent of total exports. This share fell from a very high 80 percent in the 1980s, as a result of a continuous export diversification process. Agricultural products, fish and forestry products, cellulose and fishmeal are other important export sectors that have grown rapidly in the last decade. Imports are concentrated in capital goods and fuel/energy.

The most dynamic sectors during the 1990s were transport and communications, commerce, restaurants and hotels, and fisheries, which more than tripled, and financial services and construction, which almost tripled compared with the earlier decade. However, since 1998 only the first three grew significantly, while others experienced negative (or sluggish) growth rates (manufacturing and construction).

Finally, it is important to observe that economic activity is concentrated geographically and by product. One of Chile's 13 administrative regions, the Metropolitan region, where the country's capital city Santiago is located, accounts for 43 percent of the GDP, followed by the Bío-Bío region and Valparaiso region each with 8 percent. Regional production is heavily concentrated on specific activities: mining in the north, agriculture in the centre-north, forestry, fruit and traditional agriculture in the centre-south, and salmon, tourism and methanol in the south.

10.2 SOCIAL POLICIES IN CHILE

Since 1990, public expenditure on social issues increased significantly in order to reduce the high levels of poverty. Following the basic principle of equal opportunities and an acceptable standard of living for the whole population, social policy in the last decade in Chile has been geared to improving programs and coverage of the health, education and housing sectors. In addition, efforts have been made to promote productive development in poor areas. These are discussed in the following sections.

Evolution of Social Policies in Chile

Three distinct periods can be identified in the evolution of social policies in Chile (Schkolnik and Bonnefoy 1994; Baytelman et al. 1999). During the first period (1950–73), of Universal Policies, there was a gradual growth in public social expenditure, coverage and number of beneficiaries. Programs were designed to reach everyone (universal coverage), and were aimed at health and nutrition, education, housing and sanitary infrastructure programs. However, these programs were usually underfinanced, continuously pressed the government for more resources and caused severe fiscal deficits. Moreover, since these programs were provided through formal labor and pension systems, they did not reach those in extreme poverty situations who were usually part of the informal labor force.

The second period (1973–89),[3] of Assistance and Subsidies, was undertaken during a period of intense economic and political reforms. The provision of services by the public sector was decentralized and the private sector was encouraged to produce and operate social services. Universal programs were reduced, and expenditure was focused on specific objectives. The main goal in this period was to eradicate extreme poverty, providing mother–child care and basic services. Social expenditure was severely reduced in the period. However, thanks to focusing, there were significant improvements in human development indicators such as child mortality, improved literacy and schooling, among others. The economic crises of 1975–76 and 1982–83 strengthened this trend in expenditure reduction, and consequently the quality of social goods and services progressively decayed. Poverty levels increased significantly, as 45 percent of the population was classified as poor in 1987, double that of 15 years earlier (Martín, 1998).

The third period, of Integrating Policies, began in the 1990s[4] and is currently in effect. Spending on social objectives has increased substantially, and social policies are focused on improving the quality of the services given out, and implementing specific instruments aimed at the development of skills in the low-income population. Social *investment* is preferred to assistance. This view is consistent with the new government's integral goals of economic growth and macroeconomic stability *together* with equality and poverty reduction; overcoming the approach of growth spilling over the poor as automatic solution to poverty.

Reflecting the new government's concern for reducing poverty and income inequality, social expenditure increased sharply during this decade. Between 1990 and 2002 public social expenditure grew by 136 percent (98 percent in per capita terms), representing almost 7.4 percent annual growth. This increase was much higher that the regional average for Latin America for the same period of 5.5 percent (CEPAL, 1999). Accordingly, social expenditure rose from 61 percent of total expenditure in 1990 to 66 percent in 2002. This increase in public expenditure in Chile was higher than GDP growth for the same period. The sectoral breakdown evolution of social expenditure in Chile is presented in Table 10.1. Spending on social security is by far the most important public expenditure, followed by spending on education and health.

Table 10.1 Central government social expenditures, 1990–2002 (percentages of GDP)

	1990	1992	1994	1996	1998	2000	2002
Social expenditures	12.4	12.5	12.8	12.9	14.0	15.6	16.0
Health	1.9	2.2	2.4	2.3	2.5	2.7	2.9
Housing	0.9	1.0	1.0	1.0	1.0	0.9	0.9
Social security	6.1	5.6	5.5	5.4	5.7	6.4	6.4
Education	2.4	2.6	2.7	3.0	3.5	3.9	4.3
Others*	1.1	1.1	1.2	1.2	1.4	1.6	1.6
Total expenditures	20.2	20.3	19.9	19.6	21.3	22.4	22.9
Share social/total	61.4	61.7	64.2	66.0	65.9	69.5	69.9

Note: *Includes monetary subsidies and social investment programs oriented to priority groups.

Sources: National Budget Office, Ministry of Finance; DIPRES (2003) Series Estadísticas, Estadísticas de las Finanzas Públicas 1987–2002.

Finally, during the last decade, social programs have been focalized considerably. In addition to the target groups prioritized in the 1980s – the indigent and mother–infant care other groups such as women, youth, indigenous groups, elderly and handicapped persons were also targeted. Integral policies have been designed, aimed at the specific problems of each of these vulnerable groups. As a result of focalization, expenditure in the main social programs such as education, health and monetary subsidies, are received by the poorest 69.4 percent of households (MIDEPLAN, 1999a). In terms of income, these social programs represented 45.5 percent and 19.8 percent of total income for the first and second quintiles respectively (based on the every other year national survey, CASEN, which stands for characterization of social and economic conditions). Consequently, focalization has allowed the share in total income of the first quintile to increase from 3.7 percent when social expenditure is not considered to 6.3 percent when it is included. For the second quintile it increases from 8 percent to 9.3 percent of total income when social expenditures are included.

Health Sector

Status of the health sector in 1990

In 1980, intense reforms were introduced, changing both the structure and the financing of the health sector in Chile. These reforms included: (1) the creation of the National Health Fund (FONASA), a financial institution created to collect, manage and distribute fiscal resources earmarked for health of the poorer sectors; (2) creation of the Private Health Institutions (ISAPRES) to provide health care to the more affluent; (3) decentralization of the National Health Service (SNS) through 27 autonomous health services; (4) decentralization of primary care; (5) in 1985 an additional payment called 'co-payment' was introduced for the users of the public system, depending on income levels (Titelman, 1999). All hired workers in the private or public system are required to pay, as a minimum, 7 percent of their income for health.

These reforms fostered the creation of a private health system, parallel to the public health service.[5] The private system experienced an explosive growth since its creation, increasing its coverage from 3.1 percent of the population in 1984 to a peak of 24.7 percent in 1996. However, in the last few years, this trend has been slightly reversed, and consequently in 2000 67 percent of the population declared itself affiliated to the public health system (nearly 10 million people), 20 percent to the ISAPRE system (around 3 million people), and 3 percent to a social security system belonging to the armed forces. Nearly 11 percent declare that they are not affiliated to any health system.

The increasingly sophisticated private health system was in stark contrast to the highly deteriorated public health system at the beginning of the decade. The share of fiscal contribution to health decreased from 62 percent in 1974 to a meager 38 percent in 1990. During the 1980s, sectoral investment in health averaged only 14 million dollars per year. As a result of this reduction, there was a significant deficit of investment in infrastructure and technological obsolescence of the medical and industrial equipment in the public sector. Medical coverage and attention for the poorest two-thirds of the population was insufficient, and people had to wait months and even years to get attention. Moreover, the patient's contribution to medical expenses increased from 14 percent in 1974 to 45 percent in 1990, making it a hot political issue.

Policies, expenditure and investments in the health system in the 1990s

Beginning in 1990, new criteria for health policies were defined to included care for the poorest groups, recovery of the public system and an increase in the quality of attention. Under these premises, the main goals for health policies have been to:

1. improve access to health;
2. solve the hospital crisis and lack of infrastructure that affected the public sector
3. strengthen the institutional capacity of the sector;
4. enhance prevention and protection of people's health;
5. improve environmental quality.

In order to achieve these goals, public investment and expenditure were increased substantially, and new legislation was developed to reorganize the coexistence between the public and private systems.[6] Between 1990 and 2000 public expenditure in health increased by 147 percent (see Table 10A.3, in Annex 10A). The share of public expenditure in health, which decreased to levels under 40 percent in the 1980s, was increased to 46 percent in 2000. Public expenditure on health as a share of social public expenditure increased from 15 percent to 18 percent, and also grew as a share of GDP from 2 to 2.9 percent (Table 10.2). The average expenditure per beneficiary increased from US$ 100 in 1990 to US$ 134 in 2000, showing significant increments in a relatively short period of time.

Table 10.2 Central government health expenditures as percentage of social expenditures and GDP, 1990–98

Year	Health/ Social expenditures	Health/GDP
1990	15.3	1.9
1991	16.5	2.0
1992	17.4	2.2
1993	17.8	2.3
1994	18.5	2.4
1995	17.9	2.2
1996	17.7	2.3
1997	17.8	2.3
1998	17.9	2.5
1999	17.1	2.6
2000	17.5	2.7
2001	17.8	2.8
2002	18.1	2.9
Average (90–02)	17.5	2.4

Sources: National Budget Office, Ministry of Finance; DIPRES (2003) Series Estadísticas, Estadísticas de las Finanzas Públicas 1987–2002.

Average sectoral investment in health during the 1990s increased six-fold compared with the 1980s, reaching 87 million dollars per year (MINSAL, 1999, see Table 10.3) resulting in a significant decrease in the notorious deficit of infrastructure. Between 1990 and 1998 12 hospitals were built or rebuilt, 71 were modernized, 126 new clinics were built and 69 have been recovered, in addition to 13 new specialized centers, 117 new consulting rooms and 50 Primary Emergency Attention Services (SAPUs). This has paved the way for recovering part of the hospital capacity and increasing the access to health, especially for the poor.

Table 10.3 Investment in health, 1990–99 (1999 million US$)***

Year	Amount
1990	17.0
1991	23.0
1992	107.0
1993	107.2

1994	121.8
1995	111.9
1996	111.2
1997	107.0
1998	92.1
1999	75.1
Total investment, 1990–99	873.2
Annual average	87.3

Notes: *Consists of investment undertaken by Health Services in autonomous institutions and the Health Ministry. Decentralized investment.
** Based on the average dollar observed in 1999.

Source: Own elaboration, based on MINSAL (1999).

The results of this important financial effort include: (1) extension of equality policies including health check-up for children, pre-natal check-up, Complementary Feeding Programs (PNACs), general morbidity control and free attention for the poorest segments of the public; (2) reinforcement of primary attention with the creation of Emergency Primary Attention Services (SAPUs), a third working shift, rural health programs, Bronchial Obstruction and Acute Respiratory Infections Program; (3) reduction of waiting lists; (4) creation of dental departments; (5) solutions for hospitals considered to be in financial crisis in 1990; (6) prevention and protection programs, including mental health, prevention and control of AIDS disease, and vaccination programs; and (7) reformulation of the national complementary food program,[7] which distributes food for free to minors under six years, and pregnant women with health controls. Additionally, patients' contributions to total costs have been reduced from 45 percent in 1990 to 37 percent in 2002 (see Table 10.4).

Table 10.4 Income structure of the public health sector, 1990 and 2002 (in percentages)

Source	1990	2002
Fiscal contribution	37.5	46.1
Legal payment (7%)	44.6	36.6
Operation income	8.1	6.3
Other income	9.8	10.9
Total	100	100

Source: Own elaboration, based on MIDEPLAN (1998b); FONASA (2003).

Despite these improvements, the public system is still weak. There is a need to focus more on vulnerable groups and decrease the extensive gap between expenditure by beneficiaries in the public and private sectors. Finally, risk discrimination should be eliminated in the private sector, since it leads to a greater affiliation of elders (80 percent) in the public system, increasing their relative weight.

Education[8]

Status of education in 1990

At the beginning of the 1980s, Chile's educational system experimented with a profound reform whose main feature was the decentralization of the administration of publicly funded schools that was transferred to the municipalities. The reform also allowed the private sector to play a more active role as a supplier of education, introducing a subsidy per student. This subsidy – which covers all operational costs – can be used to pay for schooling either in a municipality school or in a subsidized private school, as chosen by the parent. The main objective of this reform was to promote competition among schools to attract and retain students, which would result in greater efficiency and a higher quality of education. This change resulted in the creation of a large number of schools by the private sector, and the definition of three types of schools: municipal schools that are financed by the state subsidy and are operated by municipalities (55 percent of school students); private subsidized schools that are operated by the private sector but financed by the subsidy (34 percent); and private paid schools that are financed exclusively by parents and are operated privately (11 percent).

This educational policy has allowed an increase in access to both elementary and high school education. The access to elementary school[9] education reached an average of 98.6 percent compared with 95 percent in 1980, and 81 percent compared with 65 percent in 1980 in high school. However, there was a shortage in access to pre-elementary education, which only reached 21 percent of the student population.

The increase in access did not improve the quality of the education, and important differences between private and subsidized schools became increasingly apparent. According to an exam given regularly in fourth grade by all elementary schools (SIMCE),[10] public subsidized schools, usually attended by the low-income population, showed a poor level of achievement. It also showed a broad gap between these schools and private paid ones (MIDEPLAN, 1999b). Problems in the quality of education were especially severe in municipal schools.

At the end of the 1980s there were more problems in the sector: a high number of drop-outs from school, almost 20 percent of teenagers between 14 and 17 years old; a deterioration in technical education; financial, administrative and management problems in the Education Secretariat; a significant deterioration in teacher's salaries, among other problems (MIDEPLAN, 1996a). Moreover, public expenditure in education was reduced during the 1980s, from 3.5 percent to 2.5 percent of GDP, particularly affecting the poorest segments of the population.

Main policies, programs and expenditure in education in the 1990s

In 1990, the new government maintained the structure of the educational system. However, specific objectives were proposed for this sector: (1) improve the quality of education; (2) more equality in the access to education; (3) increase access to education; (4) promote the participation of different sectors and institutions in educational development. In 1995 emphasis was given to promoting a general education of a similar quality for everybody, reforming high school education in order to be modern and diversified, strengthening teachers' skills, modernizing the management of the educational system, increasing investment in education using both public and private funds and strengthening scientific and technological research. A strong accent was put on increasing teachers' salaries significantly.

A number of programs have been designed in order to achieve these objectives. The most important include:

- P-900 – Program for a Better Quality Education in Elementary Schools of Poor Areas. In 1990 the Program for a Better Quality Education in Elementary Schools of Poor Areas, called P-900, was initiated, which focused on schools with the lowest 10 percent in learning results. The program was directed at improving infrastructure, teachers' formation, provision of texts and materials, libraries and school reinforcement.
- MECE – Program for the Improvement of the Quality and Equality of Education. This program was initiated in 1992, and was designed to spend around US$ 243 million in a five-year period. The main objectives of the MECE program were to:
  - substantially improve the quality of elementary education, while seeking a more equal distribution among sectors (US$ 178 million over five years);
  - increase in access and quality of pre-elementary schools (US$ 40 million);
  - improve the management at the level of the secretary of education

  (US$ 19 million);
  - evaluate different alternatives of institutional reforms in the high school education to improve quality, equity and belonging (US$ 2.5 million).
- For each educational level a specific program was developed:
  - Pre-elementary. This level focused on increasing access and supply quality for children under the age of six.
  - Elementary. The main programs implemented included the improvement of rural schools, the access to computers (ENLACES NET) among others.
  - High school. This program was launched in 1994 and focused mainly on increasing libraries, textbooks, infrastructure and the access to the ENLACES NET.

These changes required significant increases in public expenditure on education. Tables 10.5 and 10.6 show the evolution of fiscal and public expenditure since 1990: public expenditure increased by 177 percent between 1990 and 2000, the share of public expenditure on education compared with the rest of the social public expenditure also increased from 19.6 percent to 25.1 percent, while public expenditure in education as percentage of GDP grew from 2.4 percent to 3.9 percent in the same period. These indicators are consistent with the priority that has been given to this sector in the last decade. The increase in per capita public expenditure in education between 1990 and 2000 is 128 percent (Table 10A.5, Annex A).

*Table 10.5 Evolution of public and fiscal expenditure, 1990–2000 (2000 million US$)**

Year	Public expenditure	Fiscal expenditure
1990	1054.7	1040.9
1991	1196.4	1168.8
1992	1375.5	1339.4
1993	1493.3	1436.1
1994	1628.5	1593.1
1995	1818.9	1789.2
1996	2054.4	2060.4
1997	2263.0	2320.7
1998	2520.6	2500.8
1999	2.6958	2.7090
2000	2.9232	2.9353

Note: * Based on the average dollar observed in 2000.

Source: www.mideplan.cl.

Table 10.6 Public expenditure in education/social public expenditure and public expenditure in education/GDP, 1990–2000 (in percentages)

Year	PE education/ social PE	PE education/GDP
1990	19.6	2.4
1991	20.2	2.5
1992	21.0	2.6
1993	20.8	2.7
1994	21.3	2.7
1995	22.2	2.7
1996	22.9	3.0
1997	23.9	3.1
1998	24.7	3.5
1999	24.5	3.8
2000	25.1	3.9
Average (1990–2000)	22.4	3.0

Source: National Budget Office, Ministry of Finance, DIPRES (2003) Series Estadísticas, Estadísticas de las Finanzas Públicas 1987–2002.

It is interesting to examine fiscal expenditure in education. According to Table 10.7, most expenditure is dedicated to elementary education, specifically for subventions.[11] Spending in elementary education is almost six times higher than expenditure in pre-elementary, and 2.6 times more than high school expenditure. According to Cox and Gonzalez (1997), approximately half of the increase in public spending has been used to raise teachers' salaries, and the rest has been directed to the programs to improve quality and equality and access to university education.

*Table 10.7 Fiscal expenditure in education, 1996 (1998 million US$)**

	Total	% of Fiscal expenditure
Pre-elementary		
Subventions MINEDUC	76.68	3.6
JUNJI expenditure	65.33	3.1
INTEGRA expenditure	31.08	1.5
Total	173.08	8.1

	Total	% of Fiscal expenditure
Elementary		
Subventions MINEDUC	847.01	39.8
PAE elementary	108.01	5.1
School props	1.21	0.1
School texts	6.23	0.3
Oral Health	1.33	0.1
School Health	3.15	0.1
Total	966.95	45.4
High School		
Subventions scientific–humanist	154.96	7.3
PAE High School	7.20	0.3
Subventions technical–professional	173.13	8.1
Transfers to corporations with delegate adm.	34.96	1.6
Total technical–professional**	208.09	9.8
Total	370.24	17.4
Adults		
Subventions	17.90	0.8
University credits	41.40	1.9
Total	1569.57	73.8
Total other expenditures	558.13	26.2
Total fiscal expenditure	2127.70	100.0

Notes: *Based on the average dollar observed in 1999.
**Subventions and transfers to corporations.

Source: Own elaboration based on MIDEPLAN (1999b) and MINEDUC (1999).

Distribution of education expenditure among quintiles of income

One of the major achievements of social policy in the past decade has been the focalization of public programs. The share of public expenditure focused on lower income groups (that is, the lowest two quintiles of income) has steadily increased in the decade, reaching 63 percent in 2000 (Table 10.8).

Table 10.8 Expenditure in education by quintile of income, 2000 (in percentages)

	I	II	III	IV	V	Total
Pre-elementary	32.4	30.9	18.3	13.4	4.9	100.0
Elementary	38.2	26.7	18.6	11.4	5.1	100.0
High School	29.2	28.1	22.8	14.2	5.7	100.0
Adults	25.1	33.1	21.3	14.8	5.7	100.0
Total expenditure in education	35.2	27.6	19.6	12.3	5.2	100.0

Notes:
Pre-elementary includes subventions, JUNJI and INTEGRA.
Elementary includes subventions, School Food Programs, school props and texts and school and oral health.
High School includes subventions, transfers to corporations of Delegate Adm., School Food program and School Props program.
Adults includes subventions.

Source: MIDEPLAN (2001).

Results

Although difficult to evaluate in a short period, some indicators suggest that the effort to improve education has been partly successful. The average monthly wage received by teachers in the municipality sector increased significantly from US$ 477 to US$ 1063 between 1990 and 1999.

Between 1990 and 1998 the average educational years for the population over 15 increased from 9 to 9.7 years. In terms of quality, the SIMCE tests of the past years have shown a systematic reduction in the gap between subsidized and private schools, as well as the gap between municipal schools and the rest.[12]

Coverage increased by 30 percent in pre-elementary school and 10 percent in high schools. However, there is still the need to increase levels of coverage in the poorest sectors of the population. The last CASEN showed that the lower two quintiles of income had 23 percent and 29 percent of coverage in pre-elementary school, while the highest quintile reached 40 percent. Similarly, high school education also has a gap in the access level: for the population of the lowest quintile the share of attendance was 77 percent (compared with 98 percent in the highest income quintile), and for rural areas it decreased to 69 percent.

Another important indicator is school attendance, which averaged 92 percent in 1998 for Chile, 33 percent higher than Argentina, Brazil and Paraguay. This could be explained by the subsidies that are paid to schools based on actual attendance by students, giving incentives for schools to facilitate attendance.[13]

Housing

The general goals of housing policies have been to reduce the housing deficit and improve the precarious conditions of the houses of the poor. As in the other sectors examined, housing policy implemented since the late 1970s focused on the poor, and emphasized the subsidiary role of the state, with private agents playing an active role in the design, location, and financing of the houses. The private sector also defined standards, costs and quantity of houses, whereas the state's main role was to channel direct and indirect demand subsidies.

Housing sector in the 1990s

Two housing programs existed in the early 1990s. The first, oriented to the poorest 40 percent of the population, consisted of constructing social housing and sanitation. People had to save a certain amount during a period of time, and the state then subsidized the rest of the cost of the house, up to a fixed amount. Sanitation was improved in urbanizing properties while putting property titles in order. The other main programs included demand subsidies to sectors with larger savings capability and access to mortgages (MIDEPLAN, 1996a). In both cases, private construction firms built the houses. Nevertheless, while in the first program costs were set from the start, in the second program they could compete in price and quality to attract potential buyers with subsidies.

This housing policy was underfinanced, resulting in it being unable to satisfy the increasing demand for houses, thereby increasing the housing deficit during the 1980s. Over 25 percent of the population (920000 families), lived as *allegados*[14] of other families. There were 290000 people living in a house with extensive material damage, another 260000 did not have access to minimum sanitation, in particular water, and 120000 families had both deficits (MIDEPLAN, 1996b).

To prevent this deficit, it was estimated that 100000 units should be built per year during the 1990s. This was considered a great challenge, considering that between the early 1970s and late 1980 only 37000 new houses were built per year. Additionally, the increase in land prices and speculation made the solutions more expensive.

Housing policy, expenditure and programs in the 1990s

Housing policy in the 1990s was aimed at reducing the deficit substantially and improving the instruments used. More importance was given to the active participation of the beneficiary families in the design as well as in the execution and development of solutions. Private sector participation was encouraged, not only as constructors and financiers, but was extended to incorporate solutions by NGOs and community social organizations. The specific objectives for the sector in the period were:

- to seek more social equality, redistributing resources in favor of the poorest 40 percent;
- to prioritize the solutions for the regions with a greater lack of housing, especially in rural areas;
- participation of the private agents (broad concept);
- integration with other social programs related to the local and neighborhood life quality;
- to improve efficiency of the mechanisms and instruments in housing policy implementation.

Public expenditure in housing has increased considerably in the last decade. In the 1980s, it fluctuated between 1.3 percent and 7.7 percent of the share of total public expenditure, while between 1990 and 2000 it averaged 8.0 percent (Table 10.9). There has been a constant increase in fiscal and public expenditure in housing of 112 percent and 53 percent respectively (Table 10.10). Despite this growth in absolute terms, as a share of GDP, public expenditure in housing stabilized at around 1.1 percent between 1990 and 2000.

Table 10.9 Public expenditure in housing/social public expenditure and public expenditure housing/GDP, 1990–98 (in percentages)

Year	PE Housing/ Social PE	PE Housing/GDP
1990	8.1	1.0
1991	8.2	1.1
1992	8.3	1.2
1993	8.3	1.2
1994	8.2	1.2
1995	8.0	1.1
1996	8.2	1.2
1997	7.3	1.1

Year	PE Housing/ Social PE	PE Housing/GDP
1998	7.0	1.1
1999	6.4	1.3
2000	5.8	1.0
Average (1990-2000)	8.0	1.1

Source: National Budget Office, Ministry of Finance; DIPRES (2003) Series Estadísticas, Estadísticas de las Finanzas Públicas 1987–2002.

Table 10.10 Public and fiscal expenditure in housing (2000 million US$) and fiscal expenditure in housing/public expenditure in housing 1990–2000 (in percentages)*

Year	Public expenditure	Fiscal expenditure	Fiscal expenditure/ Public expenditure (%)
1990	436.82	272.49	62.4
1991	486.71	329.03	67.6
1992	542.62	425.30	78.4
1993	595.58	515.90	86.6
1994	623.19	550.02	88.3
1995	651.20	571.78	87.8
1996	728.31	611.64	84.0
1997	689.34	614.60	89.2
1998	710.48	604.14	85.0
1999	699.47	598.86	85.6
2000	667.84	576.62	86.3

Note: *Based on the average dollar observed in 1998.

Source: www.mideplan.cl.

The main public programs undertaken in the decade were:

- Creation of the Progressive House program, focused on housing solutions for the most needy. It consists of progressive phases in order to integrate the families in its development.[15]
- Special program for rural villages, created to give housing solutions to the rural areas with higher deficits.
- The Chile Neighborhood Program aimed at contributing to improve conditions of the poor in basic settlements, giving them

opportunities for residential and habitat improvement, as well as opportunities for social and labor insertion.

- The Basic Housing program was destined to give solutions to low income families who live as *allegados*, or who rent a place. Another special program was created to give basic housing to elders.
- The Unified General Subsidy program, which provides non-refundable money aid of up to a prespecified amount to those who buy a house in the market.
- The Workers Special program, which subsidizes the acquisition of houses preferably by organized groups from private and public institutions.
- The Rural Subsidy program aimed at the poorest families of rural areas.
- The program for Urban and Neighborhood Improvement whose goal is to provide resources for sanitation for villages and construction of lots with services.

Results of the programs

Table 10.11 summarizes the results of the effort to improve housing. Between 1990 and 1998, over 800000 housing solutions were delivered, more than 91000 per year. This is a significant increase compared with the previous period, where on average only 37000 were delivered per year. It also came very close to the estimated 100000 per year required to eliminate the accumulated deficit.

Table 10.12 presents how the funds were allocated to each program. Over 80 percent of the budget was used directly on housing (MIDEPLAN, 1998b, 1999a), while 43 percent of social investment on housing was channeled through the program of Social Housing, particularly the Basic Housing program. The subsidy programs were also very important, and accounted for 41 percent of investment, most of it for the General Unified Subsidy.

Table 10.11 Number of subsidies and housing contracts, 1990–98 (units)

Programs	1990	1991	1992	1993	1994	1995	1996	1997	1998	Total
Social Housing										
Basic	19.141	25.322	25.862	25.868	26.468	23.580	23.230	20.729	21.600	211.800
Progressive	4.482	9.208	13.077	4.689	3.427	3.683	3.722	3.529	3.209	49.026
Subsidies										
Basic	0	0	0	0	0	4.972	7.132	7.298	6.042	25.444
Progressive Phase I	0	0	0	7.002	8.737	6.261	10.324	8.683	9.201	50.208
Progressive Phase II	0	4.532	1.932	2.010	2.428	2.238	3.103	15.670	2.245	20.055
Rural	7.579	7.564	7.748	7.802	7.793	8.245	8.697	11.033	10.186	76.647
Workers	15.640	16.252	12.628	15.035	18.079	17.545	16.246	11.901	12.131	135.457
General unified	28.958	28.780	28.530	30.359	29.947	29.546	28.517	24.364	24.740	253.741
Total housing solution programs	75.800	91.658	89.777	92.765	96.879	96.070	100.971	89.104	89.354	822.378

Source: Own elaboration based on MIDEPLAN (1996a); MINVU (1999).

*Table 10.12 Housing investment, 1990–98 (1998 million US$)**

Programs	1989	1990	1991	1992	1993	1994	1995	1996	1997	1998	Total 90–98 US$	Total 90–98 %
Social Housing												43.0
Basic	102.77	99.15	164.32	145.96	168.80	197.07	198.91	190.65	177.90	170.57	1.51	37.4
Progressive	—	3.22	27.43	36.67	69.24	22.07	13.80	17.84	19.61	16.29	226.18	5.6
Subsidies												40.9
Basic	—	—	—	—	—	—	3.42	11.44	9.84	12.88	37.58	0.9
Progressive	—	—	—	—	—	26.95	34.61	34.19	23.67	21.01	140.42	3.5
Rural	—	17.87	15.35	29.22	23.92	25.77	26.85	20.17	29.92	34.08	223.15	5.5
Worker	35.14	32.63	33.73	52.94	37.88	42.73	44.92	38.59	33.05	30.36	346.84	8.6
General Unified	121.23	105.98	96.06	89.25	97.53	93.56	90.95	92.15	83.52	75.62	824.63	20.4
Otros	—	30.82	10.34	13.00	10.07	4.97	5.01	3.48	1.15	5.05	83.89	2.1
Housing investment Subtotal	259.13	289.67	347.24	367.05	407.44	413.12	418.48	408.50	378.66	365.86	3.39	83.9
Urban and Neighborhood Improvement Program	54.98	60.28	61.48	60.50	48.65	53.01	80.65	88.07	101.46	99.40	653.51	16.1
Total solutions	314.12	349.96	408.73	427.55	456.09	466.13	499.13	496.57	480.12	465.26	4.04	100.0

Note: *Based on the average dollar observed in 1998.

Source: Own elaboration based on MIDEPLAN (1996a); MINVU (1999).

In terms of focalization of the housing programs, the survey CASEN shows that 54 percent of the benefits given out by the social programs were received by the poorest 40 percent of the population in 1998. The benefits received by the first quintile grew from 30 percent in 1996 to 32.1 percent in 1998.

Table 10.13 Distribution of benefits per period, among homes by quintiles of income (in percentages)*

Period	Quintile					Total
	I	II	III	IV	V	
1990–93	28.9	23.0	21.3	18.8	8.0	100.0
1994–97	29.5	22.4	20.2	17.8	10.1	100.0
1998	32.1	21.4	25.8	15.1	5.6	100.0

Note: *Homes that have been declared to receive help by the state.

Source: MIDEPLAN (1999d).

The increase in social investment in housing, together with a better focalization of social programs has reduced the significant housing problem of the beginning of the decade. In quantitative measures, the housing deficit in 1990 reached nearly 900000 families. The 1996 CASEN study showed a reduction in this number of around 19 percent, reducing the deficit to 740000 families. Consequently, and despite the significant increase in investment in the period, the problem is still striking!

There have also been important qualitative improvements. According to the last CASEN (1998) deficit of material (material damage) was reduced by 39 percent while deficits in sanitation by 14 percent and the number of houses with both problems was reduced by 47 percent. Even so, there are still around half a million homes with some kind of qualitative deficit.

Productive Development in Poor Areas

Social policies and productive development in the 1990s

During the 1980s, little attention was put on improving productivity. Promotion of production was focused on modern sectors of the economy, concentrating incentive policies on the export sector and bigger companies, which was consistent with the prevailing economic policy of the 1980s. At the end of the 1980s, direct support through subsidies for small and medium enterprises was given, to keep them active due to their strong impact on employment. Usually, there was little concern for reduced productivity levels, and in general little attention was given to technological innovation, incorporation into markets and modern schemes of production and management (MIDEPLAN, 1996).

This changed during the 1990s, as at the beginning of the decade it was clear that to help the poor, it was necessary that small producers be included in the process of national development: the unemployment rate for 1990 was 8.3 percent, informal employment reached 27 percent, and the poverty level was almost 40 percent. Consequently, the promotion of productive development focused on strengthening the productive opportunities of these producers, and included actions that increased human capital, such as reconversion policies or labor training, as well as initiatives that increased the productivity of micro-enterprises. The specific objective of policies in this area is to complement the development of policies undertaken in other areas of the state, with the goal of overcoming poverty. It is expected that through the use and development of their own potentials, persons and communities can improve their living conditions through a gradual and sustained process, while developing a process of social integration.

Table 10.14 Budget evolution of FOSIS, 1995–2002 (2002 million US$)

	1995	1997	1999	2002
Revenue				
Fiscal contribution	27 812.14	34 995.20	37 924.28	38 179.86
Other income	12 692.22	3 326.95	1 021.11	739.95
Total	40 504.36	38 322.15	38 945.40	38 919.81
Expenditure				
Current transfers	21 633.99	19 996.06	10 848.07	10 378.71
Sector investment assigned by region	15 610.82	0.00	11 857.57	0.00
Capital transfers	0.00	16 094.73	14 123.04	22 163.77
Other expenditure	3 259.57	2 231.37	2 116.72	6 377.32
Total	40 504.36	38 322.15	38 945.40	38 919.81
% of MIDEPLAN	44.5	40.3	39.5	27.71

Source: Own elaboration based on the budgetary laws for 1995–2002.

This new criteria in social policies gave away in 1990 to the creation of FOSIS (Fund for Solidarity and Social Investment), which was aimed at financing the promotion of productive development of the weaker sectors of the economy. Since 1995, over 50 million dollars has been used with this. Table 10.14 shows the evolution of fiscal contribution through MIDEPLAN to FOSIS.

The main programs to promote production in small and medium-sized firms in the decade have been:

- Credit Assistance program through banks, aimed at poor micro-entrepreneurs, facilitating their inclusion into bank system benefits;
- Financial Intermediation program, similar to the above, but through Intermediate Development Institutions, and NGOs focused on the promotion of productive micro-entrepreneurs with smaller activities;
- Micro-entrepreneur program, which contributed to the development and continuity of poor micro-enterprises, through training, technical assistance and management counseling;
- CIEM program, aimed at supporting productive development of poor micro-entrepreneurs through a research center;
- Rural Production Promotion program, which aimed at supporting the generation and financing of rural productive projects, preferably non-agricultural in nature, to be developed by groups, organizations or poor rural families;
- Peasant Forestation program and Soil Recuperation
- Young Chile Joven program, developed in order to support technical training for the poor and the excluded younger segment of the population;
- Artisan Fishermen program, aimed at giving credit to poor fishing ports to renew equipment and improve infrastructure.

Table 10.15 summarizes the expenditure in each program and the number of beneficiaries. Accumulated investment between 1991 and 1999 in these programs exceeds 175 million dollars. Between 1995 and 1999 nearly 57 percent of the FOSIS budget was targeted to programs related to poor productive sectors, through investment support and generation of socio-productive capacities.

*Table 10.15 Total investment FOSIS programs (1998 thousand US$)**

	FOSIS Contribution	Coverage**
Program for Credit Assistantship through Banks	12 961.17	119 499
Chile Joven Program	47 375.16	39 862
Program for Artisan Fisheries	532.67	153***
CIEM Program	2 226.70	6 919
Microenterprise Program	41 317.87	98 923
Rural Forestation and Soil Recovery Program	9 570.33	42 983
Rural Productivity Support Program	13 627.28	28 670
IFIS OID's Program	6 217.79	40 609
Programs Total	175 770.66	377 618

Notes:
* Based on the average dollar observed in 1998.
** Persons.
*** Enterprises.

Source: Own elaboration based on FOSIS (2000).

Another important consideration in funding has been that it must support all regions, and be assigned and used with a high degree of decentralization. According to FOSIS (1997) close to 50 percent of investment for 1998[16] was assigned to regions.

Environmental Status and Issues of Concern

Since the beginning of the century, Chile had developed a considerable amount of environmental regulations and standards up to 1990. These were of diverse nature, dispersed among different sectors, fragmented, and without any coordination among them. These regulations were reactions to specific environmental problems at a given time, and not part of a coherent policy. As a result, many of the regulations were not applied, due to the uncertainty as to their validity, and moreover, a high degree of non-compliance. Nevertheless, environmental protection received strong support in the 1980 Constitution.

Based on the deteriorated environmental quality, particularly in Santiago, and the need to have an effective environmental policy to defend exports against accusations of ecological dumping, the democratic government, elected in 1990, initiated the restructuring of the sector by setting up the Special Commission for Metropolitan Region

Decontamination to improve Santiago's deteriorated environmental quality. A few months later, the National Commission for the Environment (CONAMA) was established. In 1994, the General Environmental Framework Law was passed. It reinforced the previous institutional framework by setting the foundations for the National System for Environmental Management. This institutional development also reinforced environmental expenditures. Thus, the environment-related expenditures by CONAMA, Ministries of Economy and Mining and Forestry National Corporation are now 50 times more than in 1990 (Brzovic et al., 2002), rising to over 2 percent of the public budget in 2000. The distribution of the expenditures by objectives is presented in Table 10.16. It is also important to observe that environmental authorities regulate and control some activities instead of intervening directly, allowing environmental expenditures to be transferred to the private sector (for example, in air emissions abatement).

Table 10.16 Environmental expenditures by objective, 1999–2001 (thousand US$)

Objectives according to CEPA[a] 2000	1999	2000	2001[b]
1 Protection of air and clime	6337	13440	6204
2 Management of liquid waste	12960	17428	3833
3 Management and protection of land, underground water and superficial waters	41087	60055	48693
4 Noise pollution abatement	81	347	305
5 Waste management	45568	43754	5352
6 Protection of the biodiversity	41922	39654	20305
7 Others activities of environmental Protection (including management)	149332	127292	70747
Total environmental expenditure	297286	301970	155439

Notes:
[a] Classification of Environmental Protection Activities and Expenditure.
[b] Preliminary commitments.
Current values at the annual averaged observed dollar (B. Central).

Source: O'Ryan et al. (2004).

Despite these progresses, policies and programs for sustainable development still play a secondary role in Chile, resulting in the accumulation of countless environmental problems, of which the most important include:

1. Air pollution, linked to urban areas, industrial activities (pulp and paper, fishmeal), mining and electricity generation. In specific areas, emissions of different pollutants exceed the national norm or international recommendations.
2. High levels of water pollution caused by domestic and industrial effluents without treatment, thereby affecting surface water, ground water and coastal seawater.
3. Water scarcity at the regional level.
4. Inadequate urban development management, high levels of pollution, scarcity of green or recreational areas etc.
5. Inappropriate solid waste management and disposal, in particular hazardous wastes.
6. Land erosion and degradation, associated to poor agricultural and forestry techniques, urban growth and inadequate solid waste management, primarily affecting agricultural land and river basins.
7. Threats to native forests due to overexploitation (increase of forestry activity, coal mining, wood collection) and absence of effective protection.
8. Hydro-biological resource overexploitation and biomass exhaustion.
9. Poor management of hazardous chemical substances.

The trade-off between a better environment and growth, required to solve the important social problems discussed in the previous sections, is very clear in the case of Chile. Many of the most important economic sectors are related to natural resources (mining, forestry, agriculture and fishery), thus any action that reduces activity in these sectors may have regional and/or countrywide impacts. Investment in pollution reduction, in particular in Santiago, will require significant layouts, not necessarily paid exclusively by those affected. In the following sections, Chile's main environmental problems are discussed.

Urban Pollution

Rapid and unmanaged urbanization, fueled by economic growth, has led to moderately to severe air and water pollution in many of Chile's cities. Preventive costs, health damages and productivity losses, particularly in Santiago, have been estimated as significant.

Waste generation in Chile is unevenly distributed with the Metropolitan region generating 60 percent of domestic waste, while housing only 40 percent of the population. The total production of domestic waste is also growing in Chile. In six years, waste generation increased from 200 tons/month in 1990 (or 19 kg/person/month), to 278 tons/month in 1996 (or 23 kg/person/month). The Santiago Metropolitan area has a system for the declaration of the quantity and type of waste and its final disposal. However, this system is restricted to this region and the problem of undeclared waste disposal still exists. The region's control is very lax.

In Chile, recycling is a significant business, with a recycling rate of 52 percent for cardboard and paper which exceeds the corresponding rates in many industrial countries. Approximately 30 000 people in Santiago earn their livelihood from collection of recyclable material, most of them informally and as a way to fight for their living. Around 12 500 are informally employed in this sector. The high level of material use efficiency will be harder to maintain as incomes rise and the opportunity costs of labor increase.

Industrial Pollution

Industrial pollution went largely uncontrolled until 1990. During the 1990s, significant efforts were made to complete an inventory of sources of industrial air pollution in Santiago for particulates. However, in other parts of the country, and for other pollutants, information is scarce. Currently, there are standards for all criteria of pollutants, noise coming from fixed sources (1998) and liquid industrial waste discharges to sewage. Standards for emission of liquid effluents on superficial water, and arsenic emissions are being implemented.

Non-urban industrial pollution arises primarily from the mining and smelter operations in the north and center of the country as well as petroleum-based industries in Concepción and Valparaiso areas. Mining activities are site-specific but the environmental impacts are large. The mining sector plays a key role in the Chilean economy but is also the largest source of industrial pollution especially of sulfur dioxide, particulates, arsenic and metallic residues.

Under a 1992 decree, implementation of decontamination plans is required for all existing plants including the worst offenders – state-owned smelters. Up to 1998, there were four plans being executed[17] and one more under promulgation.[18] The cost of implementing these plans is estimated at US $1 billion for the state enterprises alone. The cost of abating arsenic has recently been evaluated, and emission standards for seven smelters have recently been approved. Environmental costs associated with small-scale mining need to be evaluated.

Other important sources of industrial pollution include fossil fuel users, as well as the pulp and paper industry in Regions VII through IX (sulfuric acid), and fishmeal industry in Region VIII (sulfuric acid and trimethylamine).

Air Pollution

Air pollution in Santiago is the most obvious environmental problem in the country, although other cities are also being affected. In Santiago, natural variables, demographic growth, fixed and mobile sources are principal causes. The total amount of vehicles in Chile has grown from 1.1 million in 1990 to over 2.1 million by 2000. However, important reductions in PM10 and PM2.5 (23.3 percent and 46 percent respectively) have been achieved since 1989. The Metropolitan Region's Air Pollution Prevention and Clean-up Plan, the elimination of 3000 highly polluting buses, the incorporation of natural gas in the productive process of fixed sources, and the introduction of catalytic converters in all new vehicles (as a result 50 percent of cars in Santiago had converters in 1999) are main determinants of this improvement.

The Plan is based on emergency procedures; when the air quality index exceeds some levels an episode is declared and gradual compulsory measures are applied. Some of these measures are restrictions on vehicle use, residential heating and industrial production. Despite all efforts, in 2003 there were five environmental pre-emergency events (Table 10.17), and 21 alerts.[19]

Table 10.17 Santiago environmental situations in the 1990s

Year	Pre-emergency	Emergency	Year	Pre-emergency	Emergency
1990	11	2	1997	13	0
1991	9	2	1998	12	1
1992	14	2	1999	14	1
1993	8	0	2000	11	0
1994	3	0	2001	4	0
1995	2	0	2002	11	0
1996	6	0	2003	5	0

Source: SESMA (2004).

The transport sector makes the largest contribution to air pollution. Transport is directly responsible for most of PM10 emissions, the most critical environmental problem in the city: 25 percent are emitted directly and another 50 percent resuspended by vehicles on paved and unpaved roads. This sector is also responsible for 50 percent of PM2.5 emissions. Furthermore, the transport sector is also responsible for 94 percent of carbon monoxide (CO) emissions, 83 percent of nitrogen oxides (NO_x) emissions, and 42 percent of volatile organic compound (VOC) emissions. Private transport is generally more polluting in terms of concentration of pollutants per vehicle mile traveled than public transport, except for PM10 emissions.

The Table 10.18 shows Santiago's air quality compared with other major cities that are highly polluted, indicating that air quality is a major problem in the city. Tables 10.19 and 10.20 look at air pollution in Santiago for 1995 and 2000. In addition, air pollution in Santiago is subject to climate variables and pollution strongly varies among seasons.

Table 10.18 City comparison of air pollution

City (Population in 1000s)	Total suspended particles	Sulfur dioxide	Nitrogen dioxide
Calcutta (11923)	375	49	34
Beijing (11299)	377	90	122
Mexico City (16562)	279	74	130
Tehran (6836)	248	209	–
Bombay (15138)	240	33	39
Bangkok (6547)	223	11	23
Santiago (4891)[20]	210	29	81
Manila (9286)	200	33	–
Athens (3093)	178	34	64
Sao Paolo (16533)	86	43	83
Lisbon (1863)	61	8	52
Ankara (2826)	57	55	46
Tokyo (26959)	49	18	68
WHO Recommendations	60–90	40–60	–

Notes:
Because of differences in location and measurement, city comparisons are only indicative.
Commercial city center, $\mu g/m^3$ annual averages, 1995.

Source: World Bank databases (SIMA).

Table 10.19 Air pollution in Santiago, 1995

	CO[b]	Ozone[c]	PM10[a]	PM2.5[a]	SO_2[a]	NO_2[a]	TSP[a]
Max.	35.6	224	302	174	161	254	621
Min.	0.1	1	8	4	7	4	31
Average[21]	2.04	13	87	42	17.8	64.8	186.3

Notes:
[a] Data in µg/m3. [b] In ppm. [c] In ppb.

Source: SESMA, INE.

Table 10.20 Air pollution in Santiago, 2000

	CO[b]	Ozone[c]	PM10[a]	PM10-2.5[a]	PM2.5[a]	SO_2[a]
Max.	19.3	162	230	105	153	135
Min.	0.1	1	5	1	4	1
Average[22]	1.1	16	87	35.8	34.8	4.7

Note:
[a] data in µg/m3. [b] In ppm. [c] In ppb.

Source: SESMA, INE

Other problem areas in Chile include poor air quality in Concepción-Talcahuano from steel, petroleum, fishmeal, paper and pulp industries and high levels of ground level ozone in Valparaiso-Viña del Mar (see Tables 10.21 and 10.22). The Talcahuano environmental recovery plan is operating and air monitoring systems are being established in several cities with the goal of identifying saturated zones.

Table 10.21 Estimates of air pollution emissions for Valparaiso-Viña del Mar in 1997 (ton/year)

Source	PM10	SO_2	NO_X	CO	COV
Mobile sources	1641	1897	12669	93237	11.8
Fixed sources	25	99	217	144	0.4
Total	1666	1996	12886	93381	12

Source: Universidad de Chile (2000).

Table 10.22 Emission inventory for Concepción-Talcahuano in 1980

Emission Source	Pollution* (ton/year)					
	Total	PM	SO_2	NO_X	HCT	CO
Boiler	69	1173	5338	2331	462	609
Furnace	53	49	–	–	128	395
Incinerator	63	10879	3110	2414	6673	823
Industry	19084	161	252	1195	1196	9069
Railroad station	1	86	288	36	85	884
Total		12348	8988	5976	8544	11280

Note: *Does not include emissions of HS 0.3, trimethylamine 9.3 and mercury 0.6 ton/year, from industrial process.

Source: Universidad de Chile (2000).

Tables 10.23 and 10.24 summarize air quality problems by regions and cities.

Table 10.23 Air quality problems by region

Pollutant	Source	Affected Area
PM10	Copper smelting	II, III, V, VI regions
	Petroleum refinery	V region
	Cement production	V region
	Diesel motors	Metropolitan
SO_2	Copper smelting	II, III, V, VI regions
	Petroleum refinery	V region
	Cement production	V region
Ozone	Copper smelting	V region
	Petroleum refinery	V region
	Cement production	V region
	Vehicles	Metropolitan
Sulfuric acid	Pulp and paper	VII, VIII and IX regions
	Fishmeal industry	VIII region
Trimethylamine	Fishmeal industry	VIII region
CO and CO_2	Vehicles	Metropolitan
NO_x	Vehicles	Metropolitan

Source: CONAMA-Univ. de Talca-Univ. de Concepción (1998).

Table 10.24 Summary of air quality in Chile's major cities

City	Region	Exceeds PM-10 standard?	Other pollutants with problems?	Main emitting sources
Arica	I	Yearly standard is exceeded	Probably sulfates	No information
Iquique	I	Daily standard was exceeded 8 times, and yearly standard exceeded	No	Fixed and mobile sources
Antofagasta	II	Daily standard was exceeded 2 times	Particulates	No information
Calama	II	Daily and yearly standard exceeded	SO_2	Fixed sources
Valparaíso-Viña del mar	V	Daily standard was exceeded 3 times . Yearly average is very close to being exceeded	NO_2, SO_2, ozone	Mobile sources
Santiago	Metropolitan	Daily standard was exceeded 138 times. Yearly average exceeded	PM-2.5, Ozone and CO	Streets, vehicles, and industry
Rancagua	VI	Daily standard was exceeded 11 times. Yearly average exceeded	Ozone	Mobile sources
Concepción-Talcahuano	VIII	Daily standard was exceeded 3 times	SO_2	No information
Temuco	IX	Daily standard was exceeded 9 times	No	Fixed sources

Source: Summarized from Universidad de Chile (2002).

The biggest threat to health from air pollution is from fine particles (PM2.5). Studies indicate that there are significant effects on human health. For this reason, several territories have been declared 'saturated areas' (see Table 10.25) for specific pollutants. Santiago Metropolitan region was declared saturated of PM10, CO_2, O_3 and latent of NO_x in 1996.

Water Supply and Quality

Chile has considerable surface water resources from a series of river systems originating in the Andes and draining into the Pacific Ocean. However, water scarcity is becoming a critical issue in many regions, especially in the northern regions and the Central Valley, where traditional use in agriculture and cities is competing strongly with increasing demand by mining and hydropower generation sectors. Recently, periodic droughts have made the situation worse. Precipitation varies widely among Chilean regions (Table 10.26), resulting in water availability per person being extremely different between northern and southern regions, with strong scarcity problems from Region I even to Region VI (Figure 10.1).

Table 10.25 Saturated areas in Chile

Region	Territory	Saturated of:	Year
II	Maria Elena, Pedro de Valdivia areas	PM10	1993
II	Chuquicamata camp	SO_2, PM10	1991
II	Potrerillos smelter area	SO_2, PM10	1997
III	Hernán videla smelter area	SO_2	1993
V	Chagres village	Latent SO_2	1991
V	Ventanas smelter area	SO_2, PM10	1993
VI	Caletones area	SO_2, PM10	1994
RM	Santiago Metropolitan area	PM10, CO_2, O_3, latent NO_x	1996

Source: CONAMA.

Table 10.26 Precipitation and drains by region

Region	Precipitation		Drains	
	m^3/s	mm	m^3/s	mm
I	157	93.6	11.9	7.09
II	182	44.5	0.93	0.23
III	205	82.4	1.88	0.76
IV	281	222.0	22.2	17.5
V	211	434.0	40.7	83.7
MR	335	650.0	103.0	200.0
VI	508	898.0	205.0	32.0
VII	1 347	1 377.0	767.0	784.0
VIII	2 467	1 766.0	1 638.0	1 173.0
IX	1 451	2 058.0	1 041.0	1 476.0
X	6 319	2 970.0	5 155.0	2 423.0
XI	11 763	3 263.0	10 134.0	2 818.0
XII	11 748	2 713.0	10 124.0	2 338.0
Chile	36 947	1 522.0	29 244.0	1 204.0

Source: Dirección General de Aguas (DGA), 1987.

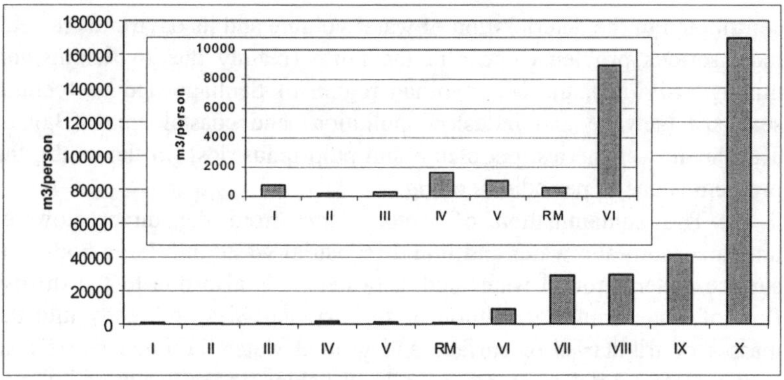

Source: Universidad de Chile (2000), on the basis of data from the General Water Directorate of Chile (DGA).

Figure 10.1 Water availability per person per region

Sectors demanding water are very different. Non-consumptive use, that is, which are injected back to the system after use, for example, in the case of hydropower generation, and for consumption, accounts for 68 percent of water used per person/day. However, agriculture spends 84 percent of consumptive water (Figure 10.2).

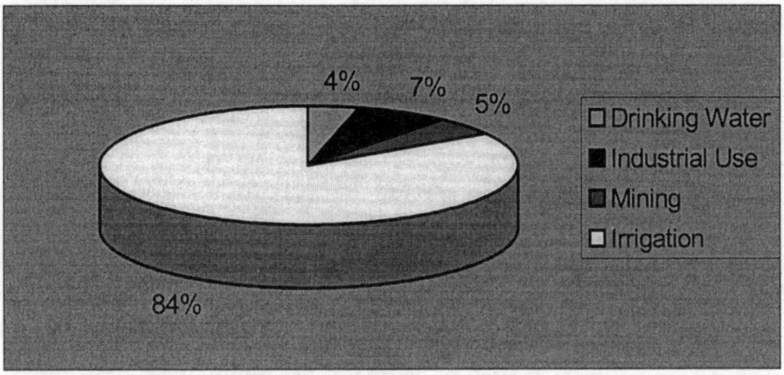

Source: Dirección General de Aguas (1999).

Figure 10.2 Demands for water by use

Water pollution is another problem. Factors such as demographic growth, industrialization and concentration of urban areas, have contributed to the deterioration of water volume and its environment. The most serious problems occur in the north (mainly due to fishing and mining activities), the Metropolitan region of Santiago and the central seaboard (sewage and industrial pollution) and coastal areas (Bay of Talcahuano – fisheries, petroleum and pulp industries). In the south, the problem is one of periodic flooding.

The contamination of water stems from the direct flow of untreated domestic water and liquid industrial waste into large bodies of surface water, ground water and seawater. It is also due to the diffuse flow of water from agricultural or forestry activities, indirectly into the masses or tributaries of surface and ground water. Polluted rivers also contaminate coastal areas, affecting local fishing operations in addition to defiling recreational and tourist sites. Table 10.27 summarizes the main problems per region

Table 10.27 Main water pollutants per region

Pollutant	Source	Affected Area
Organic Material	Domestic waste Industrial waste	Rivers: Aconcagua, Maipo, Andalien and Bio-Bio. Bays of Valparaiso and San Vicente (Concepción)
Nitrogen and Phosphorus	Domestic waste Industrial waste	II, III, V and VIII regions
TSS and TDS	Domestic waste Industrial waste	II, III, V and VIII regions
Metals (Copper, Cadmium, Lead and Zinc)	Domestic waste Industrial waste mining	II, III, V and VIII regions
Arsenic	Mining	Elqui Valley
Fats	Domestic waste Industrial waste	II, III, V and VIII regions

Source: CONAMA-Univ. de Talca-Univ. de Concepción (1998).

Studies show that the main water quality issue is microbiological contamination. While sanitation services are quite well developed in Chile – 91 percent of households have access to potable water[23] (95 percent to safe water) and 76 percent[24] have adequate sewerage – the *disposal* of collected waste water is inadequate. Waste treatment facilities are very few and small in scale. The rivers running through Santiago and surrounding areas (especially coastal) are particularly affected by the dumping of untreated sewage into open watercourses.

Table 10.28 Water contamination, an international comparison

River	BOD5 (mg/l)	Suspended solids (mg/l)	Fecal coliform (per 100 ml)
Garang, Indonesia	2.30	245.00	82500
Maipo, Chile	15.00	8.00	53447
Rapel, Chile	1.29	0.24	44391
Mataquito, Chile	0.50	0.15	33086
Yellow River, Huanghe, China	1.18	6822.00	2950
Mississippi, Vicksburg, USA			1473
Chilean Water Quality Standard for Irrigation			1000
US Ambient Water Quality Standards	4.00		500
WHO Drinking Water Guidelines		1000	0–10

Note: List includes rivers in Chile's central regions with a flow of more than 250 million m^3 /month.

Source: World Bank Report No. 13061-CH.

The concentration of fecal coliform exceeds the irrigation water standard of 1000 fecal coliform per 100 ml in almost all rivers reaching levels above 100000 FC per 100 ml in the worst cases. Table 10.28 compares water pollution in some rivers in Chile to others in the world.

Water pollution due to agricultural runoff is an issue, although little information is available on the extent of the problem. Fortunately, since a significant part of the agricultural output is exported (non-traditional crops increase its used land by 21 percent during the 1990s), its production processes have to meet relatively stringent requirements from importing countries. As a result, the rates for soil and water runoffs are lower than would otherwise be the case. Nevertheless, increases in productivity have required more fertilizer and pesticide use. Also, the agricultural output intended for domestic consumption does not meet the same standards and higher quantities of agrochemicals are usually applied. Livestock – increase in pigs from 1.6 to 2.8 million between 1990 and 1998 – is another important source of water pollution by organic residues.

Steffen (1993) believed that the use of water for agricultural, forestry and aquacultural purposes, as well as the increase of human effluents in the lakes in southern Chile has significantly increased the growth of nutrients (acting as pollutants) in these water systems, thereby leading to a buildup of algae and a drop in biodiversity.

Lastly, ground water pollution is an emerging problem. In Chile, ground water has been widely used as a source for drinking water, and it is foreseen that it will be used more and more in the future.

Renewable Natural Resources

The most pressing natural resource management issues in Chile are those associated with forestry and fisheries. These industries have rapidly expanded in response to a favorable macroeconomic policy framework and strong external demand.

Forestry

Chile has great potential for forestry development, as soils are naturally suitable for forestry in much of the country. Of the total continental surface area of 75.7 million hectares (Mha), it is estimated that 44.6 percent (33.8 Mha) is suitable for forestry, 18 percent is suitable for livestock and agriculture, while the remaining 29.4 percent is land that is unsuitable for agriculture or forestry. According to the recent forestry cadastre (Universidad Austral de Chile and others, 1997), the total surface area of Chile covered by forest is approximately 15.65 Mha, of which 86.5 percent (slightly over 13.5 Mha) contains native forests[25] and the remaining 13.5 percent (2.12 Mha) is planted (see Table 10.29). This means that only 46.3 percent of land suitable for forestry is currently forested, indicating a great potential for the development of new forests. Moreover, inasmuch as this potential is not realized, the lack of tree cover leads to increasing soil degradation.

Of native forests, 29 percent (3.92 Mha) is publicly owned and comes under the State-Protected Forestry Areas System (SNASPE), while the remaining 71 percent is privately owned. Although the total surface area of native forest within SNASPE is significant, representation of the different types of native forest is highly varied. For some forest types more than half the existing stock is within the SNASPE, whereas in other types the proportion is less than 2 percent.

Annual extraction of native forests amounts to 9.3 million m^3, of which 6.1 million m^3 is used for firewood and charcoal (INFOR, 1993), mainly for domestic use in the south of the country, and 3.2 million m^3 for industrial use (INFOR, 1995). The industrial use of native wood is divided into two-thirds for the production of lumber chips and one-third for sawn lumber and panels.

Native wood currently accounts for just 15 percent of the total consumption of the forestry industry, while the rest comes from Monterrey pine (*pino radiata*) and eucalyptus plantations. Thus, plantations are the fundamental source of timber, and restrictions on their development for environmental or other reasons would have a significant impact on the sector.

From the global point of view, the extraction of 9.3 million m^3 of timber per year from native forests does not necessarily put them in danger. As that level of extraction is well below the annual rate of forest growth, the country can expand its forestry stock in terms of native species. Of course, what is true for the whole country is not necessarily true at the local level or for certain individual species nor does it ensure adequate protection of the biodiversity associated with native forests.

With regard to existing plantations, reports state that the annual rate of forestation in the last 20 years, which approaches 63 000 ha/yr, has generated a forest mass of over 2.1 million ha. The resulting availability of timber over the next two decades will make it possible to double current physical production volumes. In other words, the forestry industry could grow from using 17 million m^3 per year at present to over 36 million m^3 in the year 2017 (INFOR, 1995). The period 1990–94 showed the highest rate of growth in plantations, with an average increase in plantation forest of 115 318 ha per year.

Table 10.29 Chilean forestry area

Forest structure	% Forestry	% National
Native forest	85.9	17.8
Plantation forest	13.5	2.8
Mixed forest	0.5	0.1
Total	100	20.8

Source: CONAMA (1997).

Biodiversity

Loss of biodiversity is a concern in Chile. Chilean forests contain several types of unique and localized forest systems including an important share of the world's temperate rainforests. Although they are not very biologically diverse, many forest ecosystems are unique to Chile. If present practices continue, unique plant and animal communities could be seriously affected. Table 10.30 presents the limited information available on this subject.

Table 10.30 Biodiversity and protected areas

Nationally protected areas (% of total)	Threatened/Total species		
	Mammals	Birds	Higher plants
18.3	11/91	15/448	292/5125

Biodiversity concerns are not exclusively related to forest management practices however. Table 10.31 shows that 35 percent of all species in Chile are affected. The conservation level and the distribution of threatened species within land vertebrates present some disparities. Non-sea fish are seriously threatened.

Table 10.31 Threatened species

	Mammals	Birds	Reptiles	Amphibians	Fishes	Total
Extinct	1	1	0	0	0	2
In Danger	15	10	1	6	18	50
Vulnerable	15	32	13	9	23	92
% Species with problems	51	17	58	79	100	35

Source: Glade (1988).

Fisheries

Chile has one of the five largest fishing industries in the world. Of the total catch, 88 percent is industrial while 12 percent is from small-scale activities. The rapid growth of this sector fueled over-investment and large-scale exertion, putting pressure on resource stocks. Between 1990 and 1998, this sector more than doubled its GDP and total extraction increased by more than 20 percent in the decade.

Catch has increased from 0.9 million tons in 1975 to over 6 million tons in recent years, resulting in a negative impact on biomass of certain marine species. A study by the Institute of Fishery Development (1991) indicated that the majority of important commercial species in Chile have been overexploited. Furthermore, a study by Gomez-Lobo in 1991 concluded that the overexploitation of mackerel and sardines for export substantially reduced the stock

The commercially most important fisheries are in a state of exploitation. The current situation implies significant risks given the natural volatility of some species, the uncertainties about stock size, reproduction and interactions between species. Though a mechanism for individual transferable quotas has been implemented to complement the existing overall quotas on an annual basis, it is only being applied to small fisheries.

Land Degradation

Land pollution and erosion are also issues of increasing concern. With regard to land pollution, despite the generally acceptable situation, there are abnormal concentrations of copper and lead in areas near copper mining activities. Fertilizer and pesticide residues in soil and water runoff is becoming a problem (Table 10.32).

Table 10.32 Major land pollutants, source and affected areas

Pollutant	Source	Affected area
Copper	Copper mining	Aconcagua, Mapocho and Cachapoal Valleys, and Puchuncavi Sector
Lead	Copper mining	Aconcagua, Mapocho and Cachapoal Valleys and Puchuncavi Sector
Fertilizers and pesticides	Agriculture and livestock	Region V and South of Chile

Source: CONAMA-Univ de Talca-Univ. de Concepción.

Land erosion affects 60 percent of the Chilean territory. Regions I to VIII, XI and XII are affected. The loss of vegetation that protects soils due to the loss of forest by piecemeal extraction and forest fires, is intensified by water erosion. Urban expansion, salinity increase, pollution and land nutrient loss are other causes of land degradation (Table 10.33).

Table 10.33 Origin of land degradation in Chile (in percentages)

Burning, deforestation and organic material loss	22.8
Erosion by water	19.3
Urban and industrial expansion	16.7
Chemical degradation	15.8
Erosion by wind	10.5
Salinity increase	7.0
Others	7.9

Source: CONAMA (1994).

Emerging Issues

Toxic substances

The management of toxic substances and hazardous waste received little attention in Chile. Limited information is available regarding the severity of this problem. Standards for 21 chemical substances and some regulations concerning transport, storage, information, etc., have been set and related international agreements have been signed. Nevertheless, classification and the implementation of policies for control and management are required.

Light contamination

Light contamination is defined as the brightness or glare of light in the night sky produced by the reflection and diffusion of artificial light in gases and air particles that disperses light toward telescope beams. This is affecting telescope vision and capacity at the observatories in the north of Chile.

Noise

Noise in urban areas is an increasing problem. Santiago shows extremely high levels of noise pollution. A study done in 1989[26] found that 65 percent of the 134 districts of exclusively residential, or mixed residential-commercial land use were unsuitable for residential use according to the noise criteria used by the Department of Housing and Urban Development in the USA. On the basis of a more sophisticated indicator,[27] it was found that nearly 50 percent of these districts were suffering from pollution of their acoustic environment. Moreover, there is no district whose main highways are suitable for residential use in housing of normal construction (that, without special acoustic treatment).

The risk of hearing loss is significant. Nearly 50 000 people are exposed to a high risk of hearing loss – 21 percent of the city's population is exposed to noise levels which constitute a moderate risk and 57 percent to noise levels representing a small probability of hearing loss. In addition, nearly 70 percent have a high risk of having their sleep affected due to the level of night-time noise.

The above means that in 1989, 41 percent of the population included in the study area – approximately 1.1 million people – were affected by some degree of significant nuisance due to noise pollution.[28] Considering the significant increase in vehicle circulation and congestion in the past seven years, there can be no doubt that the situation is even worse today.

Ozone layer and climate change

Chile will be adversely affected by ozone layer depletion as long as the Southern Hemisphere, particularly regions close to the South Pole, exhibits strong accumulated depletion (7 percent estimated decline). The magnitude of depletion is not equal in all parts. There are regions, such as between Puerto Montt (Chile) and the Antarctic Peninsula, where accumulated ozone depletion is estimated to have reached 13 percent.

10.3 INSTITUTIONAL FRAMEWORK AND ENVIRONMENTAL AND SECTORAL POLICIES THAT AFFECT THE ENVIRONMENT

Environmental Institution, Legal Framework and Policies

Since the beginning of the century and up to 1990, Chile had developed a considerable amount of environmental regulations and standards. These were of diverse nature, dispersed among different sectors, fragmented and without any coordination between them. In general these regulations were the reaction to a specific environmental problem in a given moment of time, and not part of a policy. As a result, many of the regulations were not applied, questioned in terms of their validity, and suffered from a high degree of non-compliance. These problems were reinforced by the secondary role played by sustainable development and environmental policies in relation to economic interests.

The 1980 Constitution established three provisions related to the environment: the right to live in an environment free of pollution (therefore the state should ensure this right and defend the preservation of nature); the right to bear property that shall be restricted by its social function, including the conservation of the environmental heritage; and the right of a person suffering a loss, disturbance, etc. in his or her rights (by arbitrary act or illegal charge from the authority or other person) to appeal for protection. Therefore, environmental protection received strong support by the Constitution, but was not applied.

Based on the deteriorated environmental quality, in particular in Santiago, and the need to have an effective environmental policy to defend exports against accusations of ecological dumping, the newly elected democratic government in 1990 initiated the restructuring of the sector. A month after coming into office, it set up the Special Commission for Metropolitan Region Decontamination, to improve Santiago's deteriorated environmental quality. A few months later, the National Commission for the Environment (CONAMA) was established.

In 1994, the General Environmental Framework Law was passed, reinforcing the previous institutional framework by setting the foundations for the National System for Environmental Management, a transversal and decentralized institutional framework with CONAMA coordinating other public institutions, the productive sectors and citizen participation.

The establishment of CONAMA as the national environment agency, with inter-ministerial character, to coordinate and implement environmental policies, strategies and action plans has been a significant step towards a comprehensive national environmental policy. Sectoral institutions or ministries work through their Environmental Units in collaboration with CONAMA. Nevertheless, this new institution has had to cope with significant barriers. In particular, since CONAMA is only a coordinating body, it must convince ministries and sectoral policy makers to accept its proposed policies. In many cases, non-environmental institutions maintain their own objectives and sectoral approximations, and give priority to these over environmental aspects, resulting in long-term environmental policies being difficult to sustain.

The General Environmental Law or 'Base Law' as it is usually referred to, requires that large private and public sector projects undergo an environmental impact assessment (EIA), for which unified procedures have been laid out. These cut through all the large and sometimes contradictory set of sectoral rules that prevailed before, in addition to increasing coordination among the participating actors. The EIA process applies to projects of industrial scale and projects that are identified with certain characteristics indicating potential environmental problems such as: health hazard for the population; significant adverse effects on renewable natural resources; resettlement of human community; significant changes in the way of life and habits of human groups; proximity to a protected community, resource or zone; changes in the scenic or tourist value of an area; and alteration of the cultural heritage. Some projects require comprehensive environmental impact studies, while others need only a simplified impact declaration. This process ensures that delays and uncertainties do not discourage new investment.

The 'Base Law' requires that improvement in environmental quality be based on objective indicators, thus prioritizing environmental quality standards and emission standards as the basic instruments. If a zone is considered in non-compliance (saturated zone) of a given standard, and only in this case, it is required to develop a Decontamination Plan. The Law also considers the promotion of environmental education and research, procedures for setting emission standards as well as standards for ambient quality, preservation of nature, conservation of natural heritage and the management of renewable natural resources and biological diversity. Commitment proposed for the year 2000 by CONAMA are summarized in Table 10.34.

Table 10.34 Objectives and instruments proposed for the year 2000

Objective	Instruments
Restore and improve environmental quality	Environmental quality standards Decontamination plans Specific environmental policies
Prevent environmental deterioration	Environmental impact assessment system Environmental dimension in all public policies Environmental education Quality and emission standards Prevention plans Scientific-technological research
Protect the environmental heritage and the use of sustainable natural resource	Regulatory framework Conservation measures Sustainable management of territory Ecosystem study
Introduce environmental considerations in the productive sectors	Eco-labeling and certification procedures ISO 14.000 standards accreditation Clean production promotion
Involve citizens in environmental management	Participation in environmental agreements Stimulation of co-responsibility
Full application of the National System of Environment Management	Strengthen environmental public institutions (local and national) Empowering regional capacity Develop a comprehensive, coherent and effective regulatory body

Source: CONAMA.

Multiple international agreements subscribed to by Chile reinforce the environmental institutions and policies. The main international environmental conventions in which Chile is participating actively include: Antarctica utilization; wetlands of international importance protection; international trade of endangered species of wild flora and fauna control; protection of the ozone layer and control of the ozone layer depleting substances; control of transboundary movement of hazardous waste and their disposal, coordination of environmental protection with Argentina; Agenda 21; climate change; promotion of sustainable use of biological diversity; desertification issues; use of persistent organic pollutants; joint control of the international trade of dangerous chemical components and pesticides, among others.

The goals are now clear, and are substantial. However, little effective progress will be made without administrative support, adequate financing and specific environmental regulations, better monitoring and enforcement. Centralization is also a problem, which can hamper efficient regulation. Although decentralization efforts have been made, management of environmental policy in Chile tends to be concentrated in the center, with little concern for regional development priorities.

Clearly, during the 1990s, a significant institutional and legislative effort was undertaken to put environmental issues under control. The insufficient capability of CONAMA to design, implement, monitor and control environmental regulation and to settle disputes among public institutions, and those with private institutions, are issues that need to be solved in the following years.

Environmental Management and Economic Instruments

Economic instruments are explicitly contemplated by the General Environmental Law only within Prevention and Decontamination Plans. Tradable emission permits, emission taxes, tariffs to users, instruments supporting environmental restoration, etc., although applicable, have only a complementary character.

For *air pollution*, a compensation system for particulate material from large fixed sources (volumes of up to 1000 m^3/hour), was begun in 1992 in the Metropolitan Region. This tradable emissions permit programme allows sources emitting less than their goal to sell their emitting capacity. Even though the system has been in place for four years, few trades have occurred. Moreover, there is a general debate (ideological more than technical) as to whether this instrument is appropriate in Chile. Additionally, public transport route tenders must compete for some of the most important roads they use within Santiago. A parameter considered to assign these routes – among others – is the emission characteristics of vehicles. Regulatory measures as environmental quality standards and a system of Environmental Impact Assessment are also applied.

In the *forestry sector*, regulations considered reforestation subsidies since 1974. In 1984, a new law ratified industrial plantation subsidies, and since 1994 these have been modified to focus on the poorer segments. For *water resources*, water rights have been in place for a long time. The system was revamped in the water code of 1980, establishing a market for these rights. The results have been mixed. However, there is a consensus that the environmental issues, legal aspects, provision of infrastructure, and care for underground water, are unsolved problems. The market has operated in a limited way, and the water code, aimed initially at agricultural users, assumes that it can be expanded to other sectors: mining, urban and electrical.

There is a fixed charge to partially finance collection, transport and disposal of *urban solid wastes*, which is included in the tax applied to urban properties. Studies on domestic and industrial solid wastes that introduce variable taxation and refundable deposit systems for some specific products such as batteries, industrial oils, medicines, have been proposed but not implemented.

Industrial fishing is regulated through extraction quotas on an annual cost basis, allocated by public auctions. This instrument helps in resource valuation although its protection is not guaranteed.

The research, introduction and application of economic instruments for environmental management requires solid institutions with a capacity for administration and control, flexibility, communication networks and qualified personnel. To evaluate an economic instrument, several criteria should be taken into account: partial equilibrium analysis, general equilibrium analysis, indirect effects considerations, dynamic efficiency, existing tax burden, uncertainty, double dividend, incentive effects, administrative requirements, legal considerations, political acceptability, etc. In this sense, instrument feasibility can be divided in technical and legal/political feasibility.[29] Results for Chile per polluting sector are given in Tables 10.35 to 10.38.

Table 10.35 Instruments to reduce air pollution

Instrument	Objective	Technical feasibility	Political feasibility	Advantages	Disadvantages
Emission taxation (SO_2, ozone, etc.)	Reduce emission (saturated areas)	***	*	Incentive to clean technology investment (high taxation)	Distributive effects, environmental effects uncertainty, difficulties in calculating the tax

Gasoline differentiated taxation	Reduce vehicle emission (lead)	**	**	Easy to administer, fiscal income increase	Slight relation with environment, environmental effects uncertainty
Vehicle licenses (year, type of gasoline, kms)	Reduce vehicle emission	**	**		
Technological Taxation	Reduce emission Sulfuric acid, Trimethylamine (pulp and paper and fishmeal industry)	**	**	Incentive to clean technology investment (high taxation)	
Tax Exemption	Reduce emissions by technological investment	**	*	Popular, easy to apply	Budgetary costs (fiscal income reduction), incentive to produce

Source: Own elaboration based on workshop 'Análisis de Aplicabilidad y Propuestas de Instrumentos Tributarios para la Política Ambiental', CONAMA-Univ. de Talca-Univ. de Concepción, March 1998. Key: * low; ** medium; ***high.

Table 10.36 Instruments to reduce water pollution

Instrument	Objective, source	Technical feasibility	Political feasibility
Treatment Charges	Organic material (DBO), domestic	***	*
	Organic material, industrial	**	*
	Nitrogen and phosphorus, domestic	***	**
	Nitrogen and phosphorus, industrial	**	*
	TSS and TDS, domestic	***	**
	TSS and TDS, industrial	**	*
Emission taxation	Metals, mining	***	*
Spilling charges	Fats, industrial	**	**

Source: Own elaboration based on workshop 'Análisis de Aplicabilidad y Propuestas de Instrumentos Tributarios para la Política Ambiental', CONAMA-Univ. de Talca-Univ. de Concepción (1998). Key: * low; ** medium; ***high.

Table 10.37 Instruments to reduce land pollution

Instrument	Objective, source	Technical feasibility	Political feasibility
Emission taxation	Copper, mining	***	*
Tax to products	Fertilizers and pesticides	***	**

Source: Own elaboration based on workshop 'Análisis de Aplicabilidad y Propuestas de Instrumentos Tributarios para la Política Ambiental', CONAMA-Univ. de Talca-Univ. de Concepción, March 1998.

Table 10.38 Instruments to reduce solid waste pollution

Instrument	Objective, source	Technical feasibility	Political feasibility
Tax exemption to recycled products or inputs	Recycling	*	*
Charge for waste collection	Recycling	***	*
Exemption to charge for waste collection in case of waste selection	Recycling	**	**

Source: Own elaboration based on workshop 'Análisis de Aplicabilidad y Propuestas de Instrumentos Tributarios para la Política Ambiental', CONAMA-Univ. de Talca-Univ. de Concepción (1998). Key: * low; ** medium; ***high.

10.4 CONCLUSIONS

During the 1990s, there has been significant progress in environmental stewardship in Chile. A continued effort has been undertaken to get air pollution in Santiago under control. Emissions from copper smelters have been regulated and water discharge standards are in place. Legislation is being developed for both fishing and forestry, though with problems. Important institution building processes and coordination of the legislation has been carried out.

However, significant insufficiencies exist in each of the above-mentioned sectors, as there is still a long way to go before improvements can be considered sustainable. Coordination efforts and a strategic view of what the environment should be in Chile are just starting. Moreover, key efforts have been aimed at 'visible' and immediate problems. Medium and long-term problems are usually brushed aside, as there is neither sufficient time nor resources to identify and evaluate them, nor the possibility to design policies. Native forest depletion, management of water resources, soil degradation, loss of biodiversity, regulation of toxic substances, closure and abandonment of mines, among others, in most cases have been postponed due to the need for responding to other urgent needs.

Whether or not these problems are significant, or how they will evolve, is hard to determine with current information. For example, emissions of toxic substances and noise in Santiago are two problems that are probably important, but are not being addressed. Therefore, an important insufficiency is that there is no ranking of risks or environmental efforts. What should be done first? What later? A systematic approach to respond is lacking.

A very important insufficiency is the lack of integration between environmental policy, sectoral policies and economy-wide policies. Economy-wide policies or sectoral policies, geared to promote economic development, and improve welfare, frequently have negative environmental impacts. For instance, industry accounts for approximately 40 percent of exports and as liberalization and trade promotion continue, greater growth and expansion of this sector should be expected, which could lead to greater air pollution. Given the more stringent regulations, the decontamination plan, as well as emissions trading schemes, pose constraints in the Santiago Metropolitan region, which could mean a shift of pollution to other urban and rural areas. As is already seen, other cities are 'catching up' with Santiago in terms of air pollution.

Energy policy is not related – except circumstantially – with its environmental impacts. Environmental taxes differentiated by fuel type can be used to internalize environmental costs in the energy sector and create efficient incentives for electricity producers and consumers. Alternatively, they could be used to promote the use of natural gas. Promotion of research in energy efficiency, dissemination of information, technical assistance and development of markets will help reduce social costs of generation. Active promotion of energy efficiency investments and demand-side management is beneficial as energy utilities usually have access to more favorable credit terms than consumers and apply a lower discount rate to their decisions. Therefore, both consumers and utilities could gain if demand-side efficiency investments are financed at utilities' lower cost of capital. Moreover, consumers often do not possess the relevant information for assessing the energy savings potential. Further expansion of hydropower capacity may lead to increasing environmental costs as the most favorable locations have already been tapped. Thus, demand-side management initiatives can reduce inefficient environmental damage resulting from unnecessary power system expansion. Although continually mentioned, there is no systematic effort to evaluate and develop a consistent and integrated energy management system for the country, including both the demand and supply sides, and integrating it with environmental policy.

There is also no relation between urban development policies, transport policies and environmental impacts. Clearly low-density urban growth, lack of development of subcenters and decentralization policies, insufficient management of the biophysical environment, among others, affect urban environmental quality. A decontamination plan or air quality standards are not the instruments required to change this.[30] Transport policies are not coordinated with environmental policies, even though they are the main source of air pollution and noise. Policies that encourage the use of public transport, investments in public transport, use of 'eco-friendly' adaptations in all kind of vehicles – such as filters, better quality (especially lead free) fuel, better maintenance of vehicles, etc. – would be beneficial. Even though the general economic policy discourages the use of subsidies in the different sectors, policies that encourage differentials in prices or deposit refund schemes to reduce the level of pollution should be considered and evaluated, given the significant externalities.

Poverty is another issue that is not sufficiently considered in connection with environmental problems. The poor are both agents for and victims of environmental degradation. Over 20 percent of the population live in meager sanitary conditions with health risks. In Region X, almost 75 percent of total wood collected from native forests is for use as fuel by the poor, leading to extensive environmental degradation (World Bank, 1994a). The costs of environmental degradation as well as the benefits of environmental improvements are not equally distributed among the population. Environmental degradation usually affects the poor more severely. High pollution leads to lower property values and therefore housing areas with greater pollution, noise levels and inadequate sanitation are more affordable to the poor. The level of respiratory disease from air pollution in Santiago is disproportionately high among the poor, resulting from dust from unpaved roads, lack of heating and poor diets. Again, the poor lack the means for defensive expenditures against environmental degradation and have fewer savings to bridge the loss of earning from pollution-related illnesses. In rural areas, the poor are pushed into degraded lands of low value, and are forced to encroach onto forestlands. Moreover, farming by the poor with insufficient investment on marginal lands tends to accelerate land degradation. Unregulated small-scale mining by the rural poor is a potentially large source of pollution in some regions.

In the short run, investments in environmental improvements compete for resources with expenditures on social policies. In the long run, however, good environmental policies reduce government expenditures directed at environmental damage especially health costs. Moreover, environmental improvements have direct implications for the well-being of the population. There tends to be a positive linkage between the objectives of policies for poverty alleviation and environmental improvements. However, if policies affect subsistence goods, the poor are likely to be worse off. Also, tighter environmental standards may lead to closure of production facilities that provide employment to the poor who would be willing to accept work in inferior environmental conditions.

These factors highlight the importance of analyzing in detail the distributive consequences of environmental policies. Identifying the effects of the policies would make it possible to compensate the poor with direct transfers.

Each of these activities – energy, urban development, transport policy, and poverty reduction – are in the hands of institutions with a sectoral perspective and objectives in contrast to environmental improvement. Consequently, the coordination approach adopted for CONAMA does not ensure that these externalities are effectively internalized in the decisions made by each sectoral institution. Experience shows that the contrary usually occurs. When budgets are reduced or when there is conflict between environmental and sectoral interests, the latter tends to prevail. As a result, the strength with which policies are applied and their permanence in time depend greatly on the pressures from stakeholders.

The lack of integrated pollution control is another significant weakness. The discussion thus far has had a medium-specific focus, that is, the regulations address problems specific to a single medium (for example, water or air), following the regulating practice in Chile (and most other countries for that matter). This allows regulators to focus on the numerous sources and substances of concern to a specific medium, without having to comprehend and craft rules to address all the possible transfers and transformations affecting other media. However, as media-specific expertise has grown, so has awareness of potential inter-media effects. In particular, differences in the standards governing releases to each medium and in the costs of controlling them, has led some firms to shift pollutants to the medium with the least stringent regulations or the least expensive control costs. Unfortunately, the least costly releases may not pose the least risk to human health or the environment. Policies that protect one medium may result in more pollution in another: for example the use of a wet scrubber to capture particles from a rotary kiln incinerator emitted to the air will generate great volumes of waste water. The choice of control technology may also affect the volume and toxicity of releases to other media. In the previous example, if a dry scrubber is used, waste water is reduced six times. Finally, releases to one medium may also be transferred to another medium in the environment. For example, disposal of the pollutants collected by the dry scrubber into land may result in air emissions or leaching of toxins to ground water. An integrated approach is required so that more preventive or protective, and more efficient decisions can be taken from more accurate identification of the problems and possible solutions.

In conclusion, despite Chile's successful economic growth and stability, performance in social and environmental sectors remains poor. As illustrated in the previous chapters, democratic governments have reinforced policies to overcome the main deficiencies and problems. In Chile, these socio-environmental policies are founded on: (a) the sustained and equitable improvement of the quality of live of all individuals without comprising the expectations of future generations; (b) the necessary balance between socioeconomic development and environmental sustainability (changing the contradictory focus between the economy and the environment); and (c) social equity and overcoming the poverty.

Both the Chilean government and the World Bank are interested in maintaining the sources of growth and promoting poverty reduction. Research on links between pro-economic growth policies, policies directed to reduce poverty and inequality, and policies that focus on environmental protection are relevant in order to explore double/triple dividend policies. Instruments that allow better analysis should be developed. Direct effects could be exhaustively examined by partial analysis. However, indirect and non-intuitive effects are very difficult to capture with this approach. General equilibrium analysis, although less robust in analyzing direct effects, permits discovering all indirect and non-intuitive effects as well as double dividend possibilities.

The following chapter presents several policy experiments simulated with a CGE model. They will give some insights about the convenience of applying economic instruments for environmental management and show the linkages between economic growth, social welfare and environmental protection, which force policy makers to adopt an integrated approach.

ANNEX 10A OTHER IMPORTANT ECONOMIC AND SOCIAL DATA

Table 10A.1 Important economic indicators

Year	1990	1992	1994	1996	1998	2000	2002
Growth of GDP (%)	3.7	12.3	5.7	7.4	3.1	4.6	2.2
Current account deficit % of GDP	−1.6	−2.3	−3.1	−4.3	−5.1	−1.2	−1.4
Central Bank reserves (Millions of US$)	5357.5	9009.2	13466.5	15474.0	15991.8	14741.4	15351.1
Inflation (%)	27.3	12.7	8.9	6.6	4.7	4.5	2.8
Unemployment (%)	6.0	4.9	6.0	6.5	6.3	9.2	9.0

Source: Central Bank and National Bureau of Statistics.

Table 10A.2 Distribution of population in the health system by quintile of per capita income, 1990–98 (in percentages)

Quintile of Income	Year	Health System				
		Public	Armed Forces	ISAPRE	Private	Others
I	1990	85.5	0.7	2.8	8.9	2.6
	1998	86.2	0.5	4.0	8.5	0.9
II	1990	78.6	2.1	6.5	10.0	2.8
	1998	73.9	1.7	13.2	10.1	1.2
III	1990	69.6	2.6	11.3	13.3	3.2
	1998	62.4	3.5	21.3	11.3	1.6
IV	1990	57.6	3.9	21.6	14.1	2.9
	1998	47.1	5.4	33.0	13.1	1.4
V	1990	36.8	3.9	41.2	14.9	3.0
	1998	26.0	4.9	55.4	12.6	1.2
Total	1990	67.6	2.5	15.1	12.0	2.9
	1998	618.0	3.0	23.1	109.0	1.2

Source: Based on surveys CASEN, in 1990 and 1998.

*Table 10A.3 Evolution of health public and fiscal expenditure, 1990–2000 (2000 million US$)**

Year	Public expenditure	Fiscal expenditure	Fiscal/Public expenditure (%)
1990	826.1	309.8	37.5
1991	973.0	390.9	40.2
1992	1137.4	482.8	42.4
1993	1275.0	572.3	44.9
1994	1405.4	663.0	47.2
1995	1464.4	680.8	46.5
1996	1590.8	743.1	46.7
1997	1686.2	804.3	47.7
1998	1824.1	843.1	46.2
1999	1880.0	891.9	47.4
2000	2037.3	940.1	46.1

Note: *Based upon the average dollar observed in 2000.
Source: Own elaboration based on MIDEPLAN, 2003.

Table 10A.4 Distribution of public health expenditure by service delivered, 1996

	Amount (1998 million US$)	(%)
Rest of public expenditure	116383	6.7
Health attentions in the SNSS	1252667	72.1
MLE Net private use	109998	6.4
PNAC	72821	4.2
Maternity subsidy benefit	101436	5.8
Other social security benefits	83932	4.8
Total expenditure	1737420	100.0

Source: Own elaboration based on MIDEPLAN, 1998a.

*Table 10A.5 Per capita public expenditure in education, 1990–2000 (2000 US$)**

Year	Per capita PE education
1990	362.5
1991	413.3
1992	469.7
1993	500.5
1994	538.9
1995	590.1
1996	635.2
1997	689.8
1998	757.6
1999	782.5
2000	826.7

Note: * Based upon the average dollar observed in 2000.

Source: Own elaboration based on MIDEPLAN, 2003.

NOTES

1. The growth rate of GDP fell from 7.6 percent in 1997, to 3.4 in 1998 and to approximately −1.1 percent in 1999.
2. The figures are presented in Table 10A.1, Annex10A.
3. Applied during the military government.
4. The change in focus is coincidental with the change to a democratic government in Chile.
5. Individuals who contribute can choose between public insurance (FONASA) or private insurance (ISAPREs). Contribution to a health insurance program is compulsory for all-dependent workers and pensioned persons, and constitutes 7 percent of total income. If this contribution goes to FONASA, both the contributor and his or her dependents are subject to the public health system, which allows them to make use of public establishments through the Institutional modality or to private establishments and professionals through the Free Election modality. The exceptions to this are indigents who do not contribute to any institution. These persons only have access to the Institutional modality. If the compulsory contribution is deposited in an ISAPRE, the contributor becomes part of the private health system. There are 35 ISAPREs in Chile, 15 of which are closed (contracts for a defined group), and 20 open ones.
6. In 1995 a law was passed that regulates the ISAPREs behavior in various aspects: exclusion of older people, fixed rates that gives transparency and comparability to health plans, clear norms on contracts, complaint procedures that protect the user's rights within the system, etc. The requirement of a guarantee check for emergencies was regulated in 1999.

7. Since 1991 there is a change in the products given out. Cereal milk is replaced by whole milk for children between 1 and 2, and skimmed milk is replaced by 26 percent fat milk for pregnant women.
8. University education is not considered.
9. The educational system in Chile is divided into four different stages – pre-elementary (until kindergarten), elementary (1st through 8th Grades), high school (9th through 12th or 13th depending on scientific or technical schools) and university. In Chile they are respectively called, *pre-básica*, *básica*, *media* and *superior*.
10. SIMCE, which stands for: Sistema de Medición de la Calidad de la Educación, is a test to measure the level of comprehension in different subjects (mainly Math and Spanish). This test has been done since 1988, every two years to the 4th Grades; since 1989 to the 8th Grades and since 1993 to the 10th Grades.
11. Unfortunately there is no more current information on the breakdown of educational expenditure.
12. For further results see Gonzalez (1999).
13. And of course to inflate figures of attendance as much as possible.
14. *Allegados* can represent extended family if they are relatives, or composite family if they are not related.
15. Phase I consists in giving urbanized lots with basic infrastructure, while Phase II considers the improvement of the house until it reaches the standard of a basic house.
16. In the area of decentralization, FOSIS has transferred to its regional offices the operation of the centralized assignment programs. Also, regional juries have been constituted for the selection of projects. Moreover, through the Regional Investment of Local Assignment (IRAL) the municipalities have been engaged in the focalization of investments, while the municipal councils have become selection juries of projects.
17. Caletones smelter plan, Chuquicamata-Paipote-Ventanas smelter plans.
18. Potrerillos smelter plan.
19. An Emergency Program has being applied since 1990. It establishes several levels of air quality. When pollution exceeds the 300-air quality index, a pre-emergency is declared, and when 500 is exceeded it is deemed an emergency situation. Alert was established in 1997 as a way to anticipate pre-emergency situations. This level is associated with the following:

Index	CO ppm	SO_2 μg/m³	NO_2 μg/m³	O_3 μg/m³	Particulate μg/m³
301–400	30	1.493	2.110	780	240
501 –>	50	2.620	3.750	1.400	330

20. Average is not relevant in Santiago due to the the wide range of variation between the highest and lowest concentrations.
21. The annual average is calculated as the annual average per month of all monitoring stations.
22. The annual average is calculated as the annual average per month of all monitoring stations.
23. 1999 Human Development Report.
24. This is 82.7 percent according to Chile Sustentable
25. The cadastre uses the definition recommended by FAO: 'The native forest is a natural ecosystem in which the tree layer consists of native species more than 2 meters tall and with a canopy cover of over 25 percent.'

26. Intendencia Metropolitana (1989, p. 102).
27. Compensated District Level. This considers real spatial and temporal variations in the sound level to which the inhabitants of a district are exposed (ibid. p. 36).
28. Intendencia Metropolitana (1989, p. 102).
29. Discussed in the workshop 'Análisis de Aplicabilidad y Propuestas de Instrumentos Tributarios para la Política Ambiental', CONAMA-Univ. de Talca-Univ. de Concepción, March 1998.
30. See O'Ryan and del Valle (1996).

11. Policy applications

The model allows several alternatives to formalize an environmental policy option. Three are worth singling out:

1. To set – exogenously – a tax associated to the emission of one unit of a specified pollutant in order to attain some specified reduction in the overall economy's level of emissions:

$$\tau_{Poll} = P \cdot \overline{\tau}_{Poll}$$

2. To fix a maximum level of emissions for one or every pollutant. In this case the tax is not determined exogenously but as the shadow price that results from including this new environmental constraint in the optimization function.
3. Taxing (subsidizing) the use of one or more polluting inputs.

Here, we focus in the last two alternatives. Twelve simulations are presented:[1] taxes on PM10, SO_2 and NO_2 emissions compensated by a reduction of either the tax on corporate income or the value added tax; a fuel tax with the same offsetting alternatives; the elimination of coal subsidies and an increase of transfers to households financed by a rise of either the tax on corporate income, the tax on households income or the VAT.

11.1 TAXES ON PM10, SO_2, AND NO_2 EMISSIONS

The objective of this study is to determine the impact on the level of SO_2, NO_2, CO, VOC, PM10 emissions that may result from applying environmental taxes to emissions of a specified pollutant. To develop this analysis we simulate three scenarios where a 10 percent reduction in the emissions of the respective pollutant is set, namely PM10, NO_2 and finally SO_2.

In all the scenarios the environmental tax is offset by reducing another tax in such a way that real public savings does not vary from its initial situation. Corporate-earning taxes and VAT are the offsetting taxes used in all three experiments.

The comparative analysis of the results shows that taxing PM10 emissions to reduce them by 10 percent brings about larger reductions in the rest of the pollutants than the cases where emissions of NO_2 or SO_2 are taxed. These results persists independently of the offsetting tax.

Table 11.1 Reduction of PM10 emissions by 10 percent

Policy impacts		Compensatory tax	
		Corporate tax %	VAT %
Macro	GDP Volume*	0.0	0.0
	Investment	0.2	−0.3
	Consumption	−0.4	−0.2
	Exports	−1.5	−1.5
	Imports	−1.5	−1.6
Sectoral	Water	1.3	3.3
	Electricity	0.7	1.4
	Gas	0.5	2.3
	Other Transports	−3.4	−3.4
	Oil Extraction	−4.5	−4.5
	Refinery	−11.2	−11.2
Distributive	Real YD-I Quintile	−0.8	0.2
	Real YD-II Quintile	−0.6	0.2
	Real YD-III Quintile	−0.4	0.1
	Real YD-IV Quintile	−0.4	−0.1
	Real YD-V Quintile	−0.3	−0.5
Environmental	Emissions SO_2	−11.0	−11.1
	Emissions NO_2	−11.0	−11.0
	Emissions CO	−3.2	−3.0
	Emissions VOC	−2.3	−1.7
	Emissions PM10	−10.0	−10.0

Note: * GDP volume at factor costs.

The only exception is CO emissions. In this case, a tax on emissions of SO_2 that is offset by a rise of corporate taxes triples the reduction in CO emissions induced indirectly (see Table 11.1 and Figure 11A.1 in Annex 11A) due to the relative fall in the coal sector's production associated to its lower relative absorption. In the other scenarios, the coal sector's absorption also decreases, although in this case its relative reduction is much larger. This occurs because of the larger emissions of SO_2, when coal is used, compared with the use of the rest of the energy-producing inputs and the fact that the coal sector is not comparatively so affected by the earnings tax cut. Section 11.2 analyzes in detail the coal sector with specific policy simulations (especially those associated with the coal sector).

Once the environmental impacts of emissions are analyzed, the study focuses on macro-sectoral and social consequences of applying environmental policies. None of the applied policies has a significant effect on macroeconomic variables. The marginally negative (non-significant) sign of impacts on total output, consumption, imports and exports, is linked to slight declines in the model's price indexes, because the GDP volume is not affected. Thus, real GDP at market prices could decrease only by 0.2 percent. In all cases, the costs of adjustment will depend on how steadily these policies are implemented. The possibilities of substituting among production factors and/or between energy-producing inputs, the degree of capital mobility among sectors, the technological changes affecting both the productive processes and consumption patterns, among others, determine the cost of the adjustment.

With regard to the sectors, there are many similarities between winners and losers in the simulated scenarios. In general, the most penalized sectors are those directly linked to the production of petroleum-derived fuels, or those that require them as inputs. Nevertheless, in the case of taxing SO_2, coal output is the most affected, decreasing by up to 14.3 percent.

With any of the applied policies, transport activity has been the most affected in the group of non-energy-producing sectors. The other transport sector (Tables 11.1 through 11.3), which basically includes air, sea and railroad transport, has been more affected than freight transport or highway use by passengers, but differences are not substantial. The negative impact on the highway transport sector's output fluctuates between a drop of 2.3 percent (tax on PM10 emission offset by a corporate tax) and an increase of 2.0 percent (tax on SO_2 emission offset by VAT).

The remaining sectors are not affected significantly, although there are differences in signs depending on the offsetting tax imposed (Figure 11A.3 Annex 11A). For example, the construction and service sectors are negatively affected by VAT increases, and positively if the offsetting tax is the corporate tax. The opposite is true for the food and textile industries.

Table 11.2 Reduction of NO_2 emissions by 10 percent

Policy impacts		Compensatory tax	
		Corporate tax %	VAT %
Macro	GDP Volume	0.0	0.0
	Investment	0.2	−0.2
	Consumption	−0.4	−0.2
	Exports	−1.4	−1.4
	Imports	−1.4	−1.5
Sectoral	Water	1.2	3.0
	Electricity	0.6	1.2
	Gas	0.5	2.1
	Other Transports	−3.1	−3.1
	Oil Extraction	−4.1	−4.1
	Refinery	−10.2	−10.2
Distributive	RealYD-IQuintile	−0.8	0.2
	RealYD-IIQuintile	−0.5	0.2
	RealYD-IIIQuintile	−0.4	0.1
	RealYD-IVQuintile	−0.3	−0.1
	RealYD-VQuintile	−0.3	−0.4
Environmental	Emissions SO2	−10.1	−10.1
	Emissions NO2	−10.0	−10.0
	Emissions CO	−3.0	−2.8
	Emissions VOC	−2.1	−1.6
	Emissions PM10	−9.1	−9.1

As for income distribution, the results systematically infer that to offset environmental taxes with corporate earnings taxes is less redistributive than doing so with VAT (Tables 11.1 through 11.3 and Figure 11A.4 Annex 11A). Also, real disposable income of the poorest 20 percent of the population – group of people living below the poverty line in Chile – slightly increases when the VAT decreases.

Nevertheless environmental taxes are very harmful to the poorest when they are offset by reductions of corporate taxes. Furthermore, in that case, the real income in all quintiles decreases notwithstanding the pollutant taxed, although more in the lower-income quintiles. This is associated with a larger relative decline in unskilled labor wages. Offsetting with VAT reductions results in 60 percent of the lower-income population improving their income, while income of the following 20 percent of the population will decline by around one-third less than with a corporate tax cut, and finally the wealthiest 20 percent of the population would reduce their real disposable income by no more 0.5 percent.

Table 11.3 Reduction of SO_2 emissions by 10 percent

Policy impacts		Compensatory tax	
		Corporate tax %	VAT %
Macro	GDP Volume	0.0	0.0
	Investment	0.1	−0.2
	Consumption	−0.3	−0.2
	Exports	−1.4	−1.4
	Imports	−1.4	−1.4
Sectoral	Water	1.4	3.0
	Electricity	0.3	1.2
	Gas	0.8	2.1
	Other Transports	−3.2	−3.1
	Oil Extraction	−3.4	−4.1
	Refinery	−9.7	−10.1
Distributive	Real YD-I Quintile	−0.8	0.2
	Real YD-II Quintile	−0.5	0.2
	Real YD-III Quintile	−0.4	0.1
	Real YD-IV Quintile	−0.3	−0.1
	Real YD-V Quintile	−0.2	−0.4
Environmental	Emissions SO_2	−10.0	−10.0
	Emissions NO_2	−10.0	−9.9
	Emissions CO	−9.0	−2.7
	Emissions VOC	−2.0	−1.6
	Emissions PM10	−9.8	−9.1

In terms of welfare, equivalent and compensatory variations were calculated for each quintile, with similar results to those of income. Since variations are not very significant (less than 1 percent), we agree with the thesis of Engel et al. (1998) that the Chilean tax structure has little direct effect on income distribution.

11.2 FUEL TAXES

The fourth environmental policy refers to an increase of fuel taxes. The objective was to raise this tax until a 10 percent reduction in PM10 emissions was achieved. A 150 percent increase in the tax rate on fuels was necessary. As in previous simulations, real public saving is kept at the reference level and the same offsetting scenarios are proposed, that is, a corporate tax cut and a reduction in the VAT.

The results obtained were very similar to those in the scenario where PM10 emissions are taxed. In both offsetting scenarios, VOC emissions are reduced by almost twice as much as when taxing PM10. Offsetting through increases in corporate taxes appears better in terms of relative emissions.

Table 11.4 Increase in fuel tax by 150 percent

Policy impacts		Compensatory tax	
		Corporate tax %	VAT %
Macro	GDP Volume	0.0	0.0
	Investment	0.5	0.2
	Consumption	−0.9	−0.8
	Exports	−2.1	−2.0
	Imports	−2.1	−2.1
Sectoral	Water	1.1	2.1
	Electricity	0.7	1.0
	Gas	1.4	2.4
	Other Transports	−3.1	−3.0
	Oil Extraction	−7.5	−7.4
	Refinery	−20.9	−20.5
Distributive	Real YD-I Quintile	−1.1	−0.5
	Real YD-II Quintile	−0.9	−0.4
	Real YD-III Quintile	−0.8	−0.5
	Real YD-IV Quintile	−0.9	−0.7
	Real YD-V Quintile	−0.9	−1.0
Environmental	Emissions SO_2	−11.2	−10.9
	Emissions NO_2	−11.0	−10.7
	Emissions CO	−3.2	−3.0
	Emissions VOC	−4.0	−3.6
	Emissions PM10	−9.9	−9.6

Macroeconomic impacts are slightly bigger and at the sector level more disparities arise (Table 11.1 versus Table 11.4). Real GDP at market prices can decrease by 0.3 percent when corporate taxes rises; although, in general, all GDP measures remain the same as in the previous simulations. Sectors related to fuel production, transformation and sale suffer from this tax more intensely, and their sectoral output is reduced by roughly twice as much as if a tax is imposed on PM10 emissions. The gas sector appears as the 'winner'. Offsetting by VAT appears slightly better in terms of macro-sectoral impacts.

In terms of distribution, taxing fuels has a larger negative impact on all income quintiles, although offsetting with VAT is relatively better. On the other hand, taxing fuels appears to be a more regressive tax as it causes larger reductions in the lowest-income quintile (the relative weight of fuels in their consumer basket is higher). To introduce a fuel tax along with corporate tax reductions is the worst policy to confront poverty.

Taking a closer look at the economic, distributive and environmental impacts together, taxing fuels appears to be less desirable than taxing PM10 emissions.

11.3 TAX SYSTEM

The closure rule applied in all the simulations consists of keeping government savings constant. To do so in the previous experiments presented here, either VAT or corporate tax cuts offset any environmental tax.

Table 11.5 Changes in tax rates when emissions are reduced

Tax	Reducing	ΔTax Rate (%)
PM10 Emissions	Corporate	−30.8
	VAT	−18.8
NO_2 Emissions	Corporate	−28.1
	VAT	−17.2
SO_2 Emissions	Corporate	−32.9
	VAT	−17.1
Fuel	Corporate	−18.2
	VAT	−10.6

Offsetting VAT reductions range from 10 percent to 19 percent of the existing tax rate in terms of current collection (Table 11.5), whereas corporate tax reductions vary between 18 percent and 33 percent.[2]

11.4 COAL SECTOR

One limiting factor associated with CGE models is the number and quality of the required data, in particular the social accounting matrix (SAM). The SAM used herein, updated from the 1986 SAM of Chile, overestimates the coal sector in relation to the current Chilean conditions. The presence of subsidies, which do not exist today, made this energy-producing input 'profitable' for producers and consumers. As of today, coal production has decreased dramatically, from 1667341 tons in 1994 to 378654 in 1998 along with the elimination of these subsidies (Central Bank, 1999).

In order to further understand the implications of this process, we simulate the results of removing all subsidies to coal. We also reassign these resources as transfers to households, in such a way as to keep public saving constant (a realistic scenario considering that redundant workers of the coal sector are being 'helped' by the government). This simulation attempts to replicate what occurs today in the sector in addition to those related to it.

From a macroeconomic perspective, there are no changes in the aggregate variables of the economy. Real GDP, Absorption, Consumption, Investment, Exports, Imports, etc. are not altered at all. From the standpoint of income distribution, this scenario is believed to be positive because the income of the first (poorest) quintile increases by 0.7 percent, whereas in the fifth (wealthiest group of people) it decreases by barely 0.1 percent. The remaining quintiles show a slight increase in real income, due to the increase of 1.7 percent in transfers to households, which is associated with resources arising from the elimination of the coal sector's subsidy. Regional considerations are not included as ECOGEM-Chile is a national-wide model.

Total emissions of air pollutants are not significantly altered. The exception is carbon monoxide: its emissions decrease by 7.8 percent. PM10 emissions are only reduced by 0.8 percent. This policy appears correct and shows a modest evidence of double dividend since there is no impact in macroeconomic terms, and from the environmental and distributive viewpoints impacts are slightly positive.

Impacts are greatest at the sector level – valued coal production falls by 43.2 percent associated with a 61 percent loss in the rate of return and the impossibility of translating the reduction in the subsidy to a price increase (it may only rise by 8 percent because the domestic coal (−17.3 percent) is being replaced by imported (+6.3 percent), and the absorption of this input is decreasing by 4.6 percent). The drop in production is even larger if measured in physical units than in money value. Other sectors show no impact, because the possible effects of an increase of the price of coal are offset by a greater demand by the rest of the economy linked to the fresh resources released through transfers.

These results enhance understanding of the previous studies presented in this chapter (environmental taxation). In the earlier scenarios, the coal sector was subsidized. By taxing emissions, this sector would keep some 'premium' returns over other energy-producing sectors (that is, gas, oil, electricity) as a result of the aforesaid subsidies. Therefore, the maximization process followed by producers was biased by the subsidies, which proved that the expected substitutions among energy inputs towards gas or electricity, and among inputs, capital and labor in and between sectors were not 'optimal', from the economic and the environmental points of view, as in the case of an economy without distortions. In any case, this fact that introduces an inefficiency in the market's allocation system only underestimates the possibility of reducing emissions of pollutants without suffering economic costs.

Another important outcome of this scenario is that the model reproduces trends and figures observed in Chile.

11.5 SOCIAL POLICIES

During the 1990s, Chile made a noticeable effort to reduce poverty and improve income distribution. There was an increase in health, housing and education expenditures as well as other direct and indirect transfers to households. This section analyzes the impact of social policies consisting of increases in direct government transfers to households on the environment.

Transfers to households increase their available income, resulting in increases in consumption patterns of each household. In the model, consumption is divided by quintiles of income, thus differentiating the composition of the consumption basket among income groups.

The simulations examine the macro, sectoral, distributive and environmental impacts of a 10 percent increase of current transfers to households. The distribution pattern of transfers between income groups has not been altered; that is, each income group increases their received transfers by 10 percent in relation to the initial situation. Obviously, the wealthiest groups receive less transfers in the initial situation (5.9 percent of total transfer), so the additional amount is lower.

In relation to real public savings/debt in the social calibrations, we have followed the same assumption as in environmental calibrations previously presented (that is, it remains constant). In order to cover the new public disbursement (due to the transfer increase), increases in different types of taxes have been assumed: corporate tax, VAT and households (HH) income tax.

Table 11.6 Increase in household transfers by 10 percent

Policy impacts		Compensatory tax		
		Corporate tax %	VAT %	HH income tax %
Macro	GDP Volume	0.0	0.0	0.0
	Investment	−0.4	−0.1	0.1
	Consumption	0.2	0.0	0.0
	Exports	−0.1	−0.1	0.0
	Imports	−0.1	−0.1	0.0
Sectoral	Textiles	0.1	−1.0	0.0
	Gas	0.3	−0.9	0.1
	Water	0.4	−0.9	0.2
	Chemicals	0.0	−0.7	0.0
	Food Industry	0.2	−0.7	0.1
	Refinery	0.0	−0.5	−0.1
Distributive	Real YD-I Quintile	4.9	4.1	4.2
	Real YD-II Quintile	2.2	1.7	1.7
	Real YD-III Quintile	0.8	0.5	0.5
	Real YD-IV Quintile	−0.1	−0.3	−0.3
	Real YD-V Quintile	−0.8	−0.7	−0.9
Environmental	Emissions SO_2	0.0	−0.5	−0.1
	Emissions NO_2	0.0	−0.5	−0.1
	Emissions CO	0.0	−0.3	0.0
	Emissions VOC	0.0	−0.4	0.0
	Emissions PM10	0.0	−0.4	−0.1

The impact of income distributive policies that drain resources from high to low income groups (transfer increase defrayed with some tax increase) is assessed. The adjustment has been assumed in a medium-range period (long-term elasticity but with no capital mobility), in a similar way to the previous simulations.

Although it is true that investment is affected in a more negative way when a corporate tax increase is chosen to finance transfers, none of the social policies simulated have significant impacts on macroeconomic variables. All GDP figures remain unchanged. .

There are very small effects on the sectoral activity. The sectoral output is more negatively affected when transfers are financed through VAT increases, although not significantly. In this case, the positive income effect over private consumption from the increase of transfers to households is more than compensated for by the negative price effect generated by the VAT increase. The rest of the simulations show different results that depend on the type of good (inferior, normal or superior) and how transfers and taxes affect the economy. Hence, in the case in which transfers are financed with an increase of households income tax, there is a clear redistribution of revenue from higher to lower income population. Thus, the more a sector depends on basic/inferior goods consumption (their consumption increases in less proportion than income), the more it benefits from rising revenues through private income taxes to finance additional transfers. Thus, food, load and passenger transportation and water show a positive impact, whereas sectors less related to basic needs are the most negatively affected (textiles, fuels and, above all, services).

From a distributive point of view the impact of any of the three simulated cases is very positive. The lower income quintile shows an increase in real disposable income from 4.1 percent (if the financing tax is the VAT) to 4.9 percent (if corporate taxes are increased).[3] From the point of view of poverty and income distribution, financing transfers with corporate taxes is the 'best' option. The resulting increases of effective tax rates are presented in Table 11.7. Notice that they represent, respectively, the results of their own policy simulation; but total fiscal revenues from all taxes varies in each of the three social scenarios.

Table 11.7 Increase of effective tax rate

Tax	Increase of effective tax rate
Corporate tax	13.0
VAT	22.1
HH income tax	76.9

Environmentally, as well as sectorally, the aggregated impacts from this social policy are relatively insignificant notwithstanding the financing tax considered. However, it is possible to achieve reductions of almost 2 percent in emissions of particulates, SO_2 and NO_x in the gas sector, that can be derived from the category of normal/superior good that may be assigned to the consumption of this good. On the other hand, financing transfers with VAT can reach the greatest reductions of all pollutants, but always with figures below 0.5 percent. Thus, the increase of transfers has no negative environmental impacts since scale effects are mitigated by the increase of a tax. Alternatively, no positive effects can be derived either. A comparative indication of the three policies is given in Table 11.6.

In conclusion, there is no clear evidence that increases in low levels of income may generate increases in emissions of air pollutants. Higher capacity of consumption might directly or indirectly increase pollution in a partial equilibrium context, but in a general equilibrium framework income and scale effects can be diluted.

11.6 CONCLUSION

This section analyzes the impact of different tax reforms that may improve the environment, and compares their effects on aggregate output, output by sector and income distribution. Within the ECOGEM-Chile model's framework, four possible environmental taxes were tested, each of them being offset in such a way that public savings (expenditure) remained the same as in the base scenario. Environmental taxes were applied on fuels and emissions of PM10, SO_2 and NO_2. Offsetting taxes chosen to keep public saving constant included earnings taxes and VAT. The objective was to reduce the emissions of the taxed pollutant by 10 percent; and, in the case of gasoline, it was to achieve a reduction in PM10 emissions of almost 10 percent. Most outstanding findings are:

1. Taxing PM10 emissions leads to larger reductions in the emissions of the other pollutants (SO_2, NO_2, CO, VOC) than taxing emissions of SO_2 or NO_2. This result was independent of the offsetting tax, with the exception of CO.
2. The most severely penalized sectors are those directly related to the production of oil-derived fuels and transportation. The most favored ones are those related to production of alternative energy-producing inputs.

3. Income distribution is not affected significantly by the chosen tax scheme. Still, it can be inferred that offsetting the environmental tax with a cut on corporate taxes is less progressive than doing it with VAT. However, from a narrow environmental perspective, an offset with a VAT reduction is associated with smaller reduction in emissions of pollutants.
4. Taking a closer look at the economic, environmental and distributive impacts, the fuel tax appears to be less advantageous than a tax on PM10 emissions. Moreover, although taxing fuels reduces VOC emissions more, it appears to be the most regressive tax scheme, adversely affecting the population in the poorest income quintile.
5. The fourth simulation shows two important results. Firstly, it demonstrates that eliminating coal subsidies is an efficient policy and, despite what has been said, it does not negatively affect the poor. Secondly, this simulation enhances the model`s results, in the sense that it can replicate genuine policies in place in Chile with a good degree of precision.
6. The final simulation shows that there is no clear evidence that an increase in the resources of the poorer income groups of population may generate increases in emissions of air pollutants, basing it on income and scale effects.

Ultimately, as a policy objective and from an environmental standpoint, taxing PM10 emissions appears to be the best choice. If distribution improvements are also sought, this tax will have to be offset with a reduction in VAT although, in any case, the Chilean tax structure does not seem to materially affect income distribution.

ANNEX 11A EFFECTS OF TAXES

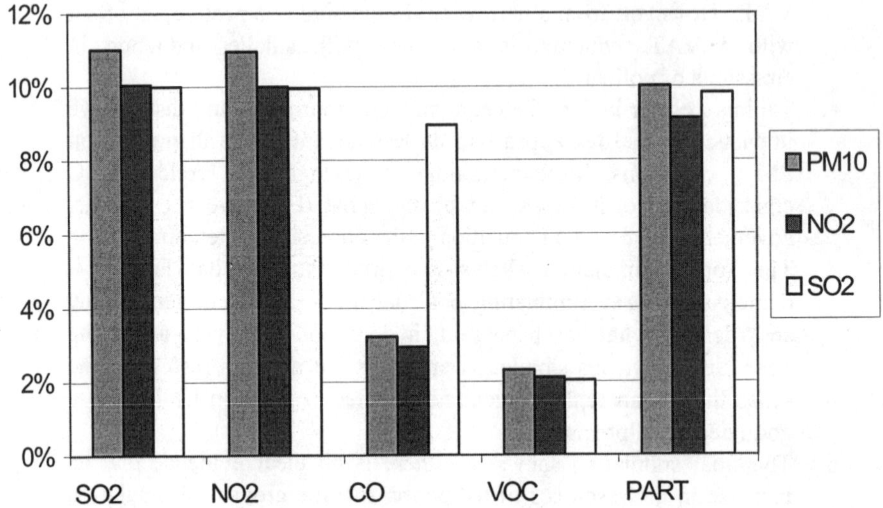

Figure 11A.1 Reduction of total emissions when taxing emissions of PM10, NO_x, SO_2 reducing corporate taxes

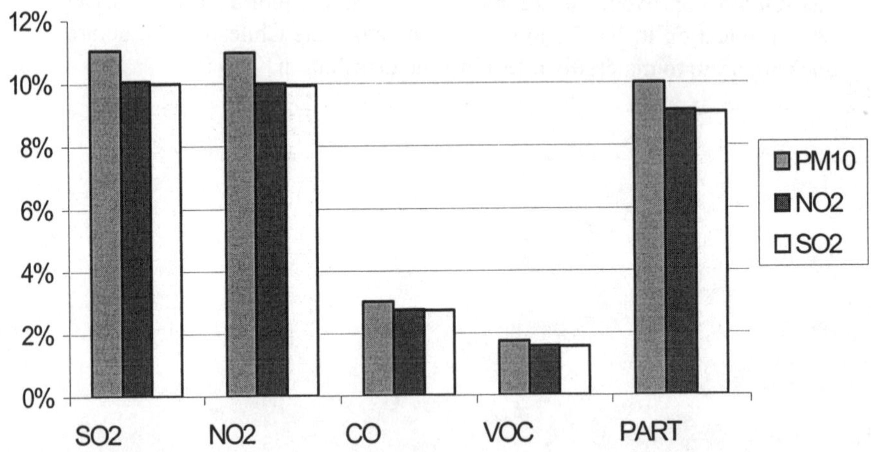

Figure 11A.2 Reduction of total emissions when taxing emissions of PM10, NO_x, SO_2 reducing VAT

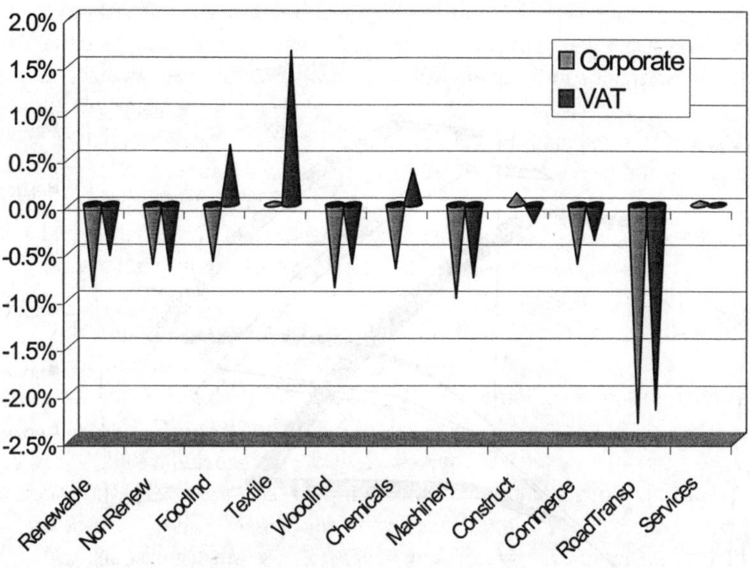

Figure 11A.3 Sectoral impact of taxing emissions of PM10, compensating with a reduction of VAT and corporate taxes

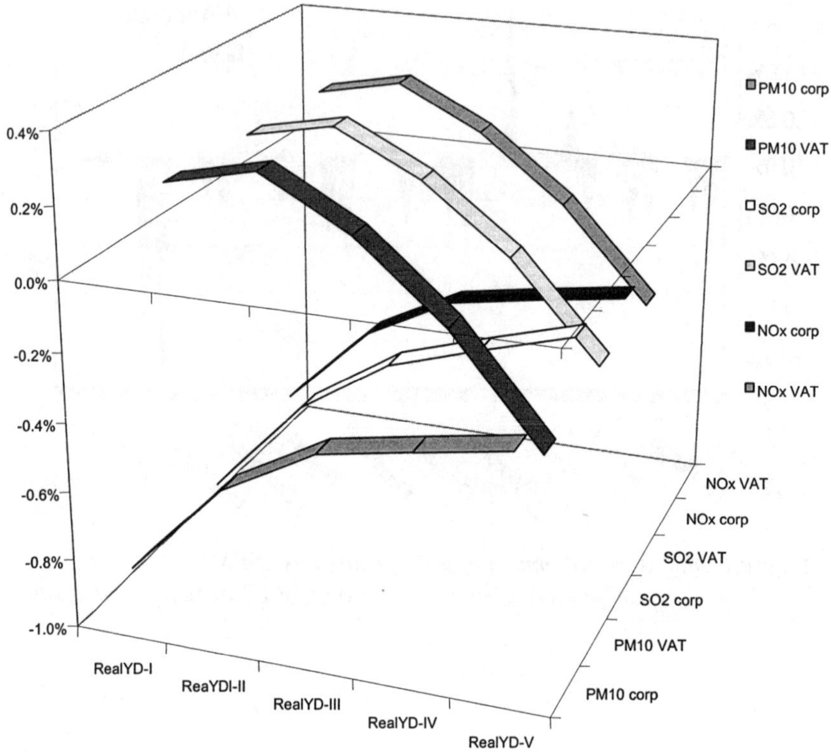

Figure 11A.4 Distributive impact (real disposable income by quintile) of taxing PM10, SO_2 or NO_x emissions, compensating with a reduction of VAT or corporate taxes

NOTES

1. Long-term substitution elasticities and no capital mobility between sectors are assumed in the scenarios analyzed in the chapter. It allows some degree of intrasectoral adjustments but limits intersectoral ones, therefore it is not a long-term context. Additionally, all simulations maintain real public savings constant.
2. Note that the model considers effective revenue; therefore, tax rates existing in Chile for VAT or corporate taxes will not necessarily match the respective payments by sector.
3. In Chile, the lowest quintile of income represents the population under the poverty line.

12. Conclusions and future research

Evaluating social and environmental policies has become a complex but necessary task in Chile. A first reason for this is that improving the environment can be costly and important sectors may be adversely affected. Resources allocated to improving the environment compete with alternative uses, making it necessary to evaluate all relevant social, macroeconomic, environmental and sectoral impacts. Additionally, economic growth, trade and external shocks will affect the environment in ways that are difficult to predict due to the complex interactions among key agents and sectors. For this reason it is necessary to develop a tool capable of evaluating systematically and consistently the relevant effects of environmental policies and Chile's expected development process. An example of this tool is the ECOGEM model.

The ECOGEM model is a static computable general equilibrium model. The current version is a static model that considers multiple sectors (72 productive sectors in the SAM), labor differentiation (20 labor categories), five different households (divided by income distribution), trade partners (27 countries and regions trade with Chile), among other features. It is a neoclassic model, which is savings-driven and incorporates energy-input substitution to reduce emissions. Five different air pollutants (PM10, SO_2, NO_x, CO and VOC) are related to the use of intermediate inputs and not only to production levels. Finally, the model also includes abatement technology as an option to reduce emissions.

This model allows for evaluating pro-poor policies applied in Chile. During the last decade, social programs have been focalized considerably. In addition to the target groups prioritized in the 1980s –the indigent and mother–infant care – other groups such as women, youth, indigenous groups, elder and handicapped persons were also targeted. As a result, integral policies have been designed, aimed at the specific problems of each of these vulnerable groups. Focalization has resulted in expenditure on the main social programs in education, health and monetary subsidies, to be received by the poorest 69 percent of households. In terms of income, these social programs represented 46 percent and 20 percent of total income for the first and second quintiles respectively. Consequently, focalization has allowed the share in total income of the first quintile to increase from 3.7 percent, when social expenditure is not considered, to 6.3 percent when it was included. The second quintile saw an increase from 8 percent to 9.3 percent.

Between 1990 and 2000 expenditure in the public health sector increased by 147 percent. Consequently, the expenditure in health grew as a share of GDP from 2 to 2.9 percent. The average expenditure per capita increased from US$ 100 in 1990 to US$ 134 in 2000. As a result of this important financial effort, the hospital crisis and lack of infrastructure that affected the public sector were ameliorated. Additionally, improved access to health with extension of equality policies; free attention for the poorest segments of the population; reinforcement of primary attention; reduction of waiting lists and prevention and protection programs have been implemented among others.

In education, public expenditure increased by 177 percent between 1990 and 2000. As a result, expenditure on education has grown as a percentage of GDP from 2.5 percent to 3.9 percent. Multiple new programs were created, including: Program for a Better Quality Education in Elementary Schools of Poor Areas, Program for the Improvement of the Quality and Equality of Education. In addition, the average monthly wage received by teachers in the municipality sector was increased significantly, more than doubling over the decade.

Expenditure in housing for the poor has also increased substantially. Public and fiscal expenditure on housing, between 1990 and 2000, increased by 53 percent and 112 percent respectively. The general goals of housing policies have been to reduce the housing deficit and improve the precarious conditions of the houses of the poor. Over 800 000 housing solutions were delivered, reducing the housing deficit by nearly 20 percent.

The promotion of productive development has focused on strengthening productive opportunities of the poor sector. They include actions that increase human capital, such as labor training, in addition to initiatives that increase the productivity of micro-enterprises. The specific objective of policies in this area is to complement the development of policies undertaken in other areas of the state, with the goal of overcoming poverty. In 1990 the FOSIS (Fund for Solidarity and Social Investment) was created, aimed at financing the promotion of productive development in the weaker sectors of the economy, utilizing over 50 million dollars per year since 1995.

Policies and strong economic growth has resulted in a fall in the the level of poverty from over 40 percent of the population in 1990, to almost half by the end of the decade. Despite these improvements income distribution has not improved in the last decade. Chile has a very bad record in terms of distribution and policies have not been able to change this state of affairs.

Expenditure on social policies has increased significantly in the period, with policies being increasingly focused on the more vulnerable groups. Although there have been significant improvements, poverty is still an issue in Chile and income distribution must be improved. The ECOGEM model examines the impact of policies in this direction.

Additionally the model helps evaluate the impacts of environmental policy. In 1990 there was a historical lack of environmental regulations and laws, or their ineffective application, which resulted in the accumulation of numerous environmental problems. There were serious problems related to air and water pollution, land and urban pollution, natural resource depletion, land erosion, water scarcity and inappropriate solid waste management and disposal.

During the past decade several initiatives were undertaken to improve the environmental situation. In 1994, the General Environmental Framework Law was passed, which reinforced the previous institutional framework by setting the foundations for the National System for Environmental Management, a transversal and decentralized institutional framework with the Environmental National Commission (CONAMA) coordinating other public institutions, the productive sectors and citizen participation. Several remedial instruments were implemented in the period. A continued effort has been undertaken to get air pollution in Santiago under control. Emissions from copper smelters have been regulated, and water discharge standards are in place. Legislation is being developed for both fishing and forestry, though with problems. Additionally, the requirement of Environmental Impact Assessments for large projects is a great leap in preventing major future problems. Significant institution building and coordination of the legislation also took place. However, the insufficient capability of CONAMA to design, implement, monitor and control environmental regulation and to settle disputes among public and private institutions, are important aspects that need to be solved in the following years. In conclusion, more environmental regulations can be expected, with the corresponding overall and sectoral economic impacts.

The ECOGEM model has been built to analyze social and environmental policies. The main features that allow this are the differentiation among quintiles of income and labor categories regarding social policies, and the input-based emissions and abatement technologies regarding environmental policy. Another important feature is the way taxes, subsidies and transfers are modeled, allowing the increase or reduction of each one separately and for specific sectors if necessary.

The static model is currently working and has been applied to four specific cases (12 simulations). In each case macroeconomic, sectoral, distributive and environmental impacts have been evaluated. First, the impact of setting emission taxes on PM10, SO_2 and NO_x was analyzed, while reducing two possible taxes: corporate taxes and VAT. The results show that a tax on PM10 leads to larger reductions in the emissions of other pollutants (SO_2, NO_x, CO, VOC) than doing so on emissions of SO_2 or NO_x. The most severely penalized sectors are those directly related to the production of oil-derived fuels or transportation. The most favored are those related with the production of alternative energy-producing inputs. Income distribution is not affected significantly by the chosen tax scheme. It can still be inferred that offsetting the environmental tax with a cut on corporate taxes is more regressive than with VAT.

Next, the impact of raising fuel taxes in order to achieve a 10 percent reduction in PM10 emissions was analyzed. The economic, environmental and distributive impacts show that the fuel tax is less advantageous than a tax on PM10 emissions. The third simulation in this study is the elimination of coal subsidies, transferring those resources directly to households. Elimination of subsidies is seen to be an efficient policy (that is, it allows most sectors to grow as well as consumption to rise). Additionally, it does not affect the poor negatively, since the poorest quintile is not affected. Moreover, this simulation is a good test of the model's predictive capacities since the results replicate closely what actually happened when these subsidies were eliminated in the mid 1990s.

Finally the impacts of raising household direct transfers are analyzed. The increase of transfers does not produce negative environmental effects, as could be expected due to an increase in consumption of the poor. The reason is that aggregate consumption remains the same since transfers are completely financed by an increase in another tax and there is a redistributive effect. Alternatively, no positive effects are derived either. In consequence, for the specific transfer considered there is no clear evidence that increases in low levels of income may generate increases in emissions of air pollutants, basing this on consumption patterns and in a higher capacity of consumption of the poor.

In conclusion, the ECOGEM-Chile model is capable of evaluating social and environmental policies in Chile. This is a very powerful tool that can determine which policies are most suitable for attaining the goals of sustainable development, focusing on the social, economic and environmental issues, as well as sectoral and labor impacts.

However, the model has certain limitations that should be overcome in order to improve its analytical capabilities. The first and maybe most important limitation, is the data used in the model. The social accounting matrix (SAM) used was built for 1992, but based on the 1986 input–output (I–O) matrix. During the past decade the production structure has changed considerably, consequently, it is imperative to generate a new SAM. At the end of 2002 the Central Bank released the 1996 I–O matrix and a SAM will be available for use in the near future .

Another limitation of the current model is that it does not consider household preferences for a better environmental quality. Thus, decisions to improve the environment must be imposed exogenously to the model. In order to address this problem, a specific module must be developed to include household preferences for environmental 'goods'.

Finally, the need for prospective analysis requires a dynamic framework. In order to achieve this, it is necessary to include dynamic features in the model to be able to analyze long-run sustainability and policies that may achieve a more sustainable growth path, addressing environmental, social and economic issues.

Bibliography

Abaza, H. (1995), 'UNEP/World Bank Workshop on the Environmental Impacts of Structural Adjustment Programmes – New York, 20–21 March 1995', *Ecological Economics*, **14** (1), pp. 1–5.

Adelman, I. and Robinson, S. (1978), *Income Distribution Policy in Developing Countries*, Stanford University, California.

Almeida, Luciana T. (1997), *Politica Ambiental: Uma Análise Econômica*, UNESP/Papirus, Campinas.

Alonso, E. and Roland-Holst, D.W. (1995), 'A Detailed Social Accounting Matrix for Chile', Working Paper, Department of Economics, Mills College.

Alston, L.J., Libecap, G.D. and Schneider, R. (1995), 'Property Rights and the Preconditions for Markets: The Case of the Amazon Frontier', *Journal of Institutional Theoretical Economics*, **151**, pp. 89–107.

Alston, L.J., Libecap, G.D. and Schneider, R. (1996), 'The Determinants and Impact of Property Rights: Land Titles on the Brazilian Amazon', NBER Working paper 5405.

Alston, L.J., Libecap, G.D. and Mueller, B. (2000), 'Land Reform Policies: the Sources of Violent Conflict and Implications for Deforestation in the Brazilian Amazon', *Journal of Environmental Economics and Management*.

Alves, D.S. (1999), 'An Analysis of the Geographical Patterns of Deforestation in Brazilian Amazônia in the 1991–1996 Period', Paper presented at the Conference on Patterns and Processes of Land Use and Forest Change in the Amazon, University of Florida, Gainesville.

Andersen, L.E. and Reis, E.J. (1997), 'Government Policies and Deforestation', Rio de Janeiro, IPEA, n. 513.

Andersen, L.E. et al. (1996), 'Report on Amazon Deforestation', Working Paper, UCSD.

Andersen, L.E., Granger, C.W.J. and Reis, E.J. (1997), 'A Random Coefficient VAR Transition Model of the Changes in Land Use in the Brazilian Amazon', *Revista de Econometria*, **17** (1).

Andersen, L.E., Granger, O., Areis, E.J., Weinhold, D. and Wunder, S. (2002), *The Dynamics of Deforestation and Development in the*

Brazilian Amazon, mimeo, IPEA DIMAC Seminar, January.

Andrade, T.A. (1998), 'Aspectos Distributivos na Determinação de Preços Públicos', IPEA, Rio de Janeiro.

Angelsen, A. (1999), 'Why Do Farmers Expand their Land into Forests? Theories and Evidence from Tanzania', *Environment and Development Economics*, **4**, pp. 313–31.

Angelsen, A. and Kaimowitz, D. (1999), 'Rethinking the Causes of Deforestation: Lessons from Economic Models', *The World Bank Research Observer*, **4** (1), pp. 73–98.

Ardila, S., Quiroga, R. and Vaugham, W.J. (1998), *A Review of the Use of Contingent Valuation Methods in Project Analysis at the Inter-American Development Bank*, Report of the Vanderbilt University, Nashville.

Aronsson, T. and Lofgren, K.G. (1998), 'Green Accounting: What Do We Know and What Do We Need to Know ?', in T. Tietenberg and H. Folmer (eds), *International Yearbook of Environmental and Resource Economics 1998/99*, Edward Elgar, Cheltenham, UK and Lyme, USA, Chapter 6.

Arrow, K.J. and Hahn, F. (1971), *General Competitive Analysis*, Holden-Day, San Francisco.

Atkinson, G., Dubourg, R., Hamilton, K., Munasinghe, Mohan, Pearce, D. and Young, C. (1997), *Measuring Sustainable Development*, Edward Elgar, Cheltenham, UK and Lyme, USA.

Auerbach, A. (1985), 'The Theory of Excess Burden and Optimal Taxation', in A.J. Auerbach and M. Feldstein (eds), *Handbook of Public Economics*, vol. I, Amsterdam, North Holland.

Babiker, M.H., Metcalf, G.E. and Reilly, J. (2003), 'Tax Distortions and Global Climate Policy', *Journal of Environmental Economics and Management*, **46**, 269–87.

Barbier, Edward (1988), 'The Economics of Farm-level Adoption of Soil Conservation Measures in the Uplands of Java', Environment Department Working Paper 11, Environment Department, World Bank, Washington DC.

Barbier, E.B. (1999), 'Institutional Constraints and Deforestation: An Empirical Application', Paper presented at the European Environmental Economic Association Meeting.

Barros, R.P., Henriques, R. and Mendonça, R. (2000), 'A Estabilidade Inaceitável: Desigualdade e Pobreza no Brasil', in R. Henriques (ed.), *Desigualdade e Pobreza no Brasil*, Rio de Janeiro, IPEA.

Bartelmus, P., Stahmer, C. and van Tongeren, J. (1991), 'Integrated Environmental and Economic Accounting: Framework for an SNA

Satellite System', *Review of Income and Wealth*, **37** (2), pp. 111–48, June.

Batabyal, A.A. (1994), 'An Open Economy Model of the Effects of Unilateral Environmental Policy by a Large Developing Country', *Ecological Economics*, **10** (3), pp. 221–32.

Bates, R., Cofala, J. and Toman, M. (1995), 'Alternative Policies for the Control of Air Pollution in Poland', Environment Paper 7, World Bank, Washington, DC.

Baytelman, Y., Cowan, K., De Gregorio, J. and González, P. (1999), 'Política Económica-Social y Bienestar: El Caso de Chile', Documento preparado para proyecto de UNICEF.

Beghin, J. and Dessus, S. (1999), 'Double Dividend with Trade Distortions. Analytical Results and Evidence from Chile', mimeo.

Beghin, J., Bowland, B., Dessus, S., Roland-Holst, D. and Van der Mensbrugghe, D. (1996a), 'Trade Reforms, Environmental Policy, and Urban Public Health in Chile', OECD Development Centre, prepared for presentation at CONAMA and Universidad de Chile.

Beghin, J., Dessus, S., Roland-Holst, D. and Van der Mensbrugghe, D. (1996b), 'General Equilibrium Modelling of Trade and The Environment', Technical Paper, Nº 116, Paris, OECD Development Centre.

Beghin, J., Roland-Holst, D. and Van der Mensbrugghe, D. (2002a), *Trade and the Environment in General Equilibrium: Evidence from Developing Economies*, Kluwer Academic Publishers, the Netherlands.

Beghin, J., Dessus, S., Roland-Holst, D. and Van der Mensbrugghe, D. (2002b), 'Empirical Modelling of Trade and the Environment', Chapter 3 in J. Beghin, D. Roland-Holst, and D. Van der Mensbrugghe, *Trade and the Environment in General Equilibrium: Evidence from Developing Economies*, Kluwer Academic Publishers, the Netherlands

BEN (1997), *Balanço Energético Nacional*, Ministério de Minas e Energia, Brasília.

Bento, A.M. and Rajkumar, A.S. (1998), 'Rethinking the Nature of the Double Dividend Debate', Document presented at 'World Congress of Environmental and Resource Economists', Venezia, Italia, 25–27 June.

Bergman, L. (1990), 'Energy and Environmental Constraints on Growth: A CGE Modeling Approach', *Journal of Policy Modeling*, **12** (4), Winter, pp. 671–91.

Bergman, Lars (1991), 'General Equilibrium Effect of Environmental

Policy: A CGE Modeling Approach', *Environmental and Resource Economics*, **1**, 43–61.

Binswanger, Hans (1989), 'Brazilian Policies that Encourage Deforestation in the Amazon', Environment Working Paper 16, Environment Department, World Bank, Washington, DC.

Binswanger, H.P. (1991). 'Brazilian Policies that Encourage Deforestation in the Amazon', *World Development*, **19** (7), pp. 821–9.

Birdsall, Nancy and Wheeler, D. (1992), 'Trade Policy and Industrial Pollution in Latin America: Where are the Pollution Havens?', in P. Low (ed.), *International Trade and the Environment*, World Bank Discussion Paper 159, World Bank, Washington, DC.

BNDES/CNI/SEBRAE (1998), *Pesquisa Gestão Ambiental na Indústria Brasileira*, BNDES, Rio de Janeiro, Brasília, CNI, SEBRAE.

Bonelli, R. (1998), 'A Note on Foreign Direct Investment (FDI) and Industrial Competitiveness in Brazil', Discussion paper, IPEA, n. 584.

Bosello, F., Carraro, C. and Galeotti, M. (1998), 'The Double Dividend Issue: Modeling Strategies and Empirical Findings', Paper presented at the Symposium on 'Environment, Energy, Economy. A Sustainable Development', October, Rome.

Bovenberg, L. and De Mooij, R. (1994), 'Environmental Levies and Distortionary Taxation', *American Economic Review*, **84**, pp. 1085–9.

Bovenberg, L. and Goulder, L.H. (1996), 'Optimal Taxation in the Presence of Other Taxes: General Equilibrium Analyses', *American Economic Review*, **86**, pp. 985–1000.

Brandao, A.S.P. (1988), 'Mercado da Terra e Estrutura Fundiaria em A.S.P. Brandao (ed)', *Os Principais Problems da Agricultura Brasileira: Analise e Sugestoes*, PNP/IPEA, Rio de Janeiro.

Breuil, J.M. (1992), 'Input–output Analysis and Pollutant Emission in France', *The Energy Journal*, **13** (2), pp. 173–84.

Brown, D.K., A.V. Deardorff and R.H. Stern (1991), 'A North American Free Trade Agreement: Analytical Issues and a Computational Assessment', Unpublished manuscript, University of Michigan.

Brzovic, F., S. Miller and C. Lagos (2002), 'Gasto, inversion y financiamiento para el desarrollo sostenible en Chile', Serie medio ambiente y desarrollo No 57 DDSAH-CEPAL, Diciembre.

Bueno, E. (1998), 'Náufragos, Traficantes e Degredados: as Primeiras Expedições ao Brasil', Coleção Terra Brasilis, v.2. Rio de Janeiro, Objetiva.

Burmeister, E. and Dobell, R., (1971), *Mathematical Theories of Economic Growth*, Macmillan, New York.

Bussolo, M., Mizala, A. and Romaguera, P. (1998), 'Beyond Heckscher-Ohlin: Trade and Labour Market, Interactions in a Case Study for Chile', *Serie Documentos de Trabajo*, FEDESARROLLO, Agosto.

Carvalho, P.G.M., and Ferreira, M.T. (1992), 'Poluição e Crescimento na Década Perdida', *Políticas Governamentais,* **80** (Mai/Jun), pp. 10-12.

Cavalcanti, M.A.F.H., Ribeiro, F.J. and Castro, A.S. (1998), in 'Desempenho Recente e Perspectivas das Exportações Brasileiras', *Revista Brasileira de comércio Exterior*, **57**, pp. 39–46.

CEPAL (1999), *Panorama social en América Latina 1998*, Naciones Unidas, Santiago de Chile, LC/G. 2050-P.

CETESB (1998), *Relatório de qualidade do ar no Estado de São Paulo – 1997.*

Chomitz. K.M. and Gray, D.A. (1996), 'Roads. Land Use and Deforestation: a Spatial Model Applied to Belize', *The World Bank Economic Review,* **10** (3), pp. 487–512.

Chomitz, K.M. and Thomas, T.S. (2000), 'Geographic Patterns of Land Use and Land Intensity in the Brazilian Amazon', World Bank, mimeo.

Cleaver, Kevin and Schreiber. G., (1991), 'The Population, Environment, and Agriculture Nexus in Sub-Saharan Africa', Africa Region Technical Paper, World Bank, Washington, DC.

Coeymans, J.E. and Larraín, F. (1994), 'Efectos de un Acuerdo de Libre Comercio entre Chile y Estados Unido: Un Enfoque de Equilibrio General', *Cuadernos de Economía*, **31** (94), pp. 357–99.

CONAMA (1994), *Propuesta Plan Nacional de Conservación de Suelos. Comisión Nacional de Medio Ambiente y Ministerio de Agricultura*, Chile.

CONAMA (1997), *Memoria Anual 1997*, Santiago, Chile.

COPPE (2002), *Primeiro Inventário Brasileiro de Emissões Antrópicas de Gases de Efeito Estufa. Relatórios de Referência. Emissões de Gases de Efeito Estufa por Queima de Combustíveis. Abordagem Bottom-Up*, Brasília, Ministério de Ciência e Tecnologia.

Cornia, G.A., Jolly, R. and Stewart, F. (1992), *Adjustment with a Human Face*, Vol. 1, *Protecting the Vulnerable and Promoting Growth*, Clarendon Press, Oxford.

Cox, D. and Harris, R. (1991), 'North America Free Trade and its Implications for Canada: Results from a CGE Model of North American Trade', mimeo.

Cox, C. and González, P. (1997), 'Educación: de Programas de Mejoramiento a Reformas', in R. Cortazar and J. Vial (eds), *Construyendo Opciones – Propuestas Económicos y Sociales para el Cambio de Siglo*, CIEPLAN, Dolmen ediciones.

Crespo et al. (1999), *O Que o Brasileiro Pensa sobre Meio Ambiente, Desenvolvimento e Sustentabilidade*, MMA/MAST/ISER, Brasília.

Cropper, M. and Griffiths, C. (1994), 'The Interaction of Population Growth and Environmental Quality', *American Economic Review*, **84** (2), pp. 250–54.

Cropper, M. and Griffiths, M. (1999), 'Roads, Population, and Deforestation in Thailand, 1976–1989', *Land Economics*, **75** (1), pp. 58–73.

Cruz, Wilfredo and Gibbs, C. (1990), 'Resource Policy Reform in the Context of Population Pressure, and Deforestation in the Philippines', *American Journal of Agricultural Economics*, **72** (5).

Cruz, Wilfredo and Repetto, Robert (1992), *The Environmental Effects of Stabilization and Structural Adjustment Programs: The Philippines Case,* World Resources Institute, Washington, DC.

Cruz, Wilfredo, Munasinghe, Mohan and Warford, Jeremy (1997), *The Greening of Economic Policy Reform*, Vol. 1 (Principles) and Vol. 2 (Case Studies), World Bank, Washington, DC.

Daly, H.E. (1991), 'Elements of Environmental Macroeconomics', in R. Costanza (ed.), *Ecological Economics: The Science and Management of Sustainability*, Columbia University Press, New York, NY, Chapter 3.

Daly, H.E. and Cobb, W. (1989), *For the Common Good: Redirecting the Economy Toward Community, the Environment and a Sustainable Future*, Beacon Press, Boston.

Dasgupta, P. and Mäler, K.G. (1998), 'Analysis, Facts, and Prediction', *Environmental and Development Economics*, **3** (4), October.

Deacon, R.T. (1995), 'Assessing the Relationship between Government Policy and Deforestation', *Journal of Environmental Economics and Management*, **28**, pp. 1–18.

Dean, Warren (1995), *With Broadax and Firebrand.. The Destruction of the Brazilian Atlantic Forest*, Berkeley, California University Press.

Debreu, G. (1959), *Theory of Value*, Wiley, New York.

de Bruyn, S. and Heintz, R.J. (1999), 'The Environmental Kuznets Curve Hypothesis', in J.C.J.M. van den Bergh (ed.), *Handbook of Environmental and Resource Economics*, Chapter 46, Edward Elgar, Cheltenham, UK and Northampton, MA, USA.

De Haan, H. (1994), 'Kaleckian computable general equilibrium models:

an evolutionary perspective', in R. Delorme and K. Dopfer (eds), *The Political Economy of Diversity*, Edward Elgar, Aldershot, UK and Brookfield, US.

De Miguel, C. and Miller, S. (1998), 'Macroeconomía, Medio Ambiente, y Modelos de Equilibrio General', Working Paper, Programa de Desarrollo Sustenable, Centro de Análisis de Políticas Públicas, Universidad de Chile, Santiago, November.

Dervis, K., de Melo, J. and Robinson, S. (1982), *General Equilibrium Models for Development Policy*, World Bank, Washington, DC.

Devarajan, Shantayanan (1997), 'Can Computable General Equilibrium Models Shed Light on the Environmental Problems of Developing Countries?', in P. Dasgupta, and K.G. Maler (èds), *The Environment and Emerging Development Issues*, vol. 1, Clarendon Press, Oxford.

Dessus, S., Roland-Holst, D. and Van der Mensbrugghe, D. (1994), 'Input-based Pollution Estimates for Environmental Assessment in Developing Countries', Technical paper 101, Paris, Organisation for Economic Cooperation and Development, Development Center.

DGA (1987), *Balance Hidrico de Chile, Dirección General de Aguas*, Ministerio de Obras Públicas, Santiago, Chile.

DIPRES (2003), 'Estadísticas de las Finanzas Públicas 1987–2002', *Series Estadísticas*, Santiago.

Dorfman, R. (1954), 'The Nature and Significance of Input–Output', *Review of Economics and Statistics*, **36**.

Dufournaud, M., Harrington, J. and Rogers, P. (1988), 'Leontief's Environmental Repercussions and the Economic Structure Revisited: A General Equilibrium Formulation', *Geographical Analysis*, **20** (4) pp. 318–27.

ECLAC (Economic Commission for Latin America and the Caribbean) (1989), 'Crisis External Debt, Macroeconomic Policies, and Their Relation to the Environment in Latin America and the Caribbean', Paper prepared for the meeting of high-level government experts on Regional Co-operation in Environmental Matters in Latin America and the Caribbean, United Nations Environmental Programme, Brasilia.

Ecological Economics (1998), *Special Issue on the Environmental Kuznets Curve.*

Edwards, Sebastian (1992), 'Structural Adjustment and Stabilization: Issues on Sequencing and Speed', EDI Working Papers, Economic Development Institute, World Bank, Washington, DC.

Engel, E., Galetovic, A. and Raddatz, C. (1998), 'Taxes and Income Distribution in Chile: Some Unpleasant Redistributive Arithmetic', Working Paper, series 6828.

England, R.W. (2000), 'Natural Capital and the Theory of Economic Growth', *Ecological Economics*, **34** (3), pp. 425–31, September.

Environment and Development Economics (1997), *Special Issue on the Environmental Kuznets Curve. Structural Adjustment and the Environment.*

Feder, Gershon, Ochan, T., Chalamwong, Y. and Hongladarom, C. (1988), *Land Policies and Farm Productivity in Thailand*, Johns Hopkins University Press, Baltimore, MD.

Fernside, P.M. (1996), 'Deforestation in Brazilian Amazonia: Comparison of Recent Landsite Estimates', INPA, mimeo.

Ferraz, C. (2001), 'What Causes Agriculture Expansion and Deforestation? Evidence for the Brazilian Amazon, 1980–1995', mimeo IPEA.

Ferraz, C. and Seroa da Motta, R. (1999), 'Automobile Pollution Control in Brazil', Discussion Paper 670, IPEA.

FONASA (2003), Estadísticas, www.fonasa.gov.cl.

Førsund, F.R. (1985), 'Input–Output Models, National Economic Models, and the Environment', in V. Kneese and J.L. Sweeney (eds), *Handbook of Natural Resource and Energy Economics*, vol. 1, Amsterdam, Elsevier.

Førsund, F. and Storm, S. (1988), *Environmental Economics and Management: Pollution and Natural Resources*, New York, Croom Helm Press.

FOSIS (1997), 'Proyecto de Presupuesto 1998'.

FOSIS (2000), 'Memoria de Fomento Productivo, 1990–2000', Document in preparation.

Foster, A.D., Rosenzweig, M.R. and Behrman, J.R. (forthcoming), 'Population Growth. Income Growth and Deforestation: Management of Village Commons in India', *Quarterly Journal of Economics*.

Freeman, A. Myrick. (1993), *The Measurement of Environmental and Resource Values: Theory and Methods*, Resources for the Future, Washington, DC.

Fullerton, D. and Metcalf, G.E. (1997), 'Environmental Taxes and the Double-Dividend Hypothesis: Did You Really Expect Something for Nothing?', NBER Working Paper, 6199, September.

Fullerton, D. and West, S. (1999), 'Can Taxes on Cars and Gasoline Mimic an Unavailable Tax on Emissions?', NBER Working Paper, 7059, March.

Furtado, C. (1959), *Formação Econômica do Brasil*, Rio de Janeiro, Fundo de Cultura.

Girma, M. (1992), 'Macropolicy and the Environment: A Framework for Analysis', *World Development*, **20** (4), pp. 531–40.

Glade, A.A. (ed.) (1988), *Libro Rojo de los Vertebrados Terrestres de Chile*, Conaf, Santiago.

Glomsrod, S., Monge, M.D. and Vennemo, H. (1998), 'Structural Adjustment and Deforestation in Nicaragua', *Environment and Development Economics*, **4** (1), pp. 19–43, February.

Goldin, I. and Roland-Host, D. (1997), 'Economic Policies for Sustainable Resource Use in Morocco', in W. Cruz, M. Munasinghe and J. Warford (eds), *The Greening of Economic Policy Reform*, Vol. II: Case Studies, World Bank, Washington, DC, Chapter 3.

Goldin, I. and Winters, A. (1992), *Open Economies: Structural Adjustment and Agriculture*, Cambridge University Press, London.

Gómez-Lobo, A. (1991), 'Desarrollo Sustentable del Sector Pesquero Chileno en los años 80', in J. Vial (ed.), *Desarrollo y Medio Ambiente: Hacia un Enfoque Integrador*, CIEPLAN, Santiago.

González, P. (1999), 'Reforma del Sistema Escolar en Chile', mimeo.

Goulder, L. (1993), 'Energy Taxes, Traditional Efficiency Effects, and Environmental Implications', NBER Working Paper, 4582.

Goulder, L. (1994), 'Environmental Taxation and the "Double Dividend": A Readers Guide', NBER Working Paper, 4896, October.

Goulder, L. (1995), 'Effects of Carbon Taxes in an Economy with Prior Tax Distortions: An Intertemporal General Equilibrium Analysis', *Journal of Environmental Economics and Management*, 29, 271–97.

Granger, C.W.J. and Hyung, N. (1997), 'Correlacao Espuria em Modelos de Painel: uma Analise do Desmatamento na Amazonia', *Pesquisa e Planejamento Economica*, **27** (3).

Grossman, G. and Krueger, A. (1993), 'Environmental Impacts of a North American Free Trade Agreement', in Peter Garber, *The Mexico–US Free Trade Agreement*, The MIT Press, Cambridge.

Grossman, G.M. and Krueger, A.B. (1995), 'Economic Growth and the Environment', *Quarterly Journal of Economics*, **CX**, pp. 353–77, May.

Gunning, J. and Keyser, M. (1993), 'Applied General Equilibrium Models for Policy Analysis', in T.N. Srinivisan and J. Behrman (eds), *Handbook of Development Economics III*, North-Holland, Amsterdam.

Hansen, L.G. (1998), 'Is there a weak double dividend?' Presented at 'The World Congress of Environmental and Resource Economists', Venice, Italy, 25–27 June.

Harrison, G., Rutherford, T.F. and Tarr, D.G. (1997), 'Opciones de

Política Comercial para Chile: Una evaluación cuantitativa', *Cuadernos de Economía*, **31**.

Harrison, G., Rutherford, T.F. and Tarr, D.G. (2002), 'Chile's Regional Arrangements: The Importance of Market Access and Lowering the Tariff to Six Percent', prepared for the Central Bank of Chile conference on General Equilibrium Models for the Chilean Economy, Santiago, 4/5 April.

Hazilla M. and Koop, R. (1990), 'Social Cost of Environmental Quality Regulations: A General Equilibrium Analysis', *Journal of Policy Modeling*, **98** (4), pp. 853–73.

Helfand, S. (1999), 'The 1995/1996 Agriculture Census: Fiction or Fact?', paper presented at the NEMESIS/PRONEX meeting, IPEA, Rio de Janeiro, December.

Hettige, Hemamala, Martin, Paul, Singh, Manjula and Wheeler, David (1994), *IPPS – The Industrial Pollution Projection System*, World Bank, Washington, DC.

Heyes, A. (2000), 'A Proposal for the Greening of Textbook Macroeconomics: IS-LM-EE', *Ecological Economics*.

Holden, S.T., Taylor, J.E. and Hampton, S. (1998), 'Structural Adjustment and Market Imperfections: A Stylized Village Economy-wide Model with Non-separable Farm Households', *Environment and Development Economics,* **4** (1), pp. 69–87, February.

Holland, D., Figueroa, E. Alvarez, R. and Gilbert, J. (2002), 'Imperfect Labor Mobility, Urban Unemployment and Agricultural Trade Reforms in Chile', prepared for the Central Bank of Chile conference on General Equilibrium Models for the Chilean Economy, Santiago, 4/5 April.

Hotelling, Harold (1931), 'The Economics of Exhaustible Resources', *Journal of Political Economy*, **39** (2), pp. 137–75.

Hultkrantz, L. (1992), 'National Account of Timber and Forest Environmental Resources in Sweden', *Environmental and Resource Economics*, **2** (3), pp. 283–305.

IBAMA (1997), *Portaria de Biodiversidade*, **62**.

IBGE (Brazilian Institute of Geography and Statistics) (1998), *Anuário Estatístico do Brasil*, IBGE.

INFOR (1993), 'Evaluación del Consumo de Leña en Chile 1992', National Energy Commission, Santiago, Chile.

INFOR (1995), 'Estadísticas Forestales 1994', *Boletín Estadístico*, **40**, Santiago, Chile.

INPE (2000), *Relatório Anual de Desflorestamento na Amazônia*, São

José dos Campos.

Intendencia Región Metropolitana (1989), 'Estudio Base de Generación de Niveles de Ruido en Santiago', Santiago de Chile.

Islam, S., Munasinghe, M. and Clarke, M. (2003), 'Making Long-term Economic Growth More Sustainable: Evaluating the Costs and Benefits', *Ecological Economics*, **47** (2–3), pp. 149–66.

Jaeger, W.K. (1999), 'Double Dividend Reconsidered', Paper presented at EAERE Ninth Annual Conference, Oslo, Norway, 25–27 June.

Johansen, L. (1960), *A Multisector Study of Economic Growth*, North-Holland, Amsterdam.

Jorgenson, D.W. and Wilcoxen, P. (1990), 'Intertemporal General Equilibrium Modeling of U.S. Environmental Regulation', *Journal of Policy Modeling*, **12** (4), pp. 715–44.

Jorgenson, D.W. and Wilcoxen, P. (1993), 'Reducing U.S. Carbon Dioxide Emissions: An Assessment of Different Instruments', *Journal of Policy Modeling*, **15** (5) pp. 491–520.

Kahn, M.E. (1998), 'A Household Level Environmental Kuznets Curve', *Economic Letters*, 59, pp. 269–73.

Kaimowitz, D. and Angelsen, A. (1998), 'Economic Models of Tropical Deforestation: A Review', CIFOR, Bogor, Indonesia.

Kessler, J.J. and Van Dorp, M. (1998), 'Structural Adjustment and the Environment: The Need for an Analytical Methodology', *Ecological, Economics*, **27** (3), pp. 267–81, December.

Ketkar, K.W. (1983), 'The Allocation and Distribution Effects of Pollution Effects of Pollution Abatement Expenditures on the US Economy', *Resources and Energy*, **5**, pp. 261–283.

Kiuila, O. (2003), 'Economic Repercussions of Sulfur Regulations in Poland', *Journal of Policy Modelling*, **25**, pp. 327–33.

Kneese, A. (1998), 'No Time for Complacency', *Environmental and Development Economics*, **3** (4), October.

Koopmans T.C. (1973), 'Some Observations on "Optimal" Economic Growth with Exhaustible Resources', Cowles Foundation Discussion Paper No. 356.

Koskela, E., Schöb, R. and Sinn, H. (1999), 'Green Tax Reform and Competitiveness', NBER Working Paper, 6922, February.

Krugman, P. (1979), 'Increasing Return, Monopolistic Competition, and International Trade', *Journal of International Economics*, **9**, pp. 469–79.

Larson, B. and Bromley Daniel, (1991), 'Natural Resource Prices, Export Policies, and Deforestation: The Case of Sudan', *World Development*.

Lele, U. and Stone, S. (1989), 'Population Pressure, the Environment, and

Agricultural Intensification: Variations on the Boserup Hypothesis', MADIA Discussion Paper 4, World Bank, Washington, DC.

Leonard, H.J. (1988), *Pollution and the Struggle for the World Product*, Cambridge University Press, Cambridge, UK.

Leontief, W. (1970), 'Environmental Repercussions and the Economic Structure: An Input–Output Approach', *Review of Economics and Statistics*, **52**, pp. 262–71.

Lewis, J. (1993), 'Energy Pricing, Economic Distortion and Air Pollution in Indonesia', Discussion Paper 455, Harvard Institute for International Development, Harvard University.

Li, P. and Rose, A. (1995), 'Global Warming and the Pennsylvania Economy: A Computable General Equilibrium Analysis', unpublished paper, MIT.

Low, P. (1992), 'International Trade and the Environment', World Bank Discussion Paper, 159, World Bank, Washington, DC.

Low, P. and Yeats, A. (1992), 'Do "Dirty" Industries Matter?', in P. Low (ed.), *International Trade and the Environment*, World Bank discussion paper no.159, Washington, DC.

Lucas, R., Wheeler, D. and Hettige, H. (1992), 'Economic Development, Environmental Regulation and the International Migration of Toxic Industrial Pollution: 1960–1988', Patrick Low (ed.), in *International Trade and the Environment*, World Bank Discussion Paper No. 159, pp. 67–88, Washington, DC.

Madrid-Aris, M.E. (1998), 'International Trade and the Environment: Evidence from the North America Free Trade Agreement (NAFTA)', Presented at 'World Congress of Environmental and Resources Economics', Venice, 25–27 June.

Mahar, D.J. (1988), 'Government Policies and Deforestation in Brazil's Amazon Region', Washington DC, World Bank.

Maler, K.G. and Munasinghe, M. (1996), 'Macroeconomic Policies, Second-best Theory, and the Environment' in M. Munasinghe (ed.), *Environmental Impacts of Macroeconomic and Sectoral Policies*, World Bank, Washington, DC.

Malthus, Thomas (1798), *On Population*, Modern Library Edition, Random House, New York.

Mani, M. and Wheeler, D. (1998), 'In Search of Pollution Havens? Dirty Industry in the World Economy, 1960–1995', in *Trade, Global Policy, and the Environment*, World Bank Disc. Paper No. 402, World Bank, Washington, DC, Chapter 8.

Martin, María Pía (1998), 'Integración al Desarrollo: Una Visión de la Política Social', in C. Toloza, and E. Lahera (eds), *Chile en los*

Noventa, Presidencia de la República, Dolmen ediciones.

Martini, A., Rosa, N. and Uhl, C. (1994), 'An Attempt to Predict which Tree Species may be Threatened by Logging Activities', *Environmental Conservation*, **21** (2), pp. 152–62.

Max-Neef, M. (1995), 'Economic Growth and Quality of Life: A Threshold Hypothesis', *Ecological Economics*, **15**, pp. 115–18.

Meier, Peter, Munasinghe, Mohan and Siyambalapitiya, Tilak (1995), 'Energy Sector Policy and the Environment: A Case Study of Sri Lanka', in M. Munasinghe (ed.), *Environmental Impacts of Macroeconomic and Sectoral Policies,* World Bank, Washington, DC.

Mendes, F.E. (1994), 'Uma Avaliacão Crítica dos Custos de Controle da Poluição Hídrica de Origem Industrial no Brasil', Tese de Mestrado, COPPE/UFRJ, Rio de Janeiro.

MIDEPLAN (Ministerio de Planificación Nacional y Política Económica) (1996a), *Balance Seis Años de las Políticas Sociales: 1990–1996*, Santiago de Chile.

MIDEPLAN (1996b), *Encuesta de Caracterización Económica* (CASEN), Santiago de Chile.

MIDEPLAN (1998a), 'Impacto de las Políticas Públicas en la Situación de Salud 1990–1996', Documentos, December, Santiago de Chile.

MIDEPLAN (1998b) 'Impacto de la Política Habitacional de los Años Noventa', Documentos, Santiago de Chile.

MIDEPLAN (1999a), 'Indicadores Económicos y Sociales 1990–1998', Documentos, Santiago de Chile.

MIDEPLAN (1999b), 'Impacto de la Política Educacional, 1990–1996', Documentos, Santiago de Chile.

MIDEPLAN (1999c), 'Situación de la Educación en Chile. Resultados Encuesta CASEN 1998', Documento No. 5, Santiago de Chile.

MIDEPLAN (1999d), 'Situación Habitacional en Chile. Resultados Encuesta CASEN 1998', *Documento* No. 6, Santiago de Chile.

MIDEPLAN (2001), 'Situación de la Educación en Chile, Análisis de la VIII Encuesta de Caracterización Socioeconómica Nacional (CASEN 2000)', Documento No. 4.

MIDEPLAN (2003), Statistical Information, www.mideplan.cl.

MIND (2005), *Action Impact Matrix (AIM) Guide*, Munasinghe Institute for Development, Colombo Sri Lanka

MINEDUC (Ministerio de Educación) (1999), *Compendio de Información Estadística 1998*, Ministerio de Educación, Santiago de Chile.

MINSAL (Ministerio de Salud) (1999), 'Inversiones Sectoriales en la Década 1990–1999', Ministerio de Salud, Santiago de Chile.

MINVU (Ministerio de Vivienda y Urbanismo) (1999), *Memoria Anual, 1999*, Ministerio de Vivienda y Urbanismo, Santiago de Chile.

Miranda, K. and Muzondo, T. (1991), 'Public Policy and the Environment', *Finance and Development*, **28** (2), pp. 25–7.

Moran, D. (1996), 'Deforestation in the Brazilian Amazon', in L.E. Sponsel et al. (eds), *Tropical Deforestation: the Human Dimension*, Columbia University Press, New York.

Mueller, B. (1997), 'Property Rights and the Evolution of a Frontier', *Land Economics*, **73** (10), pp. 42–57.

Mukherjee, N. (1996), 'Water and Land in South Africa: Economy-wide Impacts of Reform', Discussion Paper, No 12, International Food Policy Research Institute, Washington, DC.

Munasinghe, M. (1992), *Environmental Economics and Sustainable Development*, Paper presented at the UN Earth Summit, Rio de Janeiro, and reprinted by the World Bank, Washington, DC.

Munasinghe, M. (1993), 'The Economist's Approach to Sustainable Development', *Finance and Development*, **30** (4), pp. 16–19.

Munasinghe, M. (1995), 'Making Growth More Sustainable', *Ecological Economics*, **15**, pp. 121–4.

Munasinghe, M. (1996), 'An Overview of the Environmental Impacts of Macroeconomic and Sectoral Policies', in M. Munasinghe (ed.), *Environmental Impacts of Macroeconomic and Sectoral Policies*, World Bank, Washington, DC.

Munasinghe, M. (2002a), 'The Sustainomics Trans-disciplinary Meta-framework For Making Development More Sustainable: Applications to Energy Issues', *International Journal of Sustainable Development* **5** (1/2), pp. 125–82.

Munasinghe, M. (ed.) (2002b), *Macroeconomics and the Environment*, Edward Elgar, Cheltenham, UK and Northampton, MA, USA.

Munasinghe, M. (2006), *Sustainomics: Conceptual Framework and Case Studies for Making Development More Sustainable*, Edward Elgar, Cheltenham, UK and Northampton, MA, USA.

Munasinghe, M. and Cruz, W. (1994), *Economywide Policies and the Environment: Lessons from Experience*, World Bank, Washington, DC.

Munasinghe, M. and Shearer, W. (eds) (1995), *Defining and Measuring Sustainability*, United Nations University and the World Bank, Tokyo and Washington, DC.

Munasinghe, M., Cruz, W. and Warford, J. (1993), 'Are Economywide Policies Good for the Environment?', *Finance and Development*, 28, pp. 25–7.

Munasinghe, M., Sunkel, O. and de Miguel, C. (eds) (2001), *The Sustainability of Long-term Growth: Socioeconomic and Ecological Perspectives*, Edward Elgar, Cheltenham, UK and Northampton, MA, USA.

Nepstad, D.C. et al. (1999), 'Large-scale Impoverishment of Amazonian Forests by Logging and Fire', *Nature*, **398**, pp. 505–8.

Nepstad, D.C. et al. (2000), 'Cenarios Futuros para a Amazonia', Avanca Brasil: Os Custos Ambientais para a Amazonia, Relatorio do projeto Belem: IPAM/Instituto Socioambiental.

Nestor, D.V. and Pasurka, C. (1994), 'Alternative Specifications for Environmental Control Costs in a General Equilibrium Framework', Economic Analysis and Research Branch, US EPA, Washington, DC.

Nestor, D.V. and Pasurka, C. (1995), 'CGE Model of Pollution Abatement Processes for Assessing the Economic Effects of Environmental Policy', *Economic Modeling*, **12** (1), pp. 53–9.

Neumayer, E. (2000), 'Pollution Heavens: Why be Afraid of International Capital Mobility', London School of Economics and Political Science, mimeo.

Nordström, Håkan and Vaughan, Scott (1999), *Trade and Environment*, WTO Special Studies 4, Geneva, World Trade Organization.

Nugent, J.B. and Sarma, C.V.S.K. (2002), 'The Three E's – Efficiency, Equity and Environment Protection – in Search of "win–win–win" policies. A CGE Analysis of India', *Journal of Policy Modeling*, **24**, pp. 19–50.

Nzomo, M. (1992), 'Beyond Structural Adjustment Programs: Democracy, Gender, Equity, and Development in Africa, with Special Reference to Kenya', in J. Nyang'oro and T. Shaw (eds), *Beyond Structural Adjustment in Africa – The Political Economy of Sustainable and Democratic Development*, Praeger, New York.

O'Ryan, R. and del Valle, A. (1996), 'Managing Air Quality in Santiago: What Needs to be Done?', *Estudios de Economía*, (23), August, Special issue on Urban Economics.

O'Ryan, R., de Miguel, C. and Miller, S. (2000), 'Ensayo sobre equilibrio general computable: Teoría y aplicaciones', Documentos de Trabajo, Serie Economía No 73, CEA-DII, Universidad de Chile, Chile, marzo.

O'Ryan, R., de Miguel, Carlos and Miller, S. (2004), 'General Equilibrium Analysis of Economywide Cross Effects in Social and Environmental Policies: Case Study of Chile', *Ecological Economics* (forthcoming).

O'Ryan, R., Miller, S. and de Miguel, C (2003), 'A CGE Framework to Evaluate Policy Options for Reducing Air Pollution Emissions in

Chile', *Environmental and Development Economics*, **8**, pp. 285–309.

Opschoor, J.B. and Jongma, S.M. (1996), 'Structural Adjustment Policies and Sustainability', *Environment and Development Economics*, **1**, pp. 183–202.

Opschoor, H. (2001), 'Economic Growth, the Environment and Welfare: are They Compatible?' in Seroa da Motta, R. (ed.), *Environmental Economics and Policy Making in Developing Countries*, Edward Elgar, Cheltenham, UK and Northampton, MA, USA.

Ostro, B.D. (1992), 'The Health Effects of Air Pollution: A Methodolgy with Applications to Jakarta', The World Bank.

Ozorio de Almeida, A.L. and Campari, J.S. (1995), 'Sustainable Settlement in the Brazilian Amazon', Oxford University Press, Oxford.

Panayotou, T. (1997) 'Demystifying the Environmental Kuznets Curve: Turning a Black Box into a Policy Tool', *Environment and Development Economics*', **2** (4), pp. 471–79.

Panayotou, T. and Susangkarn, C. (1991), 'The Debt Crisis, Structural Adjustment and the Environment: The Case of Thailand', Paper prepared for the World Wildlife Fund Project on the Impact of Macroeconomic Adjustment on the Environment, Washington, DC.

Parry, I.W. and Bento, A.M. (1999), 'Tax Deductions, Environmental Policy, and the "Double Dividend" Hypothesis', World Bank Working Paper Series 2119, May.

Parry, I.W. and Oates, W.E. (1998), 'Policy Analysis in a Second-best World', *Resources for the Future*, Discussion Paper Series, September.

Pasurka, C. (1984), 'The Short-run Impact of Environmental Protection Costs on U.S. Product Prices', *Journal of Environmental Economics and Management*, **11**, pp. 380–90.

Pearce, D. and Turner, K. (1990), *Economía de los Recursos Naturales y del Medio Ambiente*, Celeste Ediciones, Madrid, España.

Perrings, Charles (1993), 'Pastoral Stategies in Sub-Saharan Africa: The Economic and Ecological Sustainiblity of Dryland Range Management', Environment Working Paper 57 Environment Department, World Bank, Washington, DC, February.

Perroni, C. and Wigle R. (1994), 'International Trade and Environmental Quality: How Important are the Linkages?', *Canadian Journal of Economics*, **XXVII** (3).

Persson, Anika and Munasinghe, Mohan (1995), 'Natural Resource Management and Economywide Policies in Costa Rica: A Computable General Equilibrium (CGE) Modeling Approach', *World Bank*

Economic Review, **9** (2), pp. 656–77.

Pfaff, A. (1999), 'What Drives Deforestation in the Brazilian Amazon? Evidence from Satellite and Socioeconomic Data', *Journal of Environmental Economics and Management*, **37**, pp. 26–43.

Pigott, J., Whalley, J. and Wigle, J. (1992), 'International Linkages and Carbon Reduction Initiatives', in K. Anderson and R. Blackhurst (eds), *The Greening of World Trade Issues*, University of Michigan Press.

Pinto, L.M. and G. Harrison (2003), 'Multilateral Negotiations Over Climate Change Policy', *Journal of Policy Modeling*, **25**, pp. 911–30.

PMSS, Programa de Modernização do Sistema de Saneamento – Sistema Nacional de Informações Sobre Saneamento – SNIS, Diagnóstico dos Serviços de Águas e Esgotos – 1997, **3**, IPEA, Brasília.

PNAD (1998), Pesquisa Nacional de Amostra Domiciliar, IBGE, Rio de Janeiro.

Prado, E. (1981), *Estrutura tecnológica e desenvolvimento regional*, Estudos Econômicos 10, IPE/USP, São Paulo.

Ramos, L. and Vieira, P. (2000), 'Determinantes da Desigualdade de Rendimentos no Brasil in: Henriques, R. Desigualdade e Pobreza no Brasil', IPEA, Rio de Janeiro.

Reed, David (ed.) (1992), *Structural Adjustment and the Environment*, Westview Press, Boulder, CO.

Reed, David (1996), *Structural Adjustment, the Environment and Sustainable Development*, Earthscan Publishers, London.

Reis, E.J. (1996), 'Padrões Geográficos de Incidência dos Efeitos Econômicos e Ambientais do Programa Grande Carajás', in R. Varsano, (ed.), *Perspectivas da Economia Brasileira*, IPEA, Rio de Janeiro.

Reis, E.J. and Blanco, F. (1996), 'The Causes of Brazilian Amazon Deforestation', mimeo, IPEA.

Reis, E.J. and Margulis, S. (1991), 'Options for Slowing Amazon Jungle Clearing', in R. Dornbusch and J. Poterbar (eds), *Economic Policy Responses to Global Warming*, MIT Press, Cambridge, MA.

Reis, E.J. and Guzmán, R.H. (1993), 'Un Modelo Econométrico do Desflorestamento da Amazônia', *Pesquisa e Planejamento Econômico*, **23** (1).

Repetto, R. (1995), 'Jobs, Competitiveness and Regulation: What are Real Issues?', World Resources Institute, Washington, DC.

Repetto, R., Dower R., Jenkins R. and Geochegan, J. (1992), 'Green Fees: How a Tax Shift Can Work for the Environment and the Economy', World Resources Institute.

Repetto, R., Magrath, W., Wells, M., Beer, C. and Ossini, F. (1989), 'The Need for Natural Resource Accounting', in *Wasting Assets: Natural Resources in the National Income Accounts*, World Resources Institute, Washington, DC, Chapter 1.

Ricardo, David (1817), 'Principles of Political Economy and Taxation', in P. Sraffa and Maurice H. Dobb (eds), *The Works of David Ricardo*, Cambridge University Press, Cambridge.

Robinson, S. (1990), 'Pollution, Market Failure and Optimal Policy in an Economy-wide Framework', Working Paper 559, Department of Agricultural and Resource Economics, University of Berkeley, Berkeley.

Robinson, S. and Gelhar, C. (1995), 'Land, Water and Agriculture in Egypt: The Economy-wide Impact of Policy Reform', Discussion paper, International Food Policy Research Institute, Washington, DC.

Robinson, S., Subramanian, S. and Geoghegan, J. (1993), 'A Regional Environmental Computable General equilibrium Model of the Los Angeles Basin', Working Paper No. 646, Department of Agricultural and Resource Economics, University of California, Berkeley.

Rocha, S. (2000), 'Pobreza e Desigualdade no Brasil: O Esgotamento dos Efeitos Distributivos do Plano Real', Discussion paper 721, IPEA.

Rose, A. and Abler, D. (1998), 'Computable General Equilibrium Modeling in the Integrated Assessment of Climate Change', presented at the Biennial Meeting of the International Society of Ecological Economics, Santiago, Chile, November.

Rose, A., Schluter, G. and Wiese, A. (1995), 'Motor-Fuel Taxes and Household Welfare: An Applied General Equilibrium Analysis', *Land Economics*, **71** (2), pp. 229–43.

Ruiz, J. and Yarur, I. (1990), 'Un Modelo de Equilibrio General para Evaluación de Política Tributaria', Tesis para optar al título de Ingeniero Industrial y al grado de Magister en Ciencias de la Ingeniería mención Ingeniería Industrial, Universidad de Chile.

Scarf, H. and Hansen, T. (1973), *The Computation of Economics Equilibria*, Yale University Press, New Haven.

Schkolnik, M. and Bonnefoy, J. (1994), 'Una Propuesta de Tipología de las Políticas Sociales en Chile', UNICEF document.

Schneider, R. (1993), 'Land Abandonment, Property Rights, and Agricultural Sustainability in the Amazon', LATEN Dissemination Note No. 3, World Bank, Washington, DC.

Schneider, R. (1994), 'Government and the Economy on the Amazon

Frontier', Latin America and the Caribbean Technical Department, Regional Studies Program, Report No. 34, World Bank, Washington, DC.

Schneider, R.R. (1995), 'Government and the Economy on the Amazon Frontier', World Bank Environment paper No.11, The World Bank, Washington, DC.

Schneider, R.R. et al. (2000), 'Amazônia Sustentável: Limitantes e Oportunidades para o Desenvolvimento Rural', Série Parcerias Banco Mundial/Imazon, Brasília.

Seroa da Motta, R. and Ferraz, C. (2000), 'Estimating Timber Depreciation in the Brazilian Amazon', *Environment and Development Economics*, **5** (1&2).

Seroa da Motta, R., Mendes, F.E., Nascimento, C.A. and Rosito, T. (1993), *Current Status of Industrial Air Pollution Control in Brazil*, IPEA, Rio de Janeiro.

Seroa da Motta, Ronaldo (1993a), *Water Quality and Policy in Brazil*, IPEA, Rio de Janeiro.

Seroa da Motta, R. (1993b), *Política de controle ambiental e competitividade – estudo da competitividade da indústria brasileira*, IE/UNICAMP-IEI/UFRJ-FDC-FUNCEX, Campinas.

Seroa da Motta, R. (1993), 'Indicadores de poluição na indústria brasileira', *Perspectivas da Economia Brasileira – 1994*, IPEA/RJ.

Seroa da Motta, R. (1996), 'Indicadores Ambientais: Aspectos Ecológicos, de Eficiência e Distributivos', Discussion paper 399, IPEA, Rio de Janeiro.

Serôa da Motta, R. and Fernandes Mendes, Ana Paula (1996), 'Health Costs Associated with Air Pollution in Brazil', Chapter 5, in P. May and R. Seroa da Motta (eds), *Price the Earth*, Columbia Press, New York.

Seroa da Motta, R. and Rezende, L. (1999), 'The Impact of Sanitation on Waterborne Diseases in Brazil', in Peter H. May (ed.), *Natural Resource Valuation and Policy in Brazil: Methods and Cases*, pp. 174–87, Columbia University Press, New York.

SESMA (2004), www.sesma.cl.

Shoven, J. and Whalley, J. (1984), 'Applied General Equilibrium Models of Taxation and International Trade: An Introduction and Survey', *Journal of Economics Literature*, **22,** pp. 1007–51.

Silva, A.B.O. and Medina, M.H. (1999), 'Produto Interno Bruto por Unidade da Federação: 1985–1998', Discussion paper 677, IPEA.

Sobarzo, H. (1991), 'A General Equilibrium Analysis of the Gains from Trade for the Mexican Economy of a North American Free Trade

Agreement', Working Paper, El Colegio de Mexico, Mexico City.

Solow, R. (1993), 'An Almost Practical Step Toward Sustainability', *Resources Policy*, **19** (3), pp. 162–72, September.

Southgate, Douglas and Pearce, David W. (1988), 'Agricultural Colonization and Environmental Degradation in Frontier Developing Economies', Environment Working Paper 9, Environment Department, World Bank, Washington, DC.

Steffen, W. (1993), 'Aspectos de la hidrodinámica del lago Villarrica', en III Congreso Internacional de gestión en recursos naturales, Sociedad de Vida Silvestre de Chile, Pucón, Chile.

Steininger, K.W. (1999), 'General Models of Environmental Policy and Foreign Trade', in J.C.J.M. van den Bergh (ed.), *Handbook of Environmental and Resource Economics*, Edward Elgar, Cheltenham, UK and Northampton, MA, USA, Chapter 28.

Stiglitz, J. (1974), 'Growth with Exhaustible Natural Resources: Efficient and Optimal Growth Paths', *Review of Economic Studies*, **41**, Special Symposium Issue, pp. 123–37.

Stryker, J.D. et al. (1989), 'Linkages between Policy Reform and Natural Resource Management in Sub-Saharan Africa', Fletcher School, Tufts University, Bedford, MA, and Associates for International Resources and Development.

Tarp, Finn (1993), *Stabilization and Structural Adjustment: Macroeconomic Frameworks for Analyzing the Crisis in Sub-Saharan Africa*, Routledge, New York.

Taylor, L., Bacha, E., Cardoso, E. and Lysy, F. (1980), *Models of Growth and Distribution for Brazil*, Oxford University Press, London.

Taylor, L. (1990), *Socially Relevant Policy Analysis: Structuralist CGE Models for the Developing World*, The MIT Press, Cambridge.

The Economist (1997), 'Environment Scares: Plenty of Gloom', London, 20 December.

Titelman, D. (1999), 'Reformas al Financiamiento del Sistema de Salud en Chile', *Revista de la CEPAL*, No 69, December.

Tsigas, M., Gray, D. and Krissoff, B. (1997), 'Harmonization of Environmental Standards in the Western Hemisphere', Preliminar, 18 July.

Ulph, A. (1997), 'International Trade and the Environment: A Survey of Recent Economic Analysis', in H. Folmer and T. Tietenberg (eds), *The International Yearbook of Environmental and Resource Economics 1997/98*, Edward Elgar, Cheltenham, UK and Northampton, MA, USA, pp. 205–42.

UNDP (1999), *Human Development Report 1999*.

United Nations (1993), *Integrated Environmental and Economic Accounting*, Series F, No. 61, United Nations, New York.

United Nations Statistical Office (1993), *System of National Accounts 1991*, United Nations, New York

Universidad de Chile (2000), *Informe País. Estado del Medio Ambiente en Chile – 1999*, Centro de Análisis de Políticas Públicas-CONAMA-PNUMA, Santiago.

USBEA (1995), *Natural Resource and Environment Accounting*, Conference Proceedings, US Bureau of Economic Analysis, Washington, DC.

Vaughan, D. and Pasurka Jr., C.A. (1995), 'Environmental–Economic Accounting and Indicators of the Economic Importance of Environmental Protection Activities', *The Review of Income and Wealth*, **41** (3), pp. 265–88, September.

Venegas, J. (1995), 'Matriz de Cuentas Sociales 1986: Una SAM para Chile', *Serie de Estudios Económicos*, No. 39, Banco Central de Chile.

Walker, R., Moran, E. and Anselin, L. (2000), 'Deforestation and Cattle Ranching in the Brazilian Amazon: External Capital and Household Processes', *World Development*, **28** (4), pp. 683–99.

Walras, L. (1954) [1874], *Elements of Pure Economics*, Allen and Unwin, London.

Warford, Jeremy, Munasinghe, Mohan and Cruz, Wilfredo (1997), *The Greening of Economic Policy Reform*, Vol. 1 (Principles), World Bank, Washington, DC.

Weil, D.E.C., Alicbusan, A.P., Wilson, J.F., Reich, M.R. and Bradley, D.J. (1990), *The Impact of Development Policies on Health: a Review of the Literature*, World Health Organization, Geneva.

Welsch, H. (1996), 'The Carbon Tax Game: Differential Tax Recycling in a Two-region General Equilibrium Model of the European Community', *Weltwirtschaftliches Archiv*, **132** (2), pp. 356–77.

Withagen, C. (1990), 'Topics in Resource Economics', in F. van der Ploeg (ed.), *Advanced Lectures in Quantitative Economics*, Academic Press, London, pp. 381–420.

World Bank (1994a), 'Chile, Managing Environmental Problems: Economic Analysis of Selected Issues', Report No. 13061-CH, 19 December.

World Bank (1992a), *World Development Report 1992: Development and the Environment*, Oxford University Press, New York.

World Bank (1992b), *Water Quality and Pollution Control Project in Brazil*, Staff Appraisal Report, World Bank, Washington, DC.

World Bank (1992c), *The Changchun Water Supply and Environmental Project in China*, Staff Appraisal Report, World Bank, Washington, DC.

World Bank (1992d), *The Zambia Marketing and Processing Infrastructure Project*, Staff Appraisal Report, World Bank, Washington, DC.

World Bank (1993a), *The Karnataka Rural Water Supply and Environmental Sanitation Project in India*, Staff Appraisal Report, World Bank, Washington, DC.

World Bank (1993b), *Peru: Privatization Adjustment Loan*, Report No. P-5929-PE, World Bank, Washington, DC.

World Bank (1994), *Adjustment in Africa: Reforms, Results and the Road Ahead*, A World Bank Policy Research Report, Washington, DC.

World Commission on Environment and Development (WCED) (1987), *Our Common Future*, Oxford University Press, Oxford, UK.

Xie, J. (1995), 'Environmental Policy Analysis: An Environmental Computable General Equilibrium Approach to China', Ph. D. Dissertation, Cornell University.

Young, Carlos Eduardo F. (1997), *Economic Adjustment Policies and the Environment: a Case Study of Brazil*, PhD Dissertation, University College, London.

Young, C.E.F. and Bishop, J. (1995), *Adjustment Policies and the Environment: A Critical Review of the Literature*, CREED Working Paper Series No. 1, IIED, London, UK.

Index